Anonymous

The Christian Hymnary

A selection of hymns & tunes for Christian worship

Anonymous

The Christian Hymnary
A selection of hymns & tunes for Christian worship

ISBN/EAN: 9783337038656

Printed in Europe, USA, Canada, Australia, Japan

Cover: Foto ©Lupo / pixelio.de

More available books at **www.hansebooks.com**

THE

CHRISTIAN HYMNARY:

A SELECTION OF
HYMNS & TUNES FOR
CHRISTIAN WORSHIP.

"*With psalms and hymns and spiritual songs, singing with grace in your hearts unto God.*" Col. iii. 16.

CHRISTIAN PUBLISHING ASSOCIATION:
DAYTON, OHIO

PREFACE.

THE CHRISTIAN HYMNARY is a revision and enlargement of the Gospel Hymnal. It is the result of action taken by the American Christian Convention, the General Convention (South), and the Christian Publishing Association. The committee entrusted with this work represents both sections of our Zion.

The Christian Hymn Book, Christian Hymns, and Gospel Hymnal have furnished most of our hymns, yet some have been gathered from other sources. They seem to be sufficient in number and variety for the use of most congregations in their public services. Very little of music for Sunday schools and social services has been used, as there are so many books designed especially for their use. The right to use some music that greatly enriches the Hymnary, has been purchased, or free use obtained.

For the free use of their compositions, thanks are due to Dr. H. R. Palmer and Prof. W. G. Tomer.

Space has been saved by not repeating first stanzas.

To meet the wants of many we have inserted chants, responses, and responsive readings.

The indexes are sufficiently copious to render much aid in the use of the book.   *   *   *   *   *

We trust this book may aid in the service of the Lord's house, and we shall be amply compensated for our labor, which has drawn us into closer fellowship, if those who use the Hymnary may be helped to a sweeter fellowship with all true disciples, to a firmer trust in God, and to a truer Christian service.

         ALVA H. MORRILL,
         S. S. NEWHOUSE,
         W. W. STALEY,   } *Committee.*
         C. V. STRICKLAND,

First Edition, December 1, 1891.

NOTE TO SECOND EDITION.

As a new edition of the HYMNARY is needed, effort has been made to correct errors, both in music and words, so far as a careful examination has revealed them. An entire change has been made in one hymn, while slight changes have been made in two others, one at the request of its author, Rev. H. Lizzie Haley. It is hoped that the work of revision will add to the usefulness of the book.

CONTENTS.

I. PUBLIC WORSHIP—
	HYMNS.
I. SANCTUARY AND SABBATH	1–53
II. ADORATION AND PRAISE	54–95
III. MORNING AND EVENING	96–124
IV. CLOSING HYMNS	125–146

II. GOD—
I. BEING AND GREATNESS	147–160
II. IN NATURE	161–166
III. PROVIDENCE AND GRACE	167–213

III. CHRIST—
I. ADVENT	214–229
II. LIFE AND MINISTRY	230–236
III. SUFFERINGS	237–241
IV. RESURRECTION AND GLORY	242–258
V. CHARACTER AND OFFICES	259–299
VI. PRAISE TO HIM	300–311

IV. HOLY SPIRIT—
HOLY SPIRIT	312–334

V. THE BIBLE—
THE BIBLE	335–346

VI. THE GOSPEL—
I. WARNINGS AND INVITATIONS	347–382
II. BLESSINGS AND TRIUMPHS	383–390

VII. EXPERIENCE AND LIFE—
I. PENITENCE AND CONSECRATION	391–425
II. REGENERATION	426–434
III. FAITH	435–441
IV. HELP AND TRUST	442–464
V. LOVE AND OBEDIENCE	465–504
VI. PRAYER AND ASPIRATION	505–575
VII. THE CROSS	576–593
VIII. COURAGE AND ACTION	594–631
IX. TEMPTATION AND DIVINE STRENGTH	632–646
X. AFFLICTION AND COMFORT	647–676
XI. JOY, PEACE, HOPE	677–684

VIII. THE CHURCH—
	HYMNS
I. FOUNDATION AND EXCELLENCY	685–696
II. MINISTRY	697–702
III. DEDICATION	703–708
IV. ADMISSION OF MEMBERS	709–719
V. ORDINANCES	720–738
VI. FELLOWSHIP AND UNITY	739–747
VII. GROWTH AND FUTURE GLORY	748–759

IX. CHRISTIAN PHILANTHROPY—
I. MISSIONS	760–778
II. CHARITIES AND REFORMS	779–791

X. VARIOUS OCCASIONS—
I. THE NATION	792–799
II. THANKSGIVING	800–803
III. THE YEAR	804–810
IV. THE SEASONS	811–815
V. THE FAMILY	816–823
VI. YOUTH AND OLD AGE	824–831

XI. MORTALITY—
I. BREVITY OF LIFE	832–840
II. DEATH	841–870

XII. FUTURITY—
I. SECOND COMING OF CHRIST	871–872
II. HEAVEN	873–902

XIII. MISCELLANEOUS—
I. MISCELLANEOUS	903–913
II. CHANTS AND RESPONSES	914–930

XIV. INDEXES—
	PAGES
I. OF SUBJECTS	303–306
II. OF SCRIPTURE TEXTS	307–308
III. OF TUNES	309–310
IV. OF METRES	311–312
V. OF FIRST LINES	312–322

XV. RESPONSIVE READINGS	323–33.

The Christian Hymnary.

1. Ho-ly, ho-ly, ho-ly, Lord God, Al-might-y! Ear-ly in the morn-ing our song shall rise to thee; Ho-ly, ho-ly, ho-ly! mer-ci-ful and might-y! All thy works shall praise thy name in earth, and sky, and sea.

1

2 Holy, holy, holy! all the saints adore thee,
Casting down their golden crowns around the glassy sea;
Cherubim and seraphim falling down before thee,
Thou who wast, and art, and evermore shalt be.

3 Holy, holy, holy! though the darkness hide thee,
Though the eye of sinful man thy glory may not see,
Only thou art holy; there is none beside thee,
Infinite in power, in love, and purity.

Bp. Reginald Heber, 1827.

(5)

PUBLIC WORSHIP.

GERMANY. L. M.
Beethoven.

1. Thine earthly Sab-baths, Lord, we love; But there's a no-bler rest a-bove; To that our long-ing souls as-pire With ear-nest hope and strong de-sire.

2
2 No more fatigue, no more distress,
Nor sin, nor death shall reach the place;
No groans to mingle with the songs
Which warble from immortal tongues.

3 No rude alarms of raging foes;
No cares to break the long repose;
No midnight shade, no clouded sun,
But sacred, high, eternal noon.

4 O long-expected day, begin;
Dawn on these realms of woe and sin:
Fain would we leave this weary road,
And sleep in death, to rest with God.
Philip Doddridge.

3   *Rejoicing in the Sabbath.*
1 My opening eyes with rapture see
The dawn of thy returning day;
My thoughts, O God, ascend to thee;
While thus my early vows I pay.

2 I yield my heart to thee alone,
Nor would receive another guest;
Eternal King, erect thy throne,
And reign sole Monarch in my breast.

3 O, bid this trifling world retire,
And drive each carnal thought away,
Nor let me feel one vain desire,
One sinful thought, through all the day.

4 Then, to thy courts when I repair,
My soul shall rise on joyful wing,
The wonders of thy love declare,
And join the strains which angels sing.
Hutton.

4   *Public Worship.*
1 Oh come! loud anthems let us sing,
Loud thanks to our Almighty King;
For we our voices high should raise,
When our Salvation's Rock we praise.

2 Into his presence let us haste,
To thank him for his favors past;
To him address in joyful songs,
The praise that to his name belongs.

3 Oh, let us to his courts repair,
And bow with adoration there;
With joy and fear, devoutly all
Before the Lord, our Maker, fall!
Tate & Brady.

5   *The Lord will give Grace and Glory.*
1 Great God, attend, while Zion sings
The joy that from thy presence springs:
To spend one day with thee on earth
Exceeds a thousand days of mirth.

2 Might I enjoy the meanest place
Within thy house, O God of grace,
Not tents of ease, nor thrones of power,
Should tempt my feet to leave thy door.

3 God is our sun—he makes our day;
God is our shield—he guards our way
From all th' assaults of hell and sin,
From foes without and foes within.

4 All needful grace will God bestow,
And crown that grace with glory, too;
He gives us all things, and withholds
No good from pure and upright souls.
Isaac Watts.

SANCTUARY AND SABBATH.

MIGDOL. L. M. — Lowell Mason, 1840.

1. How pleasant, how di-vine-ly fair, O Lord of hosts, thy dwellings are! With long de-sires my spir-it faints To meet th'as-sem-blies of thy saints.

6 *How amiable are thy Tabernacles.*

2 Blest are the souls who find a place
Within the temple of thy grace;
There they behold thy gentler rays,
And seek thy face, and learn thy praise.

3 Blest are the men whose hearts are set
To find the way to Zion's gate:
God is their strength; and through the road
They lean upon their Helper, God.

4 Cheerful they walk with growing strength,
Till all shall meet in heaven at length;
Till all before thy face appear,
And join in nobler worship there.
Isaac Watts, 1719.

7 *Supplication.*

1 GREAT God, the followers of thy Son,
We bow before thy mercy-seat,
To worship thee, the Holy One,
And pour our wishes at thy feet.

2 O, grant thy blessing here to-day;
O, give thy people joy and peace;
The tokens of thy love display,
And favor that shall never cease.

3 We seek the truth which Jesus brought;
His path of light we long to tread;
Here be his holy doctrines taught,
And here their purest influence shed.

4 May faith, and hope, and love abound;
Our sins and errors be forgiven;
And we, from day to day, be found
Children of God and heirs of heaven.
Henry Ware, Jr.

8 *The Sabbath.*

1 ANOTHER six days' work is done,
Another Sabbath is begun;
Return, my soul! enjoy thy rest,
Improve the day thy God has blessed.

2 Oh, that our thoughts and thanks may rise,
As grateful incense to the skies;
And draw from heaven that sweet repose,
Which none, but he that feels it, knows.

3 This heavenly calm, within the breast,
Is the dear pledge of glorious rest,
Which for the church of God remains—
The end of cares, the end of pains.
Stennett.

9 *Surely the Lord is in this Place.*

1 Lo, God is here! let us adore,
And humbly bow before his face:
Let all within us feel his power,
Let all within us seek his grace.

2 Lo, God is here! him, day and night,
United choirs of angels sing:
To him, enthroned above all height,
Heaven's host their noblest praises bring.

3 Being of beings, may our praise
Thy courts with grateful incense fill;
Still may we stand before thy face,
Still hear and do thy sovereign will.
G. Tersteegen. Tr. John Wesley, 1739.

PUBLIC WORSHIP.

ALL SAINTS. L. M.
W. Knapp, 1768.

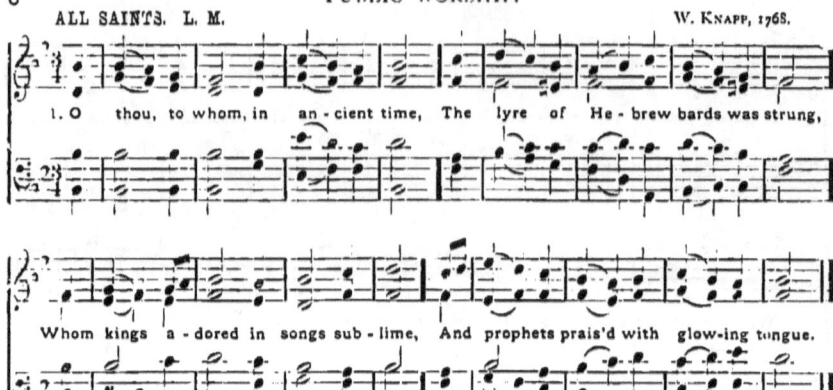

1. O thou, to whom, in an-cient time, The lyre of He-brew bards was strung, Whom kings a-dored in songs sub-lime, And prophets prais'd with glow-ing tongue.

10 *Every place a Temple.*

2 Not now on Zion's height alone
Thy favored worshipers may dwell;
Nor where at sultry noon, thy Son
Sat weary, by the patriarch's well.

3 From every place below the skies,
The grateful song, the fervent prayer,
The incense of the heart,—may rise
To Heaven, and find acceptance there.

4 To thee shall age, with snowy hair,
And strength, and beauty, bend the knee,
And childhood lisp, with reverent air,
Its praises and its prayers to thee.
John Pierpont.

11 *The Hour of Prayer.*

1 Blest hour! when mortal man retires,
To hold communion with his God,
To send to heaven his warm desires,
And listen to the sacred word.

2 Blest hour! for, where the Lord resorts,
Foretastes of future bliss are given;
And mortals find his earthly courts
The house of God, the gate of heaven!

3 Hail, peaceful hour! supremely blest,
Amid the hours of worldly care,
The hour that yields the spirit rest,
That sacred hour, the hour of prayer.

4 And, when my hours of prayer are past,
And this frail tenement decays,
Then may I spend, in heaven, at last,
A never-ending hour of praise.
Thomas Raffles, 1826.

12 *The Sacrifice of the Heart.*

1 When, as returns this solemn day,
Man comes to meet his Maker, God,
What rites, what honors shall he pay?
How spread his sovereign name abroad?

2 From marble domes and gilded spires
Shall curling clouds of incense rise,
And gems, and gold, and garlands deck
The costly pomp of sacrifice?

3 Vain, sinful man! creation's Lord
Thy golden offerings well may spare,
But give thy heart, and thou shalt find
Here dwells a God who heareth prayer.
Mrs. Barbauld.

13 *The Close of the Sabbath.*

1 Sweet is the light of Sabbath eve,
And soft the sunbeams lingering there;
For these blest hours the world I leave,
Wafted on wings of faith and prayer.

2 The time how lovely and how still!
Peace shines and smiles on all below;
The plain, the stream, the wood, the hill,
All fair with evening's setting glow.

3 Season of rest—the tranquil soul
Feels the sweet calm, and melts in love;
And, while these sacred moments roll,
Faith sees a smiling heaven above.

4 Nor will our days of toil be long;
Our pilgrimage will soon be trod;
And we shall join the ceaseless song,
The endless Sabbath, of our God.
James Edmeston.

SANCTUARY AND SABBATH.

BERA. L. M.   John E. Gould, 1846.

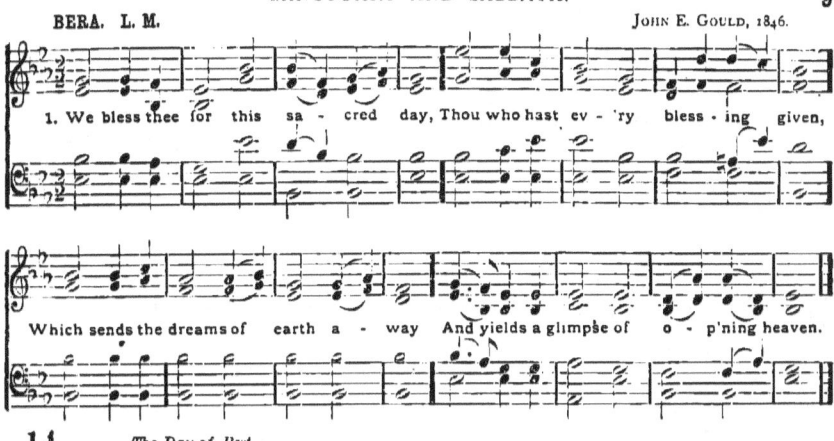

1. We bless thee for this sacred day, Thou who hast ev'ry blessing given,
Which sends the dreams of earth away And yields a glimpse of op'ning heaven.

14   *The Day of Rest.*

2 Rich day of holy, thoughtful rest,
  May we improve thy calm repose,
And, in God's service truly blest,
  Forget the world, its joys, its woes.

3 Lord, may thy truth upon the heart
Now fall and dwell as heavenly dew,
And flowers of grace in freshness start
Where once the weeds of error grew.

4 May Prayer now lift her sacred wings,
  Contented with that aim alone
Which bears her to the King of kings,
  And rests her at his sheltering throne.
Mrs. Gilman.

MEAR. C. M.   Welsh Air. Aaron Williams, 1760.

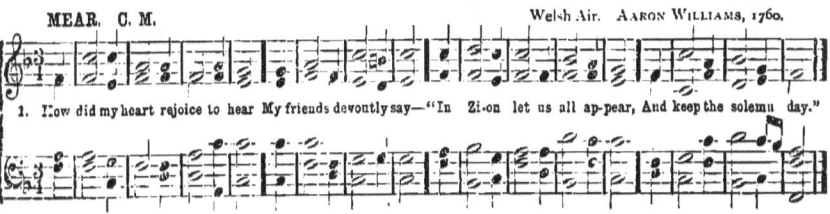

1. How did my heart rejoice to hear My friends devoutly say—"In Zion let us all appear, And keep the solemn day."

15   *How Lovely is Zion.*

2 I love her gates, I love the road;
  The church adorned with grace,
Stands like a palace built for God,
  To show his milder face.

3 Peace be within this sacred place,
  And joy a constant guest!
With holy gifts and heavenly grace
  Be her attendants blest!

4 My soul shall pray for Zion still,
  While life or breath remains;
There my best friends, my kindred, dwell,
  There God, my Saviour, reigns.
Isaac Watts, 1719.

16   *Prayer for special Favor.*

1 Within thy house, O Lord, our God,
  In glory now appear;
Make this a place of thine abode,
  And shed thy blessings here.

2 When we thy mercy-seat surround,
  Thy spirit, Lord, impart;
And let thy gospel's joyful sound
  With power reach every heart.

3 Here let the blind their sight obtain;
  Here give the mourners rest;
Let Jesus here triumphant reign,
  Enthroned in every breast.

4 Here let the voice of sacred joy
  And humble prayer arise,
Till higher strains our tongues employ
  In realms beyond the skies.

PUBLIC WORSHIP.

10. DAY OF REST. C. M.
L. V. Wheeler.

1. This is the day the Lord hath made; He calls the hours his own;
Let heav'n rejoice, let earth be glad, And praise surround the throne.

17 *This is the Day which the Lord hath made.*

2 To-day he rose and left the dead,
And Satan's empire fell;
To-day the saints his triumph spread,
And all his wonders tell.

3 Blest be the Lord who comes to men
With messages of grace,—
Who comes, in God his Father's name
To save our sinful race.

4 Hosanna in the highest strains
The church on earth can raise;
The highest heavens in which he reigns
Shall give him nobler praise.
Isaac Watts.

18 *Joy of Worship.*

1 With joy we hail the sacred day,
Which God has called his own;
With joy the summons we obey
To worship at his throne.

2 Spirit of grace, O, deign to dwell
Within thy church below;
Make her in holiness excel,
With pure devotion glow.

3 Let peace within her walls be found,
Let all her sons unite
To spread with grateful zeal around
Her clear and shining light.
Henry F. Lyte.

19 *Homage and Devotion.*

1 With sacred joy we lift our eyes
To those bright realms above,
That glorious temple in the skies,
Where dwells eternal love.

2 Before the gracious throne we bow
Of heaven's almighty King;
Here we present the solemn vow,
And hymns of praise we sing.

3 O Lord, while in thy house we kneel
With trust and holy fear,
Thy mercy and thy truth reveal,
And lend a gracious ear.

4 With fervor teach our hearts to pray,
And tune our lips to sing;
Nor from thy presence cast away
The sacrifice we bring.
Thos. Jarvis.

20 *Early will I seek thee.*

1 Early, my God, without delay,
I haste to seek thy face;
My thirsty spirit faints away
Without thy cheering grace.

2 I've seen thy glory and thy power
Through all thy temple shine;
My God, repeat that heavenly hour,
That vision so divine.

3 Not life itself, with all its joys,
Can my best passions move,
Or raise so high my cheerful voice,
As thy forgiving love.

4 Thus, till my last expiring day,
I'll bless my God and King,
Thus will I lift my hands to pray,
And tune my heart to sing.
Isaac Watts, 1719.

SANCTUARY AND SABBATH.

DOWNS. C. M.   LOWELL MASON

1. What shall I ren-der to my God For all his kindness shown? My feet shall visit thine abode, My songs address thy throne.

Used by per Oliver Ditson Co., owners of Copyright.

---

21   *What shall I render unto the Lord?*

2 Among the saints that fill thy house
    My offerings shall be paid;
There shall my zeal perform the vows
    My soul in anguish made.

3 How happy all thy servants are!
    How great thy grace to me!
My life, which thou hast made thy care,
    Lord, I devote to thee.

4 Here in thy courts I leave my vow,
    And thy rich grace record;
Witness, ye saints, who hear me now,
    If I forsake the Lord.
                    Isaac Watts.

22   *Pure Worship.*

1 THE offerings to thy throne which rise,
    Of mingled praise and prayer,
Are but a worthless sacrifice
    Unless the heart is there.

2 Upon thine all-discerning ear
    Let no vain words intrude;
No tribute but the vow sincere—
    The tribute of the good.

3 My offerings will indeed be blest,
    If sanctified by thee—
If thy pure spirit touch my breast
    With its own purity.

4 O, may that spirit warm my heart
    To piety and love,
And to life's lowly vale impart
    Some rays from heaven above.
                    Sir John Bowring.

23   *Languid Devotion lamented.*

1 FREQUENT the day of God returns
    To shed its quickening beams;
And yet, how slow devotion burns!
    How languid are its flames!

2 Increase, O Lord, our faith and hope,
    And fit us to ascend
Where the assembly ne'er breaks up,
    And Sabbaths never end;—

3 Where we shall breathe in heavenly air,
    With heavenly lustre shine,
Before the throne of God appear,
    And feast on love divine.

4 There shall we join, and never tire,
    To sing immortal lays,
And, with the bright, seraphic choir,
    Sound forth Immanuel's praise.
                    Brown.

24   *God present in the Sanctuary.*

1 My soul, how lovely is the place
    To which thy God resorts!
'Tis heaven to see his smiling face,
    Though in his earthly courts.

2 There the great monarch of the skies
    His saving power displays,
And light breaks in upon our eyes,
    With kind and quickening rays.

3 With his rich gifts, the heavenly Dove
    Descends and fills the place,
While Christ reveals his wondrous love,
    And sheds abroad his grace.
                    Isaac Watts

PUBLIC WORSHIP.

AVONDALE. C. M. — S. K. WHITING.

1. Again our earthly cares we leave, And to thy courts repair;
Again, with joyful feet, we come To meet our Saviour here.

25 *A Blessing sought.*

2 The feeling heart, the melting eye,
The humble mind, bestow;
And shine upon us from on high,
To make our graces grow.

3 May we in faith receive thy word,
In faith present our prayers,
And in the presence of our Lord
Unbosom all our cares.

4 Show us some token of thy love,
Our fainting hope to raise;
And pour thy blessing from above,
That we may render praise.
Anon.

26 *The Lord's Day—Morning.*

1 Again the Lord of life and light
Awakes the kindling ray,
Unseals the eyelids of the morn,
And pours increasing day.

2 O, what a night was that which wrapped
The heathen world in gloom!
O, what a sun which broke, this day,
Triumphant from the tomb!

3 This day be grateful homage paid,
And loud hosannas sung;
Let gladness dwell in every heart,
And praise on every tongue.

4 Ten thousand different lips shall join
To hail this welcome morn,
Which scatters blessings from its wings
To nations yet unborn.
Wm. Barbauld.

27 *Blest Day of God.*

1 Blest day of God, most calm, most bright,
The first and best of days;
The laborer's rest, the saint's delight,
The day of prayer and praise.

2 My Saviour's face made thee to shine;
His rising thee did raise,
And made thee heavenly and divine
Beyond all other days.

3 The first-fruits oft a blessing prove
To all the sheaves behind;
And they who do the Sabbath love,
A happy week will find.
Anon.

28 *Love of Sabbath Service.*

1 How sweet, upon this sacred day,
The best of all the seven,
To cast our earthly thoughts away,
And think of God and heaven!

2 How sweet to be allowed to pray
Our sins may be forgiven—
With filial confidence to say,
"Father, who art in heaven!"

3 And if, to make our sins depart,
In vain the will has striven,
He who regards the inmost heart,
Will send his grace from heaven.

4 Then hail, thou sacred, blessed day,
The best of all the seven,
When hearts unite their vows to pay
Of gratitude to heaven.
Mrs. Follen.

SANCTUARY AND SABBATH.

NUREMBURG. 7s. Arr. by Dr. Mason.

1. Lord, be-fore thy pres-ence come, Bow we down with ho-ly fear:
Call our err-ing foot-steps home, Let us feel that thou art near.

29 *Engagedness in Devotion.*

2 Wandering thoughts and languid powers
Come not where devotion kneels;
Let the soul expand her stores,
Glowing with the joy she feels.

3 At the portals of thine house,
We resign our earth-born cares:
Nobler thoughts our souls engross,
Songs of praise and fervent prayers.
John Taylor.

30 *Communion Hymn.*

1 JESUS, we thy promise claim:
We are met in thy dear name;
In the midst do thou appear;
Manifest thy presence here.

2 Sanctify us, Lord, and bless;
Breathe thy spirit, give thy peace;
Thou thyself within us move:
Make our feast a feast of love.

3 Give to us thy humble mind,
Patient, fearless, just, and kind;
Meek and lowly let us be,—
Full of goodness, full of thee.
Wesleyan.

31 *God's Presence Invoked.*

1 SOVEREIGN and transforming grace!
We invoke thy quickening power;
Reign the spirit of this place,
Bless the purpose of this hour.

2 Holy and creative Light!
We invoke thy kindling ray,
Dawn upon our spirits' night,
Turn our darkness into day.

3 Give the struggling peace for strife,
Give the doubting light for gloom,
Speed the living into life,
Warn the dying of their doom.

4 Work in all,—in all renew,
Day by day, the life divine;
All our wills to thee subdue,
All our hearts to thee incline.
F. H. Hedge.

32 *Did not our Heart burn within us?*

1 To thy temple I repair;
Lord, I love to worship there,
When within the veil I meet
Christ before the mercy-seat.

2 While thy glorious praise is sung,
Touch my lips, unloose my tongue,
That my joyful soul may bless
Thee, the Lord, my Righteousness.

3 While thy word is heard with awe,
While we tremble at thy law,
Let thy gospel's wondrous love
Every doubt and fear remove.

4 From thy house when we return,
Let our hearts within us burn;
That at evening we may say,—
"We have walked with God to-day."
James Montgomery.

PUBLIC WORSHIP.

SABBATH. 7s. 6l.   LOWELL MASON, 1824.

1. Safe-ly thro' an-oth-er week, God has bro't us on our way; Let us now a blessing seek, Waiting in his courts to-day: Day of all the week the best, Emblem of e-ter-nal rest; Day of all the week the best, Emblem of e-ter-nal rest.

---

33   *The Sabbath of Rest.*

2 While we seek supplies of grace,
  Through the dear Redeemer's name,
Show thy reconciling face—
  Take away our sin and shame;
From our worldly cares set free,—
  May we rest this day in thee.

3 Here we come thy name to praise,
  Let us feel thy presence near;
May thy glory meet our eyes.
  While we in thy house appear.
Here afford us, Lord, a taste
  Of our everlasting rest.

4 May thy gospel's joyful sound
  Conquer sinners, comfort saints,
Make the fruits of grace abound,
  Bring relief from all complaints:
Thus may all our Sabbaths prove
  Till we join the church above.
                    John Newton, 1779.

---

34   *The Accepted Offering.*

1 LORD, what offering shall we bring,
  At thine altars when we bow?—
Hearts, the pure, unsullied spring
  Whence the kind affections flow;
Soft compassion's feeling soul
  By the melting eye expressed;
Sympathy, at whose control
  Sorrow leaves the wounded breast

2 Willing hands to lead the blind;
  Bind the wounded, feed the poor;
Love, embracing all our kind;
  Charity, with liberal store.
Teach us, O Thou heavenly King,
  This to show our grateful mind,
Thus the accepted offering bring,—
  Love to thee and all mankind.
                    John Taylor, 1795.

---

35   *The House of Prayer.*

1 IN this peaceful house of prayer,
  Stronger faith, O God, we seek;
Here we bring each earthly care,
  Thou the strengthening message speak.
In our greatest trials we,
  Calm, through thee, the way have trod:
In the smallest, may we feel
  Thou art still our Helper-God!

2 Of thy presence and thy love
  We more steadfast feeling need,
Till the high and holy thought
  Hallow every simplest deed.
In our work and in our homes
  Christian men we fain would be;
Learn how daily life affords
  Noblest opportunity.
                    Hymns of the Spirit.

SANCTUARY AND SABBATH.

36 *The Courts of the Lord.*

1 PLEASANT are thy courts above
In the land of light and love;
Pleasant are thy courts below
In this land of sin and woe.
Oh, my spirit longs and faints
For the converse of thy saints,
For the brightness of thy face,
For the fulness of thy grace.

2 Happy birds that sing and fly
Round thy altars, O Most High;
Happier souls that find a rest
In a heavenly Father's breast;
Like the wandering dove that found
No repose on earth around,
They can to their ark repair,
And enjoy it ever there.

3 Happy souls, their praises flow,
Even in this vale of woe;
Waters in the deserts rise,
Manna feeds them from the skies;
On they go from strength to strength,
Till they reach thy throne at length,
At thy feet adoring fall,
Who hast led them safe through all.
Henry F. Lyte, 1834.

37 *For a general blessing.*

1 LORD, we come before thee now,
At thy feet we humbly bow;
O, do not our suit disdain;
Shall we seek thee, Lord, in vain?

2 Lord, on thee our souls depend;
In compassion now descend;
Fill our hearts with thy rich grace,
Tune our lips to sing thy praise.

3 Comfort those who weep and mourn·
Let the time of joy return;
Those that are cast down lift up;
Make them strong in faith and hope.

4 Grant that all may seek and find
Thee, a gracious God and kind:
Heal the sick, the captive free;
Let us all rejoice in thee.
Anon.

38 *The Temple.*

1 IN thy courts let peace be found;
Be thy temple full of love;
Here we tread on holy ground,
All serene around, above.

2 While the knee in prayer is bent,
While with praise the heart o'erflows,
Tranquilize the turbulent,
Give the weary one repose.

3 Be the place for worship meet,
Meet the worship for the place—
Contemplation's blest retreat,
Shrine of guilelessness and grace!

4 As an infant knows its home,
Lord, may we thy temple know;
Hither for instruction come,
Hence by thee instructed go.
Sir John Bowring

39 *Sabbath Evening.*

1 SOFTLY fades the twilight ray
Of the holy Sabbath day;
Gently as life's setting sun
When the Christian's course is run.

2 Night her solemn mantle spreads
O'er the earth as daylight fades;
All things tell of calm repose
At the holy Sabbath's close.

3 Peace is on the world abroad;
'Tis the holy peace of God—
Symbol of the peace within
When the spirit rests from sin.

4 Saviour, may our Sabbaths be
Days of peace and joy in thee,
Till in heaven our souls repose,
Where the Sabbath ne'er shall close.
S. F. Smith.

40 *Feast of Love.*

1 COME, and let us sweetly join
God to praise in hymns divine;
Give we all, with one accord,
Glory to our common Lord.

2 Hands and hearts and voices raise;
Sing as in the ancient days;
Taste e'en now the joys above,
Find the heaven of mutual love.

3 Jesus, we thy promise claim,
We are met in thy great name;
In the midst do thou appear,
Manifest thy presence here.

4 Make us all in thee complete,
Make us all for glory meet,—
Meet to appear before thy sight,
Partners of the saints in light.
Charles Wesley.

PUBLIC WORSHIP.

LISCHER. H. M.   Friedrich Schneider, 1840.

1. Welcome, delightful morn; Thou day of sa-cred rest,
 I hail thy kind return: Lord, make these moments blest.
 From low desires and fleeting toys I soar to reach immortal joys, I soar to reach immortal joys.

41 *Sabbath Morning.*

2 Now may the King descend
 And fill his throne of grace;
 Thy sceptre, Lord, extend,
 While saints address thy face.
Let sinners feel thy quickening word,
And learn to know and fear the Lord.

3 Descend, celestial Dove,
 With all thy quickening powers,
 Disclose a Saviour's love,
 And bless the sacred hours.
Then shall my soul new life obtain,
Nor Sabbaths be enjoyed in vain.
Hayward, 1806.

42 *A Day in thy Courts.*

1 Lord of the worlds above,
 How pleasant and how fair
 The dwellings of thy love,
 Thine earthly temples are!
To thine abode | With warm desires
My heart aspires, | To see my God.

2 O, happy souls that pray
 Where God appoints to hear!
 O, happy men that pay
 Their constant service there!
They praise thee still; | Who love the way
And happy they | To Zion's hill.

3 They go from strength to strength
 Through this dark vale of tears,
 Till each arrives at length,
 Till each in heaven appears.
O, glorious seat, | Shall thither bring
When God our King | Our willing feet.
Isaac Watts, 1719.

43 *Ask, and it shall be given you.*

1 O Thou, that hearest prayer,
 Attend our humble cry,—
 And let thy servants share
 Thy blessing from on high:
We plead the promise of thy word;
Grant us thy Holy Spirit, Lord.

2 If earthly parents hear
 Their children when they cry,
 If they, with love sincere,
 Their children's wants supply,
Much more wilt thou thy love display,
And answer when thy children pray.

3 Our heavenly Father, thou;
 We, children of thy grace:
 O, let thy Spirit now
 Descend and fill the place,
That all may feel the heavenly flame,
And all unite to praise thy name.
Burton.

SANCTUARY AND SABBATH.

WAYNE. H. M. — L. M Gordon, 1830.

1. A-wake, ye saints, a-wake! And hail this sacred day; In loftiest songs of praise Your joy-ful hom-age pay; Come, bless the day that God hath blest, The type of heav'n's, the type of heav'n's e-ter-nal rest. Come, bless the day that God hath blest, The type of heav'n's e-ter-nal rest.

44 *The Day that God hath blessed.*

2 On this auspicious morn
The Lord of life arose;
He burst the bars of death,
And vanquished all our foes;
And now he pleads our cause above,
And reaps the fruit of all his love.

3 All hail, triumphant Lord!
Heaven with hosannas rings,
And earth, in humbler strains,
Thy praise responsive sings,—
Worthy the Lamb, that once was slain,
Through endless years to live and reign.
Thomas Cotterill.

SPRAGUE. S. M. — A. N. Johnson, by per.

1. Sweet is the work, O Lord, Thy glorious name to sing; To praise and pray, to hear thy word, And grateful off'rings bring.

Used by per. Oliver Ditson Co., owners of Copyright.

45 *Enjoyment in Worship.*

2 Sweet, at the dawning hour,
Thy boundless love to tell;
And, when the night-wind shuts the flower,
Still on the theme to dwell.

3 Sweet, on this day of rest,
To join, in heart and voice,
With those who love and serve thee best,
And in thy name rejoice.

4 To songs of praise and joy
Be every Sabbath given,
That such may be our blest employ,
Eternally in heaven. Spirit of the Psalms.

46 *"Even thine altars, O Lord of Hosts."*

1 How charming is the place
Where my Redeemer, God,
Unveils the beauties of his face,
And sheds his love abroad!

2 Not the fair palaces,
To which the great resort,
Are once to be compared with this,
Where Jesus holds his courts.

3 Here on the mercy-seat,
With radiant glory crowned,
Our joyful eyes behold him sit,
And smile on all around.

4 Give me, O Lord, a place
Within thy blest abode,
Among the children of thy grace,
The servants of my God.
Stennett.

PUBLIC WORSHIP.

LISBON. S. M.
DANIEL READ, 1885.

1. Welcome, sweet day of rest, That saw the Lord a-rise,—Welcome to this re-viving breast And these rejoicing eyes.

47 *The Sabbath welcomed.*

2 The King himself comes near,
And feasts his saints to-day;
Here may we sit, and see him here,
And love, and praise, and pray.

3 One day amid the place
Where Christ, my Lord, hath been,
Is sweeter than ten thousand days
Of pleasure and of sin.

4 My willing soul would stay
In such a frame as this,
And sit and sing herself away
To everlasting bliss.
Isaac Watts, 1709.

48 *This is the Lord's Doing.*

1 THIS is the glorious day
That our Redeemer made;
Let us rejoice, and sing, and pray,
Let all the church be glad.

2 The work, O Lord, is thine,
And wondrous in our eyes;
This day declares it all divine,
This day did Jesus rise.

3 Hosanna to the King,
Of David's royal blood;
Bless him, you saints, he comes to bring
Salvation from your God.
Anon.

49 *Invitation to the House of God.*

1 COME to the house of prayer,
O thou afflicted, come;
The God of peace shall meet thee there,
He makes that house his home.

2 Come to the house of praise,
Ye who are happy now;
In sweet accord your voices raise,
In kindred homage bow.

3 Thou, whose benignant eye
In mercy looks on all,
Who seest the tear of misery,
And hear'st the mourner's call,—

4 Up to thy dwelling-place
Bear our frail spirits on,
Till they outstrip time's tardy pace,
And heaven on earth be won.
Emily Taylor.

GREENVILLE. 8s & 7s.
ROUSSEAU.

{ Far from mortal cares retreating, Sordid hopes and vain desires, } From the Fount of glory beaming, Light celestial cheers our
{ Here, our willing footsteps meeting, Ev'ry heart to heav'n aspires. }   [eyes,
D.C.—Mercy from above proclaiming Peace and pardon from the skies.

50 *The Fount of Blessing.*

2 Who may share this great salvation?
Every pure and humble mind,
Every kindred, tongue, and nation,
From the stains of guilt refined.

Blessings all around bestowing,
God withholds his care from none,
Grace and mercy ever flowing
From the fountain of his throne.
J. Taylor.

SANCTUARY AND SABBATH.

BADEA. S. M. — German Melody.

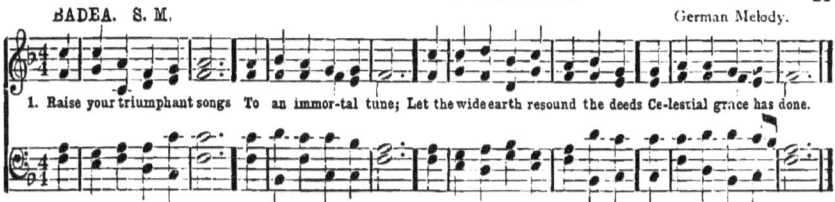

1. Raise your triumphant songs To an immor-tal tune; Let the wide earth resound the deeds Ce-lestial grace has done.

51 *Break forth into joy.*

2 Sing how Eternal Love,
   His chief belovéd chose,
And bade him raise our wretched race
   From their abyss of woes.

3 Now, sinners, dry your tears,
   Let hopeless sorrow cease;
Bow to the sceptre of his love,
   And take the offered peace.

4 Lord, we obey thy call:
   We lay an humble claim
To the salvation thou hast brought,
   And love and praise thy name.
                 Isaac Watts, 1719.

52 *Heavenly Joy on Earth.*

1 Come we that love the Lord,
   And let our joys be known;
Join in a song with sweet accord,
   And thus surround the throne.

2 The sorrows of the mind
   Be banished from the place;
Religion never was designed
   To make our pleasures less.

3 The hill of Zion yields
   A thousand sacred sweets,
Before we reach the heavenly fields
   Or walk the golden streets.

4 Then let our songs abound,
   And every tear be dry;
We're marching thro' Immanuel's ground
   To fairer worlds on high.
                 Isaac Watts, 1709.

EDINBURGH. 11s. — "Modern Harp."

1. Approach not the altar with gloom in thy soul, Nor let thy feet fal-ter from terror's control;
God loves not the sadness of fear and mistrust; Oh, serve him with gladness—the Loving and Just.

53 *I will be glad in the Lord.*

2 Come not to his temple with pride in thy mien,
But lowly and simple, in courage serene;
Bring meekly before him the faith of a child,
Bow down and adore him with heart undefiled.

3 His bounty is tender, his being is love;
His smile fills with splendor the blue arch above;
Confiding, believing. O, enter always
His courts with thanksgiving, his portals with praise.
                 Frances Osgood.

PUBLIC WORSHIP.

ESTELLA. L. M.   From MENDELSSOHN.

1. Come, O my soul! in sa-cred lays, At-tempt thy great Cre-a-tor's praise;
But, oh, what tongue can speak his fame!} What mor-tal verse can reach the theme!

Used by per. Oliver Ditson Co., owners of Copyright.

54

2 Enthroned amidst the radiant spheres,
He glory like a garment wears;
To form a robe of light divine,
Ten thousand suns around him shine.

3 In all our Maker's grand designs,
Omnipotence with wisdom shines;
His works, through all this wondrous frame,
Bear the great impress of his name.

4 Raised on devotion's lofty wing,
Do thou, my soul, his glories sing;
And let his praise employ thy tongue,
Till listening worlds applaud the song.
                    Thomas Blacklock, 1754.

55   *Praises to the Eternal King.*

1 THE Lord is King; lift up thy voice,
O earth, and all ye heavens, rejoice;
From world to world the joy shall ring—
The Lord omnipotent is King.

2 The Lord is King; child of the dust,
The Judge of all the earth is just;
Holy and true are all his ways:
Let every creature speak his praise.

3 Come, make your wants, your burdens
The contrite soul he'll ne'er disown; [known;
And angel bands are waiting there,
His messages of love to bear.

4 O, when his wisdom can mistake,
His might decay, his love forsake,
Then may his children cease to sing,
The Lord omnipotent is King.
                    Conder.

56   *Bless the Lord, O my Soul.*

1 BLESS, O my soul, the living God;
Call home thy thoughts, that rove abroad;
Let all the powers within me join
In work and worship so divine.

2 Bless, O my soul, the God of grace;
His favors claim thy highest praise;
Let not the wonders he hath wrought
Be lost in silence, and forgot.

3 Let every land his power confess;
Let all the earth adore his grace;
My heart and tongue with rapture join
In work and worship so divine.
                    Isaac Watts, 1719.

57

1 SWEET is the day of sacred rest;
No mortal cares shall seize my breast;
O may my heart in tune be found,
Like David's harp of solemn sound.

2 My heart shall triumph in the Lord,
And bless his works and bless his word:
Thy works of grace, how bright they shine;
How deep thy counsels, how divine!

3 And I shall share a glorious part,
When grace hath well refined my heart,
And fresh supplies of joy are shed,
Like holy oil, to cheer my head.

4 Then shall I see, and hear, and know
All I desired or wished below,
And every power find sweet employ
In that eternal world of joy.
                    Isaac Watts.

ADORATION AND PRAISE. 21

WESTFIELD. L. M.   D. A. Winslow

1. Now to the Lord a no-ble song! A-wake, my soul; a-wake, my tongue;
Ho-san-na to th'E-ter-nal Name, And all his bound-less love pro-claim.

Used by per. Oliver Ditson Co., owners of Copyright.

58

2 See where it shines on Jesus' face,
The brightest image of his grace;
God, in the person of his Son,
Has all his mightiest work outdone.

3 Grace! 'tis a sweet, a charming theme;
My thoughts rejoice at Jesus' name!
Ye angels dwell upon the sound;
Ye heavens reflect it to the ground!

4 Oh, may I reach the happy place,
Where he unveils his lovely face!
Where all his beauties you behold;
And sing his name to harps of gold.
Isaac Watts.

59   *Worship of God.*

1 ETERNAL God, almighty cause
Of earth, and seas, and worlds unknown,
All things are subject to thy laws;
All things depend on thee alone.

2 Thy glorious being singly stands,
Of all within itself possessed:
Controlled by none are thy commands;
Thou in thyself alone art blessed.

3 Worship to thee alone belongs;
Worship to thee alone we give;
Thine be our hearts, and thine our songs,
And to thy glory may we live.
Simon Browne, 1720.

60   *Be thou exalted, O God.*

1 My God, in whom are all the springs
Of boundless love and grace unknown,
Hide me beneath thy spreading wings
Till the dark cloud is overblown.

2 My heart is fixed; my song shall raise
Immortal honors to thy name;
Awake, my tongue, to sound his praise—
My tongue, the glory of my frame.

3 High o'er the earth his mercy reigns,
And reaches to the utmost sky;
His truth to endless years remains,
When lower worlds dissolve and die.

4 Be thou exalted, O my God,
Above the heavens where angels dwell;
Thy power on earth be known abroad,
And land to land thy wonders tell.
Isaac Watts.

61   *"A Joyful Song."*

1 SING to the Lord a joyful song;
Lift up your hearts, your voices raise:
To us his gracious gifts belong,
To him our songs of love and praise.

2 For life and love, for rest and food,
For daily help and nightly care,
Sing to the Lord, for he is good,
And praise his name, for it is fair:—

3 For strength to those who on him wait,
His truth to prove, his will to do,
Praise ye our God, for he is great,
Trust in his name, for it is true;—

4 For life below, with all its bliss,
And for that life, more pure and high,
That inner life, which over this
Shall ever shine, and never die.
J. S. B. Monsell.

PUBLIC WORSHIP.

CURTIS. L. M. From "Jubilant Voices." L. V. WHEELER.

1. Be thou, O God, ex-alt-ed high; And, as thy glo-ry fills the sky, So let it be on earth dis-played, Till thou art here as there o-beyed.

62 *Be thou exalted, O God.*

2 O God, my heart is fixed; 'tis bent
 Its thankful tribute to present;
And with my heart, my voice I'll raise
 To thee, my God, in songs of praise.

3 Thy praises, Lord, I will resound
 To all the listening nations round;
Thy mercy highest heaven transcends;
 Thy truth beyond the clouds extends.
                                    Anon.

63 *Serve the Lord with Gladness.*

1 BEFORE Jehovah's awful throne,
 Ye nations bow with sacred joy;
Know that the Lord is God alone;
 He can create, and he destroy.

2 His sovereign power, without our aid,
 Made us of clay, and formed us men;
And, when like wandering sheep we strayed,
 He brought us to his fold again.

3 We'll crowd thy gates, with thankful songs,
 High as the heaven our voices raise;
And Earth, with her ten thousand tongues,
 Shall fill thy courts with sounding praise.

4 Wide as the world is thy command,
 Vast as eternity thy love;
Firm as a rock thy truth shall stand,
 When rolling years shall cease to move.
        Isaac Watts, 1719. Alt. J. Wesley, 1741.

64 *Psalm.*

1 FROM all that dwell below the skies
Let the Creator's praise arise;
Let the Redeemer's name be sung
Through every land, by every tongue.

2 Eternal are thy mercies, Lord;
Eternal truth attends thy word;
Thy praise shall sound from shore to shore,
Till suns shall rise and set no more.
                            Isaac Watts, 1719.

65 *Song of Gratitude and Praise.*

1 GOD of my life, through all my days
I'll tune the grateful notes of praise;
The song shall wake with opening light,
 Ad warble to the silent night.

2 When anxious cares would break my rest,
And griefs would tear my throbbing breast,
The notes of praise, ascending high,
Shall check the murmur and the sigh.

3 When death o'er nature shall prevail,
And all the powers of language fail,
Joy through my swimming eyes shall break,
And mean the thanks I can not speak.

4 But, oh, when that last conflict's o'er,
And I am chained to earth no more,
With what glad accents shall I rise
To join the music of the skies!

5 The cheerful tribute will I give,
Long as a deathless soul can live;
A work so sweet, a theme so high,
Demands and crowns eternity.
                            Doddridge

ADORATION AND PRAISE.

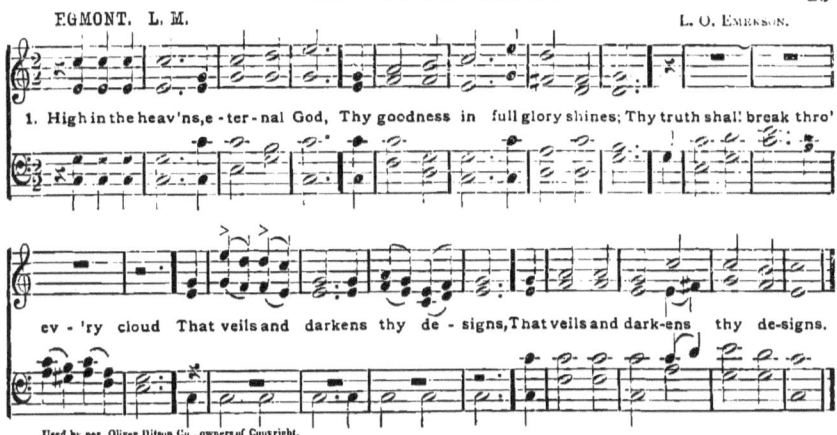

EGMONT. L. M. L. O. Emerson.

1. High in the heav'ns, e-ter-nal God, Thy goodness in full glory shines; Thy truth shall break thro' ev-'ry cloud That veils and darkens thy de-signs, That veils and dark-ens thy de-signs.

Used by per. Oliver Ditson Co., owners of Copyright.

66 *Providence.*

2 Forever firm thy justice stands,
As mountains their foundations keep:
Wise are the wonders of thy hands;
Thy judgments are a mighty deep.

3 Life, like a fountain, rich and free,
Springs from the presence of my Lord;
And in thy light our souls shall see
The glories promised in thy word.
Isaac Watts, 1719.

67 *The Lord of Life.*

1 Lord of all being, throned afar,
Thy glory flames from sun and star;
Center and soul of every sphere,
Yet to each loving heart how near!

2 Sun of our life, thy quickening ray
Sheds on our path the glow of day:
Star of our hope, thy softened light
Cheers the long watches of the night.

3 Our midnight is thy smile withdrawn;
Our noontide is thy gracious dawn;
Our rainbow arch thy mercy's sign:
All, save the clouds of sin, are thine.

4 Grant us thy truth to make us free,
And kindling hearts that burn for thee,
Till all thy living altars claim
One holy light, one heavenly flame.
O. W. Holmes, 1860.

68 *Universal Praise.*

1 Ye nations round the earth, rejoice
Before the Lord, your sovereign King;
Serve him with cheerful heart and voice;
With all your tongues his glory sing.

2 The Lord is God; 'tis he alone
Doth life, and breath, and being give;
We are his work, and not our own—
The sheep that on his pastures live.

3 Enter his gates with songs of joy,
With praises to his courts repair,
And make it your divine employ
To pay your thanks and honors there.

4 The Lord is good; the Lord is kind;
Great is his grace, his mercy sure;
And all the race of man shall find
His truth from age to age endure.
Isaac Watts, 1719.

69 *"Mightier than the mighty Sea."*

1 The floods, O Lord, lift up their voice,
The mighty floods lift up their roar;
The floods in tumult loud rejoice,
And climb in foam the sounding shore.

2 But mightier than the mighty sea,
The Lord of glory reigns on high;
Far o'er its waves we look to thee,
And see their fury break and die.

3 Thy word is true, thy promise sure,
That ancient promise, sealed in love;
Here be thy temple ever pure,
As thy pure mansions shine above.
George Burgess.

PUBLIC WORSHIP.

BRATTLE STREET. C. M. D.   Ignac Pleyel, 1791. Arr. by Nahum Mitchell, 1812.

1. While thee I seek, protecting Power! Be my vain wish-es stilled; And may this con-se-crated hour With bet-ter hopes be filled. Thy love the pow'r of tho't bestowed; To thee my tho'ts would soar. Thy mer-cy o'er my life has flow'd; That mercy I a-dore.

70

2 In each event of life how clear
   Thy ruling hand I see!
Each blessing to my soul more dear
   Because conferred by thee.
In every day that crowns my days,
   In every pain I bear,
My heart shall find delight in praise,
   Or seek relief in prayer.

3 When gladness wings my favored hour,
   Thy love my thoughts shall fill;
Resigned, when storms of sorrow lower,
   My soul shall meet thy will.
My lifted eye, without a tear,
   The gathering storm shall see;
My steadfast heart shall know no fear;
   That heart will rest on thee.
Mrs. H. M. Williams.

71   *Rejoicing in God.*

1 Rejoice, believer, in the Lord,
   Who makes your cause his own:
The hope that's built upon his word
   Can ne'er be overthrown.
Though many foes beset your road,
   And feeble is your arm,
Your life is hid with Christ in God,
   Beyond the reach of harm.

2 Weak as you are, you shall not faint,
   Or, fainting, shall not die;
For God, the strength of every saint,
   Will aid you from on high.
As surely as Christ overcame,
   And triumphed once for you,
So surely you that love his name
   Shall triumph in him too.
John Newton.

72   *Rejoice in the Lord.*

1 Now to our loving Father, God,
   A gladsome song begin;
His smile is on the world abroad,
   His joy our hearts within.
We need not, Lord, our gladness leave
   To worship thee aright;
Our joyfulness for praise receive;
   Thou make'st our lives so bright!

2 We turn to God a smiling face,
   He smiles on us again;
He loves to see our cheerfulness,
   And hear our gladsome strain.
The pure in heart are always glad,
   The smile of God they feel;
He doth the secret of his joy
   To blameless hearts reveal.
Hymns and Tunes.

ADORATION AND PRAISE.

WARWICK. C. M.   S. STANLEY.

1. Come, let us lift our joy-ful eyes Up to the courts a-bove,
And smile to see our Fa-ther there Up-on a throne of love.

73   *"Access to God by a Mediator."*

2 Come, let us bow before his feet,
   And venture near the Lord;
No fiery cherub guards his seat,
   Nor double-flaming sword.

3 The peaceful gates of heavenly bliss
   Are opened by the Son;
High let us raise our notes of praise,
   And reach th' almighty throne.

4 To thee, ten thousand thanks we bring,
   Great Advocate on high,
And glory to th' eternal King,
   Who lays his anger by.
Isaac Watts.

74   *Devotion.*

1 WE bow before thy mercy-seat,
   O Lord, our Heavenly King,
The wonders of thy grace repeat,
   And grateful tributes bring.

2 Grant us thy Holy Spirit, Lord,
   Our souls with love inspire,
And may instruction from thy word
   Increase each pure desire.

3 Where'er thy servants worship thee,
   From east to farthest west,
Upon the land, or on the sea,
   May all in thee be blessed.

4 Remember those by whom the light
   Of life and truth divine
Has not been seen,—dispel their night,—
   On them in glory shine.
B. S. Batchelor

75   *One Thing have I desired of the Lord.*

1 THE Lord of glory is my light,
   And my salvation too:
God is my strength, nor will I fear
   What all my foes can do.

2 One privilege my heart desires—
   O, grant me an abode
Among the churches of thy saints,
   The temples of my God.

3 There shall I offer my requests,
   And see thy beauty still;
Shall hear thy messages of love,
   And there inquire thy will.

4 When troubles rise and storms appear,
   There may his children hide:
God has a strong pavilion, where
   He makes my soul abide.
Isaac Watts.

76   *Psalm 65.*

1 PRAISE waits in Zion, Lord! for thee
   There shall our vows be paid;
Thou hast an ear when sinners pray
   All flesh shall seek thine aid.

2 O Lord! our guilt and fears prevail,
   But pardoning grace is thine;
And thou wilt grant us power and skill,
   To conquer every sin.

3 Thus shall the wondering nations see
   The Lord is good and just;
The distant isles shall fly to thee,
   And make thy name their trust.
Isaac Watts.

PUBLIC WORSHIP.

SILVER STREET S. M.   Isaac Smith, 1770.

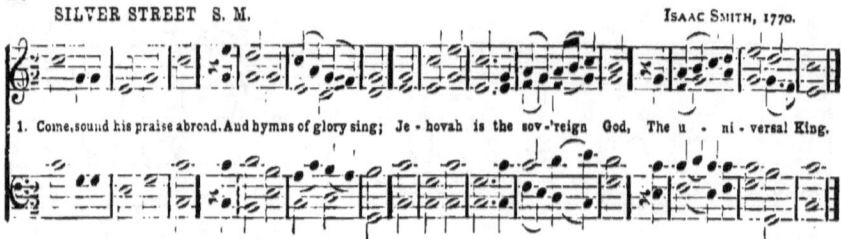

1. Come, sound his praise abroad, And hymns of glory sing; Jehovah is the sov-'reign God, The u-ni-versal King.

77   *Call to Worship.*

2 He formed the deep unknown;
   He gave the seas their bound;
The watery worlds are all his own,
   And all the solid ground.

3 Come, worship at his throne,
   Come, bow before the Lord:
We are his work, and not our own;
   He formed us by his word.

4 To-day attend his voice,
   Nor dare provoke his rod;
Come, like the people of his choice,
   And own your gracious God.
                          Isaac Watts, 1719.

78   *Praise.*

1 Stand up, and bless the Lord,
   Ye people of his choice;
Stand up, and bless the Lord, your God,
   With heart and soul and voice.

2 Though high above all praise,
   Above all blessing high,
Who would not fear his holy name,
   And laud and magnify?

3 Stand up, and bless the Lord;
   The Lord, your God, adore;
Stand up, and bless his glorious name,
   Henceforth, forevermore.
                        James Montgomery, 1825.

79   *Exhortation to Praise.*

1 Arise, and bless the Lord,
   Ye people of his choice;
Arise, and bless the Lord, your God,
   With heart, and soul, and voice.

2 O for the living flame,
   From his own altar brought,
To touch our lips, our souls inspire,
   And wing to heaven our thought!

3 God is our strength and song,
   And his salvation ours;
Then be his love in Christ proclaimed
   With all our ransomed powers.
                       James Montgomery.

80   *Praising God for Mercies.*

1 Oh bless the Lord, my soul!
   Let all within me join,
And aid my tongue, to bless his name
   Whose favors are divine.

2 Oh bless the Lord, my soul!
   Nor let his mercies lie
Forgotten in unthankfulness,
   And without praises die.

3 'Tis he forgives thy sins;
   'Tis he relieves thy pain;
'Tis he that heals thy sicknesses,
   And makes thee strong again.

4 He crowns thy life with love;
   He rescues from the grave:
He that redeemed my soul from death
   Hath sovereign power to save.
                       Isaac Watts, 1719.

81   *Goodness of God's Mercy.*

1 My soul, repeat his praise
   Whose mercies are so great,
Whose anger is so slow to rise,
   So ready to abate.

2 His power subdues our sins,
   And his forgiving love
Far as the east is from the west
   Doth all our guilt remove.

3 High as the heavens are raised
   Above the ground we tread,
So far the riches of his grace
   Our highest thoughts exceed.
                       Isaac Watts, 1719.

ADORATION AND PRAISE. 27

WILMOT. 8s & 7s. C. M. von WEBER, 1820.

1. Praise the Lord; ye heav'ns adore him; Praise him, angels, in the height;
Sun and moon, rejoice before him; Praise him all ye stars of light.

82 *Praise the Lord.*

2 Praise the Lord, for he hath spoken;
  Worlds his mighty voice obeyed:
Laws, which never can be broken,
  For their guidance he hath made.

3 Praise the Lord, for he is glorious;
  Never shall his promise fail:
God hath made his saints victorious;
  Sin and death shall not prevail.

4 Praise the God of our salvation,
  Hosts on high his power proclaim;
Heaven and earth, and all creation,
  Praise and magnify his name.
    Dublin Col.

83 *Universal Praise.*

1 PRAISE to thee, thou great Creator!
  Praise to thee from every tongue;
Join, my soul, with every creature,
  Join the universal song.

2 Father! Source of all compassion!
  Pure, unbounded grace is thine;
Hail the God of our salvation,
  Praise him for his love divine!

3 For ten thousand blessings given,
  For the hope of future joy,
Sound his praise thro' earth and heaven,
  Sound Jehovah's praise on high.

4 Joyfully on earth adore him,
  Till in heaven our song we raise;
There enraptured fall before him,
  Lost in wonder, love, and praise.
    John Fawcett, 1767.

84 *Holy, holy, holy Lord.*

1 LORD, thy glory fills the heaven;
  Earth is with its fulness stored;
Unto thee be glory given,
  Holy, holy, holy Lord.

2 Heaven is still with anthems singing;
  Earth takes up the angel's cry,
Holy, holy, holy, singing,
  Lord of hosts, thou Lord most high.

3 Ever thus in God's high praises,
  Brethren, let our tongues unite,
While our thoughts his greatness raises,
  And our love his gifts excite.

4 Thus thy glorious name confessing,
  We adopt the angel's cry:
Holy, holy, holy, blessing
  Thee, the Lord our God most high.
    Richard Mant.

PUBLIC WORSHIP.

SEYMOUR. 7s.   C. M. von Weber.   Arr. by H. W. Greatorex, 1849.

1. All ye nations, praise the Lord! All ye lands, your voices raise! Heav'n and earth, with loud accord, Praise the Lord, forever praise!

85   *Praise the Lord.*
2 For his truth and mercy stand,
  Past and present and to be,
Like the years of his right hand,
  Like his own eternity.

3 Praise him, ye who know his love!
  Praise him, from the depths beneath!
Praise him, in the heights above!
  Praise your Maker, all that breathe!
                   James Montgomery, 1822.

86   *Holy is the Lord.*
1 Holy, holy, holy, Lord,
  Be thy glorious name adored;
Lord, thy mercies never fail;
  Hail, celestial goodness, hail!

2 Though unworthy, Lord, thine ear,
  Deign our humble songs to hear;
Purer praise we hope to bring
  When around thy throne we sing.

3 While on earth ordained to stay,
  Guide our footsteps in thy way,

Then on high we'll joyful raise
Songs of everlasting praise.
                 Benjamin Williams.

87   *Lowly Praise.*
1 Lord, in heaven, thy dwelling-place,
  Hear the praises of our race,
And, while hearing, let thy grace
  Dews of sweet forgiveness pour;

2 While we know, benignant King,
  That the praises which we bring
Are a worthless offering
  Till thy blessing makes it more.

3 More of truth and more of might,
More of love and more of light,
More of reason and of right,
  From thy pardoning grace be given.

4 It can make the humblest song
Sweet, acceptable, and strong
As the strains the angels' throng
  Pour around the throne of heaven.
                 Sir John Bowring.

SAVANNAH. 10s.   Ignace Pleyel.

1. We praise thee, Lord, with earliest morning ray; We praise thee with the glowing light of day; All things that live and move, by sea and land, For-ev-er read-y at thy service stand.

88   *Universal Praise.*
2 Thy name supreme, thy kingdom, in us dwell,
Thy will constrain and feed and guide us well;
Guard us, redeem us in the evil hour;
For thine the glory, Lord, and thine the power.
                 Johann Franck.

ADORATION AND PRAISE.

ITALY. 6s & 4s.
Felice Giardini, 1760.

1. Come, thou Al-might-y King! Help us thy name to sing; Help us to praise!
{ Fa-ther all glo-ri-ous, }
{ O'er all vic-to-ri-ous, } Come and reign o-ver us, An-cient of Days!

89   *Invocation.*

2 Come, thou all-gracious Lord,
By heaven and earth adored,
  Our prayer attend!
Come, and thy children bless;
Give thy good word success;
Make thine own holiness
  On us descend.

3 Never from us depart;
Rule thou in every heart,
  Hence, evermore.
Thy sovereign majesty
May we in glory see,
And to eternity
  Love and adore.
Charles Wesley, 1757.

90   *Praise in the Courts of the Lord.*

1 Praise ye Jehovah's name,
Praise through his courts proclaim;
  Rise and adore;
High o'er the heavens above
Sound his great acts of love,
While his rich grace we prove,
  Vast as his power.

2 Now let the trumpet raise
Triumphant sounds of praise,
  Wide as his fame;
There let the harp be found;
Organs, with solemn sound,
Roll your deep notes around,
  Filled with his name.

3 While his high praise we sing,
Strike every sounding string—
  Sweet the accord.
His vital breath bestows;
Let every breath that flows
His noblest fame disclose:
  Praise ye the Lord.
Goode.

91   *Supplication.*

1 Word, whose creative thrill
Wakes in all nature still
  Life, light, and bloom!
Come with resistless ray,
Chase all our clouds away,
And with thy heavenly day
  All souls illume!

2 Spirit, in whom we live!
Thou who dost yearn to give
  All hearts thy rest!
When earthly joys take flight,
Cheer thou the earthly night,
And in the morning light
  Still be our guest!

3 And when th' eternal morn,
From death's deep night shades born,
  Our eyes shall see,
Father, thy word, thy breath,
Thy Christ who conquereth
Sorrow and sin and death,
  Our trust shall be!
Charles T. Brooks, 1779.

PUBLIC WORSHIP.

ST. CATHERINE'S. H. M. 3d P. M.   H. R. PALMER.

1. Ye boundless realms of joy, Ex-alt your Maker's fame; His praise your songs employ, A-bove the star-ry frame: Your voi-ces raise; Ye cher-u-bim, Ye cher-u-bim And ser-a-phim, To sing his praise.

92

2 Let them adore the Lord,
And praise his holy name,
By whose almighty word,
  They all from nothing came;
    And all shall last
    From changes free,
  His firm decree
Stands ever fast.

3 His chosen saints to grace,
He sets them up on high;
And favors Israel's race,
  Who still to him are nigh:
    O therefore raise
    Your grateful voice,
  And still rejoice
The Lord to praise.
             N. Tate

MERTON, C. M.   H. K. OLIVER.

1. Long as I live I'll bless thy name, My King, my God of love; My work and joy shall be the same In the bright world above.

93 *I will praise thy Name forever and ever.*

2 Great is the Lord, his power unknown;
  O, let his praise be great;
I'll sing the honors of thy throne,
  Thy works of grace repeat.

3 Fathers to sons shall teach thy name,
  And children learn thy ways,

Ages to come thy truth proclaim,
  And nations sound thy praise.

4 The world is governed by thy hand;
  Thy saints are ruled by love;
And thine eternal kingdom stands,
  Though rocks and hills remove.
             Isaac Watts.

ADORATION AND PRAISE. 31

HADDAM. H. M.

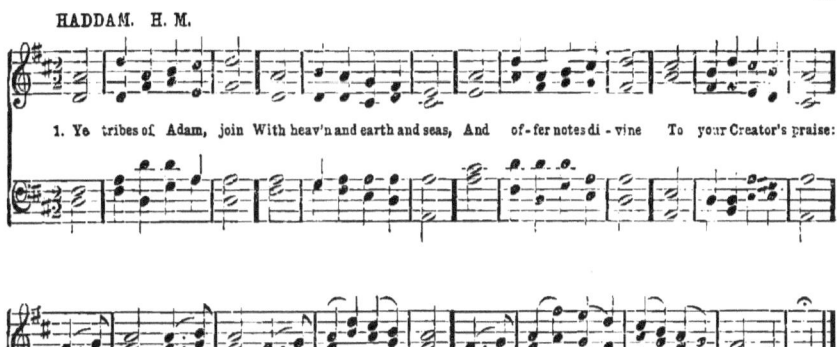

1. Ye tribes of Adam, join With heav'n and earth and seas, And of-fer notes di-vine To your Creator's praise:

Ye ho-ly throng of an-gels bright, In worlds of light, be-gin the song.

94 *Praise from all Creatures.*

2 The shining worlds above
In glorious order stand,
Or in swift courses move,
By his supreme command:
He spake the word, and all their frame
From nothing came, to praise the Lord.

3 He moved their mighty wheels
In unknown ages past,
And each his word fulfils,
While time and nature last:
In different ways his works proclaim
His wondrous name, and speak his praise.

4 Let all the nations fear
The God who rules above;
He brings his people near,
And makes them taste his love:
While earth and sky attempt his praise,
His saints shall raise his honors high.
Tate and Brady

95 *God's wondrous Love*

1 O FOR a shout of joy
High as the theme we sing!
To this divine employ
Your hearts and voices bring;
Sound, sound through all the earth abroad
The love, th' eternal love, of God.

2 Unnumbered myriads stand
Of seraphs bright and fair;
Or bow at his right hand,
And pay their homage there,
But strive in vain, with loudest chord,
To sound the wondrous love of God.

3 Yet sinners saved by grace,
In songs of lower key,
In every age and place,
Have sung the mystery,—
Have told in strains of sweet accord,
Thy love, thy sovereign love, O Lord.

4 Though earth and hell assail,
And doubts and fears arise,
The weakest shall prevail,
And grasp the heavenly prize,
And through an endless age record
The love, th' unchanging love, of God.
Young

PUBLIC WORSHIP.

PARK STREET. L. M.   F. M. A. VENUA. Arr. by LOWELL MASON.

1. Awake, my soul, and with the sun Thy daily stage of duty run; Shake off dull sloth, and joyful rise To pay thy morning sacrifice, To pay thy morning sacrifice.

96   *I will sing aloud in the Morning.*

2 Wake, and lift up thyself, my heart,
And with the angels bear thy part,
Who all night long unwearied sing
High praises to the eternal King.

3 Glory to thee, who safe hast kept,
And hast refreshed me while I slept;
Grant, Lord, when I from death shall wake,
I may of endless life partake.
Thomas Ken.

97   *Morning Prayer for Direction.*

1 GOD of the morning, at whose voice
The cheerful sun makes haste to rise,
And like a giant doth rejoice
To run his journey through the skies,—

2 O, like the sun may I fulfil
Th' appointed duties of the day;
With ready mind and active will
March on, and keep my heavenly way.

3 Lord, thy commands are clean and pure,
Enlightening our beclouded eyes,
Thy threatenings just, thy promise sure;
Thy gospel makes the simple wise.

4 Give me thy counsel for my guide,
And then receive me to thy bliss;
All my desires and hopes beside
Are faint and cold, compared with this.
Isaac Watts, 1700.

98   *Evening.*

1 AGAIN, as evening's shadow falls,
We gather in these hallowed walls,
And vesper hymn and vesper prayer
Rise mingling on the holy air.

2 May struggling hearts, that seek release,
Here find the rest of God's own peace,
And, strengthened here by hymn and prayer,
Lay down the burden and the care.

3 O God, our light, to thee we bow;
Within all shadows standest thou;
Give deeper calm than night can bring,
Give sweeter songs than lips can sing.

4 Life's tumult we must meet again,
We cannot at the shrine remain;
But in the spirit's secret cell
May hymn and praise forever dwell.
S. Longfellow, 1864.

99   *Thou shalt seek me in the Morning.*

1 Now with creation's early song,
Let us, the children of the day,
Cast off the darkness which so long
Has led our guilty souls astray.

2 O, may the morn, so pure, so clear,
Its own sweet calm in us instil—
A guileless mind, a heart sincere,
Simplicity of word and will.

3 And ever, as the day glides by,
May we the busy senses rein,
Keep guard upon the hand and eye,
Nor let the body suffer stain.

4 Give grace, O God, for love of thee,
To scorn all vanities below,
Faith to detect each falsity,
And knowledge thee alone to know.
Anon.

MORNING AND EVENING.

HEBRON. L. M. — Lowell Mason, 1830.

1. Thus far the Lord has led me on; Thus far his pow'r pro-longs my days;
And ev-'ry eve-ning shall make known Some fresh me-mo-rial of his grace.

100 *Evening Hymn.*

2 Much of my time has run to waste,
And I, perhaps, am near my home,
But he forgives my follies past,
And gives me strength for days to come.

3 I lay my body down to sleep;
Peace is the pillow for my head;
While well-appointed angels keep
Their watchful stations round my bed.

4 Thus, when the night of death shall come,
My flesh shall rest beneath the ground,
And wait thy voice to break my tomb,
With sweet salvation in the sound.
Isaac Watts, 1709.

101 *An ancient Psalm of the Morning.*

1 O Christ, with each returning morn,
Thine image to our heart be borne;
And may we ever clearly see
Our Friend and Saviour, Lord, in thee.

2 May grace each idle thought control,
And sanctify our wayward soul;
May guile depart, and malice cease,
And all within be joy and peace.

3 Our daily course, O Jesus bless;
Make plain the way of holiness;
From sudden falls our feet defend,
And cheer at last our journey's end.
Chandler.

102 *The Morning Hour.*

1 In sleep's serene oblivion laid,
I safely passed the silent night;
Again I see the breaking shade,
And drink again the morning light.

2 O, guide me through the various maze
My doubtful feet are doomed to tread,
And spread thy shield's protecting blaze
When dangers press around my head.

3 A deeper shade shall soon impend,
A deeper sleep my eyes oppress;
Yet then thy strength shall still defend,
Thy goodness still delight to bless.

4 That deeper shade shall break away,
That deeper sleep shall leave my eyes;
Thy light shall give eternal day;
Thy love, the rapture of the skies.
John Hawkesworth, 1773.

103 *Let my Prayer be as Incense.*

1 My God, accept my early vows,
Like morning incense in thy house;
And let my nightly worship rise
Sweet as the evening sacrifice.

2 Watch o'er my lips, and guard them, Lord,
From every rash and heedless word,
Nor let my feet incline to tread
The guilty path where sinners lead.

3 O, may the righteous, when I stray,
Smite and reprove my wandering way,
Their gentle words, like ointment shed,
Shall never bruise, but cheer my head.

4 When I behold them pressed with grief,
I'll cry to Heaven for their relief,
And by my warm petitions prove
How much I prize their faithful love.
Isaac Watts.

PUBLIC WORSHIP.

BROWNELL. L. M. 61. Arr. fr. HADYN.

1. As ev-ery day thy mer-cy spares, Will bring its tri-als or its cares, O Fa-ther! till my life shall end, Be thou my coun-sel-lor and friend; Teach me thy statues all di-vine, And let thy will be al-ways mine.

104 *Morning or Evening.*

2 When each day's scenes and labors close,
And wearied nature seeks repose,
With pardoning mercy, richly blest,
Guard me, my Father, while I rest;
And, as each morning's sun shall rise,
Oh lead me onward to the skies!

3 And at my life's last setting sun,
My conflict o'er, my labors done,
Father, thine heavenly radiance shed,
To cheer and bless my dying bed;
And from death's gloom my spirit raise,
To see thy face and sing thy praise.

Christian Psalmist.

FADING, STILL FADING. P. M.

105
1. Fading, still fading, the last beam is shining; Fa-ther in heav-en the day is de-clin-ing; Thine is the dark-ness, as thine is the light; We trust thee by day and we trust thee by night. From the fall of the shade till the morn-ing bells chime, Shield us from dan-ger and guard us from crime. Fa-ther, have mer-cy, Fa-ther, have mer-cy, Fa-ther, have mer-cy, thro' Je-sus Christ, our Lord. A-men.

2. Father in heav-en, oh, hear when we call, Thou the Pro-tec-tor and Sav-iour of all! Faint-ing and fee-ble, we trust in thy might; In doubt-ing and dark-ness, thy love be our light; Let us sleep on thy breast while the night-ta-per burns, And wake in thine arms when the morn-ing re-turns.

MORNING AND EVENING.

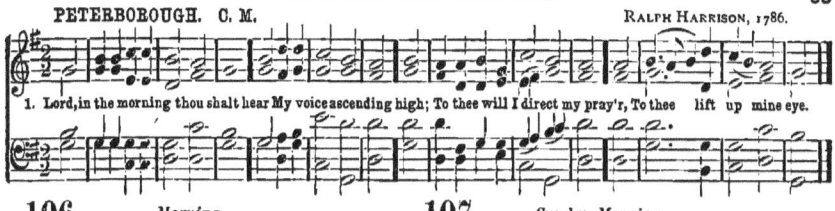
PETERBOROUGH. C. M.   RALPH HARRISON, 1786.

1. Lord, in the morning thou shalt hear My voice ascending high; To thee will I direct my pray'r, To thee lift up mine eye.

106 *Morning.*

2 Thou art a God, before whose sight
 The wicked shall not stand:
 Sinners shall ne'er be thy delight,
 Nor dwell at thy right hand.

3 But to thy house will I resort,
 To taste thy mercies there;
 I will frequent thy holy court,
 And worship in thy fear.

4 Oh, may thy Spirit guide my feet
 In ways of righteousness!
 Make every path of duty straight
 And plain before my face.
                 Isaac Watts.

107 *Sunday Morning.*

1 How sweet, how calm, this sacred morn!
 How pure the air that breathes,
 And soft the sounds upon it borne
 And light its vapor wreaths!

2 It seems as if the Christian's prayer,
 For peace and joy and love,
 Were answered by the very air
 That wafts its strains above.

3 Let each unholy passion cease,
 Each evil thought be crushed;
 Each anxious care that mars thy peace
 In faith and love be hushed.
                 Anon.

WOODLAND. C. M.   N. D. GOULD.

1. Once more, my soul, the ris-ing day Sa-lutes thy waking eyes: Once more, my voice, thy trib-ute pay, Once more, my voice, thy trib-ute pay To Him who rules the skies.

108 *Day unto Day uttereth Speech.*

2 Night unto night his name repeats;
 The day renews the sound,
 Wide as the heavens on which he sits
 To turn the seasons round.

3 Great God, let all my hours be thine,
 While I enjoy the light;
 Then shall my sun in smiles decline,
 And bring a peaceful night.
                 Isaac Watts.

109 *He was there alone.*

1 I LOVE to steal awhile away
 From every cumbering care,
 And spend the hours of setting day
 In humble, grateful prayer.

2 I love to think on mercies past,
 And future good implore,
 And all my cares and sorrows cast
 On Him whom I adore.

3 I love by faith to take a view
 Of brighter scenes in heaven;
 The prospect doth my strength renew,
 While here by tempests driven.

4 Thus, when life's toilsome day is o'er,
 May its departing ray
 Be calm as this impressive hour,
 And lead to endless day.
                 P. H. Brown.

PUBLIC WORSHIP.

STATE STREET S. M.   J. C. WOODMAN, 1844.

1. How sweet the melt-ing lay, That breaks up-on the ear, When, at the hour of ris-ing day, Chris-tians u-nite in prayer.

110 *Morning Prayer.*

2 The breezes waft their cries
   Up to Jehovah's throne;
He listens to their burning sighs,
   And sends his blessings down.

3 So Jesus rose to pray,
   Before the morning light;
Once on the chilling mount did stay,
   And wrestle all the night.
                                Anon.

111 *Begin with God.*

1 BEGIN the day with God;
   He is thy sun and day;
He is the radiance of thy dawn:
   To him address thy lay.

2 Cast every weight aside;
   Do battle with each sin;
Fight with the faithless world without,
   The faithless heart within.

3 The first transaction be
   With God himself above:
So shall thy business prosper well,
   And all the day be love.
                          Horatius Bonar.

112 *Evening Reflections.*

1 THE day is past and gone,
   The evening shades appear;
O, may we all remember well
   The night of death draws near.

2 Lord, keep us safe this night,
   Secure from all our fears;
May angels guard us while we sleep,
   Till morning light appears.

3 And if we early rise,
   And view th' unwearied sun,
May we set out to win the prize,
   And after glory run.

4 And when our days are past,
   And we from time remove,
O, may we in thy bosom rest,
   The bosom of thy love.
                          J. Leland.

113

1 THE day is past and gone,
   Great God, we bow to thee;
Again, as shades of night steal on,
   Unto thy side we flee.

2 O when shall that day come,
   Ne'er sinking in the West,
That country and that happy home
   Where none shall break our rest;

3 Where all things shall be peace,
   And pleasure without end,
And golden harps, that never cease,
   With joyous hymns shall blend;

4 Where we, preserved beneath
   The shelter of thy wing,
For evermore thy praise shall breathe,
   And of thy mercy sing.
                   Rev. Wm. John Blew.

MORNING AND EVENING.

STOCKWELL. 8s & 7s.   D. E. Jones

1. Sav-iour, breathe an eve-ning bless-ing, Ere re-pose our spir-its seal;
Sin and want we come con-fess-ing, Thou canst save, and thou canst heal.

114 *The darkness hideth not from Thee.*

2 Though destruction walk around us,
Though the arrow near us fly,
Angel guards from thee surround us;
We are safe if thou art nigh.

3 Though the night be dark and dreary,
Darkness cannot hide from thee;
Thou art He who, never weary,
Watcheth where thy people be;

4 Should swift death this night o'ertake us,
And our couch become our tomb,
May the morn in heaven awake us,
Clad in light and deathless bloom.
Edmeston.

115 *Evening Sacrifice.*

1 On the dewy breath of even
Thousand odors mingling rise,
Borne like incense up to heaven—
Nature's evening sacrifice.

2 With her favorite offerings blending,
Let our glad thanksgiving be,
To thy throne, O Lord, ascending—
Incense of our hearts to thee.

3 Thou whose favors without number
All our days with gladness bless,
Let thine eye, that knows no slumber,
Guard our hours of helplessness.

4 Then, though conscious we are sleeping
In the outer courts of death,
Safe beneath a Father's keeping,
Calm we rest in perfect faith.
Anon.

116 *Tarry, Saviour, at Evening.*

1 Tarry with me, O my Saviour,
For the day is passing by;
See! the shades of evening gather,
And the night is drawing nigh.

2 Deeper, deeper grow the shadows,
Paler now the glowing west;
Swift the night of death advances;
Shall it be the night of rest?

3 Tarry with me, O my Saviour;
Lay my head upon thy breast
Till the morning; then awake me—
Morning of eternal rest.
Mrs C. S. Smith.

117 *Blessing sought.*

1 Gracious Saviour, thus before thee,
With our varied want and care;
For a blessing we implore thee,
Listen to our evening prayer.

2 By thy favor safely living,
With a grateful heart we raise
Songs of jubilant thanksgiving;
Listen to our evening praise.

3 Thro' the day, Lord, thou hast given
Strength sufficient for our need;
Cheered us with sweet hopes of heaven,
Helped and comforted indeed.

4 Lord, we thank thee, and adore thee,
For the solace of thy love;
And rejoicing thus before thee,
Wait thy blessing from above!
Henry Bateman.

PUBLIC WORSHIP.

VESPER HYMN.* 8s & 7s.
Russian Air.

* *Double, by singing small notes.*

118 *Jubilate.*

1 Soft as fades the sunset splendor,
    And the light of day grows dim,
We to thee our praises render;
    Sing we thus our vesper hymn:
        Jubilate! Amen!
Father, gracious, loving, tender,
    O, accept the loving strain.

2 Day by day comes rich in blessing;
    Night by night brings holy calm;
Lord, to thee our praise addressing,
    Rises thus our joyful psalm:
        Jubilate! Amen!
But, unworthiness confessing,
    Into silence fades again.
                    S. Longfellow.

119 *Vesper Hymn.*

1 Hark! the vesper hymn is stealing
    O'er the waters soft and clear;
Nearer yet, and nearer pealing,
    Now it bursts upon the ear!
        Jubilate! Amen!
Farther now, now farther stealing,
    Soft it fades upon the ear.

2 Now like moonlight waves retreating
    To the shore, it dies along;
Now like angry surges meeting,
    Breathes the mingled tide of song,
        Jubilate! Amen!
Hush! again like waves retreating
    To the shore, it dies along.
                    James Montgomery.

MORNING AND EVENING.

SALISBURY. L. M. D.   Arr from HAYDN, by DR. MASON.

How shall we praise thee, Lord of light! How shall we all thy love de-clare!
The earth is veiled in shades of night, But heav'n is o - pen to our pray'r—
That heav'n so bright with stars and suns— That glo-rious heav'n which has no bound,
Where the full tide of be - ing runs, And life and beau - ty glow a - round.

120 *Evening Worship*

2 We would adore thee, God sublime!
  Whose power and wisdom, love and grace
Are greater than the round of time,
  And wider than the bounds of space.
O, how shall thought expression find,
  All lost in thine immensity!
How shall we see thee, glorious Mind,
  Amid thy dread infinity!

3 But thou art present with us here,
  As in thy glittering high, domain;
And grateful hearts and humble fear
  Can never seek thy face in vain.
Help us to praise thee, Lord of light!
  Help us thy boundless love declare;
And, here within thy courts to-night,
  Aid us, and hearken to our prayer.
                    Sir John Bowring.

121 *Evening Hymn.*

1 O HOLY Father! 'mid the calm
  And stillness of this evening hour,
We would lift up our solemn psalm,
  To praise thy goodness and thy power:
For over us, and over all,
  Thy tender mercies still extend,
Nor vainly shall thy children call
  On thee, our Father and our Friend!

2 Kept by thy goodness through the day,
  Thanksgiving to thy name we pour!
Night o'er us, with its stars,—we pray
  Thy love. to guard us evermore!
In grief, console; in gladness, bless;
  In darkness, guide; in sickness, cheer;
Till, perfected in righteousness,
  Before thy throne our souls appear!
                    W. H. Burleigh.

PUBLIC WORSHIP.

EVENING HYMN. L. M. — TALLIS.

1. Glo-ry to thee, my God, this night, For all the bless-ings of the light;
Keep me, oh, keep me, King of kings! Be-neath thine own al-might-y wings.

122 *"Evening Song."*

2 Forgive me, Lord, for thy dear Son,
The ill which I this day have done;
That with the world, myself, and thee,
I, ere I sleep, at peace may be.

3 Teach me to live, that I may dread
The grave as little as my bed:
Teach me to die, that so I may
Rise glorious at the judgment-day.

4 Oh, let my soul on thee repose
And may sweet sleep mine eyelids close!
Sleep, which shall me more vigorous make,
To serve my God when I awake.
Thos. Ken.

ANATOLIUS. 7s, 6s & 8s. — A. H. BROWN.

1. The day is past and o-ver; All thanks, O Lord! to thee; We pray thee now that sin-less
The hours of dark may be; O Je-sus! keep us in thy sight, And save us thro' the coming night.

123 *"Guard and Save."*

2 The joys of day are over;
We lift our hearts to thee
And ask thee that offenceless
The hours of dark may be;
O Jesus! make their darkness light,
And save us through the coming night.

3 The toils of day are over;
We raise our hymn to thee;
And ask that free from peril
The hours of dark may be;
O Jesus! keep us in thy sight,
And guard us through the coming night.

4 Be thou our souls' preserver,
O God! for thou dost know
How many are the perils
Through which we have to go;
O loving Jesus! hear our call,
And guard and save us from them all.
John M. Neale.

CLOSING HYMNS. 41

DUKE STREET. L. M.   JOHN HATTON, 1709.

1. My God, how end-less is thy love! Thy gifts are ev-'ry eve-ning new;
And morning mer-cies, from a-bove, Gen-tly dis-til, like ear-ly dew.

124 *Morning or Evening Song.*
2 Thou spread'st the curtains of the night,
  Great Guardian of my sleeping hours:
Thy sovereign word restores the light,
  And quickens all my drowsy powers.

3 I yield my powers to thy command;
  To thee I consecrate my days:
Perpetual blessings from thine hand
  Demand perpetual songs of praise.
Isaac Watts.

125 *Christian Farewell.*
1 THY presence, ever-living God,
  Wide through all nature spreads abroad;
Thy watchful eyes, which never sleep,
  In every place thy children keep.

2 To thee we now commit our ways,
  And still implore thy heavenly grace;
Still cause thy face on us to shine,
  And guard and guide us still as thine.

3 Give us within thy house to raise
  Again united songs of praise;
Or, if that joy no more be known,
  Give us to meet around thy throne.
Philip Doddridge.

126 *He calleth his own Sheep by Name.*
1 Now may the Lord, our Shepherd, lead
  To living streams his little flock;
May he in flowery pastures feed,
  Shade us at noon beneath the rock.

2 Now may we hear our Shepherd's voice,
  And gladly answer to his call;
Now may our hearts for Him rejoice
  Who knows, and names, and loves us all.

3 When the chief Shepherd shall appear,
  And small and great before him stand,
O, be the flock assembling here
  Found with the sheep on his right hand.
James Montgomery.

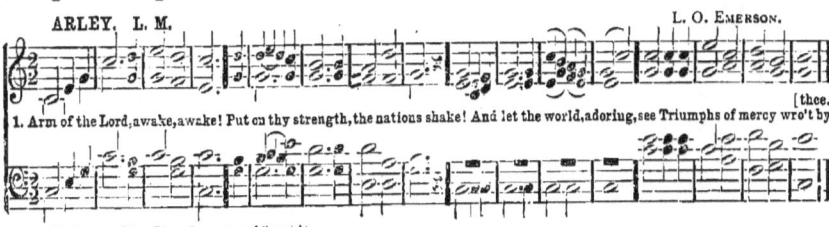

ARLEY. L. M.   L. O. EMERSON.

1. Arm of the Lord, awake, awake! Put on thy strength, the nations shake! And let the world, adoring, see Triumphs of mercy wro't by [thee.

Used y per. Oliver Ditson Co., owners of Copyright

127
2 Say to the heathen, from thy throne,
  "I am Jehovah!—God alone!"—
Thy voice their idols shall confound,
  And cast their altars to the ground.

3 Let Zion's time of favor come;
  O bring the tribes of Israel home:
And let our wondering eyes behold
  Gentiles and Jews in Christ's one fold.

4 Almighty God, thy grace proclaim,
  In every land, of every name:
Let adverse powers before thee fall,
  And crown the Saviour —LORD OF ALL!
Wm. Shrubsole.

PUBLIC WORSHIP.

128 Praise God, from whom all blessings flow; Praise him, all creatures here below; Praise him above, ye heav'n-ly host; Praise Father, Son, and Holy Ghost.

Bishop Thomas Ken.

129
To God, the great, eternal One,
To Jesus Christ, his only Son,
Be ceaseless praise and glory given,
By all on earth and all in heaven.
  N. Summerbell.

130 *Closing Hymn.*
1 COME, dearest Lord, descend and dwell
  By faith and love in every breast;
  Then shall we know, and taste, and feel
  The joys that cannot be expressed.

2 Come, fill our hearts with inward strength,
  Make our expanding souls possess
  And learn the height, and breadth, and
    length
  Of thine immeasurable grace.

3 Now to the God whose power can do
  More than our thoughts and wishes know,
  Be everlasting honors done
  By all the church, through Christ, his Son.
  Isaac Watts, 1709.

1. Ere to the world again we go, / Its pleasures, cares, and idle show, / Thy grace once more, O God, we crave, From folly and from sin to save.

131 *Close of Worship.*
2 Oh may the influence of this day,
  Long as our memory with us stay,
  And as an angel guardian prove,
  To guide us to our home above.
  Anon.

132 *Dismission.*
1 DISMISS us with thy blessing, Lord!
  Help us to feed upon thy word;
  Grant us, our few remaining days,
  To work thy will and live thy praise.

2 Teach us in life and death to bless
  Thee, Lord, our strength and righteousness;
  And grant we all may meet above,
  Where we shall better sing thy love.
  Reginald Heber

CLOSING HYMNS.

SICILY. 8s, 7s & 4s. Sicilian Melody

1. Lord, dismiss us with thy blessing;
   Let us each, thy love possessing,
   Fill our hearts with joy and peace;
   Triumph in redeeming grace;
   Oh, refresh us, Oh, refresh us,
   Trav-'ling thro' this wilderness.

133 *Dismission.*

2 Thanks we give, and adoration,
For the gospel's joyful sound;
May the fruits of thy salvation
In our hearts and lives abound:
 May thy presence
With us evermore be found.

3 Then, whene'er the signal's given,
Us from earth to call away,
Borne on angels' wings to heaven,
Glad the summons to obey,
 May we ever
Reign with Christ in endless day.
Walter Shirley, 1774.

134 *The Spirit and the Word.*

1 COME, thou soul-transforming Spirit!
Bless the sower and the seed;
Let each heart thy grace inherit;
Raise the weak, the hungry feed;
 From thy gospel,
Now supply thy people's need.

2 Oh! may all enjoy the blessing
Which thy word designs to give;
Let us all, thy love possessing,
Joyfully the truth receive;
 And forever
To thy praise and glory live.
Jonathan Evans, 1784.

135 *Close of Service.*

1 COME, Christians, brethren, ere we part;
Join every voice and every heart;
One solemn hymn to God we raise,
Our final song of grateful praise.

2 Christians, we here may meet no more,
But there is yet a happier shore;
And there released from toil and pain,
Soon, brethren, we may meet again.
Henry Kirke White, 1806.

137 "Blessing desired."

Father, bless thy word to all;
Quick and powerful let it prove;
Oh may sinners hear thy call!
Let thy people grow in love.

Thine own gracious message bless,—
Follow it with power divine;
Give the gospel great success:
Thine the work, the glory thine.

Anon.

138 Evening.

2 And when morn again shall call us
  To run life's way,
May we still, whate'er befall us,
  Thy will obey;
From the power of evil hide us,
In the narrow pathway guide us,
Nor thy smile be e'er denied us,
  The live-long day.

3 Guard us waking, guard us sleeping,
  And, when we die,
May we in thy mighty keeping
  All peaceful lie;
When the heavenly call shall wake us,
Do not thou, our God, forsake us,
But to dwell in glory take us
  With thee on high.

Bishop Reginald Heber, 1827. V. 1.
Abp. Richard Whately, 1860. Vs. 2 3.

CLOSING HYMNS. 45

SHAWMUT. S. M.   LOWELL MASON, 1832.

1. The day, O Lord, is spent; A-bide with us and rest; Our hearts' de-sires are ful-ly bent On mak-ing thee our guest.

139   *Evening.*

2 We have not reached that land,
   That happy land, as yet,
Where holy angels round thee stand,
   Whose sun can never set.

3 Our sun is sinking now;
   Our day is almost o'er:
O Sun of Righteousness, do thou
   Shine on us evermore.
                         John M. Neale, 1854.

140   *Sabbath ended*

1 THE day of praise is done;
   The evening shadows fall;
Yet pass not from us with the sun,
   True Light that lightenest all!

2 Around thy throne on high,
   Where night can never be,
The white-robed harpers of the sky
   Bring ceaseless hymns to thee.

3 Too faint our anthems here;
   Too soon of praise we tire;
But oh, the strains how full and clear
   Of that eternal choir!

4 Shine thou within us, then,
   A day that knows no end,
Till songs of angels and of men
   In perfect praise shall blend.
                         John Ellerton

141   *" At Dismission."*

1 ONCE more, before we part,
   Oh, bless the Saviour's name!
Let every tongue and every heart
   Adore and praise the same.

2 Lord, in thy grace we came,
   That blessing still impart;
We met in Jesus' sacred name,
   In Jesus' name we part.

3 Still on thy holy word
   Help us to feed, and grow,
Still to go on to know the Lord,
   And practice what we know.

4 Now, Lord, before we part,
   Help us to bless thy name:
Let every tongue and every heart
   Adore and praise the same.
                         Joseph Hart.

142   *Closing Hours.*

1 LORD, at this closing hour,
   Establish every heart
Upon thy word of truth and power,
   To keep us when we part.

2 Peace to our brethren give;
   Fill all our hearts with love;
In faith and patience may we live
   And seek our rest above.

3 Through changes, bright or drear,
   We would thy will pursue;
And toil to spread thy kingdom here,
   Till we its glory view.

4 To God, the only wise,
   In every age adored,
Let glory from the church arise
   Through Jesus Christ our Lord.
                         E. T. Fitch.

CLOSING HYMNS.

DUNDEE. C. M. [FRENCH.]   ANDRE HART'S PSALTER, 1615.

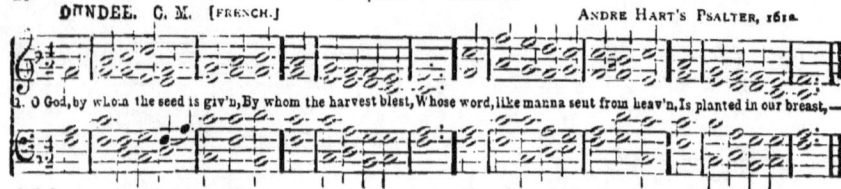

1. O God, by whom the seed is giv'n, By whom the harvest blest, Whose word, like manna sent from heav'n, Is planted in our breast,—

143   *For a Blessing on Truth.*
2 Preserve it from the passing feet,
   And plunderers of the air,
The sultry sun's intenser heat,
   And weeds of worldly care.

3 Though buried deep, or thinly strown,
   Do thou thy grace supply:
The hope in earthly furrows sown
   Shall ripen in the sky.
                Bishop Reginald Heber, 1827.

144   *Psalm 89.*
1 BLEST are the souls that hear and know
   The gospel's joyful sound;
Peace shall attend the path they go,
   And light their steps surround.

2 Their joys shall bear their spirits up
   Through their Redeemer's name;
His righteousness exalts their hope,
   Nor Satan dares condemn.

3 The Lord, our glory and defence,
   Strength and salvation gives;
Israel! thy King for ever reigns,
   Thy God for ever lives.
                Isaac Watts.

145   *Precious Seed.*
1 ALMIGHTY God, thy word is cast
   Like seed into the ground;
Now let the dew of heaven descend,
   And righteous fruits abound.

2 Let not the foe of Christ or man
   This holy seed remove,
But give it root in every heart,
   To bring forth fruits of love.

3 Let not the world's deceitful cares
   The rising plant destroy,
But let it yield, a hundred-fold,
   The fruits of peace and joy.

4 Nor let thy word, so kindly sent
   To raise us to thy throne,
Return to thee, and sadly tell
   That we reject thy Son.
                John Cawood.

GREENVILLE. 8s, 7s & 4.   ROUSSEAU.

1 God of our sal-va-tion, hear us; Bless, O, bless us ere we go;
D.C.—Sav-iour, keep us, Sav-iour, keep us— Keep us safe from ev-'ry foe.
When we join the world, be near us, Lest we cold and care-less grow:

146   *The Close of Worship.*
2 May we live in view of heaven,
   Where we hope to see thy face;
Save us from unhallowed leaven,
   All that might obscure thy grace;
     Keep us walking
Each in his appointed place.

3 As our steps are drawing nearer
   To the place we call our home,
May our view of heaven grow clearer,
   Hope more bright of joys to come,
     And, when dying,
May thy presence cheer the gloom.
                Kelly.

BEING AND GREATNESS. 47

KEENE. L. M.   L. O. Emerson.

1. A-wake, my tongue, thy trib-ute bring, To him who gave thee power to sing:
Praise him, who is all praise a-bove, The source of wis-dom and of love.

Used by per. Oliver Ditson Co., owners of Copyright.

147
2 How vast his knowledge! how profound!
A depth where all our tho'ts are drowned!
The stars he numbers, and their names
He gives to all their heavenly flames.

3 But in redemption, oh, what grace,
Its wonders, oh, what thought can trace!
Here wisdom shines forever bright,
Praise him, my soul, with sweet delight.
Needham.

148   *God Incomprehensible.*
1 GREAT God, in vain man's narrow view
Attempts to look thy nature through!
Our laboring powers with reverence own
Thy glories never can be known.

2 Not the high seraph's mighty thought,
Who countless years his God has sought,
Such wondrous height or depth can find,
Or fully trace thy boundless mind.

3 And yet thy kindness deigns to show
Enough for mortal minds to know;
While wisdom, goodness, power divine,
Through all thy works and conduct shine.

4 Oh, may our souls with rapture trace
Thy works of nature and of grace,
Explore thy sacred truth, and still
Press on to know and do thy will!
Andrew Kippis. 1795.

149   *Divine Sovereignty.*
1 LORD, my weak tho't in vain would climb,
To search the starry vault profound;
In vain would wing her flight sublime,
To find creation's outmost bound.

2 When doubts disturb my troubled breast,
And all is dark as night to me,
Here, as on solid rock, I rest;
That so it seemeth good to thee.

3 Be this my joy, that evermore
Thou rulest all things at thy will;
Thy sovereign wisdom I adore,
And calmly, sweetly trust thee still.
Ray Palmer, 1858.

150   *From everlasting thou art God.*
1 ERE mountains reared their forms sublime,
Or heaven and earth in order stood,
Before the birth of ancient time,
From everlasting, thou art God.

2 A thousand ages, in their flight,
With thee are as a fleeting day;
Past, present, future, to thy sight
At once their various scenes display.

3 But our brief life's a shadowy dream,
A passing thought, that soon is o'er,
That fades with morning's earliest beam,
And fills the musing mind no more.

4 To us, O Lord, the wisdom give,
Each passing moment so to spend,
That we at length with thee may live,
Where life and bliss shall never end.
Anon.

GOD.

LYDIAN. L. M. — L. O. Emerson.

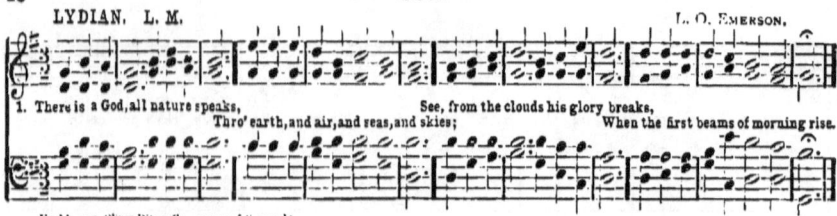

1. There is a God, all nature speaks,
Thro' earth, and air, and seas, and skies;
See, from the clouds his glory breaks,
When the first beams of morning rise.

Used by per. Oliver Ditson Co., owners of Copyright.

151 *The Sun knoweth his going down.*

2 The rising sun, serenely bright,
   O'er the wide world's extended frame,
Incribes in characters of light
   His mighty Maker's glorious name.

3 Diffusing light his influence spreads,
   And health and plenty smile around;
And fruitful fields and verdant meads
   Are with a thousand blessings crowned.

4 Ye curious minds, who roam abroad,
   And trace creation's wonders o'er,
Confess the footsteps of your God,
   Bow down before him and adore.
Steele.

152 *God in all.*

1 There's nothing bright, above, below,
From flowers that bloom to stars that glow,
But in its light my soul can see
Some feature of the Deity.

2 There's nothing dark, below, above,
But in its gloom I trace thy love,
And meekly wait the moment when
Thy touch shall make all bright again.

3 The heaven, the earth, where'er I look,
Shall be one pure and shining book,
Where I may read in words of flame,
The glories of thy wondrous name.
Thomas Moore. 1816.

BARTHOLOMEW. 10s. — Bourgeois.

1. Fa-ther, thy won-ders do not singly stand, Nor far remov'd where feet have seldom stray'd:
A-round us ev-er lies th'enchanted land, In marvels rich to thine own sons dis-play'd.

153 *Heaven not afar off.*

2 In finding thee are all things round us found;
   In losing thee are all things lost beside;
Ears have we, but in vain sweet voices sound,
   And to our eyes the vision is denied.

3 Open our eyes that we that world may see,
   Open our ears that we thy voice may hear,
And in the spirit-land may ever be,
   And feel thy presence with us always near.
Jones Very.

BEING AND GREATNESS.

DEDHAM. C. M. — Gardiner, 1820.

1. Lord, thou art good: all nature shows
Its mighty Author kind:
Thy bounty thro' creation flows,
Full, free, and unconfined.

154 *Universal Goodness of God.*

2 Long hath it been diffused abroad,
Through ages past and gone;
Nor ever can exhausted be,
But still keeps flowing on.

3 Thro' the whole earth it pours supplies,
Spreads joy through every part;
Oh may such love attract my eyes,
And captivate my heart;

4 My highest admiration raise,
My best affections move;
Employ my tongue in songs of praise
And fill my heart with love.
Simon Browne.

155 *Lord, thou hast been our Dwelling-place.*

1 Our God, our help, in ages past,
Our hope for years to come,
Our shelter from the stormy blast,
And our eternal home.

2 Beneath the shadow of thy throne
Thy saints have dwelt secure;
Sufficient is thy arm alone,
And our defence is sure.

3 Before the hills in order stood,
Or earth received her frame,
From everlasting thou art God,
To endless years the same.

4 O God, our help in ages past,
Our hope for years to come,
Be thou our guard while troubles last,
And our eternal home.
Isaac Watts.

156 *The Heavens cannot contain thee.*

1 The heaven of heavens cannot contain
The universal Lord;
Yet he in humble hearts will deign
To dwell, and be adored.

2 Where'er ascends the sacrifice
Of fervent praise and prayer,
Or on the earth, or in the skies,
The God of heaven is there.

3 His presence is diffused abroad
Through realms, thro' worlds unknown;
Who seek the mercies of our God
Are ever near his throne.
Drennan.

157 *Whither shall I go from thy Spirit.*

1 In all my vast concerns with thee,
In vain my soul would try
To shun thy presence, Lord, or flee
The notice of thine eye.

2 Thy all-surrounding sight surveys
My rising and my rest,
My public walks, my private ways,
And secrets of my breast.

3 O, wondrous knowledge, deep and high;
Where can a creature hide?
Within thy circling arms I lie,
Enclosed on every side.

4 So let thy grace surround me still,
And like a bulwark prove,
To guard my soul from every ill,
Secured by sovereign love.
Isaac Watts.

50   GOD.

VARINA. C. M. D.   Johann C. H. Rink. Arr. by Geo. F. Root, 1849.

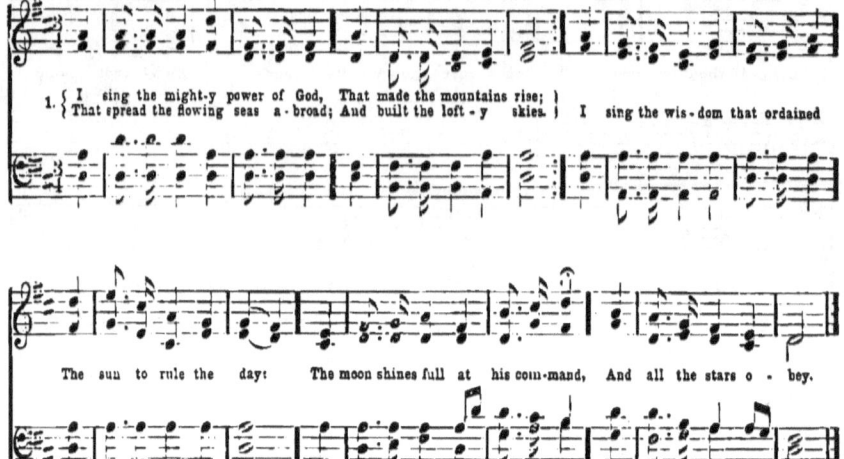

1. I sing the mighty power of God, That made the mountains rise;
That spread the flowing seas abroad; And built the lofty skies. I sing the wisdom that ordained The sun to rule the day: The moon shines full at his command, And all the stars obey.

158   *Mighty in Power.*

2 I sing the goodness of the Lord,
   That filled the earth with food;
He formed the creatures with his word,
   And then pronounced them good.
Lord, how thy wonders are displayed,
   Where'er I turn my eye;
If I survey the ground I tread,
   Or gaze upon the sky!

3 There's not a plant or flower below,
   But makes thy glories known;
And clouds arise and tempests blow,
   By order from thy throne.
Creatures that borrow life from thee
   Are subject to thy care;
There's not a place where we can flee,
   But God is present there.
                     Isaac Watts, 1709.

159   *Presence of God.*

1 Great God, thy penetrating eye
   Pervades my inmost powers;
With awe profound my wandering soul
   Falls prostrate, and adores.
To be incompassed round with God,
   The holy and the just,
Armed with omnipotence to save
   Or crumble me to dust.

2 O, how tremendous is the thought!
   Deep may it be impressed;
And may thy Spirit firmly grave
   This truth within my breast.
Begirt with thee, my fearless soul
   The gloomy vale shall tread;
And thou wilt bind th' immortal crown
   Of glory on my head.
                     Scott.

160   *Holy and reverend is his Name.*

1 Holy and reverend is the name
   Of our eternal King;
Thrice holy Lord! the angels cry;
   Thrice holy! let us sing.
The deepest reverence of the mind
   Pay, O my soul, to God;
Lift with thy hands a holy heart
   To his sublime abode.

2 With sacred awe pronounce his name,
   Whom words nor thoughts can reach;
A broken heart shall please him more
   Than noblest forms of speech.
Thou holy God, preserve my soul
   From all pollution free;
The pure in heart are thy delight,
   And they thy face shall see.
                     Needham.

IN NATURE.

WARDWELL. 7s. J. H. Tenny, by per.

1. Might-y God, the first, the last, What are a-ges in thy sight But as yes-terday when past, Or a watch within the night?

161 *All things Present to God.*

2 All that being ever knew,
  Down, far down, ere time had birth,
  Stands as clear within thy view
  As the present things of earth.

3 In thine all-embracing sight,
  Every change its purpose meets,
  Every cloud floats into light,
  Every woe its glory greets.

4 Whatsoe'er our lot may be,
  Calmly in this thought we'll rest,—
  Could we see as thou dost see,
  We should choose it as the best.
  William Gaskell.

CREATION. L. M. 6 l. HAYDN'S CREATION.

1. Thou art, O God! the life and light Of all this wondrous world we see!
Its glow by day, its smile by night, Are but re-flec-tions caught from thee.
Wher-e'er we turn, thy glo-ries shine, And all things fair and bright are thine.

162 *God the Light and Life of All.*

2 When day, with farewell beam, delays
  Among the opening clouds of e'en,
  And we can almost think we gaze
  Through golden vistas into heaven,—
  Those hues, that make the sun's decline
  So soft, so radiant, Lord, are thine.

3 When night, with wings of starry gloom
  O'ershadows all the earth and skies,—
  Like some dark, beauteous bird, whose plume
  Is sparkling with unnumbered eyes,—
  That sacred gloom, those fires divine,
  So grand, so countless, Lord, are thine.

4 When youthful spring around us breathes,
  Thy spirit warms her fragrant sigh;
  And every flower the summer wreathes
  Is born beneath thy kindling eye:
  Where'er we turn, thy glories shine,
  And all things fair and bright are thine.
  Thomas Moore, 1816.

GOD.

BYFIELD. L. M. D.   L. O. Emerson.

1. The spacious fir-ma-ment on high, With all the blue e-the-real sky, And spangled heav'ns, a shining frame, Their great O-rig-i-nal pro-claim. Th'unwearied sun, from day to day, Does his Cre-a-tor's pow'r dis-play, And publishes to ev'ry land, The work of an Al-mighty hand.

Used by per Oliver Ditson Co., owners of Copyright.

163
2 Soon as the evening shades prevail,
The moon takes up the wondrous tale,
And nightly, to the listening earth,
Repeats the story of her birth.
While all the stars that round her burn,
And all the planets in their turn,
Confirm the tidings as they roll,
And spread the truth from pole to pole.

3 What though in solemn silence, all
Move round this dark terrestrial ball?
What though no real voice, nor sound,
Amid their radiant orbs be found.
In reason's ear they all rejoice,
And utter forth a glorious voice;
Forever singing as they shine,
The hand that made us is divine.
Addison.

164 *God through all and in you all.*
1 God of the earth, the sky, the sea;
Of all above and all below,—
Creation lives and moves in thee;
Thy present life through all doth flow.
Thy love is in the sunshine's glow,
Thy life is in the quickening air;
When lightnings flash and storm-winds blow,
There is thy power; thy law is there.

2 We feel thy calm at evening's hour,
Thy grandeur in the march of night,
And, when the morning breaks in power,
We hear thy word, "Let there be light."
But higher far, and far more clear,
Thee in man's spirit we behold;
Thine image and thyself are there,—
The indwelling God, proclaimed of old,
S. Longfellow.

165 *Presence and Love of God.*
1 God reigns on earth; he reigns above;
His realm embraces every shore;
He reigns in righteousness and love,
Almighty King for evermore.
With swelling heart, I look on high;
And every light that blazes there,
Each constellation of the sky,
His wisdom and his love declare.

2 There's not a leaf in yonder bower,
Or gem that sparkles in the sea,
Or blade of grass, or tender flower,
But has a voice of love to me,—
A voice that speaks of God—my trust
When danger or when death is near;
He lifts the righteous from the dust;
He wipes away the scalding tear.
Warren Hathaway.

PROVIDENCE AND GRACE.

FEDERAL STREET. L. M. H. K. Oliver, 1832.

1. Fa-ther of lights, we sing thy name, Who kindlest up the lamp of day; Wide as he spreads his gold-en flame, His beams thy power and love dis-play.

166 *God's Love in Nature.*

2 Fountain of good, from thee proceed
The copious drops of genial rain,
Which, o'er the hill and through the mead,
Revive the grass and swell the grain.

3 O, let not our forgetful hearts
O'erlook the tokens of thy care;
But what thy liberal hand imparts,
Still own in praise, still ask in prayer.

4 So shall our suns more grateful shine,
And showers in sweeter drops shall fall,
When all our hearts and lives are thine,
And thou, O God, enjoyed in all.
Doddridge.

167 *Not that we loved God, but he us.*

1 ERE earth's foundations yet were laid,
Or heaven's fair roof was spread abroad,
Ere man a living soul was made,
Love stirred within the heart of God.

2 Thy loving counsel gave to me
True life in Christ, thy only Son.
Whom thou hast made my way to thee,
From whom all grace flows ever down.

3 O love, that, long ere time began,
This precious name of child bestowed,—
That opened heaven on earth to man,
And called us sinners, "sons of God!"

4 Could I but honor thee aright,
Noble and sweet my song should be,
That earth and heav'n should learn thy might,
And what my God hath done for me.
Anon.

168 *Perfections.*

1 THE Lord! how wondrous are his ways!
How firm his truth! how large his grace!
He takes his mercy for his throne,
And thence he makes his glories known.

2 Not half so high his power hath spread
The starry heavens above our head,
As his rich love exceeds our praise,
Exceeds the highest hopes we raise.

3 Not half so far has nature placed
The rising morning from the west,
As his forgiving grace removes
The daily guilt of those he loves.
Isaac Watts, 1719.

169 *God is Everywhere.*

1 FATHER and friend, thy light, thy love,
Beaming through all thy works, we see;
Thy glory gilds the heavens above,
And all the earth is full of thee.

2 Thy voice we hear, thy presence feel,
While thou too pure for mortal sight,
Involved in clouds, invisible,
Reignest the Lord of life and light.

3 We know not in what hallowed part
Of the wide heavens thy throne may be;
But this we know, that where thou art
Strength, wisdom, goodness, dwell with thee.

4 Thy children shall not faint nor fear,
Sustained by this delightful thought,
Since thou, their God, art everywhere,
They cannot be where thou art not.
Sir John Bowring.

GOD.

WARD. L. M.   Scotch Melody. Arr. by Dr. Mason, 1830.

1. God is the ref-uge of his saints, When storms of sharp dis-tress in-vade; Ere we can of-fer our com-plaints, Be-hold him pres-ent with his aid.

170   *Our Refuge and Strength.*

2 Loud may the troubled ocean roar;
 In sacred peace our souls abide,
While every nation, every shore,
 Trembles, and dreads the swelling tide.

3 There is a stream, whose gentle flow
 Supplies the city of our God;
Life, love, and joy, still gliding through,
 And watering our divine abode.

4 That sacred stream, thine holy word,
 Supports our faith, our fear controls;
Sweet peace, thy promises afford,
 And give new strength to fainting souls.
Isaac Watts, 1719

171   *His Mercy endureth forever.*

1 Give to our God immortal praise;
Mercy and truth are all his ways;
Wonders of grace to God belong;
Repeat his mercies in your song.

2 He built the earth, he spread the sky,
And fixed the starry lights on high:
Wonders of grace to God belong;
Repeat his mercies in your song.

3 He sent his Son with power to save
From guilt, and darkness, and the grave:
Wonders of grace to God belong;
Repeat his mercies in your song.

4 Thro' this vain world he guides our feet,
And leads us to his heavenly seat:
His mercies ever shall endure,
When this vain world shall be no more.
Isaac Watts.

172   *God is greater than our Heart.*

1 Whither. O. whither should I fly,
 But to my loving Father's breast,
Secure within thine arms to lie,
 And safe beneath thy wings to rest?

2 In all my ways thy hand I own,
 Thy ruling providence I see:
Assist me still thy course to run,
 And still direct my paths to thee.

3 Foolish, and impotent, and blind,
 Lead me a way I have not known;
Bring me where I my heaven may find,
 The heaven of loving thee alone.
Charles Wesley.

173   *Paternal Providence of God.*

1 Through all the various shifting scene
 Of life's mistaken ill or good,
Thy hand, O God! conducts, unseen,
 The beautiful vicissitude.

2 Thou givest with paternal care,
 Howe'er unjustly we complain,
To all their necessary share
 Of joy and sorrow, health and pain.

3 All things on earth, and all in heaven,
 On thine eternal will depend;
And all for greater good were given,
 Would man pursue th' appointed end.

4 Be this my care: to all beside
 Indifferent let my wishes be;
Passion be calm, and dumb be pride,
 And fixed my soul, great God, on thee.
Samuel Collett.

PROVIDENCE AND GRACE. 55

MARION. L. M.   L. V. WHEELER.

1. Kingdoms and thrones to God be-long; Crown him, ye na-tions, in your song, His wondrous name and pow'rs re-hearse; His hon-ors shall en-rich your verse.

174   *The Lord is King.*

2 He rides and thunders through the sky;
 His name, Jehovah, sounds on high:
 Praise him aloud, ye sons of grace;
 Ye saints, rejoice before his face.

3 Proclaim him King, pronounce him blest;
 He's your defence, your joy, your rest;
 When terrors rise, and nations faint,
 God is the strength of every saint.
 Isaac Watts, 1719.

175   *Every good Gift is from above.*

1 GREAT God, let all my tuneful powers
 Awake, and sing thy mighty name:
 Thy hand revolves my circling hours—
 Thy hand, from whence my being came.

2 Seasons and moons, still rolling round
 In beauteous order, speak thy praise;
 And years, with smiling mercy crowned;
 To thee successive honors raise.

3 My life, my health, my friends I owe,
 All to thy vast, unbounded love;
 Ten thousand precious gifts below,
 And hope of nobler joys above.

4 Thus will I sing till nature cease,
 Till sense and language are no more;
 And, after death, thy boundless grace
 Through everlasting years adore.
 Ottiwell Heginbotham, 1768-1794.

176   *God is Good.*

1 OUR God is good; in earth and sky,
 From ocean-depths and spreading wood,
 Ten thousand voices seem to cry,
 "God made us all, and God is good."

2 I hear it in the rushing breeze:
 The hills that have for ages stood,
 The echoing sky and roaring seas,
 All swell the chorus, "God is good."

3 Yea, God is good, all nature says,
 By God's own hand with speech endued;
 And man, in louder notes of praise,
 Should sing for joy that God is good.

4 For all thy gifts we bless thee, Lord;
 But chiefly for our heavenly food,
 Thy pardoning grace, thy quickening word:
 These prompt our song, that God is good.
 John Hampden Gurney, 1838.

177   *Behold, what Manner of Love.*

1 O LOVE of God, how strong and true!
 Eternal and yet ever new,
 Above all price, and still unbought,
 Beyond all knowledge and all thought.

2 O wide-embracing, wondrous love,
 We read thee in the sky above,
 We read thee in the earth below,
 In seas that swell and streams that flow.

3 We read thee best in Him who came
 To bear for us the cross of shame;
 Sent by the Father from on high,
 Our life to live, our death to die.

4 O love of God, our shield and stay,
 Through all the perils of our way;
 Eternal love, in thee we rest,
 Forever safe, forever blest.
 Horatius Bonar.

GOD.

GOOD SHEPHERD. L. M. 6 l.   I. B. WOODBURY.

1. The Lord my pas-ture shall pre-pare, And feed me with a shepherd's care;
His presence shall my wants sup-ply, And guard me with a watch-ful eye:
My noon-day walks he shall at-tend, And all my mid-night hours de-fend.

Used by per. Oliver Ditson Co., owners of Copyright

178

2 When in the sultry glebe I faint,
Or on the thirsty mountain pant,
To fertile vales and dewy meads
My weary, wandering steps he leads,
Where peaceful rivers, soft and slow,
Amid the verdant landscape flow.

3 Though in the verdant paths I tread,
With gloomy horrors overspread,
My steadfast heart shall feel no ill,
For thou, O Lord, art with me still:
Thy friendly crook shall give me aid,
And guide me through the dreadful shade.

4 Though in a bare and rugged way,
Through devious lonely wilds I stray,
Thy presence shall my pains beguile,
The barren wilderness shall smile,
With sudden greens and herbage crowned,
And streams shall murmur all around.
                             Addison.

179   *The Peace of God.*

1 O FATHER, lift our souls above,
Till we find rest in thy dear love;
And still that peace divine impart
Which sanctifies the inmost heart,
And make each morn and setting sun
But bring us nearer to thy throne.

2 Help us with man in peace to live,
Our brothers wrong in love forgive,
And, day and night, the tempter flee
Thro' strength which comes alone in thee!
Thus will our spirits find their rest,
In thy deep peace forever blest.
                                 Anon.

180   *"My Strength, my Tower."*

1 THEE will I love, my strength, my tower,
   Thee will I love, my joy, my crown!
Thee will I love, with all my power,
   In all thy works, and thee alone:
Thee will I love, till the pure fire
Fill my whole soul with chaste desire.

2 Uphold me in the doubtful race,
   Nor suffer me again to stray;
Strengthen my feet, with steady pace
   Still to press forward in thy way;
That all my powers with all their might,
In thy sole glory may unite.

3 Thee will I love, my joy, my crown!
   Thee will I love, my Lord, my God!
Thee will I love beneath thy frown,
   Or smile, thy sceptre or thy rod:
What though my heart and flesh decay?
Thee shall I love in endless day.
                              John Wesley, tr.

PROVIDENCE AND GRACE.

BREMEN. C. P. M. THOMAS HASTINGS.

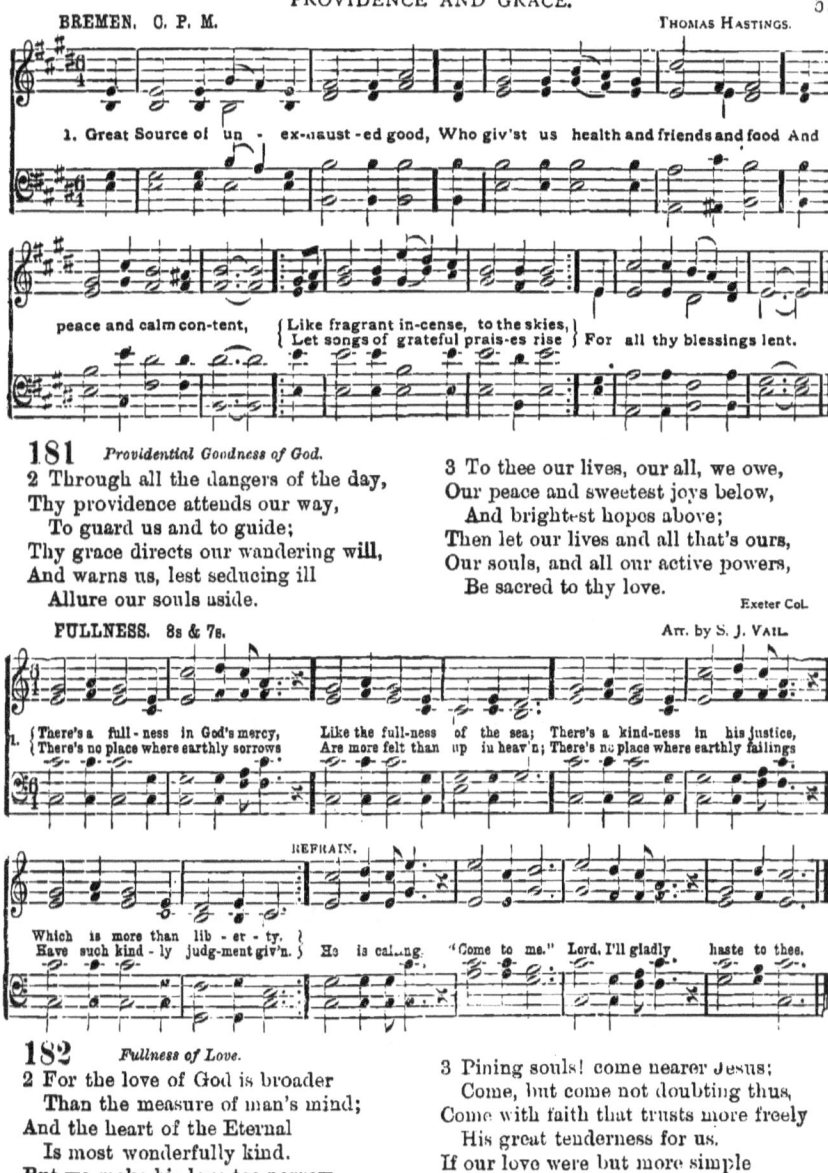

1. Great Source of un-exhaust-ed good, Who giv'st us health and friends and food And peace and calm con-tent, { Like fragrant in-cense, to the skies, / Let songs of grateful prais-es rise } For all thy blessings lent.

181 *Providential Goodness of God.*
2 Through all the dangers of the day,
  Thy providence attends our way,
   To guard us and to guide;
  Thy grace directs our wandering will,
  And warns us, lest seducing ill
   Allure our souls aside.

3 To thee our lives, our all, we owe,
  Our peace and sweetest joys below,
   And brightest hopes above;
  Then let our lives and all that's ours,
  Our souls, and all our active powers,
   Be sacred to thy love.
                                  Exeter Col.

FULLNESS. 8s & 7s. Arr. by S. J. VAIL.

{ There's a full-ness in God's mercy, Like the full-ness of the sea; There's a kind-ness in his justice,
  There's no place where earthly sorrows Are more felt than up in heav'n; There's no place where earthly failings
Which is more than lib-er-ty. }
Have such kind-ly judg-ment giv'n. } He is call-ing. "Come to me." Lord, I'll gladly haste to thee.

182 *Fullness of Love.*
2 For the love of God is broader
   Than the measure of man's mind;
  And the heart of the Eternal
   Is most wonderfully kind.
  But we make his love too narrow
   By false limits of our own;
  And we magnify his strictness
   With a zeal he will not own.—*Ref.*

3 Pining souls! come nearer Jesus;
   Come, but come not doubting thus,
  Come with faith that trusts more freely
   His great tenderness for us.
  If our love were but more simple
   We should take him at his word;
  And our lives would be all sunshine
   In the sweetness of our Lord.—*Ref.*
                          Frederick W. Faber.

58 ST. MARTIN'S. C. M. — GOD.

William Tansur, 1735.

1. O thou, to whom all crea-tures bow With-in this earth-ly frame,
Thro' all the world, how great art thou! How glo-rious is thy name!

183 *God's Condescension.*

2 When heaven, thy glorious work on high,
   Employs my wandering sight,
The moon, that nightly rules the sky,
   With stars of feebler light,—

3 Lord, what is man, that thou shouldst
   To keep him in thy mind? [choose
Or what his race, that thou shouldst prove
   To them so wondrous kind?

4 O thou, to whom all creatures bow
   Within this earthly frame,
Through all the world, how great art thou
   How glorious is thy name!
                                   Anon.

184 *Divine Goodness in Affliction.*

1 Great Ruler of all nature's frame,
   We own thy power divine;
We hear thy breath in every storm,
   For all the winds are thine.

2 Wide as they sweep their sounding way,
   They work thy sovereign will;
And, awed by thy majestic voice,
   Confusion shall be still.

3 Thy mercy tempers every blast
   To those who seek thy face;
And mingles, with the tempest's roar,
   The whispers of thy grace.

4 Those gentle whispers let me hear,
   Till all the tumult cease,
And gales of Paradise shall lull
   My weary soul to peace.
                       Philip Doddridge, 1755.

185 *The Guide of Life.*

1 I cannot walk in darkness long,
   My light is by my side;
I cannot stumble or go wrong,
   While following such a guide.

2 He is my stay and my defense,
   How shall I fail or fall?
My keeper is Omnipotence,
   My ruler ruleth all.

3 The powers below and powers above
   Are subject to his care;
I cannot wander from his love
   Whose love is everywhere.
                          Caroline A. Mason.

186 *God's Loving Grace.*

1 Come, happy souls, approach your God
   With new, melodious songs;
Come, render to almighty grace
   The tribute of your tongues.

2 So strange, so boundless was the love
   That pitied dying men,
The Father sent his only son
   To give them life again.

3 Yes, all was merciful and mild,
   And wrath forsook the throne,
When Christ on the kind errand came,
   And brought salvation down.

4 See, dearest Lord, our willing souls
   Accept thine offered grace;
We bless the great Redeemer's love,
   And give the Father grace.
                                Isaac Watts.

PROVIDENCE AND GRACE.

GENEVA. C. M.   John Cole.

1. When all thy mer-cies, O my God! My ris-ing soul sur-veys, Trans-port-ed with the view, I'm lost in won-der, love, and praise.

187   *God's Care.*

2 Unnumbered comforts on my soul
   Thy tender care bestowed,
Before my infant heart conceived
   From whom those comforts flowed.

3 Ten thousand thousand precious gifts
   My daily thanks employ;
Nor is the least a cheerful heart,
   That tastes those gifts with joy.

4 Through every period of my life
   Thy goodness I'll pursue;
And after death in distant worlds,
   The glorious theme renew.
                         Joseph Addison.

188   *The Love of God.*

1 COME, ye that know and fear the Lord,
   And raise your souls above;
Let every heart and voice accord,
   To sing that "God is love."

2 His precious truth his word declares,
   And all his mercies prove;
Jesus, the gift of gifts appears,
   To show that "God is love."

3 Behold his patience, bearing long
   With those who from him rove;
'Till mighty grace their hearts subdues
   To teach them—"God is love."

4 Oh! may we all, while here below,
   This best of blessings prove;
Till warmer hearts, in brighter worlds,
   Shall shout that "God is love."
                         George Burder. 1784.

189   *Thy Judgments are a great Deep.*

1 GOD moves in a mysterious way
   His wonders to perform;
He plants his footsteps in the sea,
   And rides upon the storm.

2 Judge not the Lord by feeble sense,
   But trust him for his grace:
Behind a frowning providence
   He hides a smiling face.

3 His purposes will ripen fast,
   Unfolding every hour;
The bud may have a bitter taste,
   But sweet will be the flower.

4 Blind unbelief is sure to err,
   And scan his work in vain;
God is his own interpreter,
   And he will make it plain.
                        William Cowper, 1779.

190   *The Earth is full of God's Goodness.*

1 THY goodness, Lord, our souls confess,
   Thy goodness we adore—
A spring whose blessings never fail,
   A sea without a shore.

2 Sun, moon, and stars thy love declare
   In every golden ray;
Love draws the curtains of the night
   And love brings back the day.

3 But chiefly thy compassion, Lord,
   Is in the gospel seen;
There, like a sun, thy mercy shines,
   Without a cloud between.
                        Thomas Gibbons.

GOD

ST. MARTIN'S. C. M. — William Tansur, 1735.

1. With rev-'rence let the saints ap-pear, And bow be-fore the lord; His high com-mands with rev-'rence hear, And trem-ble at his word.

191 *"Who can be compared with the Lord?"*

2 Great God, how high thy glories rise!
How bright thine armies shine!
Where is the power with thee that vies,
Or truth compared to thine?

3 Thy words the raging winds control,
And move the boisterous deep;
Thou mak'st the sleeping billows roll,
The rolling billows sleep.

4 Justice and judgment are thy throne,
Yet wondrous is thy grace;
While truth and mercy, joined in one,
Invite us near thy face.
Isaac Watts.

192 *All as God wills.*

1 ALL as God wills! who wisely heeds
To give or to withold,
And knoweth more of all my needs
Than all my prayers have told.

2 Enough, that blessings undeserved
Have marked my erring track;
That, wheresoe'er my feet have swerved,
Thy chastening turned me back;

3 That death seems but a covered way
Which opens into light,
Wherein no blinded child can stray
Beyond the Father's sight.

4 No longer forward or behind
I look, in hope or fear,
But grateful take the good I find,
God's blessing now and here.
John G. Whittier.

193 *The Book of Nature.*

1 THERE is a book, who runs may read,
Which heavenly truth imparts;
And all the lore its scholars need,
Pure eyes and Christian hearts.

2 The works of God, above, below
Within us and around,
Are pages in that book to show
How God himself is found.

3 The glorious sky, embracing all,
Is like the Father's love,
Wherewith encompassed, great and small,
In peace and order move.

4 Thou who hast given me eyes to see
And love this sight so fair,
Give me a heart to find out thee,
And read thee everywhere.
John Keble.

194 *Now we see through a Glass darkly.*

1 THY way, O God, is in the sea;
Thy paths I can not trace,
Nor comprehend the mystery
Of thine unbounded grace.

2 Though but in part I know thy will,
I bless thee for the sight:
When will thy love the whole reveal
In glory's clearer light?

3 With rapture shall I then survey
Thy providence and grace,
And spend an everlasting day
In wonder, love, and praise.
J. Fawcet.

PROVIDENCE AND GRACE. 61

ST. JOHN'S, C. M. English Melody.

1. Be-ing of be-ings, God of love, To thee our hearts we raise;
Thy all-sus-tain-ing power we prove, And glad-ly sing thy praise.

195 *The Fullness of God.*

2 Thine, wholly thine, we want to be;
Our sacrifice receive;
Made, and preserved, and saved by thee,
To thee ourselves we give.

3 To thee our every wish aspires:
For all thy mercy's store,
The sole return thy love requires
Is that we ask for more.

4 For more we ask; we open, Lord,
Our hearts to embrace thy will:
Renew us by thy quickening word,
And from thy fulness fill.
Charles Wesley.

196 *In Nature.*

1 LORD, when my raptured thought surveys
Creation's beauties o'er,
All nature joins to teach thy praise,
And bid my soul adore.

2 Where'er I turn my gazing eyes,
Thy radiant footsteps shine;
Ten thousand pleasing wonders rise,
And speak their source divine.

3 On me thy providence has shone
With gentle smiling rays;
Oh, let my lips and life make known
Thy goodness and thy praise.

4 All-bounteous Lord, thy grace impart!
Oh, teach me to improve
Thy gifts with humble, grateful heart,
And crown them with thy love.
Anne Steele.

197 *Nature's Worship.*

1 The harp at Nature's advent strung
Has never ceased to play;
The song the stars of morning sung
Has never died away.

2 And prayer is made, and praise is given
By all things near and far;
The ocean looketh up to heaven
And mirrors every star;

3 So Nature keeps the reverent frame
With which her years began;
And all her signs and voices shame
The prayerless heart of man.
J. G. Whittier.

198 *The Lord is thy Keeper.*

1 Up to the hills I lift mine eyes;
There all my hope is laid;
The Lord, who built the earth and skies,—
From him will come mine aid.

2 Thy foot unmoved he ever keeps,
And all thy ways will guard;
He slumbers not, and never sleeps—
Thy Keeper is the Lord.

3 The Lord, thy Keeper, shades thy way,
Preserves thee in his sight;
Nor shall the sun smite thee by day,
Nor shall the moon by night.

4 The Lord preserves thy soul from sin,
From evils great and sore—
Thy going out and coming in,
Now and for evermore.
Anon.

GOD.

SPANISH HYMN. 7s, 6 l.   Spanish Melody.

1. Oh, give thanks to Him who made Morning light and evening shade! Source and giver of all good; Nightly sleep and daily food!
D.C.—Quickener of wearied powers, Guard of our unconscious hours!

199   *Oh, give Thanks.*   [Omit Repeat.]

2 Oh, give thanks to nature's King,
Who made every breathing thing!
His our warm and sentient frame;
His the mind's immortal flame;
Oh, how close the ties that bind
Spirits to the Eternal Mind!

3 Oh, give thanks with heart and lip,
For we are his workmanship,
And all creatures are his care;
Not a bird that cleaves the air
Falls unnoticed;—but who can
Speak the Father's love to man!
                             Conder.

200   *All from God.*

1 Father, thy paternal care
Has my guardian been, my guide;
Every hallowed wish and prayer
Has thy hand of love supplied:
Thine is every thought of bliss,
Left by hours and days gone by;
Every hope thy offspring is,
Beaming from futurity.

2 Every sun of splendid ray;
Every moon that shines serene;
Every morn that welcomes day;
Every evening's twilight scene;
Every hour which wisdom brings;
Every incense at thy shrine,—
These, and all life's holiest things,
And its fairest,—all are thine.

HENDON. 7s.   C. H. A. Malan, 1850.

1. They who seek the throne of grace Find that throne in ev-ery place; If we live a life of prayer, God is pres-ent ev-ery-where, God is pres-ent ev-ery-where.

201   *God Everywhere.*

2 In our sickness and our health,
In our want and in our wealth,
If we look to God in prayer,
God is present everywhere.

3 When our earthly comforts fail,
When the woes of life prevail,
'Tis the hour for earnest prayer:
God is present everywhere.

4 Then, my soul, in every strait,
To thy Father come and wait;
He will answer every prayer;
God is present everywhere.
                       Methodist Collection

202   *The only Refuge.*

1 Holy Father, heavenly King,
O'er me spread thy guardian wing;
When by trembling fears distressed
Let me flee to thee and rest.

2 Call me, keep me by thy side;
Teach me there alone to hide;
Where for safety should I flee,
If my footsteps strayed from thee?

3 Warn me with thy gentle voice;
Point my path, and guide my choice;
Let me, Lord, in thee possess
Wisdom, peace and righteousness.
                              Anon.

PROVIDENCE AND GRACE.

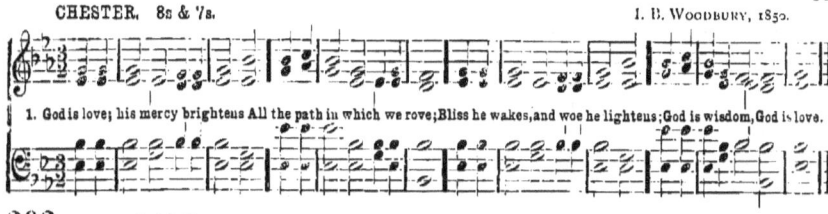

CHESTER. 8s & 7s.　　I. B. Woodbury, 1850.

1. God is love; his mercy brightens All the path in which we rove; Bliss he wakes, and woe he lightens; God is wisdom, God is love.

203　　*God is Love.*

2 Chance and change are busy ever;
　Man decays, and ages move;
But his mercy waneth never,
　God is wisdom, God is love.
3 E'en the hour that darkest seemeth
　Will his changeless goodness prove;
From the gloom his brightness streameth,
　God is wisdom, God is love.
4 He with earthly cares entwineth
　Hope and comfort from above·
Everywhere his glory shineth;
　God is wisdom, God is love.
　　　　　　　　　Sir John Bowring.

204　　*Grace.*

1 Lord, with glowing heart I'd praise thee
For the bliss thy love bestows:
For the pardoning grace that saves me,
And the peace that from it flows:

2 Help, O God, my weak endeavor;
This dull soul to rapture raise;
Thou must light the flame, or never
Can my love be warmed to praise.

3 Lord, this bosom's ardent feeling
Vainly would my lips express:
Low before thy footstool kneeling,
Deign thy suppliant's prayer to bless.

4 Let thy grace, my soul's chief treasure,
Love's pure flame within me raise;
And since words can never measure,
Let my life show forth thy praise.
　　　　　　　　　Francis Scott Keys.

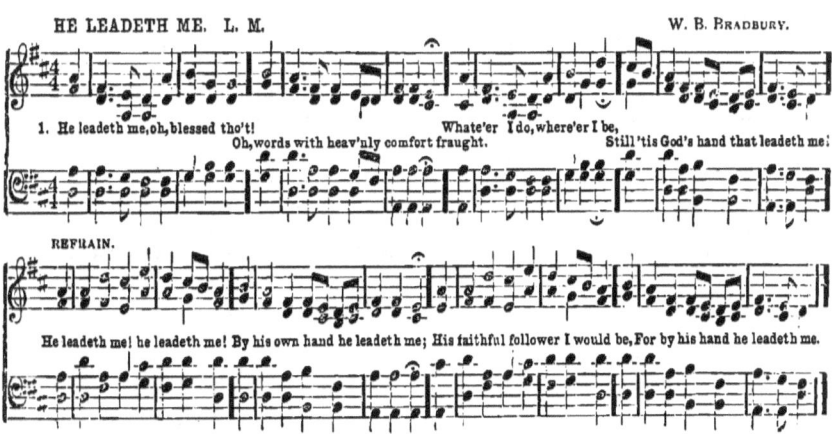

HE LEADETH ME. L. M.　　W. B. Bradbury.

1. He leadeth me, oh, blessed tho't!
Oh, words with heav'nly comfort fraught.
Whate'er I do, where'er I be,
Still 'tis God's hand that leadeth me!

REFRAIN.
He leadeth me! he leadeth me! By his own hand he leadeth me; His faithful follower I would be, For by his hand he leadeth me.

205　　*He leadeth me.*

2 Sometimes, 'mid scenes of deepest gloom,
Sometimes where Eden's bowers bloom,
By waters still, o'er troubled sea—
Still 'tis his hand that leadeth me.—*Ref.*

3 Lord, I would clasp thy hand in mine,
Nor ever murmur nor repine—

Content, whatever lot I see,
Since 'tis my God that leadeth me.—*Ref.*

4 And when my task on earth is done,
When by thy grace the victory's won,
E'en death's cold wave I will not flee,
Since God through Jordan leadeth me.—*Ref.*
　　　　　　　　　J. H. Gilmore, 1859.

GOD.

DENNIS. S. M.

1. How gentle God's commands! How kind his precepts are!
"Come, cast your burdens on the Lord, And trust his constant care."

206 *He careth for you.*

2 Beneath his watchful eye
　His saints securely dwell;
That hand which bears all nature up
　Shall guard his children well.

3 Why should this anxious load
　Press down your weary mind?
Haste to your heavenly Father's throne,
　And sweet refreshment find.

4 His goodness stands approved
　Down to the present day;
I'll drop my burden at his feet,
　And bear a song away.
　　　　　　　Philip Doddridge, 1735.

207 *The Lord is my Shepherd.*

1 The Lord my Shepherd is;
　I shall be well supplied;
Since he is mine, and I am his,
　What can I want beside?

2 He leads me to the place
　Where heavenly pasture grows,
Where living waters gently pass,
　And full salvation flows.

3 If e'er I go astray,
　He doth my soul reclaim,
And guides me in his own right way,
　For his most holy name.

4 While he affords his aid,
　I cannot yield to fear;
Tho' I should wake through death's dark
　My Shepherd's with me there. [shade,
　　　　　　　Isaac Watts, 1719.

208 *God our Benefactor.*

1 My Maker and my King,
　To thee my all I owe;
Thy sovereign bounty is the spring
　From whence my blessings flow.

2 The creature of thy hand,
　On thee alone I live;
My God, thy benefits demand
　More praise than life can give.

3 Shall I withold thy due?
　And shall my passion rove?
Lord, form this wretched heart anew,
　And fill it with thy love.
　　　　　　　Anne Steele, 1760.

209 *God our Father.*

1 My Father,—cheering name,—
　Oh! may I call thee mine?
Give me the humble hope to claim
　A portion so divine.

2 This can my fears control,
　And bid my sorrows fly:
What real harm can reach my soul,
　Beneath my Father's eye?

3 Whate'er thy will denies,
　I calmly would resign;
For thou art just and good and wise;
　Oh bend my will to thine!

4 Whate'er thy will ordains,
　Oh give me strength to bear;
Still let me know a Father reigns,
　And trust a Father's care!
　　　　　　　Anne Steele.

210

2 O, lead me to the Rock
  That's high above my head,
And make the covert of thy wings
  My shelter and my shade.
3 Within thy presence, Lord,
  Forever I'll abide;

Thou art the tower of my defence,
  The refuge where I hide.
4 Thou givest me the lot
  Of those that fear thy name;
If endless life be their reward,
  I shall possess the same.
                                    Isaac Watts.

211 *His Mercy endureth forever.*
2 How mighty is his hand!
    What wonders hath he done!
  He formed the earth and seas,
    And spread the heavens alone.
Thy mercy, Lord, | And ever sure
Shall still endure; | Abides thy word.
3 He sent his only Son
    To save us from our woe—
  From Satan, sin and death,
    And every hurtful foe.
His power and grace | And let his name
Are still the same; | Have endless praise.
4 Give thanks aloud to God,
    To God, the heavenly King;
  And let the spacious earth
    His works and glories sing.
Thy mercy, Lord, | And ever sure
Shall still endure; | Abides thy word.
                                    Isaac Watts.

212 *The Living God.*
1 THE Lord Jehovah lives,
  And blessèd be my Rock!
Though earth her bosom heaves
  And mountains feel the shock,
Though oceans rage and torrents roar,
He is the same for evermore.
2 The Lord Jehovah lives,
  The dying sinner's Friend;
How freely he forgives
  The follies that offend!
He wipes the penitential tear,
Bids faith and hope the spirit cheer.
3 The Lord Jehovah lives
  To hear and answer prayer;
Whoe'er in him believes
  And trusts his guardian care,
A Father's tender love shall know,
Whence living streams of comfort flow.
                                    Thomas Hastings.

GOD.

AMSTERDAM. 7s & 6s. [TROCHAIC.]   JAMES NARES, 1760.

1. O-pen, Lord, my inward ear, And bid my heart re-joice;
Bid my qui-et spir-it hear The comfort of thy voice.
Nev-er in the whirlwind found,
Or where earthquakes rock the place,—Still and si-lent is the sound, The whis-per of thy grace.

213   *Quiet Religion.*

2 From the world of sin and noise
   And hurry I withdraw;
For the small and inward voice
   I wait with humble awe:

Silent I am now and still,
   Dare not in thy presence move;
To my waiting soul reveal
   The secret of thy love.
Charles Wesley, 1742.

ORIENT. 11s & 10s.   MOZART.

1. Brightest and best of the sons of the morning, Dawn on our darkness, and lend us thine aid;
Star of the East, the ho-ri-zon a-dorn-ing, Guide where our infant Re-deem-er is laid.

214   *Star of the East.*

2 Cold on his cradle the dewdrops are shining;
   Low lies his head with the beasts of the stall;
Angels adore him in slumber reclining,
   Lord, and Redeemer, and Saviour of all.

3 Say, shall we yield him, in costly devotion,
   Odors of Edom, and offerings divine,
Gems of the mountain and pearls of the ocean,
   Myrrh from the forest, or gold from the mine?

4 Vainly we offer each ample oblation,
   Vainly with gifts would his favor secure;
Richer by far is the heart's adoration,
   Dearer to God are the prayers of the poor.

5 Brightest and best of the sons of the morning,
   Dawn on our darkness, and lend us thine aid;
Star of the East, the horizon adorning,
   Guide where our infant Redeemer is laid.
Bishop Reginald Heber.

ADVENT.

ASAPH. H. M. From "Jubilant Voices." L. V. WHEELER.

1. Hark! what ce-les-tial sounds, What mu-sic fills the air!
   Soft warbling to the morn, (Omit...........) It strikes the rav-ish'd ear:
   Now all is still, now wild it floats In tune-ful notes, loud, sweet, and shrill.

215 *Fear not.*

2 Th' angelic hosts descend,
   With harmony divine;
   See how from heaven they bend,
   And in full chorus join:—
'Fear not,' say they; 'great joy we bring;
Jesus, your King, is born to-day.'

3 Glory to God on high!
   Ye mortals, spread the sound,
   And let your raptures fly
   To earth's remotest bound:
For peace on earth, from God in heaven,
To man is given, at Jesus' birth.
Williams.

216 *Christmas Hymn.*

1 Lo! from the upper skies
   Angelic hosts appear;
   Hark! how their songs arise,
   In accents sweet and clear,—
The Christ of God is born to-day,
The Christ that takes our sins away.

2 The chorus swells on high,
   In melody divine;
   And lo! the Heralds nigh,
   In dazzling glory shine,
As they proclaim the Saviour's birth,—
"Good-will to men, and peace on earth."

3 The darkness falls away;
   All types and shadows flee;
   Messiah comes to-day,
   The Christ of prophecy.
Mortals, be glad; your praises bring;
All hearts, all lands, exultant sing.

4 Enter our hearts to-day,
   Thou Mystery Divine;
   Make strong and sure Thy sway,
   That we be wholly Thine.
We give ourselves,—our all to Thee,
For time and for eternity.
Rev. F. B. Wheeler, D.D.

217 *Good Tidings of Great Joy.*

1 HARK! hark! the notes of joy
   Roll o'er the heavenly plains,
   And seraphs find employ
   For their sublimest strains.
Some new delight in heaven is known,
Loud sound the harps around the throne.

2 Hark! hark! the sound draws nigh;
   The joyful hosts descend;
   Jesus forsakes the sky;
   To earth his footsteps bend:
He comes to bless our fallen race;
He comes with messages of grace.

3 Strike, strike the harps again
   To great Immanuel's name;
   Arise, ye sons of men,
   And all his grace proclaim:
Angels and men, wake every string;
'Tis Christ the Saviour's praise we sing.
A. Reed.

CHRIST.

ANTIOCH. C. M.   From G. F. HANDEL. Arr. by LOWELL MASON, 183.

1. Joy to the world! the Lord is come: Let earth re-ceive her King; Let ev-ery heart pre-pare him room, And heav'n and na-ture sing, And heav'n and na-ture sing, And heav'n, and heav'n and na-ture sing.

218 *The Mission of Christ.*

2 Joy to the earth! the Saviour reigns:
Let men their songs employ,
While fields and floods, rocks, hills, and plains
Repeat the sounding joy.

3 No more let sins and sorrows grow,
Nor thorns infest the ground:
He comes to make his blessings flow
Far as the curse is found.

4 He rules the world with truth and grace,
And makes the nations prove
The glories of his righteousness,
And wonders of his love.
                    Isaac Watts, 1719.

219 *The Birth-song of Christ.*

1 CALM on the listening ear of night
Come heaven's melodious strains,
Where wild Judea stretches far
Her silver-mantled plains.

2 Celestial choirs from courts above
Shed sacred glories there;
And angels with their sparkling lyres
Make music on the air.

3 The answering hills of Palestine
Send back the glad reply:
And greet from all their holy heights
The Dayspring from on high.

4 "Glory to God!" the sounding skies
Loud with their Anthems ring;
"Peace to the earth, good-will to men,
From heaven's eternal King."
                      E. H. Sears.

220 *Prepare ye the Way of the Lord.*

1 SING to the Lord, ye distant lands,
Ye tribes of every tongue;
His new-discovered grace demands
A new and nobler song.

2 Say to the nations, Jesus reigns,
God's own almighty Son;
His power the sinking world sustains,
And grace surrounds his throne.

3 Let an unusual joy surprise
The islands of the sea:
Ye mountains, sink; ye valleys, rise;
Prepare the Lord his way.

4 Behold, he comes; he comes to bless
The nations as their Lord,
To show the world his righteousness,
And send his truth abroad.
                      Isaac Watts, 1719.

221 *Star of Bethlehem.*

1 As SHADOWS, cast by cloud and sun,
Flit o'er the summer grass,
Lo, in thy sight, Almighty One!
Earth's generation's pass.

2 Yet doth the star of Bethlehem shed
A lustre pure and sweet;
And still it leads, as once it led,
To the Messiah's feet.

3 O Father, may that holy Star
Grow every year more bright,
And send its glorious beams afar,
To fill the world with light.
                      William Cullen Bryant.

ADVENT.

CAROL. C. M. D.   RICHARD STORRS WILLIS.

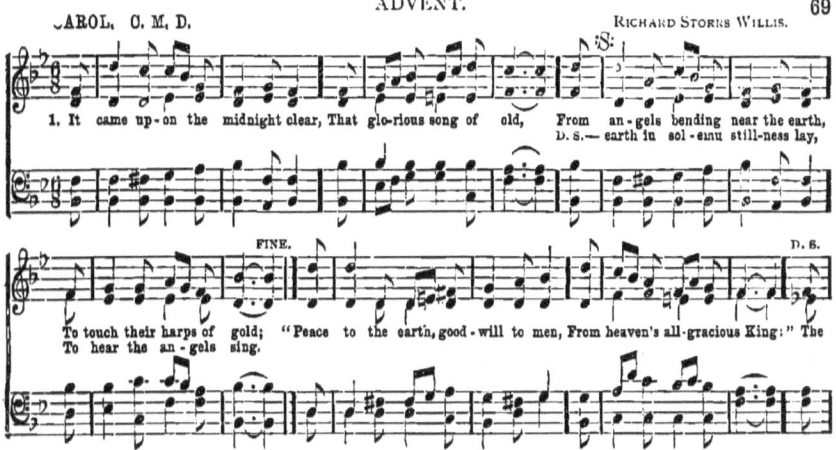

1. It came up-on the midnight clear, That glo-rious song of old, From an-gels bending near the earth,
D. S.— earth in sol-emn still-ness lay,

To touch their harps of gold; "Peace to the earth, good-will to men, From heaven's all-gracious King:" The
To hear the an-gels sing.

222 *Christmas Carol.*
2 And ye, beneath life's crushing load
  Whose forms are bending low,
  Who toil along the climbing way,
  With painful steps and slow,—
  Look now; for glad and golden hours
  Come swiftly on the wing;
  Oh, rest beside the weary road,
  And hear the angels sing!

3 For lo, the days are hastening on
  By prophet bards foretold,
  When, with the ever-circling years,
  Comes round the age of gold;
  When peace shall over all the earth
  Its ancient splendors fling,
  And the whole world send back the song
  Which now the angels sing.
  E. H. Sears.

CHRISTMAS. C. M.   HANDEL.

1. While shepherds watched their flocks by night, All seat-ed on the ground, The an-gel
of the Lord came down And glo-ry shone a-round, And glo-ry shone a-round.

223 *The Watch of the Shepherds.*
2 "To you, in Bethlehem, this day,
  Is born of David's line,
  The Saviour, who is Christ, the Lord,
  And this shall be the sign:

3 "The heavenly Babe you there shall find
  To human view displayed,
  And meanly wrapped in swathing bands,
  All in a manger laid."

4 "All glory be to God on high,
  And to the earth be peace;
  Good-will henceforth from heaven to men
  Begin, and never cease."
  Tate.

CHRIST.

ZERAH. C. M. 61. — Lowell Mason.

1. To us a child of hope is born, To us a Son is giv'n; Him shall the tribes of earth obey, Him all the hosts of heav'n; Him shall the tribes of earth obey, Him all the hosts of heav'n.

224 *Unto us a Child is Born.*

2 His name shall be the Prince of Peace,
   For evermore adored,
The Wonderful, the Counsellor,
   The great and mighty Lord.

3 His power, increasing, still shall spread;
   His reign no end shall know;
Justice shall guard his throne above,
   And peace abound below.

4 To us a Child of hope is born,
   To us a Son is given—
The Wonderful, the Counsellor,
   The mighty Lord of heaven.
Logan.

225 *The Advent.*

1 HARK! the glad sound! the Saviour comes;
   The Saviour promised long!
Let every heart prepare a throne,
   And every voice a song.

2 He comes the prisoners to release,
   In wretched bondage held;
The gates of brass before him burst,
   The iron fetters yield.

3 He comes the broken heart to bind,
   The bleeding soul to cure,
And with the treasures of his grace,
   Enrich the humble poor.

4 Our glad hosannas, Prince of Peace,
   Thy welcome shall proclaim,
And heaven's eternal arches ring
   With thy belovéd name.
Philip Doddridge.

HARWELL. 8s & 7s. — Lowell Mason, 1840.

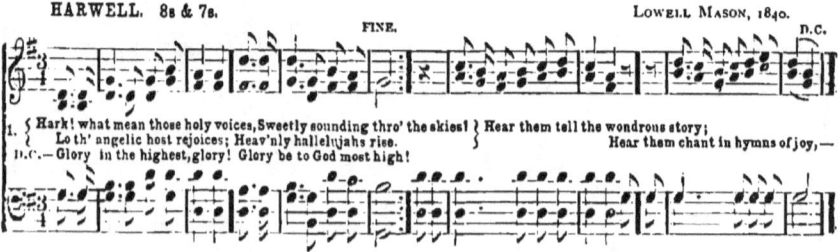

1. Hark! what mean those holy voices, Sweetly sounding thro' the skies! Hear them tell the wondrous story;
Lo th' angelic host rejoices; Heav'nly hallelujahs rise. Hear them chant in hymns of joy,—
D.C.—Glory in the highest, glory! Glory be to God most high!

226 *The Song of the Angels.*

2 'Peace on earth, good-will from heaven,
   Reaching far as man is found;
Souls redeemed, and sins forgiven!
   Loud our golden harps shall sound.
Christ is born, the great Anointed;
   Heaven and earth his praises sing;
O, receive, whom God appointed
   For our Prophet, Priest and King.'
John Cawood.

ADVENT.

HERALD ANGELS. 7s, D. Felix Mendelssohn Bartholdy, 1846.

1. Hark! the her-ald an-gels sing Glo-ry to the new-born King: Peace on earth, and mercy mild, God and sin-ners rec-on-ciled. {Joy-ful, all ye nations, rise, / Join the triumph of the skies;} With th'an-gelic host proclaim:

REFRAIN.

Christ is born in Beth-le-hem. Hark! the her-ald an-gels sing Glo-ry to the new-born King.

227 *The Herald-angels' Song.*

2 Gracious bond of earth and sky,
Born that man no more may die,
Born to raise the sons of earth,
Born to give them second birth.
Hail, the heaven-born Prince of Peace!
Hail, the Sun of Righteousness!
Light and life to all he brings,
Risen with healing in his wings.—Ref.
Charles Wesley, 1737.

228 *"The Christ of God."*

1 He has come! the Christ of God
Left for us his glad abode;
Stooping from his throne of bliss,
To this darksome wilderness.
He has come! the Prince of Peace;
Come to bid our sorrows cease;
‖:Come to scatter with his light
All the shadows of our night. :‖

2 He the mighty King has come!
Making this poor earth his home;
Come to bear our sin's sad load;
Son of David, Son of God!
He has come, whose name of grace
Speaks deliverance to our race;
‖:Left for us his high abode:
Son of Mary, Son of God! :‖

3 Unto us a child is born!
Ne'er has earth beheld a morn,
Among all the morns of time,
Half so glorious in its prime.
Unto us a Son is given!
He has come from God's own heaven,
‖:Bringing with him from above
Holy peace and holy love. :‖
Horatius Bonar.

CHRIST.

WATCHMAN, TELL US. 7s, D.
Lowell Mason, 1830.

1. Watchman, tell us of the night, What its signs of promise are; Trav'ler, o'er yon mountain's height See that glory-beaming star! Watchman, does its beauteous ray Aught of hope or joy foretell? Trav'ler, yes; it brings the day, Promis'd day of Is-ra-el.

229

2 Watchman, tell us of the night;
 Higher yet that star ascends.
Traveller, blessedness and light,
 Peace and truth its course portends.
Watchman, will its beams alone
 Gild the spot that gave them birth?
Traveller, ages are its own;
 See, it bursts o'er all the earth!

3 Watchman, tell us of the night,
 For the morning seems to dawn.
Traveller, darkness takes its flight,
 Doubt and terror are withdrawn.
Watchman, let thy wanderings cease;
 Hie thee to thy quiet home!
Traveller, lo! the Prince of Peace,
 Lo! the Son of God is come!

Sir John Bowring, 1823

WEBB. 7s & 6s.
George James Webb, 1830.

1. How lost was my con-di-tion, Till Jesus made me whole! There is but one Phy-si-cian Can cure the sin-sick soul, His wondrous pow'r to save.
D.S.—To tell to all around me Next door to death he found me, And snatch'd me from the grave,

230 *The Good Physician.*

2 A risen, living Jesus,
 Seen by an eye of faith,
At once from danger frees us,
 And saves the soul from death.

Come then to this Physician,
 His help he'll freely give;
He makes no hard condition,
 'Tis only look and live.

Anon.

LIFE AND MINISTRY. 73

ROCKINGHAM. L. M.   Dr. L. Mason.

1. How beauteous were the marks di-vine, That in thy meek-ness used to shine: That lit thy lone-ly path-way, trod In wondrous love, O Son of God!

231. *"Holy, harmless."*

2 Oh! who like thee—so calm, so bright,
So pure, so made to live in light?
Oh! who like thee did ever go
So patient through a world of woe?

3 Oh! who like thee so humbly bore
The scorn, the scoffs of men, before?
So meek, forgiving, godlike, high,
So glorious in humility!

4 Oh! in thy light be mine to go,
Illuming all my way of woe;
And give me ever on the road
To trace thy foosteps, Son of God!
A. C. Coxe.

232   *Behold how he loved Him.*

1 "See how he loved!" exclaimed the Jews,
As tender tears from Jesus fell;
My grateful heart the thought pursues,
And on the theme delights to dwell.

2 See how he loved, who traveled on,
Teaching the doctrines from the skies;
Who bade disease and pain be gone,
And called the sleeping dead to rise.

3 See how he loved, who never shrank
From toil or danger, pain or death,
Who all the cup of sorrow drank,
And meekly yielded up his breath.

4 Such love can we, unmoved, survey?
O, may our breasts with ardor glow,
To tread his steps, his laws obey,
And thus our warm affections show.
Bacbe.

233   *I will give you Rest.*

1 How sweetly flowed the gospel's sound
From lips of gentleness and grace,
When listening thousands gathered round,
And joy and reverence filled the place!

2 From heaven he came, of heaven he spoke,
To heaven he led his followers' way;
Dark clouds of gloomy night he broke,
Unveiling an immortal day.

3 'Come, wanderers, to my Father's home;
Come, all ye weary ones, and rest.'
Yes, sacred Teacher, we will come:
Obey thee, love thee, and be blest.
Sir John Bowring, 1825.

234   *Abide with us.*

1 Abide with us; the evening shades
Begin already to prevail;
And, as the lingering twilight fades,
Dark clouds along the horizon sail.

2 Abide with us; and still unfold
Thy sacred, thy prophetic lore;
What wondrous things of Jesus told!
Stranger, we thirst, we pant for more.

3 Abide with us; our hearts are cold;
We thought that Israel he'd restore;
But sweet the truths thy lips have told,
And, stranger, we complain no more.

4 Abide with us; amazed they cry,
As, suddenly, while breaking bread,
Their own lost Jesus meets their eye,
With radiant glory on his head.
Raffles.

CHRIST.

GERHARDT. 7s & 6s.   J. P. HOLBROOK.

1. O sacred Head, now wounded, With grief and shame weighed down, Now scornfully surrounded With thorns, thy only crown; O sacred Head, what glory, What bliss till now was thine! Yet, tho' despised and gory, I joy to call thee mine.

235

1 WHAT equal honors shall we bring
   To thee, O Lord our God, the Lamb,
When all the notes that angels sing
   Are far inferior to thy name?

2 Worthy is he who once was slain,
   The Prince of Peace, who groaned and died;
Worthy to rise, and live, and reign
   At his almighty Father's side.

3 Honor immortal must be paid,
   Instead of scandal and of scorn;
While glory shines around his head,
   And a bright crown without a thorn.

4 Blessings forever on the Lamb,
   Who bore the curse for wretched men:
Let angels sound his sacred name,
   And every creature say, Amen!
                              Isaac Watts.

236 *Christ our Advocate.*

1 HE lives! the Great Redeemer lives!
   What joy the blest assurance gives!
And now, before his Father, God,
   Pleads the full merits of his blood.

2 Repeated crimes awake our fears,
   And justice armed with frowns appears;
But in the Saviour's lovely face
   Sweet mercy smiles, and all is peace.

3 In every dark, distressful hour,
   When sin and Satan join their power,
Let this dear hope repel the dart,
   That Jesus bears us on his heart.

4 Great Advocate, almighty Friend!
   On him our humble hopes depend;
Our cause can never, never fail,
   For Jesus pleads, and must prevail.
                              Anne Steele.

SUFFERINGS.

PASSION CHORALE. 7s & 6s, D.   Arr. fr. Bach.

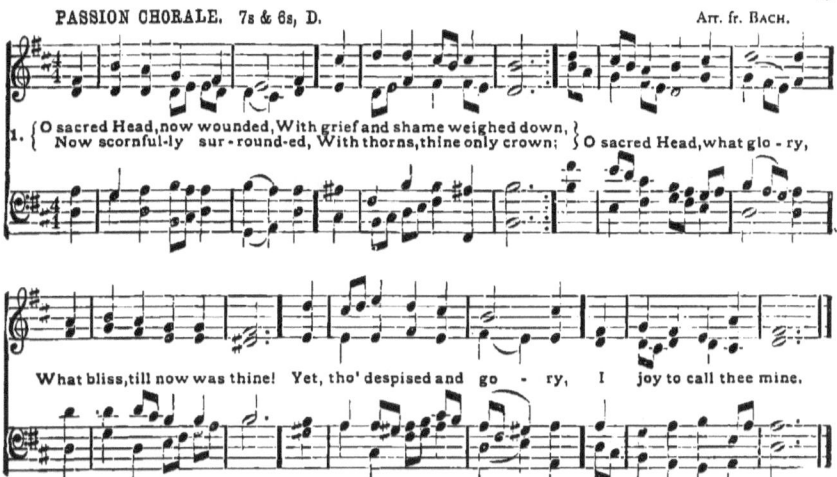

1. O sacred Head, now wounded, With grief and shame weighed down,
Now scornful-ly sur-round-ed, With thorns, thine only crown;
O sacred Head, what glo-ry, What bliss, till now was thine! Yet, tho' despised and go-ry, I joy to call thee mine.

237   *At the Cross.*

2 What language shall I borrow,
   To praise thee, heavenly Friend·
For this, thy dying sorrow,
   Thy pity without end?
Lord, make me thine forever,
   Nor let me faithless prove:
Oh! let me never, never,
   Abuse such dying love.

3 Forbid that I should leave thee;
   O Jesus, leave not me;
By faith I would receive thee;
   Thy blood can make me free:
When strength and comfort languish,
   And I must hence depart:
Release me then from anguish,
   By thine own wounded heart.

4 Be near when I am dying,
   Oh! show thy cross to me!
And for my succor flying,
   Come, Lord, to set me free:
These eyes new faith receiving,
   From Jesus shall not move;
For he who dies believing,
   Dies safely—through thy love.
                J. W. Alexander.

MISSIONARY CHANT. L. M.   Ch. Zeuner.

OLIVE'S BROW. L. M.   CHRIST.   W. B. Bradbury, 1853.

1. 'Tis midnight; and on Olive's brow
The star is dim that lately shone;
'Tis midnight; in the garden, now,
The suff'ring Saviour prays alone.

238 *Christ in Gethsemane.*

2 'Tis midnight; and from all removed,
The Saviour wrestles lone, with fears;
E'en that disciple whom he loved
Heeds not his Master's grief and tears.

3 'Tis midnight; and for others' guilt
The Man of Sorrows weeps in blood;
Yet he who hath in anguish knelt
Is not forsaken by his God.

4 'Tis midnight; from celestial plains
Is borne the song that angels know;
Unheard by mortals are the strains
That sweetly soothe the Saviour's woe.
W. B. Tappan.

2 Still near the lake with weary tread,
Lingers a form of human kind;
And on his lone, unsheltered head
Flows the chill night-damp of the wind.

3 Why seeks he not a home of rest?
Why seeks he not the pillowed bed?
Beasts have their dens, the birds their nest;
He hath not where to lay his head.

4 Such was the lot he freely chose,
To bless, to save the human race;
And through his poverty there flows
A rich, full stream of heavenly grace.
Russell.

239 *It is finished.*

1 'Tis finished! so the Saviour cried,
And meekly bowed his head, and died.
'Tis finished; yes, the race is run,
The battle fought, the victory won.

2 'Tis finished!—all that heaven foretold
By prophets in the days of old;
And truths are opened to our view
That kings and prophets never knew.

3 'Tis finished! Son of God, thy power
Hath triumphed in this awful hour;
And yet our eyes with sorrow see
That life to us was death to thee.

4 'Tis finished! let the joyful sound
Be heard through all the nations round;
'Tis finished! let the triumph rise,
And swell the chorus of the skies.
Stennett.

241 *Christ's Passion.*

1 The morning dawns upon the place
Where Jesus spent the night in prayer;
Through yielding glooms behold his face;
Nor form nor comeliness is there.

2 Brought forth to judgment, now he stands
Arraigned, condemned, at Pilate's bar;
Here, spurned by fierce prætorian bands,
There, mocked by Herod's men of war.

3 He bears their buffeting and scorn,
Mock homage of the lip, the knee,
The purple robe, the crown of thorn,
The scourge, the nail, th' accursèd tree.

4 No guile within his mouth is found;
He neither threatens, nor complains;
Meek as a lamb for slaughter bound,
Dumb, 'mid his murderers he remains.

5 But hark! he prays: 'tis for his foes:
And speaks: 'tis comfort to his friends;
Answers: and paradise bestows;
He bows his head: the conflict ends.
James Montgomery.

240 *Through his Poverty made Rich.*

1 On the dark wave of Galilee
The gloom of twilight gathers fast;
And o'er the waters heavily
Sweeps cold and drear the evening blast.

RESURRECTION.

DROSTANE. L. M. J. B. Dykes.

1. Ride on, ride on in majesty;
Hark! all the tribes Hosanna cry;
Thy humble beast pursues his road,
With palms and scattered garments strowed.

242 *Christ's Entry into Jerusalem.*

2 Ride on, ride on in majesty;
In lowly pomp ride on to die;
O Christ, thy triumphs now begin
O'er captive death and conquered sin.

3 Ride on, ride on in majesty;
Thy last and fiercest strife is nigh;

The Father, on his sapphire throne,
Expects his own anointed Son.

4 Ride on, ride on in majesty;
In lowly pomp ride on to die.
Bow thy meek head to mortal pain;
Then take, O Christ, thy power and reign.
Milman.

DUKE STREET. L. M. J. Hatton.

1. Now to the Lord, who makes us know The wonders of his dy-ing love,
Be humble hon-ors paid be-low, And strains of no-bler praise a-bove.

243

2 'Twas he who cleansed our foulest sins,
And washed us in his precious blood;
'Tis he who makes us priests and kings,
And brings us rebels near to God.

3 To Jesus, our atoning Priest,
To Jesus, our eternal King,
Be everlasting power confessed!
Let every tongue his glory sing.

4 Behold! on flying clouds he comes,
And every eye shall see him move;
Though with our sins we pierced him once,
He now displays his pardoning love.

5 The unbelieving world shall wail,
While we rejoice to see the day;
Come, Lord! nor let thy promise fail,
Nor let thy chariot long delay.
Isaac Watts.

244 *"King, Creator, Lord!"*

1 O Christ, our King, Creator, Lord!
Saviour of all who trust thy word!
To them who seek thee ever near,
Now to our praises bend thine ear.

2 In thy dear Cross a grace is found,—
It flows from every streaming wound,—
Whose power our inbred sin controls,
Breaks the firm bond, and frees our souls.

3 When thou didst hang upon the tree,
The quaking earth acknowledged thee;
When thou didst there yield up thy breath,
The world grew dark as shades of death.

4 Now in the Father's glory high,
Great Conqueror! never more to die,
Us by thy mighty power defend,
And reign through ages without end.
Ray Palmer.

CHRIST.

LUTON. L. M.   G. Burden, 1830.

1. He dies, the friend of sinners dies; Lo, Salem's daughters weep around: A solemn darkness veils the skies; A sudden trembling shakes the ground.

245   *"Christ dying, rising, and reigning."*

2 Here's love and grief beyond degree;
   The Lord of glory dies for men;
But lo, what sudden joys I see,
   Jesus, the dead, revives again.

3 Break off your tears, ye saints, and tell
   How high our great Deliverer reigns.
Sing how he spoiled the hosts of hell,
   And led the monster, Death, in chains.

4 Say, "Live forever, wondrous King,
   Born to redeem, and strong to save!"
Then ask the monster, "Where's thy sting?"
   "And where's thy vict'ry, boasting Grave?"
Isaac Watts.

246   *The King of Glory.*

1 Our Lord is risen from the dead;
   Our Jesus is gone up on high;
Lift up your heads, ye heavenly gates,
   Ye everlasting doors, give way.

2 Loose all your bars of massy light,
   And wide unfold th' ethereal scene:
He claims these mansions as his right,
   Receive the King of glory in.

3 Who is the King of glory—who?
   The Lord, who all our foes o'ercame;
Who sin, and death, and hell o'erthrew;
   And Jesus is the Conqueror's name.

4 Lo, his triumphal chariot waits,
   And angels chant the solemn lay;
Lift up your heads, ye heavenly gates,
   Ye everlasting doors, give way.
Charles Wesley.

247   *"He lives."*

1 "I know that my Redeemer lives:"
   What comfort this sweet sentence gives,
He lives, He lives, who once was dead,
   He lives, my ever-living Head.

2 He lives to bless me with His love,
   He lives to plead for me above,
He lives my hungry soul to feed,
   He lives to help in time of need.

3 He lives, and grants me daily breath,
   He lives, and I shall conquer death,
He lives, my mansions to prepare,
   He lives to bring me safely there.
Rev. Samuel Medley.

248   *The Song of Songs.*

1 Come, let us sing the song of songs—
   The saints in heaven began the strain—
The homage which to Christ belongs:
   "Worthy the Lamb, for he was slain!"

2 Slain to redeem us by his blood,
   To cleanse from every sinful stain,
And make us kings and priests to God—
   "Worthy the Lamb, for he was slain!"

3 To him, enthroned by filial right,
   All power in heaven and earth proclaim,
Honor, and majesty, and might:
   "Worthy the Lamb, for he was slain!"

4 Long as we live, and when we die,
   And while in heaven with him we reign;
This song, our song of songs shall be:
   "Worthy the Lamb, for he was slain."
James Montgomery.

249

2 Glory to God in full anthems of joy;
The being he gave us death cannot destroy.
'Sad were the life we must part with to-morrow,
If tears were our birth-right, and death were our end;
But Jesus hath cheered the dark valley of sorrow,
And bade us, immortal, to heaven ascend.
Lift, then, your voices in triumph on high,
For Jesus hath risen, and man shall not die.

ASCENSION. P. M.   CHRIST.   W. H. MONK.

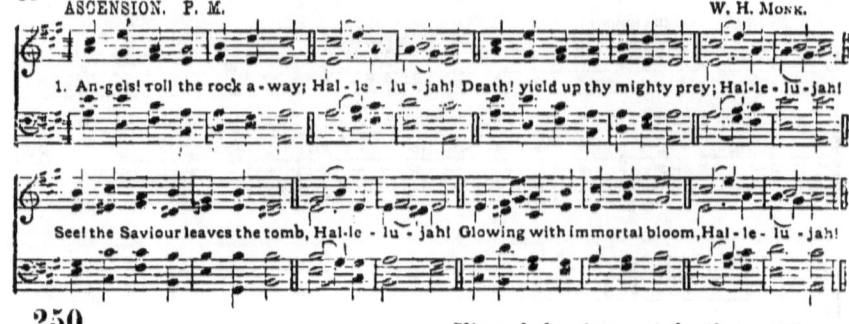

1. Angels! roll the rock away; Hallelujah! Death! yield up thy mighty prey; Hallelujah! See! the Saviour leaves the tomb, Hallelujah! Glowing with immortal bloom, Hallelujah!

250

2 Hark! the wondering angels raise
Louder notes of joyful praise;
Let the earth's remotest bound
Echo with the blissful sound.

3 Heaven unfolds its portals wide,
See the Conqueror through them ride!

King of glory! mount thy throne—
Boundless empire is thine own.

4 Praise him, ye celestial choirs!
Tune, and sweep your golden lyres;
Raise, O earth! your noblest songs,
From ten thousand thousand tongues.
T. Scott.

EASTER HYMN. 7s.   J. WORGAN.

1. Christ, the Lord, is ris'n to-day, Alleluia! Sons of men, and angels, say; Alleluia! Raise your joys and triumphs high! Alleluia! Sing, ye heav'ns, and earth, reply! Alleluia!

251   *The Lord is Risen.*

2 Love's redeeming work is done,
Fought the fight, the battle won;
Lo, our Sun's eclipse is o'er;
Lo, he sets in blood no more.

3 Vain the stone, the watch, the seal,
Christ hath burst the gates of hell;
Death in vain forbids his rise;
Christ has opened paradise.

4 Lives again our glorious King;
"Where, O Death, is now thy sting?"

Once he died our souls to save;
"Where's thy victory, boasting grave?"

5 Soar we now where Christ has led,
Following our exalted Head;
Made like him, like him we rise;
Ours the cross, the grave, the skies!

6 Christ, the Lord, is risen to-day!
Sons of men and angels say:
Sing, ye heavens, and earth reply!
Raise your joys and triumphs high!
Charles Wesley, 1739.

RESURRECTION. 81

TELEMAN'S CHANT. 7s.   Ch. Zeuner.

1. Joyful be the hours to-day; Joy-ful let the seasons be; Let us sing, for well we may: Jesus! we will sing of thee.

252 *Joy in the Lord.*

2 Should thy people silent be,
   Then the very stones would sing:
What a debt we owe to thee,
   Thee our Saviour, thee our King!

3 Joyful are we now to own,
   Rapture thrills us as we trace
All the deeds thy love hath done,
   All the riches of thy grace.

4 Thine the Name to sinners dear!
   Thine the Name all names before!
Blessèd here and everywhere;
   Blessèd now and evermore!
                             Thomas Kelly.

253 *"The Lord's Day."*

1 Hail the day that sees him rise,
   Glorious, to his native skies!
Christ, awhile to mortals given,
   Enters now the gates of heaven.

2 There the glorious triumph waits;
   Lift your heads, eternal gates!
Christ hath vanquished death and sin;
   Take the King of glory in.

3 See, the heaven its Lord receives!
   Yet he loves the earth he leaves:
Though returning to his throne
   Still he calls mankind his own.

4 What, though parted from our sight
   Far above yon starry height;
Thither our affections rise
   Following him beyond the skies.
                             Charles Wesley.

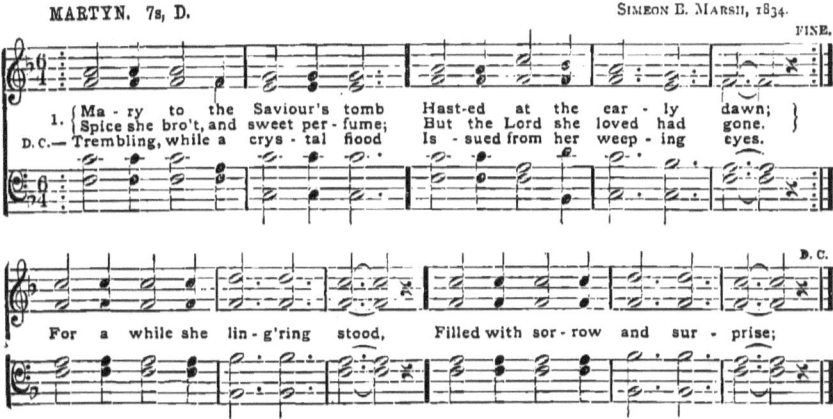

MARTYN. 7s, D.   Simeon B. Marsh, 1834.

1. Ma-ry to the Saviour's tomb Hast-ed at the ear-ly dawn;
   Spice she bro't, and sweet per-fume; But the Lord she loved had gone.
D.C.—Trembling, while a crys-tal flood Is-sued from her weep-ing eyes.

For a while she lin-g'ring stood, Filled with sor-row and sur-prise;

254 *Mary at the Tomb.*

2 But her sorrows quickly fled
   When she heard his welcome voice;
Christ had risen from the dead;
   Now he bids her heart rejoice:

What a change his word can make,
   Turning darkness into day!
Ye who weep for Jesus' sake,
   He will wipe your tears away.
                             J. Newton.

CHRIST.

FARLAND. 8s, 7s & 4s. T. HASTINGS.

1. Look, ye saints, the sight is glorious; See the Man of Sorrows now: From the fight returned victorious, Every knee to him shall bow: Crown him, crown him! Crown him, crown him! Crowns become the Victor's brow.

255 "King of kings."
2 Crown the Saviour, angels, crown him;
Rich the trophies Jesus brings;
In the seat of power enthrone him,
While the vault of heaven rings:
Crown him, crown him;
Crown the Saviour "King of kings."

3 Hark: those bursts of acclamation!
Hark, those loud triumphant chords!
Jesus takes the highest station;
Oh, what joy the sight affords:
Crown him, crown him;
"King of kings and Lord of lords."
Thomas Kelly.

DARWELL. H. M. J. DARWELL.

1. Yes, the Redeemer rose: The Saviour left the dead, And o'er our hellish foes High raised his conquering head: In wild dismay the guards around Fall to the ground and sink away.

256 Angel said He was Alive.
2 Lo, the angelic bands
In full assembly meet
To wait his high commands,
And worship at his feet:
Joyful they come, and wing their way
From realms of day to Jesus' tomb.

3 Then back to heaven they fly,
And the glad tidings bear;

Hark! as they soar on high,
What music fills the air!
Their anthems say, "Jesus who bled
Hath left the dead: he rose to-day."

4 Ye mortals, catch the sound,
Redeemed by him from hell,
And send the echo round
The globe on which you dwell;
Transported cry, "Jesus, who bled,
Hath left the dead, no more to die."
Philip Doddridge.

RESURRECTION. 83

VICTORIA. P. M.   Arr. fr. PALESTRINA.

Hal-le - lu - jah! Hal-le - lu - jah! Hal-le - lu - jah! The strife is o'er, the bat - tle done: The vic-to - ry of Life is won: The song of tri-umph has be - gun,— Hal-le - lu - jah!

257   *Captivity led captive.*
2 The powers of death have done their worst,
But Christ their legions hath dispersed;
Let shout of holy joy outburst,—
Hallelujah!

3 Lord, by the stripes which wounded thee,
From death's dread sting thy servants free,
That we may live and sing to thee,
Hallelujah!

Francis Pott, *tr.*

CORONATION. C. M.   O. HOLDEN.

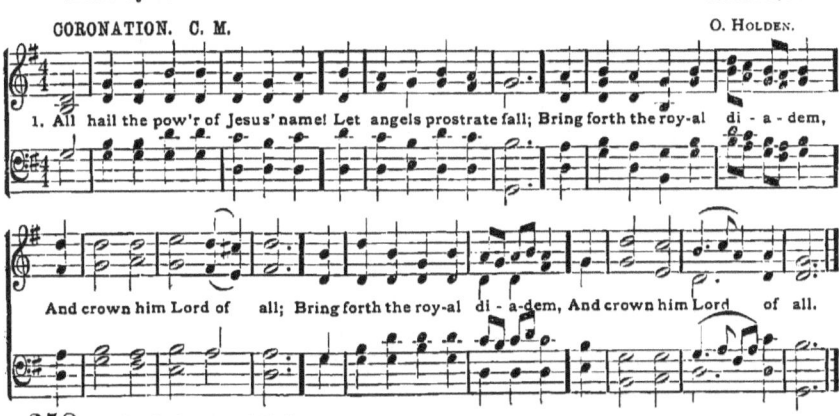

1. All hail the pow'r of Jesus' name! Let angels prostrate fall; Bring forth the roy-al di - a - dem, And crown him Lord of all; Bring forth the roy-al di - a-dem, And crown him Lord of all.

258   *The Glorification of Christ.*
2 Let every kindred, every tribe,
On this terrestrial ball,
To him all majesty ascribe,
And crown him Lord of all.

3 Oh that, with yonder sacred throng,
We at his feet may fall,
And join the everlasting song,
And crown him Lord of all!
         Edward Perronet, 1780.

259   *Christ our All.*
1 O JESUS, Lord of all below,
Thou fount of life and fire,

Surpassing all the joys we know,
All that we can desire,—

2 May every heart confess thy name,
And ever thee adore,
And seeking thee, itself inflame
To seek thee more and more.

3 Thee may our tongue forever bless,
Thee may we love alone,
And ever in our lives express,
The image of thine own.
         Bernard.

CHRIST.

HYMN. C. M. — J. E. Gould.

1. Thou art the Way; to thee alone From sin and death we flee;
And he who would the Father seek, Must seek him, Lord, by thee.

260 *The Way, the Truth, and the Life.*

2 Thou art the Truth; thy word alone
True wisdom can impart;
Thou only canst inform the mind,
And purify the heart.

3 Thou art the Life; the rending tomb
Proclaims thy conquering arm;
And those who put their trust in thee
Nor death nor hell shall harm.

4 Thou art the Way, the Truth, the Life:
Grant us to know that way,
That truth to keep, that life to win,
Which lead to endless day.
Geo. W. Doane, 1824.

261 *Lift up your Heads, O ye Gates.*

1 Lift up your heads, eternal gates;
Unfold; to entertain
The King of glory; see, he comes
With his celestial train.

2 Who is this King of glory—who?
The Lord, for strength renowned;
In battle mighty; o'er his foes
Eternal Victor crowned.

3 Who is the King of glory—who?
The Lord of hosts renowned:
Of glory he alone is King,
Who is with glory crowned.
Tate & Brady.

262 *"I have prayed for thee."*

1 I know that my Redeemer lives,
And ever prays for me;
A token of his love he gives,
A pledge of liberty.

2 I find him lifting up my head;
He brings salvation near:
His presence makes me free indeed,
And he will soon appear.

3 He wills that I should holy be:
What can withstand his will?
The counsel of his grace in me
He surely shall fulfill.

4 Jesus, I hang upon thy word;
I steadfastly believe
Thou wilt return, and claim me, Lord,
And to thyself receive.
Charles Wesley.

263 *"All in Jesus."*

1 Behold, where in a mortal form,
Appears each grace divine!
The virtues, all in Jesus met,
With mildest radiance shine.

2 To spread the rays of heavenly light,
To give the mourner joy,
To preach glad tidings to the poor,
Was his divine employ.

3 In the last hour of deep distress,
Before his Father's throne,
With soul resigned he bowed, and said,—
"Thy will, not mine, be done!"

4 Be Christ our pattern, and our guide,
His image may we bear;
Oh! may we tread his holy steps,—
His joy and glory share.
W. Enfield.

CHARACTER AND OFFICES.

ORTONVILLE. C. M. — Thomas Hastings, 1837.

1. Majestic sweetness sits enthron'd Upon the Saviour's brow;
His head with ra-diant glo -(Omit)............ ries crown'd, His lips with grace o'erflow, His lips with grace o'er- flow.

264 *He is altogether lovely.*

2 No mortal can with him compare
Among the sons of men;
Fairer is he than all the fair
Who fill the heavenly train.

3 Since from his bounty I receive
Such proofs of love divine,
Had I a thousand hearts to give,
Lord, they should all be thine.
Joseph Stennett, d. 1713.

265 *The precious Name.*

1 How sweet the name of Jesus sounds
In a believer's ear!
It soothes his sorrows, heals his wounds,
And drives away his fear.

2 It makes the wounded spirit whole,
And calms the troubled breast;
'Tis manna to the hungry soul,
And to the weary rest.

3 Dear name, the rock on which I build,
My shield and hiding-place;
My never-failing treasury, filled
With boundless stores of grace.
John Newton.

ST. LEON. C. M. — From "Sabbath Harmony," by per. L. O. Emerson.
SOLO - SOPRANO.

1. Thou dear Re-deem-er, dy-ing Lamb,.... I love to hear of thee;
No music's like thy charm-ing.... name, Nor half so sweet to me.

Used by per. Oliver Ditson Co., owners of Copyright.

266 *Sweet Name.*

2 My Jesus shall be all my theme,
While on this earth I stay;
And still I'll sing his lovely name
When all things else decay.

3 When I appear in yonder cloud,
With all his favored throng,
Then will I sing more sweet, more loud,
And Christ shall be my song.
John Cennick, 1743.

CHRIST.

COWPER. C. M. LOWELL MASON

1. Plunged in a gulf of dark despair, We wretch-ed sin-ners lay, With-out one cheer-ful beam of hope, Or spark of glimm'ring day, Or spark of glimm'ring day.

267 *Love of Christ.*

2 With pitying eyes the Prince of grace
  Beheld our helpless grief;
He saw, and—O, amazing love!—
  He ran to our relief.

3 Down from the shining seats above
  With joyful haste he fled,
Entered the grave in mortal flesh,
  And dwelt among the dead.

4 O, for this love let rocks and hills
  Their lasting silence break;
And all harmonious human tongues
  The Saviour's praises speak.

Isaac Watts.

CLEANSING FOUNTAIN. C. M.

1. There is a fountain filled with blood, Drawn from Im-manuel's veins, And sinners plunged beneath that flood,
D.S.—And sinners plunged beneath that flood,
Lose all their guil-ty stains. Lose all their guil-ty stains, Lose all their guil-ty stains;
Lose all their guil-ty stains.

268

2 The dying thief rejoiced to see
  That fountain in his day;
And there may I, though vile as he,
  Wash all my sins away.

3 Dear dying Lamb! thy precious blood
  Shall never lose its power,
Till all the ransom'd Church of God
  Are saved, to sin no more.

4 E'er since by faith I saw the stream
  Thy flowing wounds supply,
Redeeming love has been my theme,
  And shall be, till I die.

5 Then in a nobler, sweeter song
  I'll sing thy power to save,
When this poor lisping, stamm'ring tongue,
  Lies silent in the grave.

Cowper.

CHARACTER AND OFFICES. 87

CAMBRIDGE C. M. Dr. John Randall, 1790.

1. Sal-va-tion! O, the joy-ful sound! 'Tis pleasure to our ears— A sov'reign balm for ev-'ry wound, A cor-dial for our fears, A cor-dial for our fears, A cor-dial for our fears.

269 *Salvation by Christ.*

2 Salvation! let the echo fly
The spacious earth around,
While all the armies of the sky
Conspire to raise the sound.

3 Salvation! O thou bleeding Lamb,
To thee the praise belongs,
Salvation shall inspire our hearts,
And dwell upon our tongues.
Isaac Watts, 1709.

TAMPICO. C. M.

1. With joy we med-i-tate the grace Of our High Priest a-bove; His heart is made of ten-der-ness; It melts with pit-y-ing love, It melts with pitying love.

270 *Tempted like as We are.*

2 Touched with a sympathy within,
He knows our feeble frame;
He knows what sore temptations mean,
For he hath felt the same.

3 He, in the days of feeble flesh,
Poured out his cries and tears,
And, in his measure, feels afresh
What every member bears.

4 Then let our humble faith address
His mercy and his power;
We shall obtain delivering grace
In the distressing hour.
Isaac Watts, 1709.

271 *The Life was the Light of Men.*

1 O, what a treasure all divine
Is hid in Christ, the Lord!
From him what rays of glory shine!
What peace his paths afford!

2 In him our light and life are found,
Though we were dead before;
And now he makes our joys abound,
Who all our sorrows bore.

3 When sore distressed, he to our aid
On rapid pinions flies,
And to the wounds which sin has made
A healing balm applies.
Benjamin Beddome.

CHRIST.

LOVING-KINDNESS. L. M.

1. A-wake, my soul, to joy-ful lays, And sing the great Redeem-er's praise; He just-ly claims a song from me; His lov-ing-kind-ness, oh, how free! Lov-ing-kindness, lov-ing-kindness, His lov-ing-kind-ness, oh, how free!

272

2 When trouble, like a gloomy cloud,
Has gathered thick and thundered loud,
He near my soul has always stood;
His loving-kindness, oh, how good!

3 Soon shall I pass the gloomy vale,
Soon all my mortal powers must fail:

Oh, may my last expiring breath
His loving-kindness sing in death!

4 Then let me mount and soar away
To the bright world of endless day;
And sing, with rapture and surprise,
His loving-kindness in the skies!

Samuel Medley.

MEDITATION. 11s & 8s. FREEMAN LEWIS.

1. O thou in whose presence my soul takes de-light, On whom in af-flic-tion I call, My com-fort by day, and my song in the night, My hope, my sal-va-tion, my all.

273 *Whither is my Beloved gone?*

2 Where dost thou at noontide resort with thy
To feed them on pastures of love? [sheep
For why in the valley of death should I weep,
Or alone in the wilderness rove?

3 Oh why should I wander an alien from thee,
And cry in the desert for bread?

Thy foes will rejoice when my sorrows they
And smile at the tears I have shed. [see,

4 Dear Shepherd! I hear, and will follow thy
I know the sweet sound of thy voice; [call,
Restore and defend me, for thou art my all,
And in thee I will ever rejoice.

Joseph Swain.

CHARACTER AND OFFICES.

ROCKINGHAM. L. M.   Dr. L. Mason.

1. My dear Re-deem-er and my Lord, I read my du-ty in thy word;
But in thy life the law ap-pears Drawn out in liv-ing char-ac-ters.

274   *The Divine Example.*

2 Such was thy truth, and such thy zeal,
Such deference to thy Father's will,
Such love, and meekness so divine,
I would transcribe and make them mine.

3 Cold mountains and the midnight air
Witnessed the fervor of thy prayer;
The desert thy temptations knew,
Thy conflict, and thy victory too.

4 Be thou my pattern; may I bear
More of thy gracious image here;
Then, God the Judge, shall own my name
Among the followers of the Lamb.
Isaac Watts, 1709.

275   *There is none other Name.*

1 There is none other name than thine,
Immanuel Jesus, name divine,
On which to rest for sins forgiven—
For peace with God, for hope of heaven.

2 There is none other name than thine,
When cares, and fears, and griefs are mine,
That with a gracious power can heal
Each care, and fear, and grief I feel.

3 There is none other name than thine,
When called my spirit to resign,
To bear me through that latest strife,
And e'en in death to be my life.
Anon.

276   *Not to condemn the World.*

1 Not to condemn the sons of men,
Did Christ, the Son of God, appear;
No weapons in his hands are seen,
No flaming sword nor thunder there.

2 Such was the pity of our God,
He loved the race of man so well,
He sent his Son to bear our load
Of sins, and save our souls from hell.

3 Sinners, believe the Saviour's word;
Trust in his mighty name, and live;
A thousand joys his lips afford;
His hands a thousand blessings give.
Isaac Watts.

277   *Kingdom of Christ.*

1 Jesus shall reign where'er the sun
Does his successive journeys run;
His kingdom stretch from shore to shore
Till moons shall wax and wane no more.

2 People and realms of every tongue
Dwell on his love with sweetest song;
And infant voices shall proclaim
Their early blessings on his name.

3 Blessings abound where'er he reigns;
The prisoner leaps to loose his chains;
The weary find eternal rest,
And all the sons of want are blest.

4 Let every creature rise and bring
Peculiar honors to our King,
Angels descend with songs again,
And earth repeat the loud Amen.
Isaac Watts, 1719.

CHRIST.

CURTIS. L. M.   Fr. "Jubilant Voices."   L. V. WHEELER.

1. Be-hold a Stran-ger at the door; He gen-tly knocks, has knocked be-fore; Has wait-ed long, is wait-ing still; You treat no oth-er friend so ill.

278 *"Behold, I stand at the door."*
2 Oh, lovely attitude! he stands
With melting heart and open hands:
Oh, matchless kindness!—and he shows
This matchless kindness to his foes!

3 Rise, touched with gratitude divine,
Turn out his enemy and thine;
Turn out thy soul-enslaving sin,
And let the heavenly stranger in.

4 Oh, welcome him, the Prince of Peace!
Now may his gentle reign increase!
Throw wide the door, each willing mind;
And be his empire all mankind.
                         Grigg.

BUCKFIELD. L. M.

1. When strangers stand and hear me tell, What beau-ties in my Sav-iour dwell, Where he is gone they fain would know, That they may seek and love him too,

279 *Excellencies of Christ described.*
2 My best Beloved keeps his throne
On hills of light in worlds unknown;
But he descends, and shows his face
In the young gardens of his grace,—

3 He has engrossed my warmest love;
No earthly charms my soul can move;
I have a mansion in his heart;
Nor death nor hell shall make us part.

4 O, may my spirit daily rise
On wings of faith above the skies,
Till death shall make my last remove,
To dwell forever with my love.
                         Isaac Watts.

CHARACTER AND OFFICES.

YOAKLEY. L. M. W. YOAKLEY.

1. Thou hid-den source of calm re-pose, Thou all-suf-fi-cient Love di-vine,
My help, and ref-uge from my foes, Se-cure I am if thou art mine.
And, lo, from sin, and grief, and shame, I hide me, Je-sus, in thy name.

280 *Christ all in All.*

2 Jesus, my all in all thou art:
My rest in toil, my ease in pain;
The healing of my broken heart;
In strife, my peace; in loss, my gain;
My smile beneath the tyrant's frown;
In shame, my glory and my crown;—
3 In want, my plentiful supply;
In weakness, my almighty power;
In bonds, my perfect liberty;
My light in Satan's darkest hour;
Thee, in each grief, my joy I call;
My life in death, my all in all.
Charles Wesley.

281 *Unto you which believe he is precious.*

1 O, SPEAK of Jesus: other names
Have lost for me their interest now;
His is the only one that claims
To be an antidote for woe:
It falls like music on the ear
When nothing else can soothe or cheer.

2 O, speak of Jesus—of his power
As Son of God and Son of Man,
Which day by day, and hour by hour,
As he wrought out the wondrous plan,
Led him as God, to save and heal—
As man to sympathize and feel.

3 O, speak of Jesus—of his death;
For us he lived, for us he died;
"Tis finished," with his latest breath
The Lord, Immanuel-Jesus, cried.
That death of shame and agony
Won life, eternal life, for me.
Anon.

282 *Christ-like.* [Omit Repeat.]

1 MAKE us, by thy transforming grace,
Dear Saviour, daily more like thee!
Thy fair example may we trace,
To teach us what we ought to be!

2 Oh, how benevolent and kind!
How mild!—how ready to forgive!
Be this the temper of our minds,
And these the rules by which we live.

3 To do his heavenly Father's will,
Was his employment and delight;
Humility and holy zeal,
Shone through his life divinely bright.

4 But ah! how blind, how weak we are!
How frail!—how apt to turn aside!
Lord, we depend upon thy care,
And ask thy Spirit for our guide.
Anne Steele.

283 *Christ the Sun of Righteousness.*
[Omit Repeat.]

1 To thee, O God, we homage pay,
Source of the light that rules the day;
Who, while he gilds all nature's frame,
Reflects thy rays and speaks thy name.

2 In louder strains we sing that grace
Which gives the Sun of Righteousness,
Whose nobler light salvation brings,
And scatters healing from his wings.

3 Still on our hearts may Jesus shine,
With beams of light and love divine!
Quickened by him our souls shall live,
And cheered by him shall grow and thrive.
Philip Doddridge.

CHRIST.

ALETTA. 7s.   W. B. BRADBURY, 1858.

1. Fee-ble, help-less, how shall I Learn to live, and learn to die?
Who, O God, my guide shall be? Who shall lead thy child to thee?

284 *Jesus our Leader.*

2 Blessed Father, gracious One,
Thou hast sent thy holy Son:
He will give the light I need;
He my trembling steps will lead.

3 Through this world, uncertain, dim,
Let me ever lean on him:
From his precepts wisdom draw,
Make his life my solemn law.

4 Thus in deed and thought and word,
Led by Jesus Christ the Lord,
In my weakness, thus shall I
Learn to live, and learn to die;—

5 Learn to live in peace and love,
Like the perfect ones above;
Learn to die without a fear,
Feeling thee, my Father, near.
William Henry Furness.

285 *The Good Shepherd.*

1 SHEPHERD of the ransomed flock,
Lead us to the shadowing rock,
Where the cooling waters flow,
Where the freshening pastures grow.

2 Saviour, when thy loved ones stray
From the new and living way,
Gently call thine own by name,
All our wandering steps reclaim.

3 Through the hours of darksome night,
Keep us in thy watchful sight;
O'er each deadly foe prevail;
Let no harm thy fold assail.

4 Jesus, who thy life didst give,
Dying that thy sheep might live,
Let us in thy presence rest,
With eternal comfort blest.
Anon.

TOPLADY. 7s, 6l.   FINE.   Dr. THOMAS HASTINGS, 1830. D. C.

1. Rock of A-ges, cleft for me, Let me hide myself in thee! { Let the wa-ters and the blood,
D.C.—Be of sin the double cure, Cleanse me from its guilt and pow'r. { From thy riven side which flow'd,}

286 *Rock of Ages.*

2 Could my zeal no respite know,
Could my tears forever flow
All for sin could not atone;
Thou must save, and thou alone;
Nothing in my hand I bring;
Simply to thy cross I cling.

3 While I draw this fleeting breath,
When my eyelids close in death,
When I soar to worlds unknown,
See thee on thy judgment-throne,
Rock of Ages, cleft for me,
Let me hide myself in thee.
Augustus M. Toplady. 1776.

CHARACTER AND OFFICES

GORTON. S. M.   Arr. fr. BEETHOVEN.

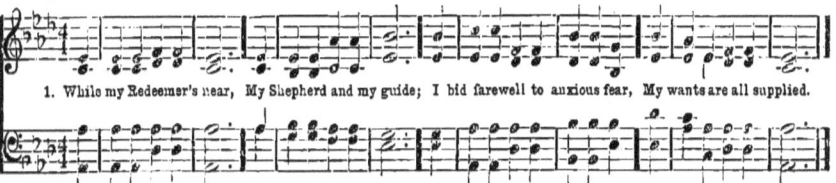

1. While my Redeemer's near, My Shepherd and my guide; I bid farewell to anxious fear, My wants are all supplied.

287 *Go in and out and find Pasture.*

2 To ever-fragrant meads,
  Where rich abundance grows,
His gracious hand indulgent leads,
  And guards my sweet repose.

3 Dear Shepherd, if I stray,
  My wandering feet restore,
To thy fair pastures guide my way,
  And let me rove no more.
Anne Steele.

288 *The Day-star from on High.*

1 WE lift our hearts to thee,
  O'Day-star from on high!
The sun itself is but thy shade,
  Yet cheers both earth and sky.

2 O let thy rising beams
  The night of sin disperse,—
The mists of error and of vice,
  Which shade the universe.

3 How beauteous nature now;
  How dark and sad before;
With joy we view the pleasing change,
  And nature's God adore.
John Wesley.

289 *Salvation by Grace.*

1 GRACE! 'tis a charming sound,
  Harmonious to the ear:
Heaven with the echo shall resound,
  And all the earth shall hear.

2 Grace first contrived a way
  To save rebellious man;
And all the steps that grace display,
  Which drew the wondrous plan.

3 Grace taught my roving feet
  To tread the heavenly road;
And new supplies each hour I meet,
  While pressing on to God.

4 Grace all the work shall crown,
  Through everlasting days;
It lays in heaven the topmost stone,
  And well deserves our praise.
Philip Doddridge.

290 *I am the Light of the World.*

1 BEHOLD, the Prince of Peace,
  The chosen of the Lord,
God's well-belovéd Son fulfils
  The sure, prophetic word.

2 The Spirit of the Lord,
  In rich abundance shed,
On this great Prophet gently lights,
  And rests upon his head.

3 Jesus, thou Light of men!
  Thy doctrine life imparts:
O may we feel its quickening power,
  To warm and cheer our hearts.

4 Cheered by its beams, our souls
  Shall run the heavenly way;
The path which thou hast marked and trod
  Will lead to endless day.
John Needham.

291 *Christ is All.*

1 O EVERLASTING Light,
  Shine graciously within;
Brightest of all on earth that's bright,
  Come, shine away my sin.

2 O everlasting Truth,
  Truest of all that's true,
Sure Guide of erring age and youth
  Lead me and teach me too.

3 O everlasting Strength,
  Uphold me in the way;
Bring me, in spite of foes, at length,
  To joy, and light, and day.

4 There night is never known,
  Nor sun's faint, sickly ray;
But glory from the eternal throne
  Spreads everlasting day.
Anne Steele.

CHRIST.

REFUGE. 7s.   Jos. P. Holbrook.

1. Jesus, lover of my soul, Let me to thy bosom fly, While the billows near me roll, While the tempest still is high; Hide me, oh, my Saviour, hide, Till the storm of life is past; Safe into the haven guide, Oh, receive my soul at last.

292. *Christ our All.*

2 Other refuge have I none,
  Hangs my helpless soul on thee,
Leave, oh, leave me not alone,
  Still support and comfort me:
All my trust on thee is stayed,
  All my help from thee I bring;
Cover my defenceless head
  With the shadow of thy wing.

3 Thou, O Christ, art all I want;
  More than all in thee I find:
Raise the fallen, cheer the faint,
  Heal the sick, and lead the blind:

Just and holy is thy name,
  I am all unrighteousness;
Vile and full of sin I am,
  Thou art full of truth and grace.

4 Plenteous grace with thee is found—
  Grace to cover all my sin:
Let the healing streams abound;
  Make me, keep me, pure within.
Thou of life the Fountain art,
  Freely let me take of thee;
Spring thou up within my heart,
  Rise to all eternity.

Charles Wesley, 1740.

MARTYN. 7s, D.   Simeon B. Marsh, 1834.

1. { Jesus, lover of my soul, Let me to thy bosom fly, } { Hide me, oh, my Saviour, hide, }
  { While the billows near me roll, While the tempest still is high; } { Till the storm of life is past; }
D.C.—Safe into the haven guide; Oh, receive my soul at last.

CHARACTER AND OFFICES.

Used by per. Oliver Ditson Co., owners of Copyright.

For other verses, see page 94. Chorus after each verse.

CHRIST.

LENOX. H. M.   JONATHAN EDSON, 1782

1. A-rise, my soul, a-rise; Shake off thy guilt-y fears; The bleed-ing Sac-ri-fice In my be-half ap-pears: Be-fore the throne my Saviour stands, My name is writ-ten on his hands, My name is writ-ten on his hands.

293 *The interceding Saviour.*
2 He ever lives above,
  For me to intercede,
  His all-redeeming love,
  His precious blood, to plead:
His blood atoned for all our race,
And sprinkles now the throne of grace.

3 The Father hears him pray,
  His dear Anointed One;—
  He cannot turn away
  The presence of his Son:
His Spirit answers to the blood,
And tells me I am born of God.
                              C. Wesley.

294 *Thou hast led Captivity captive.*
1 THE happy morn is come;
  Triumphant o'er the grave,
  The Saviour leaves the tomb,
  Almighty now to save.
Captivity is captive led;
For Jesus liveth, who was dead.

2 The ransom Christ hath paid·
  The glorious work is done;
  On him our help is laid,
  By him our victory won.
Captivity is captive led;
For Jesus liveth, who was dead.

3 All hail, triumphant Lord!
  The Resurrection thou;
  All hail, thou risen Lord!
  Before thy throne we bow
Captivity is captive led;
For Jesus liveth, who was dead.
                              Haweis.

295 *A Name above every Name.*
1 JOIN all the glorious names
  Of wisdom, love, and power,
  That ever mortals knew,
  That angels ever bore:
All are too mean to speak his worth,
Too mean to set my Saviour forth.

2 Great Prophet of our God,
  My tongue would bless thy name;
  By thee the joyful news
  Of our salvation came:
The joyful news of sins forgiven,
Of hell subdued, and peace with Heaven.

3 O thou almighty Lord,
  My Conqueror and my King,
  Thy sceptre and thy sword,
  Thy reigning grace, I sing.
Thine is the power: behold I sit,
In willing bonds, beneath thy feet.
                              Isaac Watts.

CHARACTER AND OFFICES. 97

MIDDLETON. 8s & 7s, D. Arr. by J. ZUNDEL.

Light of those whose dreary dwelling
Borders on the shades of death,
Still we wait for thine appearing,
Life and joy thy beams impart,

Come, and, thy dear self reveal-ing,
Dissipate the clouds beneath.

D.C.—Chasing all our fears, and cheering
Ev'ry poor benighted heart.

296 *Prayer for Light.*

2 Save us, in thy great compassion,
O thou God of peace and love!
Give the knowledge of salvation,
Fix our hearts on things above.
By thine all-sufficient merit,
Every burdened soul release;
Every weary, wandering spirit
Guide into thy perfect peace.
Toplady.

297 *He careth for Me.*

1 YES, for me, for me he careth
With a brother's tender care;
Yes, with me, with me he shareth
Every burden, every fear.
Yes, in me abroad he sheddeth
Joys unearthly, love and light;
And to cover me he spreadeth
His love-brooding wing of might.

2 Yes, in me, in me he dwelleth;
I in him, and he in me;
And my empty soul he filleth,
Here and through eternity.
Thus I wait for his returning,
Singing all the way to heaven;
Such the joyful song of morning,
Such the tranquil song of even.
Horatius Bonar.

298 *Christ the true Friend.*

1 ONE there is, above all others,
Well deserves the name of Friend;
His is love beyond a brother's—
Costly, free, and knows no end.

Which of all our friends, to save us,
Could or would have shed his blood?
But our Jesus died to have us
Reconciled in him to God.

2 When he lived on earth abased,
Friend of Sinners was his name;
Now, above all glory raised,
He rejoices in the same.
O for grace our hearts to soften!
Teach us, Lord, at length to love;
We, alas! forget too often
What a Friend we have above.
Newton.

299 *I am with you alway.*

1 ALWAYS with us, always with us—
Words of cheer and words of love;
Thus the risen Saviour whispers
From his dwelling-place above.
With us when we toil in sadness,
Sowing much and reaping none,
Telling us that in the future
Golden harvests shall be won;—

2 With us when the storm is sweeping
O'er our pathway dark and drear;
Waking hope within our bosoms,
Stilling every anxious fear;—
With us in the lonely valley,
When we cross the chilling stream,
Lighting up the steps to glory
With salvation's radiant beam.
Nevin.

CHRIST.

BONER. C. M. L. O. E. From "Sabbath Harmony," by per.

1. O for a thousand tongues to sing My great.... Re-deem-er's praise; The glo-ries of my Lord and King, The triumphs of his grace, The triumphs of his grace.

Used by per. Oliver Ditson Co., owners of Copyright.

300 *Praise to the Saviour.*

2 My gracious Master and my Lord,
Assist me to proclaim,
To spread through all the earth abroad
The honors of thy name.

3 Jesus! the name that calms our fears,
That bids our sorrows cease;
'Tis music in the sinner's ears,
'Tis life, and health, and peace.
Charles Wesley.

301 *Remember Me.*

1 JESUS! thou art the sinner's Friend;
As such I look to thee;
Now, in the fullness of thy love,
O Lord! remember me.

2 Remember thy pure word of grace,—
Remember Calvary;
Remember all thy dying groans,
And then remember me.

3 Lord! I am guilty—I am vile,
But thy salvation's free;
Then, in thine all-abounding grace,
Dear Lord! remember me.

4 And, when I close my eyes in death,
When earthly helps all flee,
Then, O my dear Redeemer God!
I pray, remember me.
Richard Burnham, 1782.

302 *Praising Christ for his Grace.*

1 My Saviour, my almighty Friend;
When I begin thy praise,
Where will the growing numbers end:
The numbers of thy grace?

2 Thou art my everlasting trust;
Thy goodness I adore;
And since I knew thy graces first,
I speak thy glories more.

3 My feet shall travel all the length
Of the celestial road,
And march with courage in thy strength
To see my Father, God.

4 How will my lips rejoice to tell
The victories of my King!
My soul redeemed from sin and hell,
Shall thy salvation sing.
Isaac Watts.

303 *The unsearchable Riches of Christ.*

1 To our Redeemer's glorious name
Awake the sacred song;
O, may his love—immortal flame—
Tune every heart and tongue.

2 His love what mortal thought can reach?
What mortal tongue display?
Imagination's utmost stretch
In wonder dies away.

3 Dear Lord, while we, adoring, pay
Our humble thanks to thee,
May every heart with rapture say,
"The Saviour died for me."

4 O, may the sweet, the blissful theme
Fill every heart and tongue,
Till strangers love thy charming name,
And join the sacred song.
Anne Steele.

PRAISE TO HIM.

DEVIZES. C. M.   Isaac Tucker, 1 00.

1. Come, let us join our cheer-ful songs With an-gels round the throne; Ten thousand thousand are their tongues, But all their joys are one, But all their joys are one.

304   *Worthy is the Lamb.*

2 "Worthy the Lamb that died," they cry,
"To be exalted thus;"
"Worthy the Lamb," our lips reply,
"For he was slain for us."

3 Jesus is worthy to receive
Honor and power divine;
And blessings, more than we can give
Be, Lord, forever thine.

4 Let all that dwell above the sky,
And air, and earth, and seas,
Conspire to lift thy glories high,
And speak thine endless praise.
Isaac Watts, 1709.

305   *Christ Precious.*

1 Jesus! I love thy charming name,
'Tis music to mine ear,
Fain would I sound it out so loud,
That earth and heaven should hear.

2 Yes, thou art precious to my soul,
My Transport and my Trust;
Jewels to thee are gaudy toys,
And gold is sordid dust.

3 All my capacious powers can wish,
In thee doth richly meet;
Nor to mine eyes is life so dear,
Nor friendship half so sweet.

4 Thy grace still dwells upon my heart,
And sheds its fragrance there;
The noblest balm of all its wounds,
The cordial of its care.
Philip Doddridge, 1740.

ST. THOMAS. S. M.   William Tansur, 1743.

1. A-wake, and sing the song Of Moses and the Lamb; Wake, every heart, and ev-'ry tongue, To praise the Saviour's name.

306   *The Song of Moses and the Lamb.*

2 Sing of his dying love;
Sing of his rising power;
Sing how he intercedes above
For those whose sins he bore.

3 Sing till we feel our hearts
Ascending with our tongues;
Sing, till the love of sin departs,
And grace inspires our songs.
William Hammond, 1745.

CHRIST.

ARIEL. C, P. M, — Fr. Mozart. Arr. by Lowell Mason, 1836.

1. Oh, could I speak he matchless worth, Oh, could I sound the glories forth, Which in my Saviour shine! I'd soar and touch the heav'nly strings, And vie with Gabriel while he sings In notes almost divine, In notes almost divine.

307 *Excellency of Christ.*

2 I'd sing the characters he bears,
And all the forms of love he wears,
   Exalted on his throne:
In loftiest songs of sweetest praise,
I would, to everlasting days,
   Make all his glories known.

3 Oh, the delightful day will come
When my dear Lord will bring me home,
   And I shall see his face!
Then, with my Saviour, Brother, Friend,
A blest eternity I'll spend,
   Triumphant in his grace.
                   Samuel Medley, 1789.

308 *"Complete in Him."*

1 Come join, ye saints, with heart and voice,
Alone in Jesus to rejoice,
   And worship at his feet;
Come, take his praises on your tongues,
And raise to him your thankful songs,
   "In him ye are complete!"

2 In him, who all our praise excels
The fullness of the Godhead dwells,
   And all perfections meet;
The head of all celestial powers,
Divinely theirs, divinely ours;
   "In him ye are complete!"

3 Still onward urge your heavenly way,
Dependent on him day by day,
   His presence still entreat;

His precious name forever bless,
Your glory, strength and righteousness,
   "In him ye are complete!"

4 Nor fear to pass the vale of death;
In his dear arms resign your breath,
   He'll make the passage sweet;
The gloom and fears of death shall flee,
And your departing souls shall see
   "In him ye are complete!"
                   Samuel Medley.

309 *The Saviour's Mission.*

1 Oh, let your mingling voices rise
In grateful rapture to the skies,
   And hail a Saviour's birth:
Let songs of joy the day proclaim
When Jesus all-triumphant came
   To bless the sons of earth!

2 He came to bid the weary rest,
To heal the sinner's wounded breast,
   To bind the broken heart;
To spread the light of truth around,
And to the world's remotest bound
   The heavenly gift impart.

3 He came our trembling souls to save
From sin, from sorrow, and the grave,
   And chase our fears away;
Victorious o'er death and time,
To lead us to a happier clime,
   Where reigns eternal day.
                 Jane Elizabeth Roscoe.

PRAISE TO HIM. 101

MYERS. H. M.   GEO. M. MONROE.

1. Shall hymns of grate-ful love Thro' heav'ns's high arches ring, And all the hosts a-bove Their songs of triumph sing, And shall not we take up the strain, And send the ech-o back a-gain.

And shall not we take up the strain,

310 *Response to the New Song.*

2 Shall they adore the Lord,
  Who bought them with his blood,
And all the love record
  That led them home to God,
And shall not we take up the strain,
And send the echo back again?

3 O, spread the joyful sound;
  The Saviour's love proclaim;
And publish all around
  Salvation through his name;
Till all the world take up the strain,
And send the echo back again.
James J. Cummins, 1849.

311 *The Debt of Love.*

1 COME, every pious heart,
  That loves the Saviour's name,
Your noblest powers exert
  To celebrate his fame;
Tell all above, and all below,
The debt of love to him you owe.

2 He left his starry crown,
  And laid his robe aside;
On wings of love came down,
  And wept, and bled, and died:
What he endured, no tongue can tell,
To save our souls from death and hell.

3 From the dark grave he rose—
  The mansions of the dead;
And thence his mighty foes
  In glorious triumph led;
Up through the sky the Conqueror rode,
And reigns on high, the Saviour-God.

4 Jesus, we ne'er can pay
  The debt we owe thy love;
Yet tell us how we may
  Our gratitude approve;
Our hearts, our all to thee we give;
The gift, though small, thou wilt receive.
Stennett.

HOLY SPIRIT.

MENDON. L. M.
Arr. by Dr. L. Mason.

1. Come, gracious Spirit, heavn'ly Dove, With light and comfort from above;
Be thou our guardian, thou our guide; O'er ev'ry thought and step preside.

312 *He will guide you into all Truth.*

2 To us the light of truth display,
And make us know and choose thy way;
Plant holy fear in every heart,
That we from God may ne'er depart.

3 Lead us to holiness—the road
Which we must take to dwell with God;
Lead us to Christ, the living way,
Nor let us from his pasture stray.

4 Lead us to God—our final rest,
To be with him forever blest;
Lead us to heaven, its bliss to share—
Fullness of joy forever there.
Simon Browne.

313 *He dwelleth with you.*

1 Sure, the blest Comforter is nigh;
'Tis he sustains my fainting heart;
Else would my hope forever die,
And every cheering ray depart.

2 Whene'er to call the Saviour mine,
With ardent wish my heart aspires,
Can it be less than power divine
That animates these strong desires?

3 And when my cheerful hope can say,
I love my God and taste his grace,
Lord, is it not thy blissful ray
Which brings this dawn of sacred peace?

4 Let thy kind Spirit in my heart
Forever dwell, O God of love,
And light and heavenly peace impart—
Sweet earnest of the joys above.
Anne Steele.

314 *It is the Spirit that Quickeneth.*

1 Come, Holy Spirit, calm my mind,
And fit me to approach my God;
Remove each vain, each worldly thought,
And lead me to thy blest abode.

2 Hast thou imparted to my soul
A living spark of holy fire?
O, kindle now the sacred flame,
And make me burn with pure desire.

3 A brighter faith and hope impart,
And let me now my Saviour see;
O, soothe and cheer my burdened heart,
And bid my spirit rest in thee.
George Burdett.

315 *He shall teach you all Things.*

1 Come, blessed Spirit, Source of light,
Whose power and grace are unconfined,
Dispel the gloomy shades of night,
The thicker darkness of the mind.

2 To mine illumined eyes display
The glorious truth thy work reveals;
Cause me to run the heavenly way;
The book unfold, unloose the seals.

3 Thine inward teachings make me know
The mysteries of redeeming love,
The emptiness of things below,
The excellence of things above.

4 While through this dubious maze I stray,
Spread, like the sun, thy beams abroad,
To show the dangers of the way,
And guide my feeble steps to God.
Beddome.

HOLY SPIRIT. 103

ASHFORD. L. M.   Ch. Zeuner.

1. O Source of un-cre-a-ted light, By whom the worlds were raised from night, Come, vis-it ev-'ry pi-ous mind; Come, pour thy joys on hu-man kind.

316 *Creator Spirit.*

2 Plenteous in grace, descend from high,
Rich in thy matchless energy;
From sin and sorrow set us free,
And make us temples worthy thee.

3 Cleanse and refine our earthly parts,
Inflame and sanctify our hearts,
Our frailties help, our vice control,
Submit the senses to the soul.

4 Thrice holy Fount, thrice holy Fire!
Our hearts with heavenly love inspire;
Make us eternal truths receive;
Aid us to live as we believe.
John Dryden.

317 *Creator Spirit.*

1 OH come, Creator Spirit blest!
Within these souls of thine to rest;
Come, with thy grace and heavenly aid,
To fill the hearts which thou hast made.

2 With patience firm and purpose high
The weakness of our flesh supply;
Kindle our senses from above,
And make our hearts o'erflow with love.
Breviary.

318 *Power of the Holy Spirit.*

1 ETERNAL Spirit, we confess
And sing the wonders of thy grace;
Thy power conveys our blessings down
From God the Father and the Son.

2 Enlightened by thy heavenly ray,
Our shades and darkness turn to day;
Thine inward teachings make us know
Our danger, and our refuge too.

3 The troubled conscience knows thy voice;
Thy cheering words awake our joys;
Thy words allay the stormy wind,
And calm the surges of the mind.
Isaac Watts.

319 *Thy Will be done.*

1 SPIRIT of peace, and health, and power,
Fountain of life and light below,
Around thy healing influence shower,
O'er all the nations let it flow.

2 Inspire our hearts with perfect love;
In us the work of faith fulfil;
So not heaven's host shall swifter move
Than we on earth, to do thy will.

3 Father, 'tis thine each day to yield
Thy children's wants a fresh supply;
Thou cloth'st the lilies of the field,
And hear'st young ravens when they cry.

4 To thee we pray; for all must live
By thee, who know'st their every need;
Pray for the world, that thou wilt give
All human hearts thy living bread.
John Wesley.

HOLY SPIRIT.

LOETHFIELD. C. M.   INGALLS.

1. Come, Holy Spirit, heav'nly Dove, With all thy quick'ning pow'rs, Kindle a flame of sacred love In these cold hearts of ours, In these cold hearts of ours, Kindle a flame of sacred love, Kindle a flame of sacred love.

320 *Prayer for the Holy Spirit.*

2 Look, how we grovel here below,
  Fond of these trifling toys!
Our souls can neither fly nor go
  To reach eternal joys.

3 In vain we tune our formal songs,
  In vain we strive to rise;
Hosannas languish on our tongues,
  And our devotion dies.

4 Dear Lord, and shall we ever live
  At this poor dying rate?
Our love so faint, so cold to thee,
  And thine to us so great?

5 Come, Holy Spirit, heavenly Dove,
  With all thy quickening powers;
Come, shed abroad a Saviour's love,
  And that shall kindle ours.
                    Isaac Watts, 1709

321 *"Spirit of Grace."*

1 Come, sacred Spirit, from above,
  And fill the coldest heart with love;
Oh, turn to flesh the flinty stone,
  And let thy sovereign power be known.

2 Speak thou, and from the haughtiest eyes
Shall floods of contrite sorrow rise;
While all their glowing souls are borne
To seek that grace which now they scorn.

3 Oh, let a holy flock await
  In crowds around thy temple-gate!
Each pressing on the zeal to be
A living sacrifice to thee.
                    Philip Doddridge.

322 *"Quicken me, O Lord."*

1 Come, mighty Spirit, penetrate
  This heart and soul of mine;
And my whole being with thy grace
  Pervade, O Life divine.

2 As the clear air surrounds the earth,
  Thy grace around me roll;
As the fresh light pervades the air,
  So pierce and fill my soul.

3 As from the clouds drops down in love
  The precious summer rain,
So from thyself pour down the flood
  That freshens all again.

4 Thus life within our lifeless hearts
  Shall make its glad abode;
And we shall shine in beauteous light,
  Filled with the light of God.
                    Horatius Bonar, 1857.

HOLY SPIRIT.

NEW HAVEN. 6s & 4s.   T. Hastings.

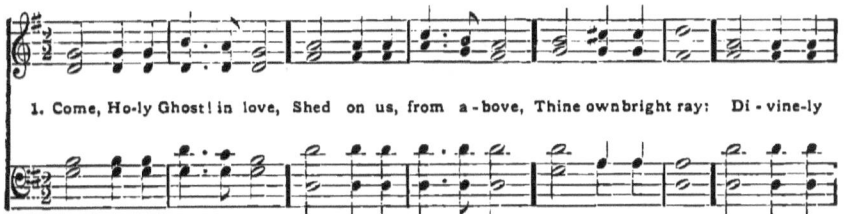

1. Come, Ho-ly Ghost! in love, Shed on us, from a-bove, Thine own bright ray: Di-vine-ly

good thou art; Thy sa-cred gifts im-part, To gladden each sad heart; Oh, come to-day!

323   *"Oh, come to-day."*

2 Come, tenderest Friend, and best,
Our most delightful Guest!
  With soothing power;
Rest, which the weary know;
Shade, 'mid the noontide glow;
Peace, when deep griefs o'erflow;
  Cheer us, this hour!

3 Come, Light serene! and still,
Our inmost bosoms fill;
  Dwell in each breast:
We know no dawn but thine;
Send forth thy beams divine,
On our dark souls to shine,
  And make us blest.

4 Come, all the faithful bless;
Let all, who Christ confess,
  His praise employ:
Give virtue's rich reward;
Victorious death accord,
And, with our glorious Lord,
  Eternal joy!
                Ray Palmer.

324   *Let there be Light.*

1 Thou, whose almighty word
Chaos and darkness heard,
  And took their flight!
Hear us, we humbly pray;
And, where the gospel day
Sheds not its glorious ray,
  Let there be light.

2 Thou, who didst come to bring,
On thy redeeming wing,
  Healing and sight!
Health to the sick in mind,
Light to the inly blind,
Oh, now to all mankind
  Let there be light!

3 Descend thou from above,
Spirit of truth and love,—
  Speed on thy flight!
Move o'er the waters' face,
Spirit of hope and grace,
And in earth's darkest place
  Let there be light!
                John Marriott, 1813.

HOLY SPIRIT.

PAX DEI. 10s.   J. B. Dykes.

1. O thou great Friend to all the sons of men, Who once appeared in humblest guise below, Sin to rebuke, to break the captive's chain, And call thy brethren forth from want and woe!

325 *"Guidance into Truth."*

2 We look to thee: thy Spirit gives the light
Which guides the nations, groping on
   their way,
Stumbling and falling in disastrous night,
Yet hoping ever for the perfect day.

3 Yes: thou art still the Life: thou art the
   Way   [of heaven;
The holiest know,—Light, Life, and Way
And they who dearest hope, and deepest pray,
Toil by the light, life, way, which thou
   last given.   Theodore Parker.

KELLOGG. H. M.   L. O. Emerson.

1. Come, Holy Spirit, come, And deign to dwell with me; Come, make my heart thy home, And bid all darkness flee. Come, sacred Guest, oh, quickly come, And make my heart thy lasting home!

Used by per. Oliver Ditson Co., owners of Copyright.

326 *Come, Holy Spirit.*

2 Exert thy mighty power,
   And banish all my sin:
In this auspicious hour,
   Bring all thy graces in.
Come, strong Deliverer, quickly come,
And make my heart thy lasting home.

3 Rule thou in every thought
   And passion of my soul,
Till all my powers are brought
   Beneath thy full control.
Come, peaceful Conqueror, quickly come,
And make my heart thy lasting home.

4 Then shall my days be thine,
   And all my heart be love;
And joy and peace be mine,
   Such as are known above;
Come, Holy Spirit, quickly come,
And make my heart thy lasting home.
                    Andrew Reed, 1842.

HOLY SPIRIT. 107

OLNEY. S. M.   LOWELL MASON, 1832.

1. Come, ho-ly Spir-it, come! Let thy bright beam a-rise;
Dis-pel the sor-rows from our minds, The dark-ness from our eyes.

327   *For the Spirit.*

2 Revive our drooping faith,
   Our doubts and fears remove,
And kindle in our breasts the flame
   Of never-dying love.

3 'Tis thine to cleanse the heart,
   To sanctify the soul,
To pour fresh life in every part,
   And new-create the whole.

4 Dwell, Spirit! in our hearts;
   Our minds from bondage free;
Then shall we know, and praise, and love,
   And rise at length to thee.
                     Joseph Hart, 1750.

328   *"The heart melted."*

1 Come, Holy Spirit, come,
   With energy divine;
And on this poor benighted soul
   With beams of mercy shine.

2 Oh, melt this frozen heart;
   This stubborn will subdue;
Each evil passion overcome,
   And form me all anew.

3 Mine will the profit be,
   But thine shall be the praise;
And unto thee will I devote
   The remnant of my days.
                     Benjamin Beddome.

329   *Divine Comforter.*

1 Blest Comforter divine,
   Let rays of heavenly light
Amidst our gloom and darkness shine,
   To guide our souls aright.

2 Draw with thy still small voice
   From every sinful way;
And bid the mourning heart rejoice,
   Though earthly joys decay.

3 By thine inspiring breath
   Make every cloud of care,
And e'en the gloomy vale of death,
   A smile of glory wear.

4 Come, Holy Spirit, come,
   With energy divine,
And on this poor benighted heart,
   With beams of mercy shine.
                     Lydia H. Sigourney, 1824.

330   *"The Light."*

1 Lord, bid thy light arise
   On all thy people here,
And when we raise our longing eyes,
   Oh, may we find thee near!

2 Thy Holy Spirit send,
   To quicken every soul;
And hearts, the most rebellious, bend
   To thy divine control.

3 Let all that own thy name
   Thy sacred image bear,
And light in every heart the flame
   Of watchfulness and prayer.

4 Since in thy love we see
   Our only sure relief,
Ah, raise our earthly minds to thee,
   And help our unbelief!
                     W. H. Bathurst.

HOLY SPIRIT.

HORTON, 7s.   Arr. by Dr. L. Mason.

1. Gracious Spirit, Love divine,
Let thy light within me shine;
All my guilty fears remove;
Fill me with thy heav'nly love.

331   *He will guide you.*

2 Speak thy pardoning grace to me,
Set the burdened sinner free;
Lead me to the Lamb of God;
Wash me in his precious blood.

3 Life and peace to me impart;
Seal salvation on my heart;
Dwell thyself within my breast,
Earnest of immortal rest.

4 Let me never from thee stray;
Keep me in the narrow way;
Fill my soul with joy divine;
Keep me, Lord, forever thine.
John Stocker, 1776.

332   *The Word.*

1 Word by God the Father sent,
Lord of all, Omnipotent;
Word for sinners' need supplied,
As their comfort and their guide!

2 Word of Life, both pure and strong,
Word for which the heathen long,
Spread abroad, till out of night
All the world awake to light!

3 Up—for, lo, earth's surface o'er,
Waving fields with ripening store;
Countless sheaves are spread around:
Few, O, few the reapers found.

4 Lord of harvest, great and kind,
Rouse to action heart and mind;
Let the gathering nations all
See thy light and hear thy call.
Cox.

333   *The Spirit Helpeth.*

1 Holy Spirit, Light divine,
Shine upon this heart of mine;
Chase the shades of night away;
Turn the darkness into day.

2 Holy Spirit, Power divine,
Cleanse this guilty heart of mine;
Long has sin, without control,
Held dominion o'er my soul.

3 Holy Spirit, Joy divine,
Cheer this saddened heart of mine;
Bid my many woes depart;
Heal my wounded, bleeding heart.

4 Holy Spirit, All divine,
Dwell within this heart of mine;
Cast down every idol throne;
Reign supreme, and reign alone.
Andrew Reed, 1842.

334   *"The things of Christ."*

1 Holy Spirit! gently come,
   Raise us from our fallen state;
Fix thy everlasting home
   In the hearts thou didst create.

2 Now thy quickening influence bring,
   On our spirits sweetly move;
Open every mouth to sing
   Jesus' everlasting love.

3 Take the things of Christ and show
   What our Lord for us hath done;
May we God the Father know
   Through his well-belovéd Son.
William Hammond.

THE BIBLE. 109

UXBRIDGE. L. M. — Lowell Mason.

1. The heav'ns declare thy glo-ry, Lord! In ev-'ry star thy wis-dom shines;
But, when our eyes be-hold thy word, We read thy name in fair-er lines.

335 *The Works and Word of God.*

2 The rolling sun, the changing light,
And nights and days thy power confess;
But the blest volume thou hast writ
Reveals thy justice and thy grace.

3 Nor shall thy spreading gospel rest
Till thro' the world thy truth has run;
Till Christ has all the nations blest,
That see the light, or feel the sun.

4 Great Sun of righteousness! arise;
Bless the dark world with heavenly light;
Thy gospel makes the simple wise,
Thy laws are pure, thy judgments right.

5 Thy noblest wonders here we view,
In souls renewed and sins forgiven;
Lord! cleanse my sins, my soul renew,
And make thy word my guide to heaven.
Isaac Watts, 1719.

336 *Excellency of the Gospel.*

1 Let everlasting glories crown
Thy head, my Saviour and my Lord;
Thy hands have brought salvation down,
And stored the blessings in thy word.

2 In vain the trembling conscience seeks
Some solid ground to rest upon;
With long despair the Spirit breaks,
Till we apply to Christ alone.

3 How well thy blessed truths agree!
How wise and holy thy commands!
Thy promises, how firm they be!
How firm our hope, our comfort stands!
Isaac Watts, 1709.

337 *The Gospel Revelation.*

1 GOD, in the gospel of his Son,
Makes his eternal counsels known;
Here love in all its glory shines,
And truth is drawn in fairest lines.

2 Here sinners of an humble frame
May taste his grace and learn his name,
May read, in characters of blood,
The wisdom, power, and grace of God.

3 Here faith reveals to mortal eyes
A brighter world beyond the skies;
Here shines the light which guides our way
From earth to realms of endless day.

4 O, grant us grace, almighty Lord,
To read and mark thy holy word,
Its truths with meekness to receive,
And by its holy precepts live.
Benjamin Beddome, 1787.

338 *O, how I love thy Law!*

1 I LOVE the sacred Book of God;
No other can its place supply;
It points me to the saints' abode,
And lifts my joyful thoughts on high.

2 Blest Book, in thee my eyes discern
The image of my absent Lord;
From thine instructive page I learn
The joys his presence will afford.

3 But while I'm here, thou shalt supply
His place, and tell me of his love;
I'll read with faith's discerning eye,
And thus partake of joys above.
Kelly.

THE BIBLE.

HUMMEL. C. M.   From DULCIMER.

1. O, how I love thy ho-ly law! 'Tis dai-ly my de-light; And thence my med-i-ta-tions draw Di-vine ad-vice by night, Di-vine ad-vice by night.

Used by per. Oliver Ditson Co., owners of Copyright.

339   *O, how I love thy Law.*

2 Thy heavenly words my heart engage,
    And well employ my tongue,
And, through my weary pilgrimage,
    Yield me a heavenly song.

3 No treasures so enrich the mind;
    Nor shall thy word be sold
For loads of silver well-refined,
    Nor heaps of choicest gold.

4 When nature sinks, and spirits droop,
    Thy promises of grace
Are pillars to support my hope,
    And there I write thy praise.
                         Isaac Watts, 1719.

340   *The Bible a Light.*

1 How precious is the Book divine,
    By inspiration given!
Bright as a lamp its doctrines shine
    To guide our souls to heaven.

2 Its light, descending from above,
    Our gloomy world to cheer,
Display's a Saviour's boundless love,
    And brings his glories near.

3 It shows to man his wandering ways,
    And where his feet have trod;
And brings to view the matchless grace
    Of a forgiving God.

4 It sweetly cheers our drooping hearts
    In this dark vale of tears;
Life, light, and joy it still imparts,
    And quells our rising fears.

5 This lamp, through all the tedious night
    Of life, shall guide our way,
Till we behold the clearer light
    Of an eternal day.
                         John Fawcett, 1872.

341   *Breathing after Holiness.*

1 Oh that the Lord would guide my ways
    To keep his statues still!
Oh that my God would grant me grace
    To know and do his will!

2 Oh, send thy spirit down, to write
    Thy law upon my heart!
Nor let my tongue indulge deceit,
    Nor act the liar's part.
                             Isaac Watts.

342   *Comfort from the Bible.*

1 Lord, I have made thy word my choice,
    My lasting heritage;
There shall my noblest powers rejoice,
    My warmest thoughts engage.

2 I'll read the histories of thy love,
    And keep thy laws in sight,
While through the promises I rove
    With ever fresh delight.

3 'Tis a broad land of wealth unknown,
    Where springs of life arise,
Seeds of immortal bliss are sown,
    And hidden glory lies.

4 The best relief that mourners have,
    It makes our sorrows blest,
Our fairest hope beyond the grave,
    And our eternal rest.
                             Isaac Watts.

THE BIBLE.

CHESTERFIELD. C. M.   Dr. Hawies.

1. A glo-ry gilds the sacred page, Ma-jes-tic like the sun: It gives a light to ev-ery age; It gives, but borrows none.

343 *Light and Glory of the World.*
2 The hand that gave it still supplies
The gracious light and heat;
His truths upon the nations rise,
They rise, but never set.

3 Let everlasting thanks be thine,
For such a bright display,
As makes a world of darkness shine
With beams of heavenly day.
William Cowper, 1779.

344 *Thy Commandment is exceeding broad.*
1 Lamp of our feet, whereby we trace
Our path, when wont to stray:
Stream from the fount of heavenly grace;
Brook by the traveler's way;—

2 Bread of our souls, whereon we feed;
True manna from on high;
Our guide and chart, wherein we read
Of realms beyond the sky;—

3 Pillar of fire, through watches dark,
Or radiant cloud by day;
When waves would whelm our tossing bark,
Our anchor and our stay;—

4 Childhood's preceptor. manhood's trust,
Old age's firm ally;
Our hope, when we go down to dust,
Of immortality!
Barton.

345 *"Delight in the Scriptures."*
1 Father of mercies, in thy word
What endless glory shines!
Forever be thy name adored
For these celestial lines.

2 'Tis here the tree of knowledge grows,
And yields a free repast;
Here purer sweets than nature knows
Invite the longing taste.

3 Here my Redeemer's welcome voice
Spreads heavenly peace around;
And life and everlasting joys
Attend the blissful sound.

4 Oh, may these heavenly pages be
My ever dear delight;
And still new beauties may I see,
And still increasing light!
Anne Steele.

346 *Value of the Scriptures.*
1 Oppressed with guilt, and full of fears,
I come to thee, my Lord,
While not a ray of hope appears
But in thy holy word.

2 The volume of my Father's grace
Does all my grief dispel;
Here I behold my Saviour's face,
And learn to do his will.

3 This is the field where hidden lies
The pearl of price unknown;
That merchant is divinely wise
Who makes that pearl his own.

4 Here living water freely flows,
To cleanse me from my sin;
'Tis here the tree of knowledge grows,
Nor danger dwells within.

5 O, may thy counsels, mighty God,
My roving feet command;
Nor I forsake the happy road
That leads to thy right hand.
Anon.

GOSPEL.

YDOLEM. C. M.   Ch. Zeuner. Fr. "Ancient Lyre," by per.

1. Let ev-'ry mor-tal ear attend, And ev'ry heart re-joice; The trumpet of the gospel sounds With an in-vit-ing voice.

347 *Ho, every one that thirsteth.*
2 Eternal wisdom has prepared
   A soul-reviving feast,
And bids your longing appetites
   The rich provision taste.

3 Ho, ye that pant for living streams,
   And pine away and die,
Here you may quench your raging thirst
   With springs that never dry.

4 Rivers of love and mercy here
   In a rich ocean join;
Salvation in abundance flows,
   Like floods of milk and wine.   *Isaac Watts.*

348 *Forsaken by the Living Fountain.*
1 How long shall dreams of earthly bliss
   Our flattering hopes employ,
And mock our fond, deluded eyes
   With visionary joy?

2 Why from the mountains and the hills
   Is our salvation sought,
While our eternal Rock's forsook,
   And Israel's God forgot?

3 The living spring neglected flows
   Full in our daily view;
Yet we, with anxious, fruitless toil,
   Our broken cisterns hew.

4 These fatal errors, gracious God,
   With gentle pity see;
To thee our roving eyes direct,
   And fix our souls on thee.   *Philip Doddridge.*

349 *Come, buy without Money.*
1 Ye wretched, hungry, starving poor,
   Behold a royal feast,
Where Mercy spreads her bounteous store
   For every humble guest.

2 See, Jesus stands with open arms;
   He calls—he bids you come;

Guilt holds you back, and fear alarms;
   But, see, there yet is room.

3 O come, and with his children taste
   The blessings of his love;
While hope attends the sweet repast
   Of nobler joys above.   *Anne Steele.*

350 *The Wicked like the troubled Sea.*
1 Sinners, the voice of God regard;
   His mercy speaks to-day;
He calls you by his sovereign word
   From sin's destructive way.

2 Like the rough sea, that cannot rest;
   You live devoid of peace,
A thousand stings within your breast
   Deprive your souls of ease.

3 But he who turns to God shall live,
   Through his abounding grace;
His mercy will the guilt forgive
   Of those who seek his face.   *Fawcett.*

351 *The Saviour's Invitation.*
1 The Saviour calls; let every ear
   Attend the heavenly sound;
Ye doubting souls, dismiss your fear;
   Hope smiles reviving round.

2 For every thirsty, longing heart
   Here streams of bounty flow,
And life, and health, and bliss impart,
   To banish mortal woe.

3 Ye sinners, come—'tis mercy's voice;
   That gracious voice obey;
'Tis Jesus calls to heavenly joys:
   And can you yet delay?

4 Dear Saviour, draw reluctant hearts;
   To thee let sinners fly,
And take the bliss thy love imparts,
   And drink, and never die.   *Anne Steele.*

WARNING AND INVITATION.

RETURN. C. M.   T. Hastings.

1. Re-turn, O wan-d'rer, to thy home, Thy Fa-ther calls for thee: No lon-ger now an ex-ile roam In guilt and mis-er-y. Re-turn, re-turn!

352 *Return to thy Home.*

2 Return, O wanderer, to thy home;
  Thy Saviour calls for thee:
"The Spirit and the Bride say, Come;"
  Oh, now for refuge flee!

3 Return, O wanderer, to thy home,
  'Tis madness to delay;
There are no pardons in the tomb;
  And brief is mercy's day!
  William Hastings.

353 *Now Return.*

1 RETURN, O wanderer, now return,
  And seek thy Father's face!
Those new desires, which in thee burn,
  Were kindled by his grace.

2 Return, O wanderer, now return!
  He hears thy humble sigh;
He sees thy softened spirit mourn,
  When no one else is nigh.

3 Return, O wanderer, now return
  Thy Saviour bids thee live:
Go to his bleeding feet, and learn
  How freely he'll forgive.

4 Return, O wanderer, now return
  And wipe the falling tear!
Thy Father calls—no longer mourn:
  His love invites thee near.
  Wm. B. Collyer, 1802.

354 *All Things ready.*

1 THE King of heaven his table spreads,
  And dainties crown the board;
Not paradise, with all its joys,
  Could such delight afford.

2 Ye hungry poor, that long have strayed
  In sin's dark mazes, come;
Come from your most obscure retreats,
  And grace shall find you room.

3 All things are ready; come away,
  Nor weak excuses frame;
Crowd to your places at the feast,
  And bless the Master's name.
  Philip Doddridge.

355 *Spiritual Banquet.*

1 Ho, YE that pant for living streams,
  And pine away and die,
There you may quench your raging thirst
  With springs that never dry.

2 Rivers of love and mercy here
  In a rich ocean join:
Salvation in abundance flows,
  Like floods of milk and wine.

3 The happy gates of gospel grace
  Stand open night and day:
Lord, we are come to seek supplies,
  And drive our wants away.
  Isaac Watts, 1709

356 *The Gospel Feast.*

2 Sent by my Lord, on you I call;
 The invitation is to all;
 Come, all the world; come, sinner, thou;
 All things in Christ are ready now.

3 Come, all ye souls by sin oppressed,
 Ye restless wanderers after rest;
 Ye poor, and maimed, and halt, and blind,
 In Christ a hearty welcome find.
Charles Wesley.

357 *Come, ye Heavy-laden.*

1 COME hither, all ye weary souls;
 Ye heavy-laden sinners come;
 I'll give you rest from all your toils,
 And raise you to my heavenly home.

2 They shall find rest who learn of me,
 I'm of a meek and lowly mind;
 But passion rages like the sea,
 And pride is restless as the wind.

3 Blest is the man whose shoulders take
 My yoke, and bear it with delight;
 My yoke is easy to his neck;
 My grace shall make the burden light.

4 Jesus, we come at thy command,
 With faith, and hope, and humble zeal;
 Resign our spirits to thy hand,
 To mould and guide us at thy will.
Isaac Watts, 1709.

358 *The Accepted Time.*

1 LIFE is the time to serve the Lord,
 The time t' insure the great reward;
 And while the lamp holds out to burn,
 The vilest sinner may return.

2 Life is the hour that God has given
 T' escape from hell and fly to heaven—
 The day of grace; and mortals may
 Secure the blessings of the day.

3 Then what my thoughts design to do,
 My hands, with all your might pursue,
 Since no device nor work is found,
 Nor faith, nor hope, beneath the ground.

4 There are no acts of pardon passed
 In the cold grave, to which we haste;
 But darkness, death, and long despair
 Reign in eternal silence there.
Isaac Watts.

359 *Waiting for a convenient Season.*

1 O, DO not let the word depart,
 And close thine eyes against the light;
 Poor sinner, harden not thy heart;
 Thou wouldst be saved: why not to-night?

2 To-morrow's sun may never rise
 To bless thy long-deluded sight;
 This is the time; O, then, be wise;
 Thou wouldst be saved: why not to-night?

3 Our God in pity lingers still;
 And wilt thou thus his love requite?
 Renounce at length thy stubborn will;
 Thou wouldst be saved: why not to-night?

4 Our blessed Lord refuses none
 Who would to him their souls unite;
 Then be the work of grace begun:
 Thou wouldst be saved: why not to-night?
Mrs. Reed.

WARNING AND INVITATION.

WOODWORTH L. M. W. B. BRADBURY, 1849.

1. With tear-ful eyes I look a-round: Life seems a dark and storm-y sea; Yet 'mid the gloom I hear a sound, A heav'n-ly whis-per, 'Come to me.'

360 *Come with me.*

2 It tells me of a place of rest;
It tells me where my soul may flee;
O, to the weary, faint, oppressed,
How sweet the bidding, 'Come to me.'

3 'Come, for all else must fail and die;
Earth is no resting-place for thee;
To heaven direct thy weeping eye;
I am thy portion; come to me.'
Mrs. C. Elliott.

361 *The Spirit's Call.*

1 SAY, sinner! hath a voice within
Oft whispered to thy secret soul,
Urged thee to leave the ways of sin,
And yield thy heart to God's control?

2 Sinner! it was a heavenly voice,—
It was the Spirit's gracious call;
It bade thee make the better choice,
And haste to seek in Christ thine all,

3 God's Spirit will not always strive
With hardened, self-destroying man;
Ye who persist his love to grieve,
May never hear his voice again.

4 Sinner! perhaps, this very day,
Thy last accepted time may be:
Oh! shouldst thou grieve him now away,
Then hope may never beam on thee.
Ann B. Hyde.

362 *One Thing Needful.*

1 WHY will ye waste on trifling cares
That life which God's compassion spares?
While in the various range of thought,
The one thing needful is forgot?

2 Shall God invite you from above?
Shall Jesus urge his dying love?
Shall troubled conscience give you pain?
And all these pleas unite in vain?

3 Not so your eyes will always view
Those objects which you now pursue:
Not so will heaven and hell appear,
When death's decisive hour is near.

4 Almighty God! thy grace impart;
Fix deep conviction on each heart;
Nor let us waste on trifling cares
That life which thy compassion spares.
Philip Doddridge.

363 *Escape for thy life.*

1 HASTE, traveler, haste; the night comes on,
And many a shining hour is gone;
The storm is gathering in the west,
And thou far off from home and rest.

2 The rising tempest sweeps the sky;
The rains descend, the winds are high;
The waters swell, and death and fear
Beset thy path—no refuge near.

3 Haste, while a shelter you may gain,
A covert from the wind and rain,
A hiding-place, a rest, a home,
A refuge from the wrath to come.

4 Then linger not in all the plain;
Flee for thy life—the mountain gain;
Look not behind—make no delay:
O, speed thee, speed thee on thy way.
Collyer.

GOSPEL.

WINDHAM. L. M.   DANIEL READ, 1785.

1. While life prolongs its precious light, But soon, ah, soon, approaching night
Mercy is found, and peace is given; Shall blot out every hope of heaven.

364   *No Hope in the Grave.*

2 While God invites, how blest the day!
How sweet the gospel's charming sound!
Come, sinners, haste, O, haste away,
   While yet a pardoning God is found.

3 Soon, borne on time's most rapid wing,
Shall death command you to the grave,
Before his bar your spirits bring,
   And none be found to hear or save.

4 Now God invites—how blest the day!
How sweet the gospel's charming sound!
Come, sinners, come, O, haste away,
   While yet a pardoning God is found.
                          Dwight.

365   *The Road to Life and to Death.*

1 BROAD is the road that leads to death,
And thousands walk together there;
But wisdom shows a narrow path,
   With here and there a traveler.

2 "Deny thyself, and take thy cross,"
Is the Redeemer's great command;
Nature must count her gold but dross,
   If she would gain this heavenly land.

3 Lord! let not all my hopes be vain,
Create my heart entirely new;
Which hypocrites could ne'er attain,
   Which false apostates never knew.
                         Isaac Watts, 1709.

HALLE. 7s, 6l.   Arr. by Dr. HASTINGS.

1. { From the cross up-lift-ed high, Where the Sav-iour deigns to die,
    { What me-lo-dious sounds we hear, Burst-ing on the rav-ish'd ear!—}
"Love's re-deem-ing work is done— Come and wel-come, sin-ner, come!

366

2 "Sprinkled now with blood the throne—
Why beneath thy burdens groan?
On my pierced body laid,
Justice owns the ransom paid—
Bow the knee, and kiss the Son—
Come and welcome, sinner, come!

3 "Spread for thee, the festal board
See with richest bounty stored;
To thy Father's bosom pressed,
Thou shalt be a child confessed,
Never from his house to roam;
Come and welcome, sinner, come!

4 "Soon the days of life shall end—
Lo, I come—your Saviour, Friend!
Safe your spirit to convey
To the realms of endless day,
Up to my eternal home—
Come and welcome, sinner, come!"
                         T. Haweis.

WARNING AND INVITATION.

HORTON. 7s. Arr. by Dr. L Mason.

1. Come, said Jesus' sacred voice; Come, and make my paths your choice; I will guide you to your home: Weary pilgrim, hither come.

367 *Come unto Me.*

2 Thou, who homeless and forlorn,
Long hast borne the proud world's scorn,
Long hast roamed the barren waste,
Weary pilgrim, hither haste.

3 Ye, who tossed on beds of pain,
Seek for ease, but seek in vain,—
Ye, whose swollen and sleepless eyes
Watch to see the morning rise,—

4 Ye, by fiercer anguish torn,
In remorse for guilt who mourn,
Here repose your heavy care:
A wounded spirit, who can bear?

5 Sinner, come; for here is found
Balm that flows from every wound,
Peace that ever shall endure,
Rest eternal, sacred, sure.
Barbauld.

368 *The Prodigal Son.*

1 BROTHER, hast thou wandered far
From thy Father's happy home,
With thyself and God at war?
Turn thee, brother, homeward come.

2 Hast thou wasted all the powers
God for noble uses gave?
Squandered life's most noble hours?
Turn thee, brother, God can save.

3 Is a mighty famine now
In thy heart and in thy soul?
Discontent upon thy brow?
Turn thee, God will make thee whole.

4 Fall before him on the ground;
Pour thy sorrow in his ear;
Seek him while he may be found;
Call upon him; he is near.
James Freeman Clarke, 1860.

369 *Why will ye die?*

1 SINNERS, turn: why will ye die?
God, your Maker, asks you why—
God, who did your being give,
Made you with himself to live.

2 Sinners, turn: why will ye die?
Christ, your Saviour, asks you why—
Christ, who did your souls retrieve,
Died himself that ye might live?

3 Will ye not his grace receive?
Will ye still refuse to live?
Why, ye long-sought sinners, why
Will ye grieve your God, and die?
Charles Wesley.

370 *The Fields are White.*

1 WORD of Life, most pure, most strong!
Lo! for thee the nations long;
Spread, till from its dreary night
All the world awakes to light.

2 Lo! the ripening fields we see:
Mighty shall the harvest be;
But the reapers still are few;
Great the work they have to do.

3 Lord of harvest, let there be
Joy and strength to work for thee,
Till the nations far and near
See thy light, thy law revere.
From the German.

118
GOSPEL.

DETROIT. C. M. E. P. Hastings.

1. The Spirit in our hearts Is whis-p'ring, 'Sin-ner, come;'
The Bride, the Church of Christ pro-claims To all his chil-dren, 'Come.'

371 *The Spirit and the Bride say, Come.*

2 Let him that heareth say
To all about him, 'Come;'
Let him that thirsts for righteousness
To Christ, the fountain, come.

3 Yes, whosoever will,
O, let him freely come,
And freely drink the stream of life:
'Tis Jesus bids him come.

4 Lo, Jesus, who invites,
Declares, 'I quickly come:'
Lord, even so; I wait thine hour:
Jesus, my Saviour, come.
Bp. H. U. Onderdonk.

372 *The accepted Time.*

1 Now is the accepted time,
Now is the day of grace;
Now, sinners, come, without delay
And seek the Saviour's face.

2 Now is the accepted time,
The Saviour calls to-day;
To-morrow it may be too late.
Then why should you delay?

3 Now is the accepted time,
The gospel bids you come;
And every promise in his word
Declares there yet is room.
John Dobell.

373 *The Open Door.*

1 On, cease, my wandering soul,
On restless wing to roam;
All this wide world, to either pole,
Hath not for thee a home.

2 Behold the home of God;
Behold the open door;
O, haste to gain that dear abode,
And rove, my soul, no more.

3 There safe thou shalt abide;
There sweet shall be thy rest;
And, every longing satisfied,
With full salvation blest.
Wm. A. Mecklenburg.

374 *Ye are not as yet come to the Rest.*

1 On, where shall rest be found—
Rest for the weary soul?
'Twere vain the ocean depths to sound,
Or pierce to either pole.

2 The world can never give
The bliss for which we sigh;
'Tis not the whole of life to live,
Nor all of death to die.

3 Beyond this vale of tears
There is a life above,
Unmeasured by the flight of years,
And all that life is love.

4 There is a death whose pang
Outlasts the fleeting breath:
O, what eternal horrors hang
Around the second death!

5 Lord God of truth and grace,
Teach us that death to shun,
Lest we be banished from thy face,
And evermore undone.
James Montgomery, 1819.

WARNING AND INVITATION.

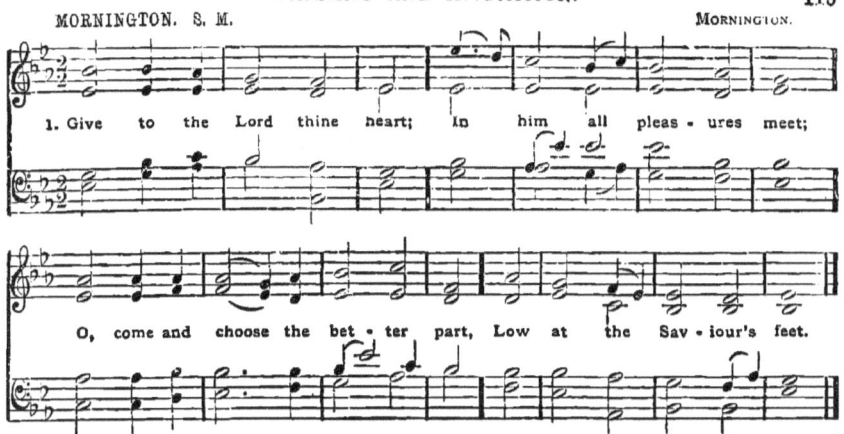

MORNINGTON. S. M. MORNINGTON.

1. Give to the Lord thine heart; In him all pleasures meet; O, come and choose the better part, Low at the Saviour's feet.

375 *Choose the good Part.*

2 Hear, and your soul shall live;
His peace shall be your stay—
Peace which the world can never give,
Can never take away.

3 Go with him to his cross;
Go with him to his tomb:
Your richest gain account but loss,
And tarry till he come.
Sabbath Hymn Book.

376

1 AND canst thou, sinner! slight
The call of love divine?
Shall God, with tenderness invite,
And gain no thought of thine?

2 Wilt thou not cease to grieve·
The Spirit from thy breast,
Till he thy wretched soul shall leave
With all thy sins oppressed?

3 To-day, a pardoning God
Will hear the suppliant pray;
To-day, a Saviour's cleansing blood
Will wash thy guilt away.
A. B. Hyde.

AVA. 6s & 4s. T. HASTINGS.

1. {Child of sin and sorrow, Filled with dismay,
   Wait not for tomorrow, Yield thee to-day;} Heav'n bids thee come, While yet there's room:
D.C.—Child of sin and sorrow, Hear, and obey.

377 *Invitation.*

2 Child of sin and sorrow,
Why wilt thou die?
Come while thou canst borrow
Help from on high:
Grieve not that love,
Which from above—
Child of sin and sorrow—
Would bring thee nigh.

3 Child of sin and sorrow,
Thy moments glide
Like the flitting arrow
Or the rushing tide;
Ere time is o'er,
Heaven's grace implore;
Child of sin and sorrow,
In Christ confide.
Thomas Hastings, 1842.

GOSPEL.

PLEADING. 8s 7s & 4.   S. K. WHITING.

Used by per. Oliver Ditson Co., owners of Copyright.

378   *The Call of Mercy.*

2 Haste, O sinner, to the Saviour;
  Seek his Mercy while you may;
  Soon the day of grace is over;
  Soon your life will pass away:
    Haste, O sinner;
  You must perish if you stay.
                                Reed.

379   *"Ho, every one that thirsteth."*

1 Come, ye sinners, poor and needy,
  Weak and wounded, sick and sore;
  Jesus ready stands to save you,
  Full of pity, love, and power.
    He is able;
  He is willing; doubt no more.

2 Let not conscience make you linger,
  Nor of fitness fondly dream;
  All the fitness he requireth
  Is to feel your need of him:
    This he gives you—
  'Tis the Spirit's rising beam.

3 Come, ye weary, heavy-laden,
  Bruised and mangled by the fall;
  If you tarry till you're better,
  You will never come at all.
    Not the righteous—
  Sinners Jesus came to call.

4 Saints and angels, joined in concert,
  Sing the praises of the Lamb,
  While the blissful seats of heaven
  Sweetly echo with his name;
    Hallelujah!
  Sinners here may do the same.
                                J. Hart.

380   *"Calls of the Spirit."*

1 SINNERS, will you slight the message
  Sent in mercy from above?
  Every sentence, O, how tender!
  Every line how full of love!
    Heavenly accents,
  Full of strength, and peace, and love.

2 Tempted souls, they bring you succor;
  Fearful hearts, they quell your fears;
  And with deepest consolation,
  Chase away the falling tears;
    Tender Heralds,
  Blessèd be their word who hears.

3 Holy Angels, hovering round us
  Waiting spirits, speed your way,
  Hasten to the court of heaven,
  Tidings bear without delay:
    Ransomed sinners
  Glad the message will obey.
                                J. Allen.

WARNING AND INVITATION. 121

GOSHEN. 11s.   Arr. by T. Hastings.

1. De - lay not, de - lay not, O sinner! draw near,
 The wa - ters of life are now (*Omit*........)
 D.C.—Redemption is purchased—sal-(*Omit*........)
 flow-ing for thee; No price is de-mand-ed, the Saviour is here,
 va - tion is free

381
Delay not.

2 Delay not, delay not, why longer abuse
 The love and compassion of Jesus our Lord?
 A fountain is opened—how canst thou refuse
 To wash and be cleansed in his pardoning blood?

3 Delay not, delay not, O sinner, to come!
 For mercy still lingers, and calls thee to-day;
 Her voice is not heard in the vale of the tomb;
 Her message, unheeded, will soon pass away.
                                   T. Hastings.

LANGRAN. 10s.   J. Langran.

1. Wea-ry of earth, and la-den with my sin, I look at heav'n and long to en-ter in,
 But there no e - vil thing may find a home: And yet I hear a voice that bids me "Come."

382
"The voice of Jesus."

2 So vile I am, how dare I hope to stand
 In the pure glory of that holy land?
 Before the whiteness of that throne appear?
 Yet there are hands stretched out to draw me near.

3 The while I fain would tread the heavenly way,
 Evil is ever with me day by day;
 Yet on mine ears the gracious tidings fall,
 "Repent, confess, thou shalt be loosed from all."

4 It is the voice of Jesus that I hear,
 His are the hands stretched out to draw me near,
 And his the blood that can for all atone,
 And set me faultless there before the throne.
                               Samuel J. Stone.

GOSPEL.

WEBB. 6s & 7s.   GEORGE JAMES WEBB, 1830.

1. The morn-ing light is break-ing; The dark-ness dis-ap-pears; The sons of earth are waking
   To pen-i-ten-tial tears: Each breeze that sweeps the o-cean Brings tidings from a-far,
   D.S.—Of na-tions in com-mo-tion,
        Prepared for Zi-on's war.

383 *Success of the Gospel.*

2 Rich dews of grace come o'er us,
  In many a gentle shower,
And brighter scenes before us
  Are opening every hour;
Each cry to heaven going,
  Abundant answers brings,
And heavenly gales are blowing,
  With peace upon their wings.

3 See heathen nations bending
  Before the God we love,
And thousand hearts ascending
  In gratitude above;
While sinners, now confessing,
  The gospel call obey,
And seek the Saviour's blessing,—
  A nation in a day.

4 Blest river of salvation!
  Pursue thine onward way;
Flow thou to every nation,
  Nor in thy richness stay:—
Stay not till all the lowly
  Triumphant reach their home;
Stay not till all the holy
  Proclaim "The Lord is come."
                       S. F. Smith.

384

1 HAIL to the Lord's Anointed,
  Great David's greater Son!
Hail in the time appointed,
  His reign on earth begun!

He comes to break oppression,
  To set the captive free,
To take away transgression,
  And rule in equity.

2 He comes with succor speedy,
  To those who suffer wrong;
To help the poor and needy,
  And bid the weak be strong;
To give them songs for sighing,
  Their darkness turn to light,
Whose souls condemned and dying,
  Were precious in his sight.

3 He shall come down, like showers
  Upon the fruitful earth,
And love, and joy, like flowers,
  Spring in his path to birth:
Before him on the mountains,
  Shall peace, the herald, go;
And righteousness in fountains,
  From hill to valley flow.

4 For him shall prayer unceasing
  And daily vows ascend;
His kingdom still increasing,—
  A kingdom without end:
The tide of time shall never
  His covenant remove;
His name shall stand forever,—
  That name to us is—Love.
                    James Montgomery.

BLESSINGS AND TRIUMPH.

HENLEY. 11s & 10s. — LOWELL MASON.

1. Come unto me when shadows darkly gather, When the sad heart is weary and distress'd, Seeking for comfort from your heav'nly Father;
D. S.—Come unto me, and I will give you rest.

385 *Come unto Me.*

2 Ye who have mourned when the spring flowers were taken,
   When the ripe fruit fell richly to the ground.
   When the loved slept, in brighter homes to waken,
   Where their pale brows with spirit-wreaths are crowned.
3 Large are the mansions in thy Father's dwelling,
   Glad are the homes that sorrows never dim;
   Sweet are the harps in holy music swelling,
   Soft are the tones which raise the heavenly hymn.
4 There, like an Eden blossoming in gladness,
   Bloom the fair flowers the earth too rudely pressed:
   Come unto me, all ye who droop in sadness,
   Come unto me, and I will give you rest. — Catherine H. Waterman.

ADRIAN. S. M. — J. E. GOULD.

1. Say not the law divine Is hidden far from thee;
   That heavenly law within may shine, And there its brightness be.

386 *The Word is nigh thee.*
2 Soar not, my soul, on high,
   To bring it down to earth;
   No star within the vaulted sky
   Is of such priceless worth.
3 Thou need'st not launch thy bark
   Upon a shoreless sea,
   Breasting its waves to find the ark,
   To bring this dove to thee.
4 Cease, then, my soul, to roam;
   Thy wanderings all are vain:
   That holy word is found at home;
   Within thy heart its reign. — Barton.

387 *Light of the World.*
1 BEHOLD the sun, how bright
   From yonder east he springs,
   As if the soul of life and light
   Were breathing from his wings!
2 So bright the gospel broke
   Upon the souls of men;
   So fresh the dreaming world awoke
   In truth's full radiance then.
3 Before yon sun arose,
   Stars clustered through the sky,
   But O, how dim, how pale were those,
   To his one burning eye! — Thos. Moore.

GOSPEL.

ZION. 8s, 7s & 4s. Thomas Hastings, 1830.

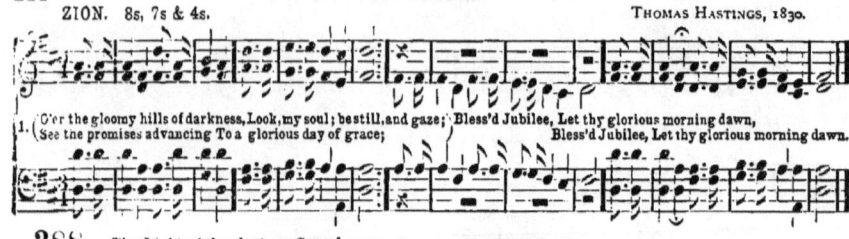

1. O'er the gloomy hills of darkness, Look, my soul; be still, and gaze; Bless'd Jubilee, Let thy glorious morning dawn,
   See the promises advancing To a glorious day of grace; Bless'd Jubilee, Let thy glorious morning dawn.

388 *The Light of the glorious Gospel.*

2 Kingdoms wide, that sit in darkness,
  Grant them, Lord, the glorious light;
Now, from eastern coast to western,
  May the morning chase the night.
    Let redemption,
  Freely purchased, win the day.

3 Fly abroad, thou mighty gospel;
  Win and conquer—never cease;
May thy lasting, wide dominions
  Multiply, and still increase:
    Sway thy sceptre,
  Saviour, all the world around.
              Williams.

389 *The Desert shall blossom.*

1 SEE, from Zion's sacred mountain
  Streams of living water flow;
God has opened there a fountain
  That supplies the world below;
    They are blessed
  Who its sovereign virtues know.

2 Through ten thousand channels flowing
  Streams of mercy find their way,
Life, and health, and joy bestowing,
  Waking beauty from decay;
    O ye nations,
  Hail the long-expected day.

3 Gladdened by the flowing treasure,
  All-enriching as it goes,
Lo, the desert smiles with pleasure,
  Buds and blossoms as the rose;
    Every object
  Sings for joy where'er it flows.
              Thomas Kelly.

LENOX. H. M. Jonathan Edson, 1782.

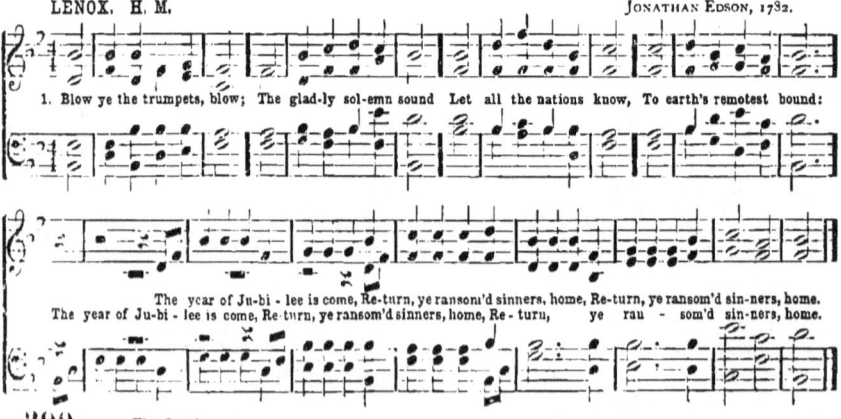

1. Blow ye the trumpets, blow; The glad-ly sol-emn sound Let all the nations know, To earth's remotest bound:
The year of Ju-bi- lee is come, Re-turn, ye ransom'd sinners, home, Re-turn, ye ransom'd sin-ners, home.

390 *The Jubilee.*

2 Jesus, our great High Priest,
  Hath full atonement made;
Ye weary spirits, rest;
  Ye mournful souls, be glad;
The year of Jubilee is come,
Return, ye ransomed sinners, home.

3 The gospel trumpet hear,
  The news of heavenly grace,
And, saved from earth, appear
  Before your Saviour's face;
The year of Jubilee is come,
Return, ye ransomed sinners, home.
              Charles Wesley, 1755.

PENITENCE AND CONSECRATION. 125

WAYNE, H. M.   L. M. Gordon, 1880.

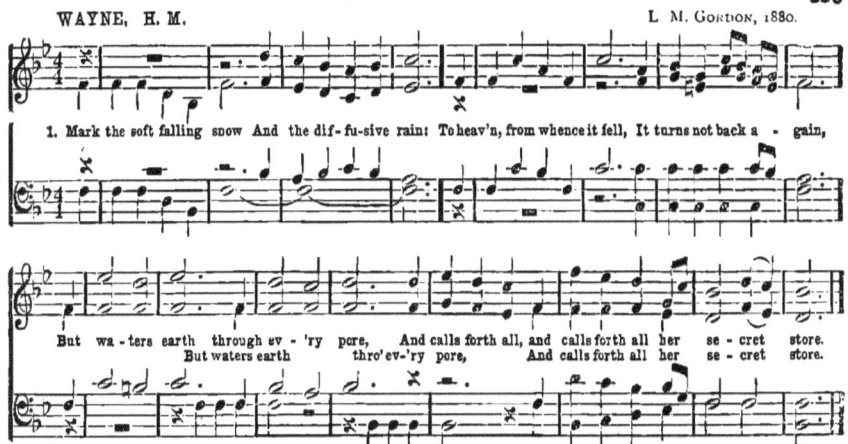

1. Mark the soft falling snow And the dif-fu-sive rain: To heav'n, from whence it fell, It turns not back a-gain, But wa-ters earth through ev-'ry pore, And calls forth all, and calls forth all her se-cret store.
But waters earth thro' ev-'ry pore, And calls forth all her se-cret store.

391   *God's Saving Word.*

2 Arrayed in beauteous green,
  The hills and valleys shine,
And man and beast are fed
  By Providence divine:
The harvest bows its golden ears,
The copious seed of future years.

3 "So," saith the God of grace,
  "My gospel shall descend.
Almighty to effect
  The purpose I intend:
Millions of souls shall feel its power,
And bear it down to millions more."
Philip Doddridge.

HAMBURG. L. M.   Gregorian.

1. Upon the gospel's sacred page The gathered beams of ages shine; And, as it hastens, ev-'ry age But makes its brightness more divine.

392   *Progress of Truth.*

2 Truth, strengthened by the strength of
  Pours inexhaustible supplies, [thought,
Whence sagest teachers may be taught,
  And Wisdom's self become more wise.

3 More glorious still as centuries roll,
  New regions blessed, new powers unfurl'd,
Expanding with th' expanding soul,
  Its waters shall o'erflow the world,—

4 Flow to restore, but not destroy;
  As when the cloudless lamp of day
Pours out its floods of light and joy,
  And sweeps each lingering mist away.
Sir John Bowring.

393   *What Sinners value, I resign.*

1 WHAT sinners value, I resign;
  Lord, 'tis enough that thou art mine;
I shall behold thy blissful face,
  And stand complete in righteousness.

2 This life's a dream, an empty show;
  But the bright world to which I go
Hath joys substantial and sincere:
  When shall I wake, and find me there?

3 O, glorious hour! O, blest abode!
  I shall be near and like my God,
And flesh and sin no more control
  The sacred pleasure of the soul.
Isaac Watts.

EXPERIENCE AND LIFE.

WARE. L. M.
George Kingsley, 1838.

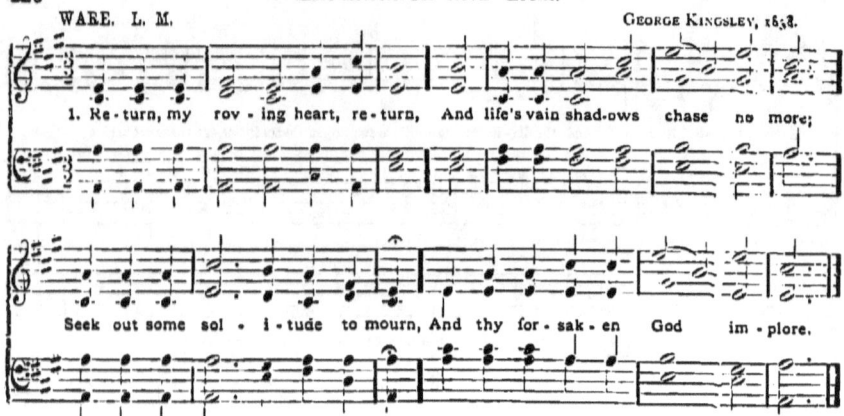

1. Re-turn, my rov-ing heart, re-turn, And life's vain shad-ows chase no more;
Seek out some sol-i-tude to mourn, And thy for-sak-en God im-plore.

394 *Commune with your Heart.*

2 O thou great God, whose piercing eye
Distinctly marks each deep retreat,
In these sequestered hours draw nigh,
And let me here thy presence meet.

3 Through all the windings of my heart,
My search let heavenly wisdom guide,
And still its radiant beams impart
Till all be known and purified.

4 Then let the visits of thy love
My inmost soul be made to share,
Till every grace combine to prove
That God has fixed his dwelling there.
Philip Doddridge.

395 *"The River of Life."*

1 GREAT Source of being and of love,
Thou waterest all the worlds above;
And all the joys we mortals know
From thine exhaustless fountain flow.

2 A sacred spring, at thy command
From Zion's mount, in Canaan's land,
Beside thy temple cleaves the ground,
And pours its limpid stream around.

3 Close by its banks, in order fair,
The blooming trees of life appear;
Their blossoms fragrant odors give,
And on their fruit the nations live.

4 Flow, wondrous stream, with glory crown'd,
Flow on to earth's remotest bound,
And bear us on thy gentle wave
To Him who all thy virtues gave.
Anon.

396 *The Stubborn Heart.*

1 Ou, for a glance of heavenly day,
To take this stubborn heart away;
And thaw, with beams of love divine,
This heart, this frozen heart of mine.

2 The rocks can rend; the earth can quake;
The seas can roar; the mountains shake:
Of feeling, all things show some sign
But this unfeeling heart of mine.

3 To hear the sorrows thou hast felt,
O Lord, an adamant would melt:
But I can read each moving line,
And nothing moves this heart of mine.

4 But power divine can do the deed;
And, Lord, that power I greatly need;
Thy Spirit can from dross refine,
And melt and change this heart of mine.
Joseph Hart, 1762.

397 *A broken and a contrite Heart.*

1 A BROKEN heart, my God, my King,
Is all the sacrifice I bring;
The God of grace will ne'er despise
A broken heart for sacrifice.

2 My soul lies humbled in the dust,
And owns thy dreadful sentence just;
Look down, O Lord, with pitying eye,
And save the soul condemned to die.

3 O may thy love inspire my tongue;
Salvation shall be all my song;
And all my powers shall join to bless
The Lord, my Strength and Righteousness.
Isaac Watts.

PENITENCE AND CONSECRATION. 127

IMLAH. L. M. Arr. fr. T.

1. O Lord, thy heavenly grace im-part, And fix my frail, in-constant heart; Henceforth my chief delight shall be To dedicate myself to thee.

398 *I delight to do thy Will.*

2 Whate'er pursuits my time employ,
One thought shall fill my soul with joy;
That silent, secret thought shall be,
That all my hopes are fixed on thee.

3 Thy glorious eye pervadeth space;
Thy presence, Lord, fills every place;
And, wheresoe'er my lot may be,
Still shall my spirit cleave to thee.

4 Renouncing every worldly thing,
And safe beneath thy sheltering wing,
My sweetest thought henceforth shall be,
That all I want I find in thee.
J. F. Oberlin, 1820.
Tr. Mrs. Daniel Wilson, 1830.

399 *Consecration to God.*

1 My gracious Lord, I own thy right
To every service I can pay,
And call it my supreme delight
To hear thy dictates and obey.

2 What is my being but for thee—
Its sure support, its noblest end?
'Tis my delight thy face to see,
And serve the cause of such a Friend.

3 Thy work my hoary age shall bless,
When youthful vigor is no more.
And my last hour of earth confess
Thy saving love, thy glorious power.
Philip Doddridge.

400 *Be Merciful.*

1 With broken heart and contrite sigh,
A trembling sinner, Lord I cry:
Thy pardoning grace is rich and free;
O God, be merciful to me!

2 I smite upon my troubled breast,
With deep and conscious guilt oppressed,
Christ and his cross my only plea:
O God, be merciful to me!

3 Far off I stand with tearful eyes,
Nor dare uplift them to the skies;
But thou dost all my anguish see:
O God, be merciful to me!

4 And when redeemed from sin and hell,
With all the ransomed throng I dwell,
My raptured song shall ever be,
God hath been merciful to me!
Cornelius Elvin.

401 *Self-consecration.*

1 I will resolve, with all my heart,
With all my powers to serve the Lord
Nor from his precepts e'er depart,
Whose service is a rich reward.

2 O, be his service all my joy;
Around let my example shine,
Till others love the best employ,
And join in labors so divine.

3 O, may I never faint nor tire,
Nor, wandering, leave his sacred ways;
Great God, accept my soul's desire,
And give me strength to live thy praise.
Anne Steele.

EXPERIENCE AND LIFE.

WOODWORTH. L. M.　　　　　　　　W. B. BRADBURY, 1849.

1. Just as I am, with-out one plea; But that thy blood was shed for me, And that thou bid'st me come to thee, O Lamb of God, I come! I come!

402　　*Just as I am.*

2 Just as I am, though tossed about
With many a conflict, many a doubt,
Fightings within, and fears without,
O Lamb of God, I come! I come!

3 Just as I am—thou wilt receive,
Wilt welcome, pardon, cleanse, relieve;
Because thy promise I believe,
O Lamb of God, I come! I come!

4 Just as I am—thy love unknown
Hath broken every barrier down;
Now, to be thine, yea, thine alone,
O Lamb of God, I come! I come!
　　　　　　　　　　　Charlotte Elliott.

403　　*Thy Will be done.*　[Repeat last line.]

1 My God, my Father, while I stray
Far from my home on life's rough way,
O, teach me from my heart to say,
　　Thy will be done.

2 What though in lonely grief I sigh
For friends beloved no longer nigh?
Submissive still would I reply,
　　Thy will be done.

3 Renew my will from day to day;
Blend it with thine, and take away
Whate'er now makes it hard to say,
　　Thy will be done.

4 Then, when on earth I breathe no more
The prayer oft mixed with tears before,
I'll sing upon a happier shore,
　　Thy will be done.
　　　　　　　　　Charlotte Elliott, 1834.

404　　*Psalm 51.*

1 Show pity, Lord! O Lord, forgive;
Let a repenting rebel live;
Are not thy mercies large and free?
May not a sinner trust in thee?

2 My crimes, though great, do not surpass
The power and glory of thy grace;
Great God, thy nature hath no bound,
So let thy pardoning love be found.

3 Oh, wash my soul from every sin,
And make my guilty conscience clean;
Here on my heart the burden lies,
And past offenses pain mine eyes.

4 Yet save a trembling sinner, Lord,
Whose hope, still hovering round thy word,
Would light on some sweet promise there,
Some sure support against despair.
　　　　　　　　　　Isaac Watts, 1719.

405

1 God calling yet; shall I not hear?
Earth's pleasures shall I still hold dear?
And life's swift-passing years all fly,
And still my soul in slumbers lie?

2 God calling yet; and shall he knock,
And I my heart the closer lock?
He still is waiting to receive;
And shall I dare his Spirit grieve?

3 God calling yet; I cannot stay:
My heart I yield without delay.
Vain world, farewell; from thee I part:
The voice of God hath reached my heart.
　　　　　　　　　　Borthwick, tr.

PENITENCE AND CONSECRATION.

129

AVON. C. M. — Hugh Wilson, 1768.

1. Alas, and did my Saviour bleed, And did my Sov'reign die? Would he devote that sacred head For such a worm as I?

406 *Christ died for our Sins.*

2 Was it for crimes that I had done
He groaned upon the tree?
Amazing pity! grace unknown!
And love beyond degree!

3 Thus might I hide my blushing face,
While his dear cross appears,
Dissolve my heart in thankfulness,
And melt mine eyes to tears.

4 But drops of grief can ne'er repay
The debt of love I owe;
Here, Lord, I give myself away—
'Tis all that I can do.
Isaac Watts, 1709.

407 *Forsaking all for Christ.*

1 AND must I part with all I have,
My dearest Lord, for thee?
It is but right, since thou hast done
Much more than this for me.

2 Yes, let it go: one look from thee
Will more than make amends
For all the losses I sustain,
Of credit, riches, friends.

3 Ten thousand worlds, ten thousand lives,
How worthless they appear,
Compared with thee, supremely good,
Divinely bright and fair!

4 Saviour of souls, could I from thee
A single smile obtain,
The loss of all things I could bear,
And glory in my gain.
Benjamin Beddome.

408 *If I perish, I perish.*

1 COME, humble sinner, in whose breast
A thousand thoughts revolve;
Come, with your guilt and fears oppressed,
And make this last resolve:—

2 I'll go to Jesus, though my sin
Hath like a mountain rose;
I know his courts: I'll enter in,
Whatever may oppose.

3 I'll to the gracious King approach,
Whose sceptre pardon gives;
Perhaps he may command my touch,
And then the suppliant lives.

4 Perhaps he will admit my plea,
Perhaps will hear my prayer;
But if I perish, I will pray,
And perish only there.
Jones.

409

1 OH! for that tenderness of heart,
That bows before the Lord;
That owns how just and good thou art,
And trembles at thy word.

2 Oh! for those humble, contrite tears,
Which from repentance flow;
That sense of guilt, which, trembling, fears
The long-suspended blow!

3 Saviour! to me in pity give,
For sin, the deep distress;
The pledge thou wilt, at last, receive,
And bid me die in peace.
Charles Wesley.

EXPERIENCE AND LIFE.

CORFU. C. M.

1. Lord, I approach the mercy-seat, Where thou dost answer prayer, There humbly fall before thy feet, For none can perish there.

410 *The Promises are Yea and Amen.*

2 Thy promise is my only plea;
With this I venture nigh;
Thou callest burdened souls to thee,
And such, O Lord, am I.

3 Bowed down beneath a load of sin,
By Satan sorely pressed,
By war without, and fear within,
I come to thee for rest.

4 O, wondrous love—to bleed and die,
To bear the cross and shame,
That guilty sinners such as I
Might plead thy gracious name!
Newton.

411 *"Remember me."*

1 O THOU, from whom all goodness flows,
I lift my soul to thee;
In all my sorrows, conflicts, woes,
O Lord, remember me!

2 When on my aching, burdened heart
My sins lie heavily,
Thy pardon grant, new peace impart,
Thus, Lord, remember me!

3 When trials sore obstruct my way,
And ills I cannot flee,
Oh, let my strength be as my day—
Dear Lord, remember me!

4 When in the solemn hour of death
I wait thy just decree;
Be this the prayer of my last breath:
Now, Lord, remember me!
Thomas Haweis.

412 *Giving all to God.*

1 How CAN I sink with such a prop
As my eternal God,
Who bears the earth's huge pillars up,
And spreads the heavens abroad?

2 How can I die while Jesus lives,
Who rose and left the dead?
Pardon and grace my soul receives
From my exalted head.

3 Yet, if I might make some reserve,
And duty did not call,
I love my God with zeal so great,
That I should give him all.
Isaac Watts.

413 *"The full Purpose."*

1 IN all my Lord's appointed ways,
My journey I'll pursue;
Hinder me not,—ye much-loved saints,
For I must go with you.

2 Thro' floods and flames, if Jesus leads,
I'll follow where he goes;
Hinder me not!—shall be my cry,
Though earth and hell oppose.

3 Through duty, and through trials too,
I'll go at his command;
Hinder me not, for I am bound
To my Immanuel's land.

4 And when my Saviour calls me home,
Still this my cry shall be,—
Hinder me not,—Come! welcome death,
I'll gladly go with thee.
J. Ryland.

PENITENCE AND CONSECRATION.

INTEGER VITÆ. 8s & 6s.
FRIEDRICH FERDINAND FLEMMING.

1. O Holy Father! Friend unseen! Since on thine arm thou bidst me lean, Help me throughout life's changing scene By faith to cling to thee!

414 *I cling to Thee.*

2 What though the world deceitful prove,
And earthly friends and joys remove;
With patient, uncomplaining love,
Still would I cling to thee!

3 If e'er I seem to tread alone
Life's weary waste, with thorns o'ergrown,
Thy voice of love, in gentlest tone,
Still whispers, "Cling to me."

4 If faith and hope are often tried,
I'll ask not, need not, aught beside;
So safe, so calm, so satisfied,
The soul that clings to thee.
Charlotte Elliott, 1834.

VARINA C. M. 6 l. (Or double, by repeating first 2 lines.) J. C. H. RINK. Arr. by GEO. F. ROOT, 1849.

1. Father, I know that all my life Is portion'd out for me; The changes that will surely come I do not fear to see: I ask thee for a present mind In-tent on pleasing thee.

415 *Become as Little Children.*

2 I ask thee for a thoughtful love,
Through constant watching wise,
To meet the glad with joyful smiles,
And wipe the weeping eyes;
A heart at leisure from itself,
To soothe and sympathize.

3 I would not have the restless will
That hurries to and fro,
That seeks for some great thing to do,
Or secret thing to know;
I would be treated as a child,
And guided where I go.

4 Wherever in the world I am,
In whatsoe'er estate,
I have a fellowship with hearts
To keep and cultivate—
A work of lowly love to do
For Him on whom I wait.
Anna L. Waring.

EXPERIENCE AND LIFE.

SPANISH HYMN. 7s. — Spanish Melody.

1. { Depths of mercy!— can there be Mercy still reserved for me?
   { Can my God his wrath forbear? Me, the chief of sinners, spare? }
   D.C.— Would not hearken to his calls; Griev'd him by a thousand falls.

I have long withstood his grace; Long provoked him to his face;

416 "*My repentings are kindled.*"

2 Kindled his relentings are;
 Me he now delights to spare;
Cries, How shall I give thee up?—
 Lets the lifted thunder drop.
There for me the Saviour stands;
Shows his wounds and spreads his hands,
God is love! I know, I feel:
Jesus weeps, and loves me still.
  C. Wesley.

417   *Conversion.*   [Omit Repeat.]

1 Jesus, Lamb of God, for me,
 Thou, the Lord of life, didst die;
Whither, whither, but to thee,
 Can a trembling sinner fly!
Death's dark waters o'er me roll,
Save, oh, save my sinking soul!

2 Never bowed a martyr's head
 Weighed with equal sorrow down,
Never blood so rich was shed,
 Never king wore such a crown:
To thy cross and sacrifice
Faith now lifts her tearful eyes.

3 All my soul, by love subdued,
 Melts in deep contrition there;
By thy mighty grace renewed,
 New-born hope forbids despair:

Lord! thou canst my guilt forgive,
Thou hast bid me look and live.

4 While with broken heart I kneel,
 Sinks the inward storm to rest,
Life, immortal life, I feel
 Kindled in my throbbing breast!
Thine, forever thine, I am;
Glory to the bleeding Lamb!
  Ray Palmer, 1863.

418   *The name "Jesus."*

1 Jesus! name of wondrous love!
Name all other names above!
Unto which must every knee
Bow in deep humilty.
Jesus! name decreed of old:
To the maiden mother told,
Kneeling in her lonely cell,
By the angel Gabriel.

2 Jesus! name of priceless worth
To the fallen sons of earth,
For the promise that it gave—
"Jesus shall his people save."—
Jesus! name of wondrous love!
Human name of God above;
Pleading only this we flee,
Helpless, O our God, to thee.
  W. W. How—

PENITENCE AND CONSECRATION.

DYKEMAN. S. M.

1. Did Christ o'er sin-ners weep, And shall our cheeks be dry?
Let floods of pen-i-ten-tial grief Burst forth from ev-'ry eye.

419 *Weeping for Sin.*

2 The Son of God in tears
  The wondering angels see:
Be thou astonished, O my soul;
  He shed those tears for thee.

3 He wept that we might weep;
  Each sin demands a tear;
In heaven alone no sin is found,
  And there's no weeping there.
Benjamin Beddome.

420 *The Penitent.*

1 O THAT I could repent,
  With all my idols part;
And to thy gracious eye present
  A humble, contrite heart.

2 Jesus, on me bestow
  The penitent desire:
With true sincerity of woe
  My aching breast inspire;

3 With soft'ning pity look,
  And melt my hardness down;
Strike with thy love's resistless stroke,
  And break this heart of stone!

4 Grant me my sins to feel,
  And then the load remove;
Wound, and pour in, my wounds to heal,
  The balm of pardoning love.
Charles Wesley, 1740.

421 *Do all to the Glory of God.*

1 TEACH me, my God and King,
  In all things thee to see;
And what I do in anything,
  To do it as for thee:

2 To scorn the senses' sway,
  While still to thee I tend;
In all I do, be thou the way,
  In all be thou the end.

3 All may of thee partake;
  Nothing so small can be
But draws, when acted for thy sake,
  Greatness and worth from thee.

4 If done beneath thy laws
  E'en servile labors shine;
Hallowed is toil, if this the cause;
  The meanest work, divine.
George Herbert, 1632.

422 *Out of the Depths have I cried unto Thee.*

1 OUT of the depths of woe,
  To thee, O Lord, I cry;
Darkness surrounds me, yet I know
  That thou art ever nigh.

2 I cast my hopes on thee:
  Thou canst, thou wilt forgive;
If thou shouldst mark iniquity,
  Who in thy sight could live?

3 I wait for thee—I wait,
  Confessing all my sin;
Lord, I am knocking at the gate;
  Open, and take me in.
James Montgomery.

EXPERIENCE AND LIFE.

THATCHER. S. M.   G. F. Handel, 1732.

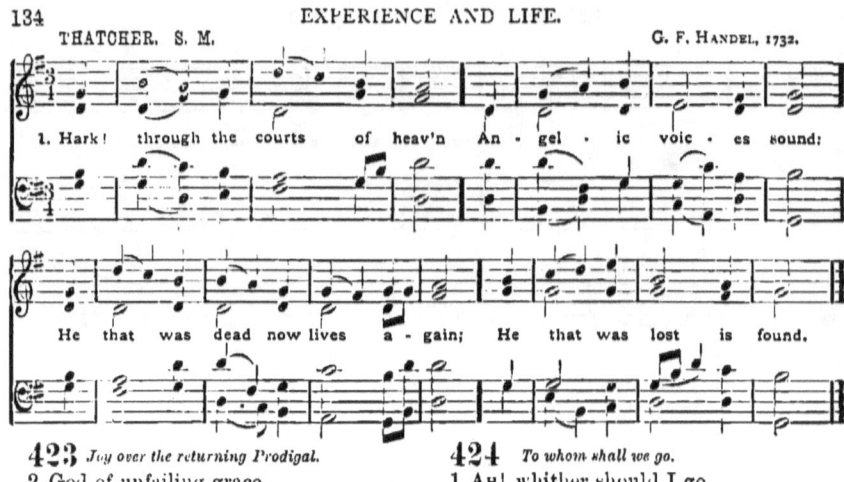

1. Hark! through the courts of heav'n Angelic voices sound: He that was dead now lives again; He that was lost is found.

423 *Joy over the returning Prodigal.*

2 God of unfailing grace,
Send down thy Spirit now;
O, raise the lowly soul to hope,
And make the lofty bow.

3 In countries far from home,
On earthly husks who feed,
Back to their Father's house, O Lord,
Their wandering footsteps lead.

4 Then, at each soul's return,
The heavenly harp shall sound—
He that was dead now lives again;
He that was lost is found.
                    Anon.

424 *To whom shall we go.*

1 Ah! whither should I go,
Burdened, and sick, and faint?
To whom should I my troubles show,
And pour out my complaint?

2 My Saviour bids me come:
Ah! why do I delay?
He calls the weary sinners home,
And yet from him I stay.

3 Jesus, the hindrance show
Which I have feared to see,
And let me now consent to know
What keeps me back from thee.
                    Charles Wesley.

PILGRIM. 8s & 7s.   Arr. fr. Mozart.

1. Jesus, I my cross have taken, All to leave and follow thee; Naked, poor, despised, forsaken,
D.S.—Yet how rich is my condition!
Thou from hence my all shalt be; Perish ev'ry fond ambition, All I've sought, or hoped, or known;
God and heav'n are still my own.

425 *Take up thy Cross.*

2 Let the world despise and leave me:
They have left my Saviour too;
Human hearts and looks deceive me;
Thou art not, like them, untrue;
And, while thou shalt smile upon me,
God of wisdom, love, and might,
Foes may hate, and friends may scorn me:
Show thy face and all is bright.
                    Henry F. Lyte, 1833.

REGENERATION.

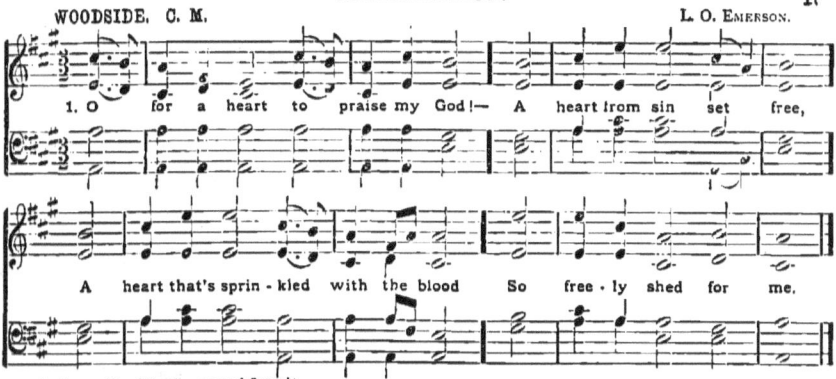

WOODSIDE. C. M. — L. O. Emerson.

1. O for a heart to praise my God!— A heart from sin set free, A heart that's sprin-kled with the blood So free-ly shed for me.

Used by per. Oliver Ditson Co., owners of Copyright.

426 *Create in me a clean Heart.*

2 O for a lowly, contrite heart,
Believing, true, and clean,
Which neither life nor death can part
From him that dwells within!

3 Thy nature, gracious Lord, impart;
Come quickly from above;
Write thy new name upon my heart—
Thy new, best name of Love.
Charles Wesley.

427 *The New Man.*

1 I PRAISE and bless thee, oh my God,
My father kind and true,
For all the old things passed away,
For all thou hast made new.

2 O God, work out thy heavenly plan,
Within my soul unfold,
The stature of the perfect man
And thine own image mould.
Hymns of the Spirit.

ATHENS. C. M. D. — Arr. fr. Giardini.

1. I heard the voice of Jesus say, "Come un-to me, and rest; Lay down, my weary one, lay down
D. S.—I found in him a resting-place,
Thy head up-on my breast;" I came to Je-sus as I was, Wea-ry, and worn, and sad;
And he has made me glad.

428 *Ye shall find Rest to your Souls.*

2 I heard the voice of Jesus say,
"Behold, I freely give
The living water: thirsty one,
Stoop down, and drink, and live."
I came to Jesus, and I drank
Of that life-giving stream—
My thirst was quenched, my soul revived,
And now I live in him.

3 I heard the voice of Jesus say,
"I am this dark world's light:
Look unto me: thy morn shall rise,
And all thy day be bright."
I looked to Jesus, and I found
In him my star, my Sun;
And in that light of life I'll walk
Till all my journey's done.
Horatius Bonar.

136 EXPERIENCE AND LIFE.

I AM TRUSTING. 7s.
Wm. G. Fisher, by per.

1. I am com-ing to the cross; I'm poor, and weak, and blind;
Chorus.—I am trust-ing, Lord, in thee; Dear Lamb of Cal - va - ry;
I am count-ing all but dross; I shall full sal - va - tion find.
Hum-bly at thy cross I bow; Save me, Je - sus, save me now.

429

2 Long my heart has sighed for thee;
Long has evil reigned within;
Jesus sweetly speaks to me,
I will cleanse you from all sin.—Cho.

3 Here, I give my all to thee,—
Friends, and time, and earthly store,
Soul and body thine to be—
Wholly thine—for evermore.—Cho.

4 Jesus comes! he fills my soul!
Perfected in love I am;
I am every whit made whole;
Glory, glory to the Lamb.

Chorus to 4th verse.

Still I'm trusting Lord, in thee,
Dear Lamb of Calvary;
Humbly at thy cross I bow—
Jesus saves me! saves me now.
Wm. McDonald.

ST. THOMAS. S. M.
William Tansur, 1743.

1. How glo-rious is the hour When first our souls a-wake,
And thro' thy Spir-it's quick-'ning pow'r Of the new life par-take!

430 *The New Life.*

2 Amid repentant tears,
We feel sweet peace within;
We know the God of mercy hears,
And pardons every sin.

3 Born of thy Spirit, Lord,
Thy Spirit may we share!
Deep in our hearts inscribe thy word,
And place thine image there.
Stephen G. Bulfinch.

REGENERATION. 137

HUMMEL. C. M.   CHARLES ZEUNER, 1832.

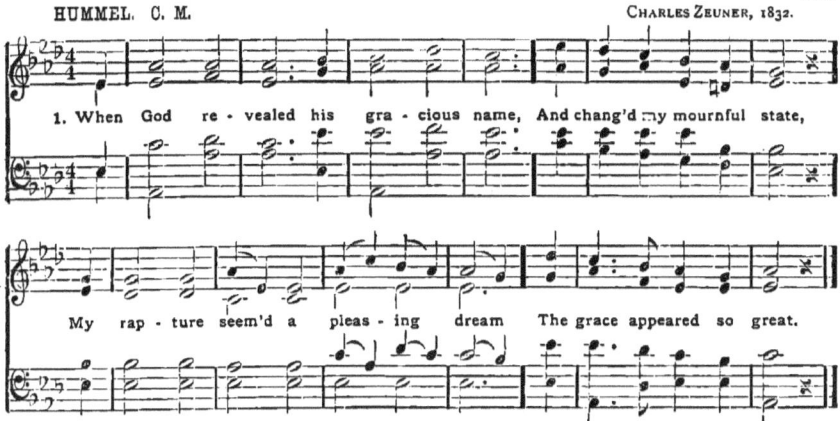

1. When God revealed his gracious name, And chang'd my mournful state, My rapture seem'd a pleasing dream The grace appeared so great.

431   *Regeneration.*
2 The world beheld the glorious change,
And did thy hand confess;
My tongue broke down in unknown strains,
And sung surprising grace.

3 "Great is the work!"—my neighbors cried,
And owned thy power divine;
"Great is the work!"—my heart replied,
And be the glory thine.

4 Let those that sow in sadness wait
Till the fair harvest come:
They shall confess their sheaves are great,
And shout the blessings home.
Isaac Watts, 1719.

432   *What shall a Man give in Exchange for his Soul?*
1 WHAT is the thing of greatest price,
The whole creation round?
Man's soul, once lost in Paradise,
But now in Jesus found.

2 God, to redeem it, did not spare
His well-belovéd Son;
Jesus, to save it, deigned to bear
The sins of all in one.

3 And is this treasure borne below
In earthen vessels frail?
Can none its utmost value know
Till flesh and spirit fail?

4 Then let us gather round the cross,
That knowledge to obtain;
Not by the soul's eternal loss,
But everlasting gain.
James Montgomery.

433   *Ye must be born again.*
1 THE Saviour speaks to every heart·
May he not speak in vain,
But unto all this truth impart—
Ye must be born again.

2 The rich, the poor, the sad, the blest,
To every class of men,
The words of Jesus are addressed,
Ye must be born again.

3 Wouldst thou be happy in the Lord,
And unto life attain?
Hear and obey the solemn word,
Ye must be born again.

4 Wouldst thou enjoy the rest above,
Beyond the reach of pain,
The Sabbath of eternal love?
Ye must be born again.
Warren Hathaway, 1862.

434   *The New Convert.*
1 SWEET was the time when I first felt
The Saviour's pardoning blood
Applied to cleanse my soul from guilt,
And bring me home to God.

2 Soon as the morn the light revealed,
His praises tuned my tongue;
And when the evening shade prevailed
His love was all my song.

3 In prayer my soul drew near the Lord,
And saw his glory shine;
And when I read his holy word,
I called each promise mine.
John Newton.

EXPERIENCE AND LIFE.

HEBER. C. M.   GEORGE KINGSLEY.

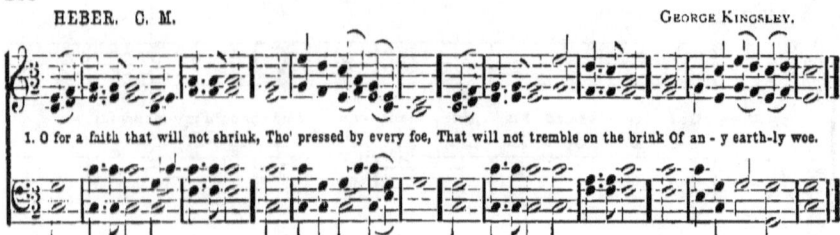

1. O for a faith that will not shrink, Tho' pressed by every foe, That will not tremble on the brink Of an-y earth-ly woe.

435

2 A faith that shines more bright and clear
  When tempests rage without;
That when in danger knows no fear,
  In darkness feels no doubt;—

3 A faith that keeps the narrow way
  Till life's last hour is fled,
And with a pure and heavenly ray
  Lights up a dying bed!

4 Lord, give us such a faith as this,
  And then whate'er may come,
We'll taste, e'en here, the hallowed bliss
  Of an eternal home.
                         Bathurst.

436   *Lord, I believe; help Thou mine Unbelief.*

1 LORD, I believe: thy power I own;
  Thy word I would obey;
I wander comfortless and lone,
  When from thy truth I stray.

2 Lord, I believe; but gloomy fears
  Sometimes bedim my sight;
I look to thee with prayers and tears,
  And cry for strength and light.

3 Lord, I believe; but oft, I know,
  My faith is cold and weak;
My weakness strengthen, and bestow
  The confidence I seek.

4 Yes, I believe; and only thou
  Canst give my soul relief;
Lord, to thy truth my spirit bow;
  Help thou mine unbelief.
                        Wreford.

437   *Power of Faith.*

1 FAITH adds new charms to earthly bliss,
  And saves us from its snares;
It yields support in all our toils,
  And softens all our cares.

2 The wounded conscience knows its power,
  The healing balm to give;
That balm the saddest heart can cheer,
  And make the dying live.

3 Wide it unveils the heavenly world,
  Where endless pleasures reign;
It bids us seek our portion there,
  Nor bids us seek in vain.

4 There, still unshaken, would we rest,
  Till this frail body dies,
And then, on faith's triumphant wing,
  To endless glory rise.
                        Turner.

438   *A Cloud of Witnesses.*

1 GIVE me the wings of faith, to rise
  Within the veil and see,
The saints above—how great their joys,
  How bright their glories be.

2 Once they were mourning here below,
  And wet their couch with tears;
They wrestled hard, as we do now,
  With sins, and doubts, and fears.

3 I ask them, whence their victory came?
  They, with united breath,
Ascribe their conquest to the Lamb,
  Their triumph to his death.

4 They marked the footsteps that he trod,
  His zeal inspired their breast,
And following their triumphant Lord,
  Possess the promised rest.

5 Our glorious Leader claims our praise
  For his own pattern given;
While the long cloud of witnesses
  Show the same path to heaven.
                    Isaac Watts, 1719.

FAITH. 139

OLIVET. 6s & 4s. LOWELL MASON, 1831.

1. My faith looks up to thee, Thou Lamb of Calvary, Saviour divine! (Now hear me while I pray,) [thine!
(Take all my guilt a-way,) Oh, let me from this day Be wholly

439 *The Life of Faith.*

2 May thy rich grace impart
Strength to my fainting heart,
My zeal inspire;
As thou hast died for me,
O, may my love to thee
Pure, warm, and changeless be—
A living fire.

3 While life's dark maze I tread,
And griefs around me spread,
Be thou my Guide:
Bid darkness turn to day,
Wipe sorrow's tears away,
Nor let me ever stray
From thee aside.
Ray Palmer.

LOUVAN. L. M. (6 lines, by repeating first two.) V. C. TAYLOR, 1847.

1. 'Tis by the faith of joys to come We walk thro' des-erts dark as night;
Till we ar-rive at heav'n, our home, Faith is our guide, and faith our light.

440 *For we Walk by Faith.*

2 The want of sight she well supplies;
She makes the pearly gates appear;
Far into distant worlds she pries,
And brings eternal glories near.

3 Cheerful we tread the desert through,
While faith inspires a heavenly ray,
Though lions roar, and tempests blow,
And rocks and dangers fill the way.
Isaac Watts, 1709.

441 *Faith without Works is dead.*

1 As BODY when the soul has fled,
As barren trees decayed and dead,
Is faith—a hopeless, lifeless thing,
If not of righteous deeds the spring.

2 One cup of healing oil and wine,
One tear-drop shed on mercy's shrine,
Is thrice more grateful, Lord, to thee,
Than lifted eye or bended knee.

3 In true and heaven-born faith, we trace
The source of every Christian grace;
Within the pious heart it plays—
A living fount of joy and praise.

4 Kind deeds of peace and love betray
Where'er the stream has found its way;
But where these spring not rich and fair,
The stream has never wandered there.
W. H. Drummond.

EXPERIENCE AND LIFE.

1. Un-shak-en as...... the sa-cred hill, And fixed as mount-ains be, Firm as..... a rock.... the soul shall rest, That leans, O Lord, on thee.

442 *They shall be as Mount Zion.*

2 Not walls nor hills could guard so well
Old Salem's happy ground,
As those eternal arms of love
That every saint surround.

3 Deal gently, Lord, with souls sincere,
And lead them safely on
Within the gates of Paradise,
Where Christ, their Lord, is gone.
Isaac Watts.

443 *Haste thee to help me.*

1 O, HELP us, Lord; each hour of need
Thy heavenly succor give;
Help us in thought, and word, and deed,
Each hour on earth we live.

2 O, help us when our spirits bleed
With contrite anguish sore;
And when our hearts are cold and dead,
O, help us, Lord, the more.

3 O, help us, through the prayer of faith,
More firmly to believe;
For still the more the servant hath,
The more shall he receive.

4 O, help us, Father, from on high;
We know no help but thee;
O, help us so to live and die,
As thine in heaven to be.
Milman.

444 *All Things work together for Good.*

1 I worship thee, sweet will of God,
And all thy ways adore;
And every day I live, I long
To love thee more and more.

2 Man's weakness, waiting upon God,
Its end can never miss;
For man on earth no work can do
More angel-like than this.

3 He always wins who sides with God;
To him no chance is lost;
God's will is sweetest to him when
It triumphs at his cost.

4 When obstacles and trials seem
Like prison-walls to be;
I do the little I can do,
And leave the rest to thee.
F. W. Faber.

445 *Submission.*

1 O LORD, my best desires fulfil;
And help me to resign
Life, health, and comfort to thy will,
And make thy pleasure mine.

2 Why should I shrink at thy command,
Whose love forbids my fears;
Or tremble at thy gracious hand,
That wipes away my tears?

3 No: let me rather freely yield
What most I prize, to thee,
Who never hast a good withheld,
Nor wilt withhold, from me.
William Cowper.

HELP AND TRUST.

1. O thou, in all thy might so far, In all thy love so near, Be-yond the range of sun and star, And yet be-side us here:

446 *Trust in God.*

2 What heart can comprehend thy name
Or, searching, find thee out?
Who art, within, a quickening flame,
A presence round about.

3 Lord, though we know thee but in part,
We ask not now for more:
Enough to us to know thou art,
To love thee and adore!
Frederick L. Hosmer, 1876.

447 *Delight in God.*

1 O Lord! I would delight in thee,
And on thy care depend;
To thee in every trouble flee,
My best, my only Friend!

2 When all created streams are dried,
Thy fullness is the same;
May I with this be satisfied,
And glory in thy name.

3 Oh! that I had a stronger faith,
To look within the veil,
To credit what my Saviour saith,
Whose word can never fail.

4 O Lord! I cast my care on thee;
I triumph and adore;
Henceforth my great concern shall be,
To love and praise thee more.
John Ryland, 1787.

448 *They shall walk and not faint.*

1 Supreme in wisdom, as in power,
The Rock of Ages stands;
We see him not, yet may we trace
The workings of his hands.

2 He gives the conquest to the weak,
Supports the fainting heart,
And courage in the evil hour
His heavenly aids impart.

3 Mere human power shall fast decay,
And youthful vigor cease;
But they who wait upon the Lord
In strength shall still increase.

4 They with unwearied feet shall tread
The path of life divine;
With growing ardor onward move,
With growing brightness shine.

5 On eagles' wings they mount, they soar—
The wings of faith and love;
Till, past the cloudy regions here,
They rise to heaven above.
Anon.

449 *Need of Help.*

1 Not only for some task sublime
Do I thy help implore;
Not only at some solemn time
Thy Holy Spirit pour!

2 But daily for each task of mine
I need thy quickening power;
I need thy presence everywhere,
I need thee every hour.

3 Each action finds in thee its spring,
Each joy thy love makes bright,
Each footstep is thine ordering,
Each grief shines in thy light.
T. H. Gill.

EXPERIENCE AND LIFE.

OLMUTZ. S. M.   Arr. by Dr. L. Mason.

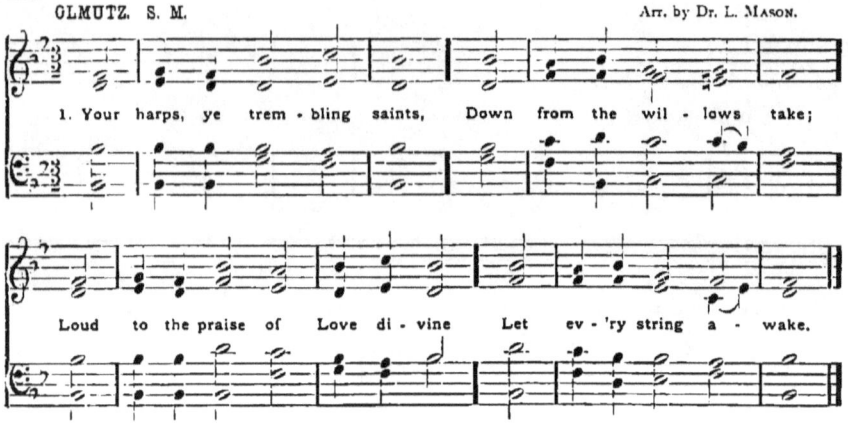

1. Your harps, ye trem-bling saints, Down from the wil-lows take;
Loud to the praise of Love di-vine Let ev-'ry string a-wake.

450   *Trust in Grace.*

2 Though in a foreign land,
   We are not far from home;
And nearer to our house above
   We every moment come.

3 His grace will to the end
   Stronger and brighter shine;
Nor present things, nor things to come,
   Shall quench the spark divine.
                            Augustus M. Toplady.

451   *To present you holy.*

1 To God, the only wise,
   Our Saviour and our King,
Let all the saints below the skies
   Their humble praises bring.

2 'Tis his almighty love,
   His counsel, and his care,
Preserves us safe from sin and death,
   And every hurtful snare.

3 He will present our souls,
   Unblemished and complete,
Before the glory of his face,
   With joys divinely great.

4 Then all the chosen seed
   Shall meet around the throne,
Shall bless the conduct of his grace,
   And make his wonders known.
                            Isaac Watts, 1719.

452   *When I am weak, then am I strong.*

1 To thee and to thy love,
   For help, O Lord, I flee;
In thy great might I must prevail;
   O Lord, deliver me.

2 It is not strength that wins;
   My weakness is my shield;
In lowly trust we fight the fight,
   And meekness wins the field.

3 Give me the lowly heart;
   Cast out each thought of pride;
Let gentleness and love come in,
   And as my guests abide.
                                 Anon.

453   *Wait thou His Time.*

1 Give to the winds thy fears;
   Hope, and be undismayed;
God hears thy sighs, God counts thy tears;
   God shall lift up thy head.

2 Thro' waves, thro' clouds and storms,
   He gently clears the way;
Wait thou his time, so shall the night
   Soon end in joyous day.

3 He everywhere hath rule,
   And all things serve his might;
His every act pure blessing is,
   His path unsullied light.

4 Thou comprehend'st him not;
   Yet earth and heaven tell
God sits as sovereign on the throne;
   He ruleth all things well.
                Paul Gerhardt, 1666. *Tr.* John Wesley, 1739.

HELP AND TRUST. 143
SEASONS. L. M.   IGNACE PLEYEL

1. We all, O Father! all are thine: All feel thy pro-vi-den-tial care;
And, thro' each vary-ing scene of life, A-like thy con-stant love we share.

454   *All things work for Good.*

2 And whether grief oppress the heart,
   Or whether joy elate the breast,
   Or life keep on its little course,
   Or death invite the heart to rest,—

3 All are thy messengers, and all
   Thy sacred pleasure, Lord, obey;
   And all are training men to dwell
   Nearer to heaven, and nearer thee.
                  George Dyer.

455   *Manna.*

1 THY bounteous hand with food can bless
   The bleak and barren wilderness;
   And thou hast taught us, Lord, to pray
   For daily bread from day to day.

2 And, oh, when through the wilds we roam,
   That part us from our heavenly home;
   When, lost in danger, want, and woe,
   Our faithless tears begin to flow,—

3 Do thou thy gracious comfort give,
   By which alone the soul can live;
   And grant thy children, Lord, we pray.
   The bread of life from day to day.
               Bishop Reginald Heber.

456   *Following after God.*

1 O GOD, thou art my God alone;
   Early to thee my soul shall cry,
   A pilgrim in a land unknown,
   A thirsty land, whose springs are dry.

2 Yet, through this rough and thorny maze,
   I follow hard on thee, my God;
   Thine hand unseen upholds my ways;
   I lean upon thy staff and rod.

3 Thee, in the watches of the night,
   When I remember on my bed,
   Thy presence makes the darkness light,
   Thy guardian wings are round my head,

4 Better than life itself thy love,
   Dearer than all beside to me;
   For whom have I in heaven above,
   Or what on earth, compared with thee?

5 Praise with my heart, my mind, my voice,
   For all thy mercy, I will give;
   My soul shall still in God rejoice;
   My tongue shall bless thee while I live.
               James Montgomery, 1872.

457   *All Things work together for Good.*

1 O FATHER, humbly we repose
   Our souls on thee, who dwell'st above,
   And bless thee for the peace which flows
   From faith in thine encircling love.

2 Though every earthly trust may break,
   Infinite might belongs to thee;
   Though every earthly friend forsake,
   Unchangeable thou still wilt be.

3 Though griefs may gather darkly round,
   They can not veil us from thy sight;
   Though vain all human aid be found,
   Thou every grief canst turn to light.

4 All things thy wise designs fulfil,
   In earth beneath and heaven above;
   And good breaks out from every ill,
   Through faith in thine encircling love.
                       Gaskell

EXPERIENCE AND LIFE.

ADVOCATE. L. M., 61. Arr. fr. Mozart.

1. O, let my trembling soul be still, While darkness veils this mortal eye, And wait thy wise, thy ho-ly will, Wrapp'd yet in fears and mys-ter-y; I can not, Lord, thy pur-pose see; Yet all is well, since ruled by thee, Yet all is well, since ruled by thee.

458 *He doeth all Things well.*

2 So, trusting in thy love, I tread
   The narrow path of duty on;
What though some cherished joys are fled?
   What tho' some flattering dreams are gone?
Yet purer, nobler joys remain,
And peace is won through conquered pain.
                                    Sir John Bowring.

459 *Thy Will be done.*

1 He sendeth sun, he sendeth shower;
  Alike they're needful for the flower;
And joys and tears alike are sent
To give the soul fit nourishment:
As comes to me or cloud or sun,
Father, thy will, not mine, be done.

2 Can loving children e'er reprove
With murmers whom they trust and love?
Creator, I would ever be
A trusting, loving child to thee.
As comes to me or cloud or sun,
Father, thy will, not mine, be done.
                                    Sarah F. Adams.

ROSEFIELD, 7s. Dr. Malan.

1. { Quiet, Lord, my froward heart; Make me teach-a-ble and mild, }
   { Upright, simple, free from art,—Make me as a lit-tle child; } From distrust and envy free, Pleas'd with all that pleases thee.

460 *Filial Trust.*

2 What thou shalt to-day provide,
   Let me as a child receive;
What to-morrow may betide,
   Calmly to thy wisdom leave.
'Tis enough that thou wilt care:
Why should I the burden bear.

3 As a little child relies
   On a care beyond his own;
Knows he's neither strong nor wise,
   Fears to stir a step alone,—
Let me thus with thee abide,
As my Father, Guard, and Guide.
                                    John Newton.

HELP AND TRUST.

AURELIA. 7s & 6s, D. S. S. WESLEY.

1. God is my strong sal-va-tion: What foe have I to fear? In darkness and temp-ta-tion, My light, my help is near.
Though hosts encamp around me, Firm in the fight I stand: What ter-ror can con-found me With God at my right hand?

461 *God is my Salvation.*

2 Place on the Lord reliance,
My soul with courage wait;
His truth be thine affiance,
When faint and desolate.

His might thy heart shall strengthen,
His love thy joy increase.
Mercy thy days shall lengthen,
The Lord will give thee peace.
James Montgomery, 1822.

ST. CATHERINE'S. H. M. 3d P. M. H. R. PALMER.

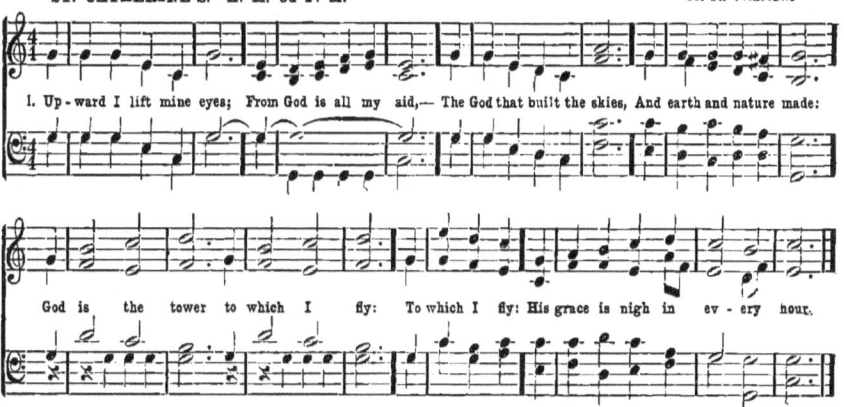

1. Up-ward I lift mine eyes; From God is all my aid,— The God that built the skies, And earth and nature made:
God is the tower to which I fly: To which I fly: His grace is nigh in ev-ery hour.

462 *God our Preserver.*

2 My feet shall never slide,
And fall in fatal snares,
Since God, my Guard and Guide,
Defends me from my fears.
Those wakeful eyes, that never sleep,
Shall Israel keep when dangers rise.

3 No burning heats by day,
Nor blasts of evening air,
Shall take my health away

If God be with me there.
Thou art my sun and thou my shade
To guard my head by night and noon.

4 Hast thou not given thy word
To save my soul from death?
And I can trust my Lord
To keep my mortal breath:
I'll go and come, nor fear to die,
Till from on high, thou call me home.
Isaac Watts, 1719.

EXPERIENCE AND LIFE.

WALES. 8s & 4s. — Welsh Melody.

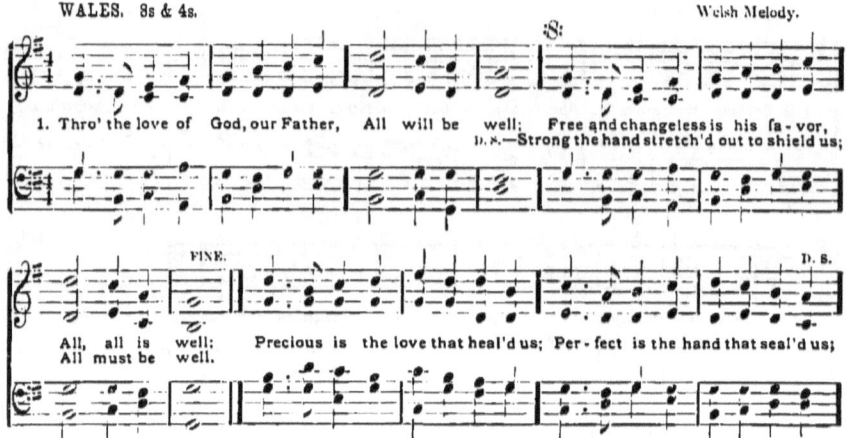

1. Thro' the love of God, our Father, All will be well; Free and changeless is his favor,
D.S.—Strong the hand stretch'd out to shield us;
All, all is well: Precious is the love that heal'd us; Perfect is the hand that seal'd us;
All must be well.

463   *All Well.*

2 Though we pass through tribulation,
   All will be well;
Ours is such a full salvation,
   All, all is well:
Happy, still in God confiding,
Fruitful, if in him abiding,
Holy, through the Spirit's guiding,
   All must be well.

3 We expect a bright to-morrow;
   All will be well;
Faith can sing through days of sorrow.
   All, all is well.
On our Father's love relying,
He our every need supplying,
Or in living, or in dying,
   All must be well.

M. B. Peters.

CALVARY. 6s & 4s. — E.

1. O strong to save and bless, My Rock and Righteousness, Draw near to me. Blessing, and joy, and might, Wisdom, and love, and light, Wisdom, and love, and light, Are all with thee.

464   *Be Thou my Strong Rock.*

2 O, answer me, my God;
Thy love is deep and broad,
   Thy grace is true.

Thousands this grace have shared,
O, let *me* now be heard,
   O, love *me* too.

Horatius Bonar.

LOVE AND OBEDIENCE.

THEODORA. 7s.   Arr. fr. HANDEL.

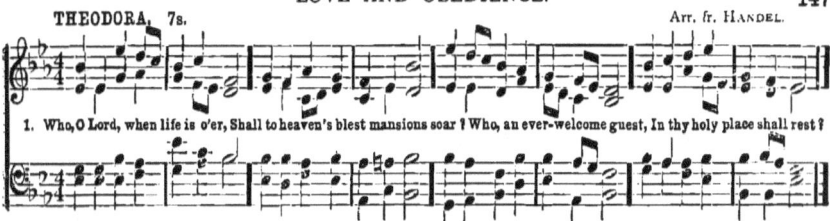

1. Who, O Lord, when life is o'er, Shall to heaven's blest mansions soar? Who, an ever-welcome guest, In thy holy place shall rest?

465 *Who shall dwell in Thy Holy Hill.*
2 He whose heart thy love has warmed;
He whose will, to thine conformed,
Bids his life unsullied run;
He whose words and thoughts are one;

3 He who shuns the sinner's road,
Loving those who love their God:
He, great God, shall be thy care,
And thy choicest blessings share.
Henry F. Lyte, 1834.

466 *He shall give his Angels Charge over thee.*
1 THEY, who on the Lord rely,
Safely dwell, though danger's nigh;
Lo, his sheltering wings are spread
O'er each faithful servant's head.

2 Vain temptation's wily snare;
They shall be the Father's care;
Harmless flies the shaft by day,
Or in darkness wings its way.

3 When they wake, or when they sleep,
Angel guards their vigils keep;
Death and danger may be near,
Faith and love can never fear.
Spirit of the Psalms.

NETTLETON. 8s & 7s, D.   A. NETTLETON, 1824.

1. { Come, thou Fount of ev'ry blessing, Tune my heart to sing thy grace; }   [above;
   { Streams of mercy, never ceasing, Call for songs of loudest praise. } Teach me some melodious sonnet, Sung by flaming tongues
D.C.—Praise the mount—I'm fix'd upon it, Mount of thy redeeming love.

467 *Memorial of Praise.*
2 Here I'll raise my Ebenezer,
Hither by thy help I'm come;
And I hope by thy good pleasure,
Safely to arrive at home.
Jesus sought me when a stranger,
Wand'ring from the fold of God,
He, to rescue me from danger,
Interposed his precious blood.

3 Oh! to grace how great a debtor,
Daily I'm constrained to be!
Let thy goodness, like a fetter,
Bind my wandering heart to thee.
Prone to wander, Lord, I feel it;
Prone to leave the God I love—
Here's my heart, oh, take and seal it;
Seal it for thy courts above.
Robert Robinson, 1758.

468 *Divine Love.*
1 LOVE divine, all love excelling,
Joy of heaven, to earth come down;
Fix in us thy humble dwelling,
All thy faithful mercies crown.
Father, thou art all compassion,—
Pure unbounded love thou art;
Visit us with thy salvation,
Enter every longing heart.

3 Breathe, oh, breathe thy loving Spirit
Into every troubled breast;
Let us all in thee inherit,
Let us find thy promised rest.
Come, almighty to deliver,
Let us all thy life receive;
Graciously come down, and never,
Never more thy temples leave.
Charles Wesley, 1747.

EXPERIENCE AND LIFE.

I WILL FOLLOW THEE. S. M.

469

2 Though the road be rough and thorny,
  Trackless as the foaming sea,
Thou hast trod this way before me,
  And I'll gladly follow thee.—Cho.

3 Though 'tis lone, and dark, and dreary,
  Cheerless though my path may be,
If thy voice I hear before me,
  Fearlessly I'll follow thee.—Cho.

4 Though I meet with tribulations,
  Sorely tempted though I be,
I remember thou wast tempted,
  And rejoice to follow thee.—Cho.

5 Though thou leadest through affliction,
  Poor, forsaken though I be,
Thou wast destitute, afflicted,
  And I only follow thee.—Cho.

6 Though to Jordan's rolling billows,
  Cold and deep, thou leadest me,
Thou hast crossed its waves before me,
  And I still will follow thee.—Cho.

Anon.

LOVE AND OBEDIENCE. 149

ERNAN. L. M.   D. Lowell Mason.

1. Had I the tongues of Greeks and Jews, And no-bler speech than an - gels use,
If love be ab - sent, I am found, Like tinkling brass, an emp ty sound.

470   *Nothing without Love.*

2 Were I inspired to preach and tell
All that is done in heaven or hell,
Or could my faith the world remove,
Still I am nothing without love.

3 Should I distribute all my store
To feed the hungry, clothe the poor,—
Or give my body to the flame,
To gain a martyr's glorious name,—

4 If love to God and love to men
Be absent, all my hopes are vain:
Nor tongues, nor gifts, nor fiery zeal,
The work of love can e'er fulfil.
Isaac Watts, 1719.

471   *A Prayer for Faith.*

1 I ask not wealth, but power to take
And use the things I have aright;
Not years, but wisdom that shall make
My life a profit and delight.

2 I ask not that for me the plan
Of good and ill be set aside,
But that the common lot of man
Be nobly borne and glorified.

3 I know I may not always keep
My steps in places green and sweet,
Nor find the pathway of the deep
A path of safety to my feet;

4 But pray that, when the tempest's breath
Shall fiercely sweep my way about,
I make not shipwreck of my faith
In the unfathomed sea of doubt.
Phœbe Cary.

472   *Living to God.*

1 O Thou who hast at thy command
The hearts of all men in thy hand!
Our wayward, erring hearts incline
To have no other will but thine.

2 Our wishes, our desires, control;
Mould every purpose of the soul;
O'er all may we victorious be
That stands between ourselves and thee.

3 Thrice blest will all our blessings be,
When we can look through them to thee,
When each glad heart its tribute pays
Of love and gratitude and praise.

4 And, while we to thy glory live,
May we to thee all glory give;
Until the final summons come,
That calls thy willing servants home.
Mrs. Joseph Cotterill, 1808.

473   *Love Divine.*

1 O Love Divine, whose constant beam
Shines on the eyes that will not see,
And waits to bless us while we dream,
Thou leav'st us when we turn from thee!

2 All souls that struggle and aspire,
All hearts of prayer, by thee are lit;
And, dim or clear, thy tongues of fire
On dusky tribes and centuries sit.

3 Nor bounds, nor clime, nor creed thou
Wide as our need thy favors fall; [know'st:
The white wings of the Holy Ghost
Stoop, unseen, o'er the heads of all.
John G. Whittier.

EXPERIENCE AND LIFE.

HEBRON. L. M.   Lowell Mason, 1830.

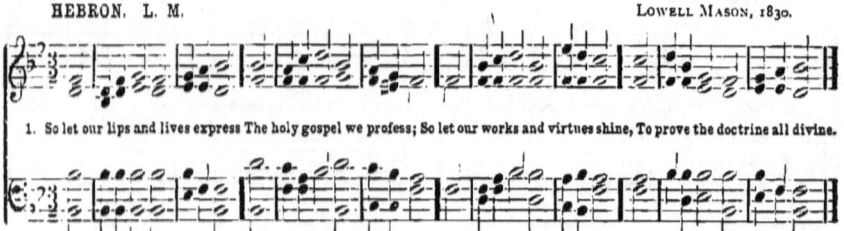

1. So let our lips and lives express The holy gospel we profess; So let our works and virtues shine, To prove the doctrine all divine.

474   *Practical Religion.*

2 Thus shall we best proclaim abroad
The honors of our Saviour God,
When his salvation reigns within,
And grace subdues the power of sin.

3 Our flesh and sense must be denied,
Passion and envy, lust and pride;
While justice, temperance, truth and love
Our inward piety approve.

4 Religion bears our spirits up,
While we expect that blessed hope,
The bright appearance of the Lord,
And faith stands leaning on his word.
                               Isaac Watts, 1709.

475   *Christian Fellowship.*

1 How BLEST the sacred tie that binds,
In union sweet, according minds!
How swift the heavenly course they run,
Whose hearts and faith and hopes are one.

2 To each, the soul of each how dear!
What jealous love, what holy fear!
How doth the generous flame within
Refine from earth and cleanse from sin!

3 In glad accord they seek the place
Where God reveals his gracious face:
How high, how strong, their raptures swell,
There's none but kindred souls can tell.

4 Nor shall the flowing flame expire
When droops at length frail nature's fire;
For they shall meet in realms above,—
A heaven of joy, because of love.
                               Anna L. Barbauld.

476   *Who shall dwell in Thy Holy Hill?*

1 Who shall ascend the heavenly place,
Great God, and dwell before thy face?
The man who minds religion now,—
And humbly walks with God below.

2 Whose hands are pure, whose heart is clean,
Whose lips still speak the things they mean;
No slanders dwell upon his tongue;
He hates to do his neighbor wrong.

3 He loves his enemies and prays
For those who curse him to his face,
And does to all men still the same
That he would hope or wish from them.

4 Yet when his holiest works are done,
His soul depends on grace alone:
This is the man thy face shall see,
And dwell forever, Lord, with Thee.
                               Isaac Watts.

477   *Who art thou that judgest?*

1 ALL-SEEING God, 'tis thine to know
The springs whence wrong opinions flow;
To judge from principles within,
When frailty errs, and when we sin.

2 Who among men, great Lord of all,
Thy servant at the bar shall call?
Judge him, for modes of faith, thy foe,
And doom him to the realms of woe?

3 Who with another's eye can read?
Or worship by another's creed?
Trusting thy grace, we form our own,
And bow to thy commands alone.

4 If wrong, correct; accept if right;
While, faithful, we improve our light,
Condemning none, but zealous still
To learn and follow all thy will.
                               Scott.

LOVE AND OBEDIENCE. 151

STONEFIELD. L. M.   SAMUEL STANLEY, 1820.

1. What precept, Jesus, is like thine—
 "Forgive, as ye would be forgiven:"
 In this we see the pow'r divine
 Which shall transform our earth to heaven.

478 "*Forgive, and ye shall be forgiven.*"

2 O, not the harsh and scornful word
 The victory over sin can gain,
 Not the dark prison, or the sword,
 The shackle, or the weary chain.

3 But from our spirits there must flow
 A love that will the wrong outweigh;
 Our lips must only blessings know,
 And wrath and sin shall die away.

4 'Twas heaven that formed the holy plan
 To win the wanderer back by love;
 Thus let us save our brother man,
 And imitate our God above.
 Mrs. Livermore.

479 *My Soul follows hard after Thee.*

1 O, THAT it were as it hath been,
 When praying in thy holy place,
 Thy power and glory I have seen,
 And marked the footsteps of thy grace!

2 Yet, through this rough and thorny maze,
 I follow hard on thee, my God;
 Thine hand unseen upholds my ways;
 I lean upon thy staff and rod.

3 Thee, in the watches of the night,
 When I remember on my bed,
 Thy presence makes the darkness light,
 Thy guardian wings are round my head.

4 Better than life itself thy love,
 Dearer than all beside to me;

For whom have I in heaven above,
 Or what on earth, compared with thee?
 James Montgomery, 1822.

480 "*The Love of God.*"

1 O SOURCE divine, and Life of all,
 The Fount of being's wondrous seal
 Thy depth would every heart appall,
 That saw not Love supreme in thee.

2 We shrink before thy vast abyss, [brood;
 Where worlds on worlds unnumbered
 We know thee truly but in this,—
 That thou bestowest all our good.

3 Bestow on every joyous thrill
 A deeper tone of reverent awe,
 Make pure thy children's erring will
 And teach their hearts to love thy law.
 John Sterling, 1839.

481 "*Jesus Our Joy.*"

1 JESUS, thou Joy of loving hearts,
 Thou Fount of Life, thou Light of men!
 From the best bliss that earth imparts,
 We turn unfilled to thee again.

2 Our restless spirits yearn for thee,
 Where'er our changeful lot is cast;
 Glad, when thy gracious smile we see;
 Blest, when our faith can hold thee fast.

3 O Jesus, ever with us stay;
 Make all our moments calm and bright;
 Chase the dark night of sin away,
 Shed o'er the world thy holy light.
 Tr. Ray Palmer, 1858.

EXPERIENCE AND LIFE.

WILLIS. 7s.   R. Storrs Willis.

1. Lord of our supreme desire! Fill us now with heav'nly fire: Nobly may we bear the strife, Keep the holiness of life,... Keep the holiness of life.

482 *Following Christ.*

2 Father, fill us with thy love;
Never from our souls remove;
Dwell with us, and we shall be
Thine through all eternity.
  Charles Wesley, 1740.

483 *Lovest thou Me?*

1 Hark, my soul; it is the Lord;
'Tis thy Saviour; hear his word;
Jesus speaks; he speaks to thee,—
"Say, poor sinner, lov'st thou me?"

2 "Thou shalt see my glory soon,
When the work of grace is done,—
Partner of my throne shalt be:
Say, poor sinner, lov'st thou me?"

3 Lord, it is my chief complaint
That my love is weak and faint,
Yet I love thee, and adore:
O for grace to love thee more!
  William Cowper, 1779.

BROWNELL. L. M. 6l.   Haydn.

1. Jesus, thy boundless love to me No tho't can reach, no tongue declare; Oh, knit my thankful heart to thee, And reign without a rival there: Thine wholly, thine alone, I am; Be thou alone my constant flame.

484 *"Thy boundless love."*

2 Oh, grant that nothing in my soul
  May dwell, but thy pure love alone:
Oh, may thy love possess me whole,—
My joy, my treasure, and my crown:
Strange flames far from my heart remove
My every act, word, thought, be love.

3 O Love! how cheering is thy ray!
  All pain before thy presence flies;
Care, anguish, sorrow, melt away,
  Where'er thy healing beams arise:
O Jesus! nothing may I see,
Nothing desire, or seek but thee!
  John Wesley, tr.

LOVE AND OBEDIENCE. 153

ARLINGTON. C. M. Thomas A. Arne, 1744.

1. Amazing grace! how sweet the sound That saved a wretch like me! I once was lost, but now am found, Was blind, but now I see.

485

2 'Twas grace that taught my heart to fear,
And grace my fears relieved;
How precious did that grace appear
The hour I first believed!

3 Through many dangers, toils and snares,
I have already come:
'Tis grace has brought me safe thus far,
And grace will lead me home.

4 Yes, when this flesh and heart shall fail,
And mortal life shall cease,
I shall possess within the vail,
A life of joy and peace.

5 The earth shall soon dissolve like snow,
The sun forbear to shine;
But God, who called me here below,
Shall be forever mine.
J. Newton.

486 *Charity thinketh no Evil.*

1 Think gently of the erring one,
And let us not forget,
However darkly stained by sin,
He is our brother yet.

2 Heir of the same inheritance,
Child of the self-same God,
He hath but stumbled in that path
We have in weakness trod.

3 Speak gently to the erring one:
Thou yet mayst lead him back,
With holy words and tones of love,
From misery's thorny track.

4 Forget not thou hast often sinned,
And sinful yet mayst be:
Deal gently with the erring one,
As God hath dealt with thee.
Miss Fletcher.

487 *Lord, my Heart is not haughty.*

1 Is there ambition in my heart?
Search, gracious God, and see;
Or do I act a haughty part?
Lord, I appeal to thee.

2 Whate'er thine all-discerning eye
Sees for thy creature fit,
I'll bless the good and to the ill
Contentedly submit.

3 Feed me, O Lord, with needful food:
I ask not wealth or fame;
Give me an eye to see thy will,
A heart to praise thy name.

4 O, may my days securely pass,
Without remorse or care;
And let me for my parting hour
From day to day prepare.
Isaac Watts.

488 *Who is thy Neighbor?*

1 Who is thy neighbor? He whom thou
Hast power to aid or bless;
Whose aching heart or burning brow
Thy soothing hand may press.

2 Thy neighbor? 'Tis the fainting poor,
Whose eye with want is dim;
O, enter thou his humble door,
With aid and peace for him.

3 Thy neighbor? He who drinks the cup
When sorrow drowns the brim;
With words of high sustaining hope,
Go thou and comfort him.

4 Thy neighbor? Pass no mourner by;
Perhaps thou canst redeem
A breaking heart from misery;
Go, share thy lot with him.
Peabody.

EXPERIENCE AND LIFE.

HUMMEL. C. M.   Charles Zeuner, 1832.

1. Do not I love thee, O my Lord? Be-hold my heart, and see;
And turn the dear-est i-dol out That dares to ri-val thee.

489   *Thou knowest that I love Thee.*

2 Do not I love thee from my soul?
   Then let me nothing love:
Dead be my heart to every joy
   When Jesus cannot move.

3 Is not thy name melodious still
   To mine attentive ear?
Doth not each pulse with pleasure bound
   My Saviour's voice to hear?

4 Thou know'st I love thee, dearest Lord;
   But, O, I long to soar
Far from the sphere of mortal joys,
   And learn to love thee more.
                    Philip Doddridge.

490   *Longing after God.*

1 I ask not now for gold to gild
   An aching, weary frame;
The yearning of the mind is stilled,—
   I ask not now for fame.

2 But, bowed in lowliness of mind,
   I make my wishes known;
I only ask a will resigned,
   O Father, to thine own.

3 And now my spirit sighs for home,
   And longs for light to see,
And, like a weary child, would come,
   O Father, unto thee.
                    John G. Whittier.

491   *Speak Gently.*

1 Speak gently—it is better far
   To rule by love than fear;
Speak gently—let no harsh word mar
   The good we may do here.

2 Speak gently to the young, for they
   Will have enough to bear;
Pass through this life as best they may,
   'Tis full of anxious care.

3 Speak gently to the aged one—
   Grieve not the care-worn heart;
The sands of life are nearly run;
   Let them in peace depart.

4 Speak gently—'tis a little thing
   Dropped in the heart's deep well;
The good, the joy that it may bring,
   Eternity shall tell.
                      Bates.

492   *The Law of Sympathy.*

1 All nature feels attractive power,
   A strong, embracing force;
The drops that sparkle in the shower,
   The planets in their course.

2 In this fine, sympathic chain
   All creatures bear a part;
Their every pleasure, every pain,
   Linked to a feeling heart.

3 More perfect bond, the Christian plan
   Attaches soul to soul;
Our neighbor is the suffering man,
   Though at the farthest pole.

4 To earth below, from heaven above,
   The faith in Christ professed
More clear reveals that God is love,
   And whom he loves is blest.
                      Drennan.

LOVE AND OBEDIENCE.

SWANWICK. C. M.   LUCAS.

1. I love the Lord; he heard my cries, And pit-ied ev-'ry groan; Long as I live, when trou-bles rise, I'll hast-en to his throne, I'll hast-en to his throne.

493 *Acknowledgment of God's Goodness.*

2 The Lord beheld me sore distressed;
He bade my pains remove;
Return, my soul, to God, thy rest,
For thou hast known his love.

3 My God hath saved my soul from death,
And dried my falling tears;
Now to his praise I'll spend my breath,
And my remaining years.
                        Isaac Watts.

494 *For a tender Conscience.*

1 I WANT a principle within
Of jealous, godly fear;
A sensibility to sin,
A pain to find it near.

2 I want the first approach to feel
Of pride, or fond desire;
To catch the wandering of my will,
And quench the killing fire.

3 From thee that I no more may part,
No more thy goodness grieve,
The filial awe, the fleshly heart,
The tender conscience give.

4 Quick as the apple of an eye,
O God! my conscience make;
Awake my soul when sin is nigh,
And keep it still awake.
                        Charles Wesley.

495 *Whom have we, Lord, in Heaven but Thee?*

1 WHOM have we, Lord, in heaven, but thee,
And whom on earth beside?
Where else for succor can we flee,
Or in whose strength confide?

2 Thou art our portion here below,
Our promised bliss above;
Ne'er may our souls an object know
So precious as thy love.

3 Lord, thou shalt be our guide thro' life,
And help and strength supply;
Sustain us in death's fearful strife,
And welcome us on high.
                        Henry F. Lyte.

496 *The New Commandment.*

1 WITH love the Saviour's heart o'erflowed;
Love spoke in every breath;
Supreme it reigned, throughout his life,
And triumphed in his death.

2 Behold, this new command he gives
To those who bear his name,—
That they shall one another love,
As he hath loved them.

3 In every action, every thought,
Be this great thought fulfilled;
Forgotten be each selfish aim,
Each angry passion stilled.

4 Let all who bear the name of Christ,
While they his sufferings view,
Think of his words, "Each other love,
As I have loved you."
                        Anon.

EXPERIENCE AND LIFE.

MANOAH. C. M. — Arr. fr. G. Rossini.

1. Blest Jesus, when my soaring thoughts O'er all thy graces rove, How is my soul in transport lost,—In wonder, joy, and love!

Used by per. Oliver Ditson Co., owners of Copyright.

---

497 *The beloved Name.*

2 Not softest strains can charm my ears
Like thy belovéd name;
Nor aught beneath the skies inspire
My heart with equal flame.

3 Where'er I look, my wondering eyes
Unnumbered blessings see;
But what is life, with all its bliss,
If once compared with thee?

4 Hast thou a rival in my breast?
Search, Lord, for thou canst tell,
If aught can raise my passions thus,
Or please my soul so well.

5 No: thou art precious to my heart,
My portion and my joy;
Forever let thy boundless grace
My sweetest thoughts employ.
Heginbotham.

498 *Ye have the Poor always with you.*

1 Lord, lead the way the Saviour went,
By lane and cell obscure,
And let our treasures still be spent,
Like his, upon the poor.

2 Like him, through scenes of deep distress,
Who bore the world's sad weight,
We, in their gloomy loneliness,
Would seek the desolate.

3 For thou hast placed us side by side
In this wide world of ill;
And, that thy followers may be tried,
The poor are with us still.

4 Small are the offerings we can make;
Yet thou hast taught us, Lord,
If given for the Saviour's sake,
They lose not their reward.
Croswell.

499 *Greater Love hath no Man than this.*

1 My blessèd Saviour, is thy love
So great, so full, so free?
Behold, I give my love, my heart,
My life, my all, to thee.

2 I love thee for the glorious worth
In thy great self I see;
I love thee for that shameful cross
Thou hast endured for me.

3 No man of greater love can boast
Than for his friend to die;
But for thy foes, Lord, thou wast slain;
What love with thine can vie?

4 O Lord, I'll treasure in my soul
The memory of thy love;
And thy dear name shall still to me
A grateful odor prove.
Anon.

500 *Ye have done it unto Me.*

1 Jesus, my Lord, how rich thy grace!
Thy bounties how complete!
How shall I count the matchless sum?
How pay the mighty debt?

2 High on a throne of radiant light
Dost thou exalted shine;
What can my poverty bestow,
When all the worlds are thine?

3 But thou hast brethren here below,
The partners of thy grace,
And wilt confess their humble names
Before thy Father's face.

4 In them thou mayst be clothed and fed,
And visited, and cheered;
And in their accents of distress
My Saviour's voice is heard.
Philip Doddridge.

LOVE AND OBEDIENCE.

LEIGHTON, S. M. GREATOREX COLLECTION.

1. O, love that casts out fear, O, love that casts out sin, Tar - ry, tar - ry ... no more with - out, But come and dwell with - in.

501 *Perfect Love casteth out Fear.*
2 True sunlight of the soul,
   Surround me as I go;
So shall my earthly way be safe,
   My feet no straying know.

3 Great love of God, come in,
   Well-spring of heavenly peace;
Thou Water of Salvation, come,
   Spring up, and never cease.

4 Love of the living God,
   And his belovéd Son,
Come into every thirsty heart;
   Fill thou each needy one.
                       Horatius Bonar.

502 *How good to dwell in Unity.*
1 BLEST are the sons of peace,
   Whose hearts and hopes are one;
Whose kind desires to serve and please
   Through all their actions run.

2 Blest is the pious house
   Where zeal and friendship meet;
Their songs of praise, their mingled vows,
   Make their communion sweet.

3 From those celestial springs
   Such streams of comfort flow,
As no increase of riches brings,
   No honors can bestow.

4 Thus, on the heavenly hills,
   The saints are blest above,
Where joy like morning dew distils,
   And all the air is love.
                       Isaac Watts, 1719.

503 *I say unto all, Watch.*
1 YE servants of the Lord,
   Each in your office wait,
Observant of his heavenly word,
   And watchful at his gate.

2 Let all your lamps be bright,
   And trim the golden flame:
Gird up your loins, as in his sight,
   For holy is his name.

3 Watch: 'tis your Lord's command;
   And while we speak, he's near;
Mark the first signal of his hand,
   And ready all appear.

4 O, happy servant he
   In such a posture found;
He shall his Lord with rapture see,
   And be with honor crowned.
                       Philip Doddridge, 1755.

504 *The Voice of Conscience.*
1 GIVE forth thine earnest cry,
   O conscience, voice of God!
To young and old, to low and high,
   Proclaim his will abroad.

2 Within the human breast
   Thy strong monitions plead;
Still thunder thy divine protest
   Against th' unrighteous deed.

3 Show the true way of peace,
   O thou our guiding light!
From bondage of the wrong release,
   To service of the right.
                       Hymns of the Spirit

EXPERIENCE AND LIFE.

REDEEMER. 3s & 7s. — O. EMERSON.

1. I would love thee, God and Father! My Redeemer and my King!
I would love thee; for without thee, Life is but a bitter thing.

Used by per. Oliver Ditson Co., owners of Copyright.

505

2 I would love thee; every blessing
Flows to me from out thy throne;
I would love thee, he who loves thee,
Never feels himself alone.

3 I would love thee; look upon me,
Ever guide me with thine eye;
I would love thee; if not nourished
By thy love, my soul would die.

4 I would love thee; may thy brightness
Dazzle my rejoicing eyes;
I would love thee; may thy goodness
Watch from heaven o'er all I prize.

5 I would love thee, I have vowed it;
On thy love my heart is set;
While I love thee, I will never
My Redeemer's blood forget.

Anon.

AMSTERDAM. 7s & 6s. [TROCHAIC.] JAMES NARES, 1760.

1. { Rise, my soul, and stretch thy wings—Thy better portion trace; }
{ Rise, from transitory things, Tow'rd heav'n, thy native place: } Sun, and moon, and stars decay,
Time shall soon this earth remove: Rise, my soul, and haste away To seats prepared above.

506 *Rise, my Soul.*

2 Rivers to the ocean run,
Nor stay in all their course;
Fire ascending seeks the sun,—
Both speed them to their source:
So a soul that's born of God
Pants to view his glorious face,
Upward tends to his abode,
To rest in his embrace.

Robert Seagrave. 1742.

PRAYER AND ASPIRATION.

1. Our heavenly Father, hear The pray'r we offer now; Thy name be hallowed far and near, To thee all nations bow, To thee all nations bow.

507 *The Lord's Prayer.*

2 Thy kingdom come; thy will
On earth be done in love,
As saints and seraphim fulfil
Thy perfect law above,

3 Our daily bread supply,
While by thy word we live;
The guilt of our iniquity
Forgive, as we forgive.

4 Thine, then, forever be
Glory and power divine;
The sceptre, throne, and majesty
Of heaven and earth are thine.
James Montgomery.

508 *Occupy till I come.*

1 A CHARGE to keep I have,
A God to glorify,
A never-dying soul to save.
And fit it for the sky.

2 To serve the present age,
My calling to fulfil:
Oh, may it all my powers engage
To do my Master's will.

3 Arm me with jealous care,
As in thy sight to live;
And oh, thy servant, Lord, prepare
A strict account to give.

4 Help me to watch and pray,
And on thyself rely,
Assured, if I my trust betray,
I shall forever die.
Charles Wesley, 1757.

509 *Desire to find God.*

1 My Father bids me come;
Oh why do I delay?
He calls the wandering spirit home,
And yet from him I stay.

2 Father, the hindrance show,
Which I have failed to see;
And let me now consent to know
What keeps me far from thee.

3 Searcher of hearts, in mine
Thy trying power display;
Into its darkest corners shine,
Take every veil away.
Anon.

510 *Spiritual Wants.*

1 My God, my strength, my hope,
On thee I cast my care,
With humble confidence look up,
And know thou hear'st my prayer.

2 Give me on thee to wait,
Till I can all things do—
On thee, almighty to create,
Almighty to renew.

3 I want a godly fear,
A quick-discerning eye,
That looks to thee when sin is near,
And bids the tempter fly;

4 A spirit still prepared,
And armed with jealous care,
Forever standing on its guard,
And watching unto prayer.
Charles Wesley.

EXPERIENCE AND LIFE.

SHIRLAND. S. M.
SAMUEL STANLEY, 1840.

1. Come at the morn-ing hour, Come, let us kneel and pray;
Prayer is the Chris-tian pil-grim's staff, To walk with God all day.

511

2 If in my Father's love
I share a filial part,
Send down thy Spirit, like a dove,
To rest upon my heart.

3 We would no longer lie,
Like slaves beneath the throne:
My faith shall Abba, Father, cry,
And thou the kindred own.
Isaac Watts, 1709.

512 *Glorious Liberty.*

1 Oh, come, and dwell with me,
Spirit of power within;
And bring the glorious liberty
From sorrow, fear, and sin!

2 Hasten the joyful day
Which shall my sins consume;
When old things shall be done away,
And all things new become.

3 I want the witness, Lord,
That all I do is right,—
According to thy will and word,—
Well pleasing in thy sight.

4 I ask no higher state:
Indulge me but in this,
And soon or later then translate
To my eternal bliss.
Charles Wesley.

513 *I will write it in their Hearts.*

1 That blessed law of thine,
Father, to me impart:
The Spirit's law of life divine,
O, write it in my heart.

2 Implant it deep within,
Whence it may ne'er remove—
The law of liberty from sin,
The perfect law of love.

3 Thy nature be my law,
Thy spotless sanctity,
And sweetly every moment draw
My happy soul to thee.
Charles Wesley.

514 *Ask, and ye shall receive.*

1 Ask, and ye shall receive:
On this my hope I build;
I ask forgiveness, and believe
My prayer shall be fulfilled.

2 Seek, and expect to find;
Wounded with sin my soul,
I seek the Saviour of mankind,
For he can make me whole.

3 Knock, and with patience wait;
By faith free entrance gain:
I stand and knock at mercy's gate
Till I thy grace obtain.

4 Shall I, then ask, in vain?
Seek, and not find the Lord?
Knock, and yet no admittance gain,
And doubt thy holy word?

5 No, Lord, thou'lt ne'er deceive:
Thy promises are sure;
In thy good time I shall receive:
What can I ask for more?
Anon.

PRAYER AND ASPIRATION. 161

LUX BENIGNA. P. M.   John Bacchus Dykes, 1861.

1. Lead, kind-ly light, a-mid th'encircling gloom, Lead thou me on; The night is dark, and I am far from home, Lead thou me on. Keep thou my feet; I do not ask to see...... The dis-tant scene, one step e-nough for me.

515

2 I was not ever thus, nor prayed that thou
   Should'st lead me on:
I loved to choose and see my path; but now
   Lead thou me on.
I loved the garish day; and, spite of fears,
Pride ruled my will; remember not past
   years.

3 So long thy pow'r has blest me, sure it still
   Will lead me on
Thro' dreary doubt, thro' pain and sorrow, till
   The night is gone.
And with the morn, those angel faces smile,
Which I have loved long since, and lost a-
   while.   John Henry Newman, 1853.

---

516 *Lead me in Thy Truth, and teach me.*

1 I ASK a perfect creed:
   O that to me were given
The teaching that leads none astray,
   The scholarship of heaven!

2 The one, whole truth I seek,
   In this sad age of strife—
The truth of Him who is the Truth,
   And in whose truth is life,—

3 Truth which contains true rest,
   Which is the grave of doubt,
Which ends uncertainty and gloom,
   And casts the falsehood out.

4 O True One, give me truth,
   And let it quench in me
The thirst of this long-craving heart,
   And set my spirit free.
                   Horatius Bonar.

EXPERIENCE AND LIFE.

RETREAT. L. M. — Thos. Hastings.

1. From ev-'ry storm-y wind that blows, From ev-'ry swell-ing tide of woes, There is a calm, a sure re-treat: 'Tis found be-neath the mer-cy-seat.

517 *The Mercy-seat.*

2 There is a scene where spirits blend,
Where friend holds fellowship with friend;
Though sundered far, by faith they meet
Around one common mercy-seat.

3 There, there on eagle wings we soar,
And sense and sin molest no more,
And heaven comes down our souls to greet,
And glory crowns the mercy-seat.
Hugh Stowell, 1832.

518 *With my Soul have I desired Thee.*

1 My God, permit me not to be
A stranger to myself and thee;
Amidst a thousand thoughts I rove,
Forgetful of my highest love.

2 Why should my passions mix with earth,
And thus debase my heavenly birth?
Why should I cleave to things below,
And let my God, my Saviour, go?

3 Call me away from flesh and sense;
One sovereign word can draw me thence;
I would obey the voice divine,
And all inferior joys resign.

4 Be earth with all her scenes withdrawn;
Let noise and vanity be gone;
In secret silence of the mind,
My heaven, and there my God, I find.
Isaac Watts.

519 *To be made perfect in Divine Love.*

1 Oh that my heart was right with thee,
And loved thee with a perfect love!
Oh that my Lord would dwell in me,
And never from his seat remove!

2 Father, I dwell in mournful night,
Till thou dost in my heart appear:
Arise, propitious Sun, and light
An everlasting morning there.

3 Oh, let my prayer acceptance find,
And bring the mighty blessing down;
Eyesight impart, for I am blind,
And seal me thine adopted Son!
Augustus M. Toplady, 1759.

520 *The Highway of Holiness.*

1 Jesus, my all, to heaven is gone—
He whom I fix my hopes upon;
His track I see, and I'll pursue
The narrow way till him I view.

2 The way the holy prophets went,
The road that leads from banishment,
The King's highway of holiness,
I'll go, for all his paths are peace.

3 This is the way I long have sought,
And mourned because I found it not,
Till late I heard my Saviour say,
Come hither, soul; I am the way.

4 Lo, glad I come; and thou blest Lamb,
Shalt take me to thee as I am;
Nothing but sin have I to give,
Nothing but love shall I receive.
John Cennick, 1743.

PRAYER AND ASPIRATION. 163

WELTON. L. M.   Rev. C. Malan.

1. Fa-ther, a-dored in worlds a-bove, Thy glorious name be hal-lowed still;
Thy king-dom come in truth and love; And earth, like heav'n, o-bey thy will.

521   *The Lord's Prayer.*

2 Lord, make our daily wants thy care,
Forgive the sins which we forsake:
In thy compassion let us share,
As fellow-men of ours partake.

3 Evils beset us every hour;
Thy kind protection we implore:
Thine is the kingdom, thine the power,
The glory thine for evermore.
Birmingham Col.

522   *Choosing the Better Part.*

1 BESET with snares on every hand,
In life's uncertain path I stand:
Father divine, diffuse thy light,
To guide my doubtful footsteps right.

2 Engage this roving, treacherous heart
Wisely to choose the better part;
To scorn the trifles of a day,
For joy that none can take away.

3 Then let the wildest storms arise,
Let tempests mingle earth and skies,
No fatal shipwreck shall I fear,
But all my treasure with me bear.

4 If thou, my Father, still be nigh,
Cheerful I live, and joyful die;
Secure, when mortal comforts flee,
To find ten thousand worlds in thee.
Philip Doddridge.

523

1 ASSIST us, Lord, to act, to be,
What nature and thy laws decree,
Worthy that intellectual flame
Which from thy breathing Spirit came.

2 Our moral freedom to maintain,
Bid passion serve, and reason reign;
Self-poised and independent still
On this world's varying good or ill.

3 May our expanded souls disclaim
The narrow view, the selfish aim;
But with a Christian zeal embrace
Whate'er is friendly to our race.

4 O Father! grace and virtue grant;
No more we wish, no more we want:
To know, to serve thee, and to love,
Is peace below,—is bliss above.
Henry Moore.

524   *This is the Gate of Heaven.*

1 How SWEET to leave the world awhile,
And seek the presence of our Lord!
Dear Saviour, on thy people smile,
And come according to thy word.

2 From busy scenes we now retreat,
That we may here converse with thee.
Ah, Lord, behold us at thy feet—
Let this the gate of heaven be.

3 Chief of ten thousand, now appear,
That we by faith may see thy face;
O, speak, that we thy voice may hear,
And let thy presence fill this place.
Thomas Kelly.

164 EXPERIENCE AND LIFE.

ORLAND. L. M.

1. Great God, my Father and my Friend, On whom I cast my constant care, On whom for all things I depend, To thee I raise......... my humble pray'r.

525 *Watchfulness.*

2 Endue me with a holy fear;
The frailty of my heart reveal;
Sin and its snares are always near—
Thee may I always nearer feel.

3 O that to thee my constant mind
May with a steady flame aspire;
Pride in its earliest motions find,
And check the rise of wrong desire!

4 O that my watchful soul may fly
The first perceived approach of sin,
Look up to thee when danger's nigh,
And feel thy fear control within!
Exeter Collection.

526 *Search me, O God, and know my Heart.*

1 O Thou to whose all-searching sight
The darkness shineth as the light,
Search, prove my heart—it pants for thee:
O, burst these bonds, and set it free.

2 Wash out its stains; refine its dross;
Nail my affections to the cross;
Hallow each thought; let all within
Be clean as thou, my Lord, art clean.

3 When rising floods my soul o'erflow,
When sinks my heart in waves of woe,
O God, thy timely aid impart,
And raise my head, and cheer my heart.

4 If rough and thorny be the way,
My strength proportion to my day,
Till toil, and grief, and pain shall cease,
Where all is calm, and joy, and peace.
John Wesley.

527 *Here have we no continuing City.*

1 We've no abiding city here;
Sad truth, were this to be our home;
But let this thought our spirits cheer—
We seek a city yet to come.

2 We've no abiding city here;
We seek a city out of sight—
Zion its name; the Lord is there:
It shines with everlasting light.

3 O, sweet abode of peace and love,
Where pilgrims freed from toil are blest!
Had I the pinions of the dove,
I'd fly to thee and be at rest.

4 But hush, my soul, nor dare repine;
The time my God appoints is best;
While here, to do his will be mine,
And his to fix my time of rest.
Thomas Kelly.

528 *For Steadiness of Principle.*

1 Amidst a world of hopes and fears,
A world of cares and toils and tears,
Where foes alarm, and dangers threat,
And pleasures kill, and glories cheat;

2 Shed down, O Lord! a heavenly ray
To guide me in the doubtful way;
And o'er me hold thy shield of power,
To guard me in the dangerous hour.

3 May never pleasure, wealth, or pride,
Allure my wandering soul aside!
But through this maze of mortal ill,
Safe lead me to thy heavenly hill.
Henry Moore.

PRAYER AND ASPIRATION.

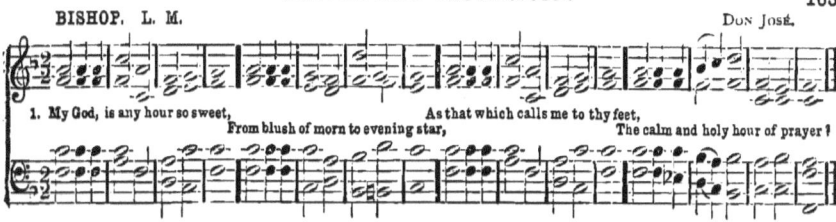

BISHOP. L. M. — Don José.

1. My God, is any hour so sweet, From blush of morn to evening star, As that which calls me to thy feet, The calm and holy hour of prayer?

529 *The Hour of Prayer.*

2 Blest is the tranquil break of morn,
And blest the hush of solemn eve,
When on the wings of prayer up-borne
This fair, but transient, world, I leave.

3 Then is my strength by thee renewed
Then are my sins by thee forgiven;
Then dost thou cheer my solitude,
With clear and beauteous hopes of heaven.

4 No words can tell what sweet relief,
There for my every want, I find;
What strength for warfare, balm for grief,
What deep and cheerful peace of mind!
C. Elliott.

STELLA. L. M. 6 l. — Crown of Jesus.

1. Lead-er of Israel's host, and guide Of all who seek the land a-bove; Be-neath thy shadow we a-bide, The cloud of thy pro-tect-ing love,—Our strength thy grace, our rule thy word, Our end the glo-ry of the Lord.

530 *God our Guide.*

2 By thine unerring spirit led,
We shall not in the desert stray,
We shall not full direction need,
Nor miss our providential way;
As far from danger as from fear,
While love, Almighty love, is near.
Wesleyan.

531 *Desire for Union with God.*

1 O Love, how cheering is the ray!
All pain before thy presence flies;
Care, anguish, sorrow, melt away,
Where'er thy healing beams arise;
O Father, nothing may I see,
And nought desire or seek, but thee.

2 O that I, as a little child,
May follow thee, and never rest
Till sweetly thou hast breathed a mild,
A lowly mind into my breast;
Nor ever may we parted be,
Till I become as one with thee.

3 Still let thy love point out my way;
How wondrous things thy love hath
Still lead me, lest I go astray; [wrought!
Direct my word, inspire my thought;
And if I fall, soon may I hear
Thy voice, and know that Love is near.
Charles Wesley.

EXPERIENCE AND LIFE.

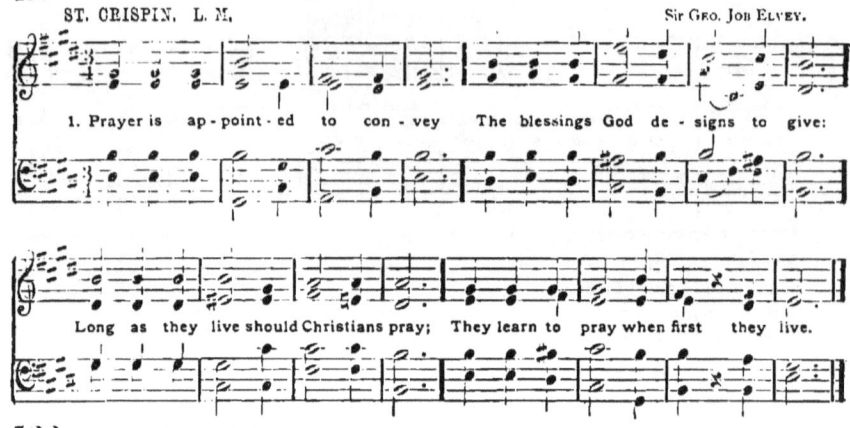

ST. CRISPIN. L. M. — Sir Geo. Job Elvey.

1. Prayer is ap-point-ed to con-vey The blessings God de-signs to give: Long as they live should Christians pray; They learn to pray when first they live.

532 *Prayer the Life of the Soul.*

2 If pain afflict or wrongs oppress,
　If cares distract or fears dismay,
If guilt deject, if sin distress,—
　In every case, still watch and pray.

3 'Tis prayer supports the soul that's weak;
　Tho' thought be broken, language lame,
Pray, if thou canst or canst not speak;
　But pray with faith in Jesus' name.

4 Depend on him—thou canst not fail:
　Make all thy wants and wishes known;
Fear not—his promise must prevail:
　Ask but in faith, it shall be done.

　　　　　　　　　　　　Joseph Hart.

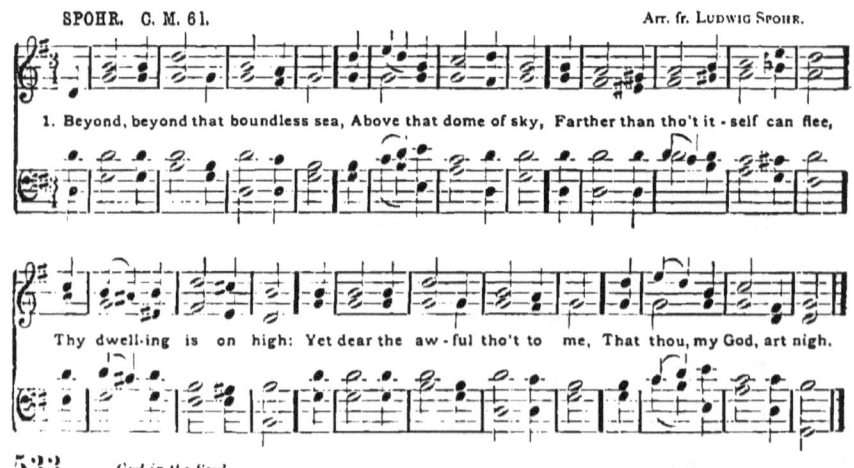

SPOHR. C. M. 61. — Arr. fr. Ludwig Spohr.

1. Beyond, beyond that boundless sea, Above that dome of sky, Farther than tho't it-self can flee, Thy dwell-ing is on high: Yet dear the aw-ful tho't to me, That thou, my God, art nigh.

533 *God in the Soul.*

2 We hear thy voice when thunders roll
　Through the wide fields of air;
The waves obey thy dread control,
　Yet still thou art not there;
Where shall I find him, O my soul,
　Who yet is everywhere?

3 O, not in circling depth or height,
　But in the conscious breast;
Present to faith, though veiled from sight,
　There does his spirit rest!
Oh, come, thou presence Infinite,
　And make thy creature blest!

　　　　　　　　　　　　Josiah Conder.

PRAYER AND ASPIRATION. 167

534 *Life more abundantly.*

2 Oh for fuller life we pine!
Let us more receive of thine;
Still for more on thee we call,
Thou who fillest all in all!

3 Live we now in thee; be fed
Daily with the living bread;
Into thee our spirits grow;
Into us thy spirit flow;

4 While we feel the vital blood,
While thy full and quickening flood
Through life's every channel rolls,
Soul of all believing souls.
Hymns of the Spirit

535 *Seeking God.*

1 THIRSTING for a living spring,
Seeking for a higher home,
Resting where our souls must cling,
Trusting, hoping, Lord, we come.

2 Glorious hopes our spirits fill,
When we feel that thou art near;
Father, then our fears are still,
Then the soul's bright end is clear.

3 Life's hard conflict we would win,
Read the meaning of life's frown;
Change the thorn-bound wreath of sin
For the spirit's starry crown.

4 Make us beautiful within
By thy spirit's holy light;
Guard us when our faith is dim,
Father of all love and might.
Frank P. Appleton.

536 *The Light of Life.*

1 LIGHT of life, seraphic fire,
Love divine, thyself impart;
Every fainting soul inspire;
Enter every drooping heart:

2 Every mournful spirit cheer;
Scatter all our doubt and gloom;
Father, in thy grace appear,
To thy human temples come!

3 Come, in this accepted hour,
Bring thy heavenly kingdom in;
Fill us with thy glorious power,
Rooting out the seeds of sin:

4 Nothing more can we require
We can rest in nothing less;
Be thou all our hearts' desire,
All our joy and all our peace.
Charles Wesley.

537 *Life in God.*

1 FATHER, we look up to thee;
Let us in thy love agree;
Thou who art the God of peace,
Bid contention ever cease.

2 Make us of one heart and mind,
Self-forgetful, true, and kind;
Strong; yet meek in thought and word,
Like thy Son, our blessed Lord!

3 Let us for each other care,
Each the other's burden bear;
Ready, when reviled, to bless;
Studious of the law of peace.

4 Free from anger, free from pride,
Let us thus in thee abide;
All the depths of love express,—
All the heights of holiness.
Charles Wesley.

EXPERIENCE AND LIFE.

ROSEFIELD. 7s, 6l.

1. As the hart, with eager looks, Pant-eth for the wa-ter-brooks,
   So my soul, a-thirst for thee, Pants the liv-ing God to see.
   When, oh! when, with fil-ial fear, Lord, shall I to thee draw near?

538 *The Soul's Cry for God.*

2 Why art thou cast down, my soul?
God, thy God, shall make thee whole;
Why art thou disquieted?

God shall lift thy fallen head,
And his countenance benign
Be the saving health of thine.

James Montgomery.

GOTTSCHALK. 7s.
Arr. by E. P. Parker.

1. Fath-er at thy foot-stool see, Those who now are one in thee!
   Each to each u-nite, and bless, Keep us in thy per-fect peace.

Used by per. Oliver Ditson Co., owners of Copyright.

539 *Following Christ.*

2 Plant in us the humble mind,
Patient, pitiful, and kind;
Meek and lowly let us be,
Full of goodness, full of thee.

Charles Wesley, 1740.

540 *Let this Mind be in you which was in Christ.*

1 Father of eternal grace,
Glorify thyself in me;
Meekly beaming in my face
May the world thine image see.

2 Humble, holy, all resigned
To thy will—thy will be done:
Give me, Lord, the perfect mind
Of thy well-belovéd Son.

3 Counting gain and glory loss,
May I tread the path he trod—
Die with Jesus on the cross,
Rise with him to thee, my God.

James Montgomery.

PRAYER AND ASPIRATION. 169

MANOAH. C. M.   GREATOREX COLLECTION.

1. Come, let us pray: 'tis sweet to feel That God him-self is near;
That, while we at his foot-stool kneel, His mer-cy deigns to hear.

541   *A Call to Prayer.*   Used by per. Oliver Ditson Co., owners of Copyright

2 Come, let us pray: the burning brow,
   The heart oppressed with care,
And all the woes that throng us now,
   Will be relieved by prayer.

3 Come, let us pray: the mercy-seat
   Invites the fervent prayer;
Our heavenly father waits to greet
   The contrite spirit there.
                           Conder.

542   *Thy Will be done.*

1 How SWEET to be allowed to pray
   To God, the Holy One,—
With filial love and trust to say,
   O God, thy will be done!

2 We in these sacred words can find
   A cure for every ill:
They calm and soothe the troubled mind,
   And bid all care be still.

3 O, let that will which gave me breath
   And an immortal soul,
In joy or grief, in life or death,
   My every wish control.

4 O, teach my heart the blessed way
   To imitate thy Son;
Teach me, O God, in truth to pray,
   Thy will, not mine, be done.
                          Mrs. Follen.

543   *Desires for Holiness.*

1 O, COULD I find, from day to day,
   A nearness to my God.
Then would my hours glide sweet away
   While leaning on his word.

2 Lord, I desire with thee to live
   . Anew from day to day,
In joys the world can never give,
   Nor ever take away.

3 O Father, come and rule my heart,
   And make me wholly thine,
That I may never more depart,
   Nor grieve thy love divine.

4 Thus, till my last expiring breath,
   Thy goodness I'll adore;
And, when my frame dissolves in death,
   My soul shall love thee more.
                          B. Cleveland.

544   *Enter into thy Closet.*

1 SWEET is the prayer whose holy stream
   In earnest pleading flows:
Devotion dwells upon the theme,
   And warm and warmer glows.

2 Faith grasps the blessings she desires;
   Hope points the upward gaze;
And Love, celestial Love, inspires
   The eloquence of praise.

3 But sweeter far the still small voice,
   Unheard by human ear,
When God has made the heart rejoice,
   And dried the bitter tear.

4 No accents flow, no words ascend;
   All utterance faileth there;
But Christian spirits comprehend,
   And God accepts the prayer.
                          Anon.

EXPERIENCE AND LIFE.

OMNISCIENCE. C. M. No. 1.   L. O. E.

1. There is an eye that nev-er sleeps Beneath the wing of night·
There is an ear that nev-er shuts, When sink the beams of light.

Used by per. Oliver Ditson Co., owners of Copyright.

545

2 There is an arm that never tires;
  When human strength gives way;
There is a love that never fails,
  When earthly loves decay.

3 That eye is fixed on seraph throngs;
  That arm upholds the sky;
That ear is filled with angel-songs;
  That love is throned on high.

OMNISCIENCE. C. M. No. 2.   L. O. E.

4. But there's power which man can wield, When mor-tal aid is vain,
That eye, that arm, that love to reach, That list-'ning ear to gain.

Used by per. Oliver Ditson Co., owners of Copyright.

5 That power is prayer, which soars on high,
  Through Jesus, to his throne;
And moves the hand which moves the world,
  To bring salvation down.

J. A. Wallace.

PRAYER AND ASPIRATION. 171

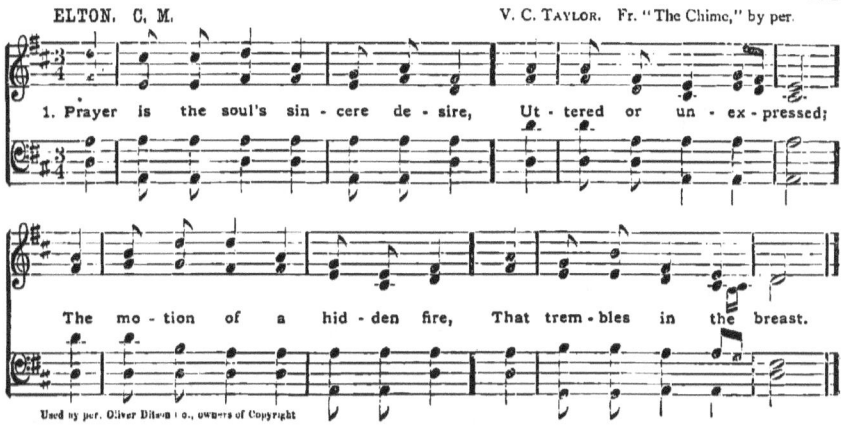

546 *Prayer.*

2 Prayer is the burden of a sigh,
  The falling of a tear,
  The upward glancing of an eye,
  When none but God is near.

3 Prayer is the simplest form of speech
  That infant lips can try;
  Prayer, the sublimest strains that reach
  The Majesty on high.

4 Prayer is the Christian's vital breath,
  The Christian's native air:
  His watchword at the gates of death—
  He enters heaven with prayer.
        James Montgomery, 1810.

547 *Prayer for Purity.*

1 BE thou, O God, by night, by day,
  My Guide, my Guard, from sin,
  My life, my trust, my light divine,
  To keep me pure within.

2 Pure as the air when day's first light
  A cloudless sky illumes,
  And active as the lark that soars
  Till heaven shines round its plumes.

3 So may my soul upon the wings
  Of faith unwearied rise,
  Till at the gate of heaven it sings,
  'Midst light from Paradise.
        Anon.

548 *Divine Help.*

1 O GRACIOUS God, in whom I live,
  My feeble efforts aid;
  Help me to watch, and pray, and strive,
  Though trembling and afraid.

2 Increase my faith, increase my hope,
  When foes and fears prevail;
  And bear my fainting spirit up,
  Or soon my strength will fail.

3 Oh keep me in thy heavenly way,
  And bid the tempter flee;
  And let me never, never stray
  From happiness and thee.
        Anne Steele, 1760.

549 *Desiring Holiness.*

1 TRY us, O God, and search the ground
  Of every sinful heart;
  Whate'er of sin in us is found,
  O, bid it all depart.

2 Help us to help each other, Lord,
  Each other's cross to bear;
  Let each his friendly aid afford,
  And feel his brother's care.

3 Help us to build each other up,
  Our heart and life improve;
  Increase our faith, confirm our hope,
  And perfect us in love.

4 Up into thee, our living Head,
  Let us in all things grow,
  Till thou hast made us free indeed,
  And spotless here below.
        Charles Wesley.

EXPERIENCE AND LIFE.

BALERMA. C. M. HUGH WILSON Arr. by LOWELL MASON, 1836.

1. Oh, for a clos-er walk with God! A calm and heav'n-ly frame! A light to shine up-on the road That leads me to.... the Lamb!

550 *Oh, for a Closer Walk.*

2 Where is the blessedness I knew
When first I saw the Lord?
Where is the soul-refreshing view
Of Jesus and his word?

3 What peaceful hours I then enjoyed!
How sweet their memory still!
But now I find an aching void
The world can never fill.

4 Return, oh, holy Dove, return,
Sweet messenger of rest;
I hate the sins that made thee mourn,
And drove thee from my breast.

5 The dearest idol I have known,
Whate'er that idol be,
Help me to tear it from thy throne,
And worship only thee.

6 So shall my walk be close with God,
Calm and serene my frame,
So purer light shall mark the road
That leads me to the Lamb.
William Cowper, 1772.

551 *Invoking God's Aid.*

1 FATHER in heaven, to thee my heart
Would lift itself in prayer;
Drive from my soul each earthly thought
And show thy presence there.

2 Oh, help me break the galling chains
This world has round me thrown,
Each passion of my heart subdue,
Each darling sin disown!

3 O Father, kindle in my breast
A never-dying flame
Of holy love, of grateful trust
In thine almighty name.
William Henry Furness, 1822.

552 *Lord. Teach us to Pray.*

1 LORD, teach us how to pray aright,
With reverence and with fear;
Though dust and ashes in thy sight,
We may, we must, draw near.

2 Burdened with guilt, convinced of sin,
In weakness, want, and woe,
Fightings without, and fears within,
Lord, whither shall we go?

3 God of all grace, we come to thee,
With broken, contrite hearts;
Give what thine eye delights to see,
Truth in the inward parts;—

4 Give deep humility; the sense
Of godly sorrow give;
A strong, desiring confidence
To hear thy voice, and live;—

5 Give these, and then thy will be done;
Thus, strengthened with all might,
We by thy Spirit and thy Son,
Shall pray, and pray aright.
James Montgomery.

PRAYER AND ASPIRATION. 173

CONWAY. C. M.

1. Father of light conduct my feet Thro' life's dark dangerous road; Let each advancing step still bring, Let each advancing step still bring Me nearer to my God.

553 *Prayer for Prudence and Wisdom.*

2 Let heaven-eyed prudence be my guide;
And, when I go astray,
Recall my feet from folly's path,
To wisdom's better way.

3 That heavenly wisdom from above
Abundantly impart,
And let it guard and guide and warm
And penetrate my heart.
Anon.

554 *Prayer for Divine Direction.*

1 ETERNAL Source of life and light,
Supremely good and wise!
To thee we bring our grateful vows,
To thee lift up our eyes.

2 Our dark and erring mind illume
With truth's celestial rays;
Inspire our hearts with sacred love,
And tune our lips to praise.

3 Safely conduct us, by thy grace,
Through life's perplexing road;
And place us, when that journey's o'er,
At thy right hand, O God!
Cappe's Selection.

555 *Make haste to help me.*

1 GREAT God, let not thy grace delay
To meet me with thy love;
Drive interposing clouds away,
And make my guilt remove.

2 We long to meet our God to-day,
And taste his grace divine,
That every soul with joy may say,
My Lord, my God, I'm thine.

3 O, how I pant, great God, to see
Thy face, and taste thy love;
O, speak, and bring me near to thee,
And all my doubts remove.

4 O God, inspire each heart and tongue
To learn thy precious name;
Redeeming love shall be my song,
While I thy love proclaim.
Anon.

556 *Prayer for Wisdom.*

1 ALMIGHTY God, in humble prayer
To thee our souls we lift;
Do thou our waiting minds prepare
For thy most needful gift.

2 We ask not golden streams of wealth
Along our path to flow;
We ask not undecaying health,
Nor length of years below;—

3 We ask not honors, which an hour
May bring and take away;
We ask not pleasure, pomp, and power,
Lest we should go astray;—

4 We ask for wisdom; Lord, impart
The knowledge how to live;
A wise and understanding heart
To all before thee give.
James Montgomery.

EXPERIENCE AND LIFE.

COVENTRY. C. M.   Arr. by LOWELL MASON.

1. Oh, could our thoughts and wish-es fly, A-bove earth's gloom-y shades, To those bright worlds be-yond the sky, Which sor-row ne'er in-vades.

557   *Immortal Joys.*

2 There joys unseen by mortal eyes,
Or reason's feeble ray,
In ever-blooming prospect rise,
Unconscious of decay.

3 Lord, send a beam of light divine,
To guide our upward aim;
With one reviving ray of thine
Our languid hearts inflame.

4 Then shall, on faith's sublimest wing,
Our ardent wishes rise,   [spring
To those bright scenes, where pleasures
Immortal in the skies.
Anne Steele.

558   *Prayer for Grace in Trial.*

1 FATHER of all our mercies, thou
In whom we move and live,
Hear us in heaven, thy dwelling, now,
And answer and forgive.

2 When, harassed by ten thousand foes,
Our helplessness we feel,
Oh give the weary soul repose,
The wounded spirit heal!

3 When dire temptations gather round,
And threaten or allure,
By storm or calm, in thee be found,
A refuge strong and sure.

4 When age advances, may we grow
In faith and hope and love,
And walk in holiness below
To holiness above!
James Montgomery.

559   *Prayer for Submission.*

1 ONE prayer I have—all prayers in one,
When I am wholly thine—
Thy will, my God, thy will be done,
And let that will be mine.

2 May I remember that to thee
Whate'er I have I owe;
And back in gratitude from me
May all thy bounties flow.

3 Thy gifts are only then enjoyed
When used as talents lent;
Those talents only well employed
When in thy service spent.

4 And though thy wisdom takes away,
Shall I arraign thy will?
No, let me bless thy name, and say,
The Lord is gracious still.
James Montgomery.

560   *Your Life is hid with Christ in God.*

1 THE Crucified is gone before
To the blest realms of light;
Oh, thither may our spirits soar,
And wing their upward flight!

2 Lord, make us to those joys aspire,
That spring from love to thee,
That pass the carnal heart's desire,
And faith alone can see.

3 To guide us to thy glories, Lord!
To lift us to the sky,
Oh, may thy spirit still be poured
Upon us from on high!
Parisian Breviary. Tr. John Chandler.

PRAYER AND ASPIRATION.

GEER. C. M.   GREATOREX COLLECTION.

561 *There Remaineth a Rest.*

2 A rest where all our soul's desire
Is fixed on things above;
Where fear, and sin, and grief expire,
Cast out by perfect love.

3 O, that I now that rest might know,
Believe, and enter in!

Now, Saviour, now the power bestow,
And let me cease from sin.

4 Remove all hardness from my heart;
All unbelief remove;
To me the rest of faith impart,
The Sabbath of thy love.

Charles Wesley.

SWEET HOME. 11s & 5s.   Sir HENRY ROWLAND BISHOP.

562 *Sweet Prayer.*

2 When far from the friends we hold dearest we part,
What fond recollections still cling to the heart!
Past converse, past scenes, past enjoyments are there;
Oh, how mournfully pleasing till hallowed by prayer!—REF.

Ann Lutua.

EXPERIENCE AND LIFE.

REGENT SQUARE. 6s, 7s & 4s. H. SMART.

1. We the weak ones, we the sinners, Would not in our poorness stay; We the low ones would be winners Of what holy height we may: Ev-er near-er, Ev-er near-er To thy pure and perfect day.

563 *Upward and Onward.*

2 By each saving word unspoken;
  By thy truth, as yet half won;
By each idol yet unbroken;
  By thy will, yet poorly done;
    Hear us, hear us,
  Thou almighty; help us on.

3 Nearer to thee would we venture,
  Of thy truth more largely take,
Upon life diviner enter,
  Into day more glorious break.
    To the ages
  Fair bequests and costly make.
      T. H. Gill.

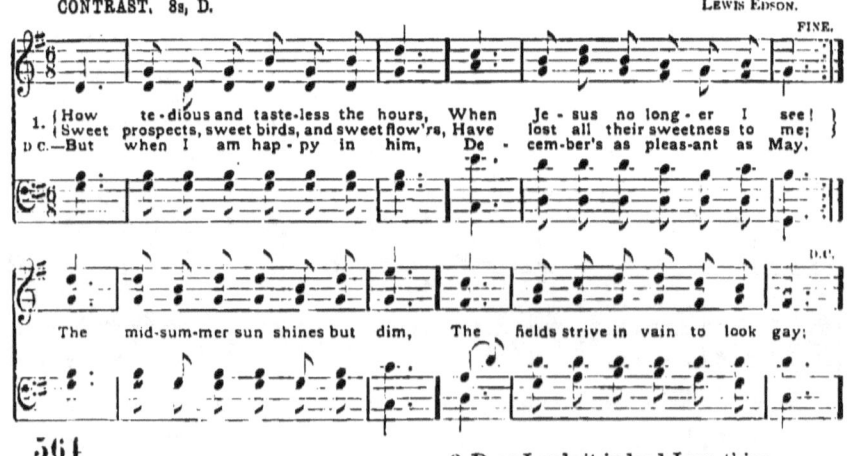

CONTRAST. 8s, D. LEWIS EDSON.

1. { How tedious and tasteless the hours, When Jesus no longer I see!
   { Sweet prospects, sweet birds, and sweet flow'rs, Have lost all their sweetness to me;
D.C.—But when I am happy in him, December's as pleasant as May.

The midsummer sun shines but dim, The fields strive in vain to look gay;

564

2 His name yields the richest perfume,
    And sweeter than music his voice;
  His presence disperses my gloom,
    And makes all within me rejoice;
  I should, were he always thus nigh,
    Have nothing to wish or to fear;
  No mortal so happy as I,—
    My summer would last all the year.

3 Dear Lord, if indeed I am thine,
    If thou art my sun and my song,
  Say, why do I languish and pine?
    And why are my winters so long?
  O drive these dark clouds from my sky!
    Thy soul-cheering presence restore;
  Or take me to thee up on high,
    Where winter and clouds are no more.
      John Newton.

PRAYER AND ASPIRATION. 177

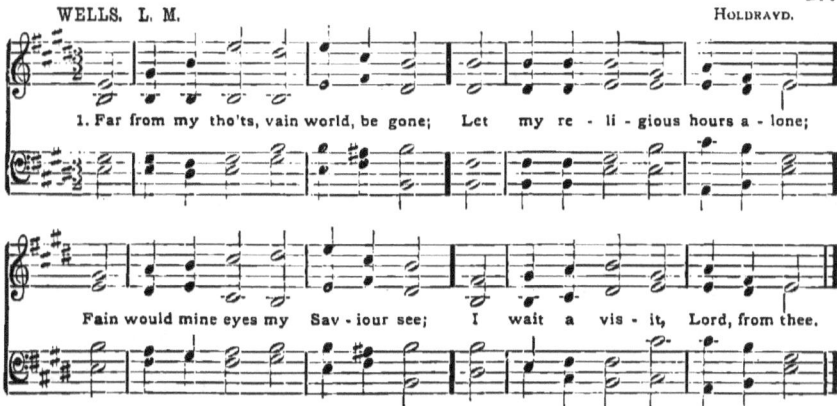

WELLS. L. M.   HOLDRAYD.

1. Far from my tho'ts, vain world, be gone; Let my re-li-gious hours a-lone; Fain would mine eyes my Sav-iour see; I wait a vis-it, Lord, from thee.

565   *O visit me with Thy Salvation.*

2 O, warm my heart with holy fire,
And kindle there a pure desire;
Come, my dear Jesus, from above,
And fill my soul with heavenly love.

3 Blest Saviour, what delicious fare!
How sweet thine entertainments are!
Never did angels taste above
Redeeming grace and dying love.

4 Hail, great Immanuel, all divine!
In thee thy Father's glories shine,
Thou brightest, sweetest, fairest One
That eyes have seen, or angels known.
Isaac Watts, 1709.

566   *Walking with God.*

1 THROUGH all this life's eventful road,
Fain would I walk with thee, my God,
And make thy presence light around,
And every step on holy ground.

2 Each blessing would I trace to thee,
In every grief thy mercy see,
And through the paths of duty move,
Conscious of thine encircling love.

3 And when the angel Death stands by,
Be this my strength, that thou art nigh;
And this my joy, that I shall be
With those who dwell in light with thee.
William Gaskell.

567   *The Kingdom of God is within you.*

1 THOU strong and loving Son of Man,
Redeemer from the bonds of sin,
'Tis thou the living spark dost fan,
That sets my heart on fire within.

2 In thee I find a nobler birth,
A glory o'er the world I see,
And Paradise returns to earth,
And blooms again for us in thee.

3 Thou openest heaven once more for men,
The soul's true home, thy kingdom, Lord,
And I can trust and hope again,
And feel myself akin to God.
Novalis.

568   *I will that they be with Me where I am.*

1 LET me be with thee where thou art,
My Saviour, my eternal Rest,
Then only will this longing heart
Be fully and forever blest.

2 Let me be with thee where thou art,
Thine unveiled glory to behold;
Then only will this wandering heart
Cease to be false to thee and cold.

3 Let me be with thee where thou art,
Where spotless saints thy name adore;
Then only will this sinful heart
Be evil and defiled no more.

4 Let me be with thee where thou art,
Where none can die, where none remove;
There neither death nor life will part
Me from thy presence and thy love.
Anon.

178   EXPERIENCE AND LIFE.

WARRINGTON. L. M.

1. O that I could for-ev-er dwell, De-light-ed at the Sav-iour's feet,
Be-hold the form I love so well, And all his ten-der words re-peat!

569   *The hidden Life.*

2 This is the hidden life I prize—
A life of penitential love;
When most my follies I despise,
And raise my highest thoughts above;—

3 When all I am I clearly see,
And freely own with deepest shame;
When the Redeemer's love to me
Kindles within a deathly flame.

4 Thus would I live till nature fail,
And all my former sins forsake,
Then rise to God within the veil,
And of eternal joy partake.
                               Anon.

570   *Did not our hearts burn within us?*

1 HATH not thy heart within thee burned
At evening's calm and holy hour,
As if its inmost depths discerned
The presence of a loftier power?

2 As they, who once with Jesus trod,
With kindling breast his accents heard,
But knew not that the Son of God
Was uttering every burning word,—

3 Father of Jesus, thus thy voice
Speaks to our hearts in tones divine;
Our spirits tremble and rejoice,
But know not that the voice is thine.

4 Still be thy hallowed accents near;
To doubt and passion whisper peace;
Direct us on our journey here,
And bid, in heaven, our wanderings cease.
                                 Bulfinch.

571   *Lo, I am with you alway.*

1 THERE'S not a hope with comfort fraught,
Triumphant over death and time,
But Jesus mingles in the thought,
Forerunner of our course sublime.

2 I see him in the daily round
Of social duty, mild and meek;
With him I tread the hallowed ground,
Communion with my God to seek.

3 I meet him at the lowly tomb;
I weep where Jesus wept before;
And there above the grave's dark gloom,
I see him rise and weep no more.
                                 Taylor.

572   *"Jesus, the Best Beloved."*

1 JESUS, my heart within me burns,
To tell thee all its conscious love;
And from earth's low delights it turns,
To taste a joy like that above.

2 When thou to me dost condescend,
In love divine, thou blessèd One,
The moments that with thee I spend,
Seem e'en as Heaven itself begun.

3 I breathe my words into thine ear;
I seem to fix mine eyes on thine;
And sure that thou dost wait to hear,
I dare in faith to call thee mine.

4 Reign, thou sole Sovereign of my heart,
My all I yield to thy control;
O let me never from thee part,
Thou best Belovèd of my soul.
                               Ray Palmer.

PRAYER AND ASPIRATION.

BETHANY. 6s & 4s. LOWELL MASON, 1859.

1. Near-er, my God, to thee, Near-er to thee; E'en though it be a cross
D.S.—Near-er, my God! to thee,—

That rais-eth me, Still all my song shall be, Near-er, my God! to thee,—
Near-er to thee.

Used by per. Oliver Ditson Co., owners of Copyright.

573 *Nearer to God.*

2 Though like the wanderer,
The sun gone down,
Darkness be over me,
My rest a stone,
Yet, in my dreams, I'd be
Nearer, my God! to thee,—
Nearer to thee.

3 There let the way appear,
Steps up to heaven;
All that thou sendest me,
In mercy given;
Angels to beckon me
Nearer, my God! to thee,—
Nearer to thee.

4 Then, with my waking thoughts
Bright with thy praise,
Out of my stony griefs
Bethel I'll raise;
So by my woes to be
Nearer, my God! to thee,—
Nearer to thee.

5 Or if, on joyful wing,
Cleaving the sky,
Sun, moon, and stars forgot,
Upward I fly,
Still all my song shall be,
Nearer, my God! to thee,—
Nearer to thee.
Mrs. Sarah Flower Adams, 1841.

574 *Closer with God.*

1 SAVIOUR, I follow on,
Guided by thee,
Seeing not yet the hand
That leadeth me;
Hushed be my heart and still,
Fear I no further ill,
Only to meet thy will
My will shall be.

2 Riven the rock for me,
Thirst to relieve;
Manna from heaven falls
Fresh every eve;
Never a want severe
Causeth my eye a tear,
But thou dost whisper near,
"Only believe!"

3 Saviour! I long to walk
Closer with thee;
Led by thy guiding hand
Ever to be;
Constantly near thy side,
Quickened and purified,
Living for him who died
Freely for me.
Charles S. Robinson, &c.

575 *"The grace of our Lord Jesus Christ be with you."*

2 God be with you till we meet again,
'Neath his wings securely hide you,
Daily manna still provide you,
God be with you till we meet again.—Cho.

3 God be with you till we meet again,
When life's perils thick confound you,
Put his loving arms around you,
God be with you till we meet again.—Cho.

4 God be with you till we meet again,
Keep love's banner floating o'er you,
Smite death's threath'ning wave before you,
God be with you till we meet again.—Cho.

J. E. Rankin, D.D.

THE CROSS. 181

DOVER. S. M.   Arr. by T. Hastings.

1. Not with our mor-tal eyes Have we be-held the Lord;
Yet we re-joice to hear his name, And love him in his word.

576 *Whom, having not seen, ye love.*
2 On earth we want the sight
Of our Redeemer's face;
Yet, Lord, our inmost thoughts delight
To dwell upon thy grace.

3 And when we taste thy love,
Our joys divinely glow
Unspeakable, like those above,
And heaven begins below.
Isaac Watts. 1709.

577 *Blessed are the pure in heart.*
1 BLEST are the pure in heart,
For they shall see their God;
The secret of the Lord is theirs;
Their soul is Christ's abode.

2 The Lord, who left the heavens,
Our life and peace to bring,
To dwell in lowliness with men,
Their pattern and their King,—

3 He to the lowly soul
Doth still himself impart,
And for his dwelling, and his throne,
Chooseth the pure in heart.

4 Lord, we thy presence seek;
May ours this blessing be;
O give the pure and lowly heart,—
A temple meet for thee.
John Keble.

578 *Spiritual Communion.*
1 OUR heavenly Father calls,
And Christ invites us near;
With both, our friendship shall be sweet,
And our communion dear.

2 God pities all our griefs;
He pardons every day,—
Almighty to protect our souls,
And wise to guide our way.

3 How large his bounties are!
What various stores of good
Diffused from our Redeemer's hand,
And purchased with his blood!

4 Here fix, my roving heart,
Here wait, my warmest love;
Till the communion be complete
In nobler scenes above.
Philip Doddridge.

579 *Christ crucified.*
1 I BLESS the Crucified,
I rest on love divine,
And, with unfaltering lip and heart,
I call this Saviour mine.

2 His cross dispels each doubt;
I bury in his tomb
Each thought of unbelief and fear,
Each lingering shade of gloom.

3 I praise my Saviour's name,
I trust his truth and might;
He calls me his, I call him mine,
My Lord, my joy, my light.

4 'Tis he who saveth me,
And freely pardon gives:
I love because he loveth me,
I live because he lives.
Horatius Bonar.

EXPERIENCE AND LIFE.

MARLOW. C. M.   English Melody. Arr. by Dr. L. Mason, 1832.

1. Walk in the light! so shalt thou know That fellowship of love His Spir-it on - ly can be-stow, Who reigns in light a-bove.

580   *"Walk in the Light."*

2 Walk in the light! and thou shalt own
   Thy darkness passed away;
Because that light hath on thee shone
   In which is perfect day.

3 Walk in the light! and e'en the tomb
   No fearful shade shall wear;
Glory shall chase away its gloom,
   For Christ hath conquered there.

4 Walk in the light! and thine shall be
   A path, though thorny, bright;
For God, by grace, shall dwell in thee,
   And God himself is light.
                    Bernard Barton.

581   *Walk with God.*

1 Walk with your God, along the road
   Your strength he will renew;
Wait on the Everlasting God,
   And he will work with you.

2 Ye shall not faint, ye shall not fail,
   Made in the spirit strong;
Each task divine ye still shall hail,
   And blend it with a song.
                    T. H. Gill.

582   *Fellowship with God.*

1 From all that's mortal, all that's vain,
   And from this earthly clod,
Arise, my soul, and strive to gain
   Sweet fellowship with God.

2 Not life, nor friendship, here below,
   Nor pleasure's flowery road,
Can to my soul such bliss impart
   As fellowship with God.

3 And when I'm made in love to bear
   Affliction's needful rod,
Light, sweet, and kind the strokes appear,
   Through fellowship with God.

4 So when the icy hand of death
   Shall chill our flowing blood;
With joy we'll yield our latest breath
   In fellowship with God.
                    Anon.

583   *Sympathy and Resignation.*

1 Let not despair nor fell revenge
   Be to my bosom known,
O, give me tears for others' woe,
   And patience for my own.

2 Feed me, O Lord, with needful food:
   I ask not wealth or fame;
Give me an eye to see thy will,
   A heart to praise thy name.

3 Whate'er thine all-discerning eye
   Sees for thy creature fit,
I'll bless the good, and to the ill
   Contentedly submit.

4 O, may my days securely pass,
   Without remorse or care:
And let me for my parting hour
   From day to day prepare.
                    Isaac Watts, 1709.

584   *The Bond of Love.*

1 Beneath the shadow of the cross,
   As earthly hopes remove,
His new commandment Jesus gives,—
   His blessèd word of love.

2 O bond of union, strong and deep;
   O bond of perfect peace!
Not e'en the lifted cross can harm
   If we but hold to this.

3 Then, Jesus, be thy Spirit ours;
   And swift our feet shall move
To deeds of pure self-sacrifice,
   And the sweet tasks of love.
                    Samuel Longfellow.

THE CROSS.

MAITLAND. C. M.   AARON CHAPIN.

1. Must Jesus bear the cross alone, And all the world go free? No, there's a cross for ev'ry one, And there's a cross for me.

585   *Cross and Crown.*
2 How happy are the saints above,
    Who once went sorrowing here!
    But now they taste unmingled love
    And joy, without a tear.
3 The consecrated cross I'll bear,
    Till death shall set me free,
    And then go home my crown to wear,
    For there's a crown for me.
4 Oh, precious cross! oh, glorious crown!
    Oh, resurrection day!
    Ye angels, from the stars come down,
    And bear my soul away.
                           G. N. Allen.

586   *I will love what God will speak.*
1 Speak with us Lord; thyself reveal,
    While here on earth we rove;
    Speak to our hearts, and let us feel
    The kindlings of thy love.
2 With thee conversing, we forget
    All toil, and time, and care;
    Labor is rest, and pain is sweet,
    If thou art present there.
3 Here then, my God, be pleased to stay,
    And bid my heart rejoice;
    My bounding heart shall own thy sway,
    And echo to thy voice.
4 Thou callest me to seek thy face
    Thy face, O God, I seek,
    Attend the whispers of thy grace
    And hear thee only speak.
                           Charles Wesley.

REDEMPTION. L. M.   Arr. fr. CHERUBINI. by L. O. EMERSON.

1. When I sur-vey the wondrous cross, On which the Prince of glo-ry died,
My rich-est gain I count but loss, And pour con-tempt on all my pride.

Used by per. Oliver Ditson Co., owners of Copyright.

587
2 Forbid it, Lord, that I should boast,
    Save in the death of Christ, my Lord:
    All the vain things that charm me most,
    I sacrifice them to his blood.
3 See! from his head, his hands, his feet,
    Sorrow and love flow mingled down!
Did e'er such love and sorrow meet,
    Or thorns compose so rich a crown?
4 Were the whole realm of nature mine,
    That were an offering far too small:
    Love so amazing, so divine,
    Demands my soul, my life, my all.
                           Isaac Watts.

EXPERIENCE AND LIFE.

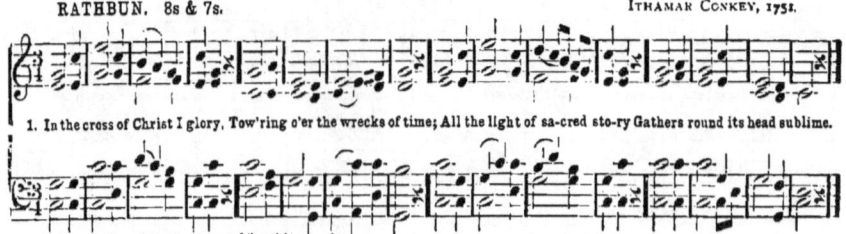

RATHBUN. 8s & 7s.   ITHAMAR CONKEY, 1751.

1. In the cross of Christ I glory, Tow'ring o'er the wrecks of time; All the light of sa-cred sto-ry Gathers round its head sublime.

Used by per. Oliver Ditson Co., owners of Copyright.

588   *In the Cross of Christ I Glory.*

2 When the woes of life o'ertake me,
  Hopes deceive, and fears annoy,
Never shall the cross forsake me;
  Lo, it glows with peace and joy.

3 When the sun of bliss is beaming
  Light and love upon my way,
From the cross the radiance streaming
  Adds more lustre to the day.

4 Bane and blessing, pain and pleasure,
  By the cross are sanctified;
Peace is there, that knows no measure,
  Joys that through all time abide.
Sir John Bowring, 1825.

589   *Before the Cross.*

1 Sweet the moments, rich in blessing,
  Which before the cross I spend,
Life, and health, and peace possessing,
  From the sinner's dying Friend.

2 Truly blessed is this station,
  Low before his cross to lie,
While I see divine compassion
  Beaming in his gracious eye.

3 Love and grief my heart dividing,
  With my tears his feet I'll bathe;
Constant still, in faith abiding,
  Life deriving from his death.

4 May I still enjoy this feeling,
  Still to my Redeemer go,
Prove his wounds each day more healing,
  And himself more truly know.
James Allen, 1757.
Alt. Walter Shirley, 1770.

590   *Work while it is Day.*

1 All around us, fair with flowers,
  Fields of beauty sleeping lie;
All around us clarion voices
  Call to duty stern and high.

2 Following every voice of mercy
  With a trusting, loving heart,
Let us in life's earnest labor
  Still be sure to do our part.

3 Now, to-day, and not to-morrow,—
  Let us work with all our might,
Lest the wretched faint and perish
  In the coming stormy night,—

4 Now, to-day, and not to-morrow,—
  Lest, before to-morrow's sun,
We too, mournfully departing,
  Shall have left our work undone.
Book of Hymns.

591   *The Prayer of Life.*

1 Father, hear the prayer we offer;
  Not for ease that prayer shall be;
But for strength, that we may ever
  Live our lives courageously.

2 Not forever in green pastures
  Do we ask our way to be;
But the steep and rugged pathway
  May we tread rejoicingly.

3 Not forever by still waters
  Would we idly quiet stay;
But would smite the living fountains
  From the rocks along our way.

4 Be our strength in hours of weakness;
  In our wanderings be our guide;
Through endeavor, failure, danger,
  Father, be thou at our side.
Hymns of the Spirit.

THE CROSS.

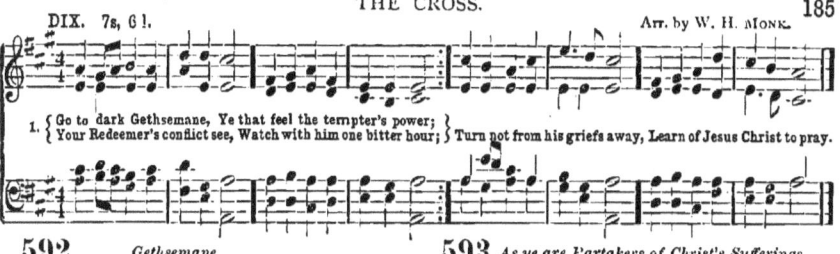

592 *Gethsemane.*

2 Calvary's mournful mountain climb;
    There, adorning at his feet,
  Mark that miracle of time,
    God's own sacrifice complete:
  "It is finished," hear him cry;—
  Learn of Jesus Christ to die.

3 Early hasten to the tomb,
    Where they laid his breathless clay;
  All is solitude and gloom,
    Who hath taken him away?
  Christ is risen;—he meets our eyes;
  Saviour, teach us so to rise!
        James Montgomery.

593 *As ye are Partakers of Christ's Sufferings.*
        [Omit Repeat.]

1 When my love to Christ grows weak,
  When for deeper faith I seek,
  Then in thought I go to thee,
  Garden of Gethsemane.

2 There behold his agony,
  Suffered on the bitter tree;
  See his anguish, see his faith;
  Love triumphant still in death.

3 Then to life I turn again,
  Learning all the worth of pain,
  Learning all the might that lies
  In a full self-sacrifice.
        Anon.

594 *Psalm of Life.*

2 Not enjoyment, and not sorrow,
    Is our destined end or way;
  But to act, that each to-morrow
    Finds us farther than to-day.
  Lives of great men all remind us
    We can make our lives sublime,
  And, departing, leave behind us
    Footprints on the sands of time:

3 Footprints, that perhaps another
    Sailing o'er life's solemn main—
  A forlorn and shipwrecked brother,
    Seeing, shall take heart again.
  Let us then be up and doing,
    With a heart for any fate;
  Still achieving, still pursuing,
    Learn to labor—and to wait.
        Longfellow.

EXPERIENCE AND LIFE.

AMES. L. M.   Dr L. Mason.

1. Stand up, my soul, shake off thy fears, And gird the gospel armor on; March to the gates of endless joy, Where Jesus, thy great Captain's gone.

595 *Captain of our Salvation.*

2 Then let my soul march boldly on,
Press forward to the heavenly gate;
There peace and joy eternal reign,
And glittering robes for conquerors wait.

3 There shall I wear a starry crown,
And triumph in almighty grace;
While all the armies of the skies
Join in my glorious Leader's praise.
                        Isaac Watts, 1709.

596 *Press on!*

1 Press on, press on! ye sons of light,
Untiring in your holy fight,
Still treading each temptation down,
And battling for a brighter crown.

2 Press on, press on! through toil and woe,
With calm resolve, to triumph go;
And make each dark and threatening ill
Yield but a higher glory still.

3 Press on, press on! still look in faith
To him who conquereth sin and death,
Then shall ye hear his word, 'Well done!'
True to the last, press on, press on!
                        William Gaskell.

597 *The Hope of Man.*

1 On, sometimes gleams upon our sight,
Through present wrong, the eternal Right,
And step by step, since time began,
We see the steady gain of man.

2 That all of good the past hath had
Remains to make our own time glad,
Our common, daily life divine,
And every land a Palestine.

3 Through the harsh noises of our day,
A low, sweet prelude finds its way;
Thro' clouds of doubt, and creeds of fear,
A light is breaking calm and clear.

4 Henceforth my heart shall sigh no more
For olden time and holier shore;
God's love and blessing, then and there,
Are now and here and everywhere.
                        J. G. Whittier.

598 *Taking the Shield of Faith.*

1 Awake, my soul, lift up thine eyes;
See where thy foes against thee rise,
In long array, a numerous host;
Awake, my soul, or thou art lost.

2 See where rebellious passions rage,
And fierce desires and lusts engage;
The meanest foe of all the train
Has thousands and ten thousands slain.

3 Thou tread'st upon enchanted ground;
Perils and snares beset thee round;
Beware of all; guard every part;
But most, the traitor in thy heart.

4 Come, then, my soul, now learn to wield
The weight of thine immortal shield;
Put on the armor from above
Of heavenly truth and heavenly love.
                        Anna L. Barbauld.

COURAGE AND ACTION.

1. Jesus, and shall it ever be, A mortal man ashamed of thee? Ashamed of thee, whom angels praise, Whose glories shine through endless days?

599

2 Ashamed of Jesus! that dear Friend,
On whom my hopes of heaven depend!
No! when I blush, be this my shame,
That I no more revere his name.

3 Ashamed of Jesus! yes, I may,
When I've no guilt to wash away;
No tear to wipe, no good to crave,
No fear to quell, no soul to save.

4 Till then, nor is my boasting vain,
Till then I boast a Saviour slain!
And, O, may this my glory be,
That Christ is not ashamed of me!
J. Grigg.

600 *He liveth long who liveth well.*

1 He liveth long who liveth well!
All other life is short and vain;
He liveth longest who can tell
Of living most for heavenly gain.

2 Be what thou seemest; live thy creed;
Hold up to earth the torch divine;
Be what thou prayest to be made;
Let the great Master's steps be thine.

3 Fill up each hour with what will last;
Buy up the moments as they go;
The life above, when this is past,
Is the ripe fruit of life below.

4 Sow love, and taste its fruitage pure;
Sow peace, and reap its harvest bright;
Sow sunbeams on the rock and moor,
And find a harvest-home of light.
Anon.

601 *Let us go forth without the Camp.*

1 Silent, like men in solemn haste,
Girded wayfarers of the waste,
We press along the narrow road
That leads to life, to bliss, to God.

2 We fling aside the weight and sin,
Resolved the victory to win;
We know the peril, but our eyes
Rest on the splendor of the prize.

3 No love of present gain or ease,
No seeking man or self to please;
With the brave heart and steady eye,
We onward march to victory.

4 What tho' with weariness oppressed?
'Tis but a little, and we rest:
Finished the toil,—the race is run!
The battle fought,—the field is won?
Horatius Bonar, 1861.

602 *The Harvest Call.*

1 Abide not in the realm of dreams,
O man, however fair it seems;
But with clear eye the present scan,
And hear the call of God and man.

2 Think not in sleep to fold thy hands,
Forgetful of thy Lord's commands;
From duty's claims no life is free,—
Behold to-day hath need of thee!

3 The present hour allots thy task:
For strength and patience ask,
And trust his love whose sure supplies
Meet all thy needs as they arise.
William H. Burleigh.

EXPERIENCE AND LIFE.

ETHEL. L. M.   L. O. Emerson.

1. Awake our souls, away our fears, Let ev-'ry trembling tho't be gone;
Awake and run the heavenly race, And put a cheer-ful cour-age on.

Used by per. Oliver Ditson Co., owners of Copyright.

603

2 From thee, the overflowing spring,
Our souls shall drink a full supply;
While such as trust their native strength,
Shall melt away, and droop, and die.

3 Swift as an eagle cuts the air,
We'll mount aloft to thine abode;
On wings of love our souls shall fly,
Nor tire amidst the heavenly road.
                      Isaac Watts.

604   "Go work To-day in my Vineyard."

1 Go, labor on; spend and be spent,
Thy joy to do thy Father's will;
It is the way the Master went;
Should not the servant tread it still?

2 Go, labor on; 'tis not for nought;
Thine earthly loss is heavenly gain;
Men heed thee, love thee, praise thee not;
The Master praises,—what are men?

3 Go, labor on; enough while here,
If he shall praise thee; if he deign
Thy willing heart to mark and cheer,
No toil for him shall be in vain.

4 Toil on, and in thy toil rejoice;
For toil, comes rest; for exile, home:
Soon shalt thou hear the Bridegroom's voice,
The midnight peal, Behold, I come!
                      Horatius Bonar.

605   The Christian Soldier.

1 The Christian warrior,—see him stand
In the whole armor of his God!
The Spirit's sword is in his hand,
His feet are with the gospel shod;

2 In panoply of truth complete,
Salvation's helmet on his head,
With righteousness, a breastplate meet,
And faith's broad shield before him spread;

3 With this omnipotence he moves,
From this the alien armies flee;
Till more than conqueror he proves,
Through God who gives him victory.
                      James Montgomery.

606   Why stand ye all the Day idle?

1 The God of glory walks his round,
From day to day, from year to year,
And warns us each with awful sound,
No longer stand ye idle here.

2 O, if the griefs ye would assuage,
That wait on life's declining year;
Secure a blessing for your age,
And work your master's business here!

3 And ye, whose locks of scanty gray
Foretell your latest travail near,
How swiftly fades your worthless day;
And stand ye yet so idle here?

4 O Thou, by all thy works adored,
To whom the sinner's soul is dear,
Recall us to thy vineyard, Lord,
And grant us grace to please thee here.
                      Bishop Reginald Heber.

COURAGE AND ACTION. 189

CHERITH. C. M.   Arr. fr. Ludwig Spohr.

1. O speed thee, Chris-tian, on thy way, And to thine ar-mor cling;
With gird-ed loins the call o-bey Which grace and mer-cy bring.

607   *The Cross before the Crown.*

2 There is a battle to be fought,
    An upward race to run,
A crown of glory to be sought,
    A victory to be won.

3 O, faint not, Christian, for thy sighs
    Are heard before the throne;
The race must come before the prize,
    The cross before the crown.
                    T. B. Onderdonk.

608   *Despise not the Day of small Things.*

1 Scorn not the slightest word or deed,
    Nor deem it void of power;
There's fruit in each wind-wafted seed,
    That waits its natal hour.

2 A whispered word may touch the heart,
    And call it back to life;
A look of love bid sin depart,
    And still unholy strife.

3 No act falls fruitless; none can tell
    How vast its power may be,
Nor what results unfolded dwell
    Within it silently.

4 Work on, despair not; bring thy mite,
    Nor care how small it be;
God is with all that serve the right,
    The holy, true, and free.
                    Anon.

609   *Working with God.*

1 Workman of God, oh, lose not heart,
    But learn what God is like!
And, in the darkest battle-field,
    Thou shalt know where to strike.

2 Oh, blest is he to whom is given
    The instinct that can tell
That God is on the field, when he
    Is most invisible!

3 And best is he who can divine
    Where real right doth lie,
And dares to take the side that seems
    Wrong to man's blindfold eye.

4 For right is right, since God is God,
    And right the day must win;
To doubt it is disloyalty;
    To falter is to sin.
                    Frederick W. Faber, 1849

610   *As the Hart panteth after the Water-brooks.*

1 As pants the hart for cooling streams,
    When heated in the chase,
So longs my soul, O God, for thee,
    And thy refreshing grace.

2 For thee, my God, the living God,
    My thirsty soul doth pine;
O, when shall I behold thy face,
    Thou Majesty divine?

3 Why restless, why cast down, my soul?
    Trust God, and he'll employ
His aid for thee, and change these sighs
    To thankful hymns of joy.

4 Why restless, why cast down, my soul?
    Hope still, and thou shalt sing
The praise of Him who is thy God,
    Thy health's eternal Spring.
                    H. F. Lyte.

EXPERIENCE AND LIFE.

LABAN. S. M.   Lowell Mason, 1830.

1. My soul, be on thy guard: Ten thousand foes a-rise; The hosts of sin are press-ing hard To draw thee from the skies.

611 *Watch and Pray.*

2 Oh, watch and fight and pray!
   The battle ne'er give o'er;
Renew it boldly every day,
   And help divine implore.

3 Ne'er think the victory won,
   Nor once at ease sit down;
Thy arduous work will not be done
   Till thou obtain thy crown.

4 Fight on, my soul, till death
   Shall bring thee to thy God:
He'll take thee, at thy parting breath,
   Up to his blest abode.
                     George Heath, 1781.

612 *Not as one that beateth the air.*

1 My soul, weigh not thy life
   Against thy heavenly crown,
Nor suffer Satan's deadliest strife
   To beat thy courage down.

2 With prayer and crying strong,
   Hold on the fearful fight;
And let the breaking day prolong
   The wrestling of the night.

3 The battle soon will yield,
   If thou thy part fulfil;
For, strong as is the hostile shield,
   Thy sword is stronger still.

4 Thine armor is divine,
   Thy feet with victory shod,
And on thy head shall quickly shine
   The diadem of God.
                           L. Swain.

613 *Put on the whole Armor of God.*

1 Soldiers of Christ, arise,
   And put your armor on,
Strong in the strength which God supplies
   Through his beloved Son.

2 Strong in the Lord of Hosts,
   And in his mighty power,
Who in the strength of Jesus trusts,
   Is more than conqueror.

3 Stand then in his great might,
   With all his strength endued;
But take, to arm you for the fight,
   The panoply of God;—

4 That, having all things done,
   And all your conflicts past,
Ye may o'ercome, through Christ alone,
   And stand entire at last.
                     Charles Wesley, 1745.

614 *Endure Hardness, as a good Soldier.*

1 Arise, ye saints, arise;
   The Lord our Leader is;
The foe before his banner flies,
   For victory is his.

2 Lead on, almighty Lord,
   Lead on to victory;
Encouraged by the bright reward,
   With joy we'll follow thee.

3 We hope to see the day
   When all our toils shall cease;
When we shall cast our arms away,
   And dwell in endless peace.

4 This hope supports us here;
   It makes our burdens light;
'Twill serve our drooping hearts to cheer
   Till faith shall end in sight;—

5 Till, of the prize possessed,
   We hear of war no more,
And —O sweet thought!—forever rest
   On yonder peaceful shore.
                             T. Kelly.

COURAGE AND ACTION. 191

GOTTSCHALK. 7s.   Arr. by E. P. Parker.

1. Sleep not, soldier of the cross; Foes are lurking all a-round; Look not here to find re-pose, This is but thy battle ground.

Used by per. Oliver Ditson Co., owners of Copyright

615   *Let us not Sleep.*

2 Up, and take thy shield and sword;
Up, it is the call of Heaven;
Shrink not, faithless, from thy Lord;
Nobly strive as he hath striven.

3 Break through all the force of ill,
Tread the might of passion down,
Struggle onward, upward still,
To the conquering Saviour's crown.

4 Through the midst of toil and pain,
Let this thought ne'er leave thy breast:
Every triumph thou dost gain
Makes more sweet thy coming rest.
William Gaskell.

616   *The Christian Warfare.*

1 BRETHREN, while we sojourn here,
Fight we must, but should not fear;
Foes we have, but we've a friend,
One who loves us to the end;

2 Forward then with courage go,
Long we shall not dwell below;
Soon the joyful news will come,
Child, your Father calls—come home.

3 In the world a thousand snares
Lay to take us unawares;
Satan with malicious art,
Watches each unguarded heart;

4 But from Satan's malice free,
Saints shall soon victorious be;
Soon the joyful news will come,
Child, your Father calls—come home.
J. Swain.

617   *Heavenly Journey.*

1 CHILDREN of the heavenly King,
As ye journey, sweetly sing;
Sing your Saviour's worthy praise,
Glorious in his works and ways.

2 We are travelling home to God,
In the way the fathers trod;
They are happy now, and we
Soon their happiness shall see.

3 Shout, ye little flock, and blest;
You on Jesus' throne shall rest;
There your seat is now prepared,
There your kingdom and reward.

4 Lift your eyes, ye sons of light;
Zion's city is in sight;
There our endless home shall be,
There our Lord we soon shall see.

5 Lord, obediently we go,
Gladly leaving all below;
Only thou our leader be,
And we still will follow thee!
John Cennick, 1742.

618   *That they go forward.*

1 OFT in sorrow, oft in woe,
Onward, Christian, onward go;
Fight the fight, maintain the strife,
Strengthened with the bread of life.

2 Onward, Christian, onward go;
Join the war, and face the foe:
Will you flee in danger's hour?
Know you not your Captain's power?

3 Let your drooping hearts be glad;
March, in heavenly armor clad;
Fight, nor think the battle long;
Soon shall victory tune your song.

4 Onward, then, to battle move;
More than conqueror you shall prove;
Though opposed by many a foe,
Christian soldier, onward go.
Anon.

EXPERIENCE AND LIFE.

WORK SONG. 7s & 6s.   Lowell Mason.

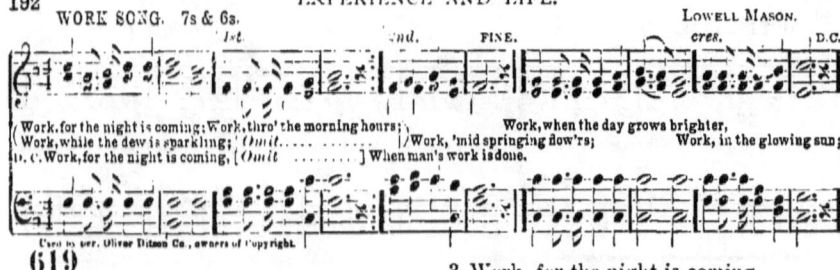

Work, for the night is coming; Work, thro' the morning hours; Work, when the day grows brighter,
Work, while the dew is sparkling; [*Omit*........]/Work, 'mid springing flow'rs; Work, in the glowing sun;
D. C. Work, for the night is coming, [*Omit*........] When man's work is done.

619

2 Work, for the night is coming,
  Work, in the sunny noon;
  Fill brightest hours with labor,
  Rest comes sure and soon.
  Give every flying minute
  Something to keep in store:
  Work, for the night is coming,
  When man works no more.

3 Work, for the night is coming,
  Under the sunset skies;
  While their bright tints are glowing,
  Work, for the daylight flies.
  Work till the last beam fadeth,
  Fadeth to shine no more;
  Work while the night is dark'ning,
  When man's work is o'er.
  A. L. Walker.

WIMBORNE. 8s & 7s.   Arr. fr. Whitaker.

1. Like the ea-gle, up-ward, on-ward, Let my soul in faith be borne;
   Calm-ly gaz-ing sky-ward, sun-ward, Let my eye un-shrink-ing turn.

620   *Upward, Onward.*

2 Where the cross, God's love revealing,
  Sets the fettered spirit free,
  Where it sheds its wondrous healing,
  There, my soul, thy rest shall be.

3 O, may I no longer, dreaming,
  Idly waste my golden day,
  But, each precious hour redeeming,
  Upward, onward, press my way!
  H. Bonar.

2 Listen, Christian; their hosanna
  Rolleth o'er thee; "God is love."
  Write upon thy red-cross banner,
  "Upward ever; heaven's above."

3 Be this world the wiser, stronger,
  For thy life of pain and peace,
  While it needs thee; oh! no longer
  Pray thou for thy quick release.

621   *Onward.*

1 Onward, Christian, though the region
  Where thou art be drear and lone;
  God has set a guardian legion
  Very near thee; press thou on.

4 Pray thou, Christian, daily rather,
  That thou be a faithful son;
  By the prayer of Jesus, "Father,
  Not my will, but thine, be done."
  Samuel Johnson, 1847.

COURAGE AND ACTION.

622

2 Like a mighty army,
  Moves the Church of God;
  Brothers, we are treading
  Where the saints have trod;
  We are not divided,
  All one body we,
  One in hope and doctrine,
  One in charity.—Cho.

3 Crowns and thrones may perish,
  Kingdoms rise and wane,
  But the Church of Jesus
  Constant will remain;
  Gates of hell can never
  'Gainst that Church prevail;
  We have Christ's own promise,
  And that cannot fail.—Cho.

4 Onward, then, ye people,
  Join our happy throng;
  Blend with ours your voices
  In the triumph-song;
  Glory, laud, and honor,
  Unto Christ the King;
  This, thro' countless ages,
  Men and angels sing.—Cho.

S. Baring-Gould.

623 *Success from God.*

1 VAINLY through night's weary hours,
  Keep we watch, lest foes alarm;—
  Vain our bulwarks, and our towers,
  But for God's protecting arm.

2 Vain were all our toil and labor,
  Did not God that labor bless;
  Vain, without his grace and favor,
  Every talent we possess.

3 Vainer still the hope of heaven,
  That on human strength relies;
  But to him shall help be given,
  Who in humble faith applies.

4 Seek we, then, the Lord's Anointed;
  He shall grant us peace and rest:
  Ne'er was suppliant disappointed,
  Who to Christ his prayer addressed.

Auber.

EXPERIENCE AND LIFE.

BELMONT. C. M.   Samuel Webbe.

1. I'm not ashamed to own my Lord, Or to defend his cause,
Maintain the honor of his word, The glory of his cross.

624 *Not ashamed of the Gospel.*

2 Jesus, my Lord, I know his name;
His name is all my trust;
Nor will he put my soul to shame,
Nor let my hope be lost.

3 Firm as his throne his promise stands,
And he can well secure
What I've committed to his hands,
Till the decisive hour

4 How long, dear Saviour, O, how long
Shall this bright hour delay?
Fly swiftly round, ye wheels of time,
And bring the welcome day.
Isaac Watts, 1709.

625

1 AWAKE, my soul, stretch every nerve,
And press with vigor on;
A heavenly race demands thy zeal,
And an immortal crown.

2 A cloud of witnesses around
Hold thee in full survey;
Forget the steps already trod,
And onward urge thy way.

3 'Tis God's all-animating voice
That calls thee from on high;
'Tis his own hand presents the prize
To thine aspiring eye;

4 That prize, with peerless glories bright,
Which shall new lustre boast,
When victors' wreaths and monarchs' gems
Shall blend in common dust.
Philip Doddridge, 1755.

626 *The Christian Soldier.*

1 AM I a soldier of the cross,
A follower of the Lamb?
And shall I fear to own his cause,
Or blush to speak his name?

2 Must I be carried to the skies,
On flow'ry beds of ease,
While others fought to win the prize,
And sailed through bloody seas?

3 Sure I must fight if I would reign;
Increase my courage, Lord!
I'll bear the toil, endure the pain,
Supported by thy word.

4 When that illustrious day shall rise,
And all thy armies shine
In robes of vict'ry through the skies,
The glory shall be thine.
Isaac Watts, 1733.

627 *He, being dead, yet speaketh.*

1 RISE, O my soul, pursue the path
By ancient worthies trod;
Aspiring, view those worthy men
Who lived and walked with God.

2 'Twas thro' the Lamb's most precious blood
They conquered every foe,
And to his power and matchless grace
Their crown of life they owe.

3 Lord, may I ever keep in view
The patterns thou hast given,
And ne'er forsake the blessed road
That led them safe to heaven.
Needham.

COURAGE AND ACTION. 195

1. Go forward, Christian sol-dier, Be-neath his banner true;
   The Lord himself, thy Leader, Shall all thy foes sub-due,
   His love foretells thy tri-als,
   He knows thine hourly need; He can, with bread of heaven, Thy faint-ing spir-it feed.

628 *Go forward, Christian Soldier.*

2 Go forward, Christian soldier,
  Nor dream of peaceful rest,
Till Satan's host is vanquished
  And heaven is all possest;
Till God himself shall call thee
  To lay thine armor by,
And wear, in endless glory,
  The crown of victory.

3 Go forward, Christian soldier,
  Fear not the gathering night:
The Lord hath been thy shelter,
  The Lord will be thy light.
When morn his face revealeth,
  Thy dangers all are past;
Oh, pray that faith and virtue
  May keep thee to the last!
  Laurence Tuttiott, 1854.

629 *Having done all, to stand.*

1 STAND up, stand up for Jesus,
  Ye soldiers of the cross;
Lift high his royal banner;
  It must not suffer loss;
From victory unto victory
  His army shall he lead,
Till every foe is vanquished,
  And Christ is Lord indeed.

2 Stand up, stand up for Jesus;
  The strife will not be long;
This day, the noise of battle:
  The next, the victor's song:

To him that overcometh
  A crown of life shall be;
He with the King of Glory
  Shall reign eternally.
  Duffield.

630 *Captain of our Salvation.*

1 OH, when shall I see Jesus,
  And reign with him above;
And from that flowing fountain
  Drink everlasting love?
When shall I be delivered
  From this vain world of sin,
And with my blessed Jesus
  Drink endless pleasures in?

2 But now I am a soldier,
  My Captain's gone before;
He's given me my orders,
  And bid me not give o'er.
If I continue faithful,
  A righteous crown he'll give,
And all his valiant soldiers
  Eternal life shall have.

3 Thro' grace I am determined
  To conquer though I die,
And then away to Jesus
  On wings of love I'll fly.
Farewell to sin and sorrow,
  I bid you all adieu;
And oh, my friends, prove faithful,
  And on your way pursue.
  Anon.

EXPERIENCE AND LIFE.

DENNIS. C. M.   Arr. fr. H. G. NAGELI.

1. Sow in the morn thy seed; At eve hold not thy hand; To doubt and fear give thou no heed; Broad-cast it o'er the land.

631 *In the Morning sow thy Seed.*

2 Beside all waters sow;
  The highway furrows stock;
Drop it where thorns and thistles grow;
  Drop it upon the rock.

3 Thou canst not toil in vain;
  Cold, heat, and moist, and dry,
Shall foster and mature the grain
  For garners in the sky.

4 Then, when the glorious end,
  The day of God, shall come,
The angel-reapers shall descend,
  And shout the harvest home.
James Montgomery, 1825.

BONAR. S. M. D.   J. P. HOLBROOK.

1. I was a wandering sheep, I did not love the fold: I did not love my Shepherd's voice, I would not be controlled;
I was a wayward child, I did not love my home, I did not love my Shepherd's voice, I loved a-far to roam.

632

2 The Shepherd sought his sheep,
  The Father sought his child;
He followed me o'er vale and hill,
  O'er deserts waste and wild;
He found me nigh to death,
  Famished, and faint, and lone;
He bound me with the bands of love;
  He saved the wandering one.

3 Jesus my Shepherd is,
  'Twas he that loved my soul.
'Twas he that washed me in his blood,
  'Twas he that made me whole:
'Twas he that sought the lost,
  That found the wandering sheep,
'Twas he that brought me to the fold—
  'Twas he that still doth keep.

4 No more a wandering sheep,
  I love to be controlled,
I love my tender Shepherd's voice,
  I love the peaceful fold:
No more a wayward child,
  I seek no more to roam,
I love my heavenly Father's voice—
  I love, I love his home.
Bonar.

TEMPTATION AND DIVINE STRENGTH.

AUTUMN. 6s & 7s, D.

1. Gen-tly, Lord! oh, gen-tly lead us, Through this lone-ly vale of tears;
Through the chang-es thou'st de-creed us, Till our last great change ap-pears:
D.S.— Let thy good-ness nev-er fail us, Lead us in thy per-fect way.
When temp-ta-tion's darts as-sail us, When in de-vious paths we stray,

633

2 In the hour of pain and anguish,
  In the hour when death draws near,
Suffer not our hearts to languish,—
  Suffer not our souls to fear;
And, when mortal life is ended
  Bid us on thy bosom rest,
Till, by angel-bands attended,
  We awake among the blest.
            T. Hastings.

634 *The End of Trials.*

1 KNOW, my soul, thy full salvation;
  Rise o'er sin and fear and care;
Joy to find, in every station,
  Something still to do or bear.
Think what spirit dwells within thee;
  Think what Father's smiles are thine;
Think what Jesus did to win thee,
  Child of heaven, canst thou repine?

2 Haste thee on from grace to glory,
  Arm'd with faith and wing'd with prayer;
Heaven's eternal day's before thee,
  God's own hand shall guide thee there.

Soon shall close thine earthly mission,
  Soon shall pass thy pilgrim-days;
Hope shall change to glad fruition,
  Faith to sight, and prayer to praise.
            Henry F. Lyte, 1833.

635 *Strength in Temptation.*

1 HOLY Father, thou hast taught me
  I should live to thee alone;
Year by year, thy hand hath brought me
  On through dangers oft unknown.
When I wandered, thou hast found me;
  When I doubted, sent me light;
Still thine arm has been around me,
  And my paths were in thy sight.

2 I would trust in thy protecting,
  Wholly rest upon thine arm,
Follow wholly thy directing,
  Thou mine only guard from harm:
Keep me from mine own undoing,
  Help me turn to thee when tried;
Still my footsteps, Father, viewing,
  Keep me ever at thy side.
            Neale.

EXPERIENCE AND LIFE.

GEER. C. M.   GREATOREX COLLECTION.

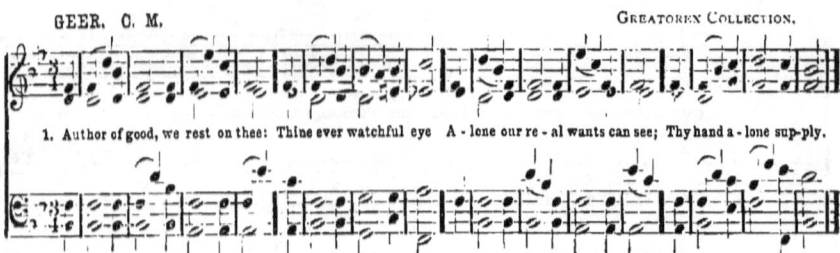

1. Author of good, we rest on thee: Thine ever watchful eye A-lone our re-al wants can see; Thy hand a-lone sup-ply.

636   *"He knoweth what ye have need of."*

2 In thine all-gracious providence
Our cheerful hopes confide:
Oh, let thy power be our defense,
Thy love our footsteps guide!

3 And since, by passion's force subdued,
Too oft, with stubborn will,
We blindly shun the latent good,
And grasp the specious ill,—

4 Not what we wish, but what we want;
Let mercy still supply:
The good unasked, O Father, grant;
The ill, though asked, deny.
James Merrick.

637   *Mine Arm also shall strengthen him.*

1 WE praise and bless thee, gracious Lord,
Our Saviour kind and true,
For all the old things passed away,
For all thou hast made new.

2 But yet how much must be destroyed,
How much renewed must be,
Ere we can fully stand complete
In likeness, Lord, to thee!

3 So shall we faultless stand at last
Before thy Father's throne;
The blessedness forever ours,
The glory all thine own.
Anon.

638   *Have Mercy on me.*

1 O THOU whose tender mercy hears
Contrition's humble sigh,
Whose hand indulgent wipes the tears
From sorrow's weeping eye,—

2 See, Lord, before thy throne of grace,
A wretched wanderer mourn;
Hast thou not bid me seek thy face?
Hast thou not said, Return?

3 Absent from thee, my Guide, my Light,
Without one cheering ray,
Through dangers, fears, and gloomy night,
How desolate my way!

4 O, shine on this benighted heart,
With beams of mercy shine;
And let thy healing voice impart
A taste of joy divine.
Anne Steele.

639   *Inconstancy lamented.*

1 LONG have I sat beneath the sound
Of thy salvation, Lord;
Yet still how weak my faith is found,
And knowledge of thy word!

2 Great God, thy sovereign power impart
To give thy word success;
Write thy salvation in my heart,
And make me learn thy grace.

3 Show my forgetful feet the way
That leads to joys on high,
Where knowledge grows without decay,
And love shall never die.
Isaac Watts.

640   *Man's Need of God's Help.*

1 WEAK and irresolute is man:
The purpose of to-day,
Woven with pains into his plan,
To-morrow rends away.

2 Bound on a voyage of fearful length,
Through dangers little known,
A stranger to superior strength,
Man vainly trusts his own.

3 But oars alone can ne'er prevail
To reach the distant coast:
The breath of heaven must swell the sail,
Or all the toil is lost.
William Cowper.

TEMPTATION AND DIVINE STRENGTH. 199

ABIDE WITH ME. 10s.   W. H. MONK.

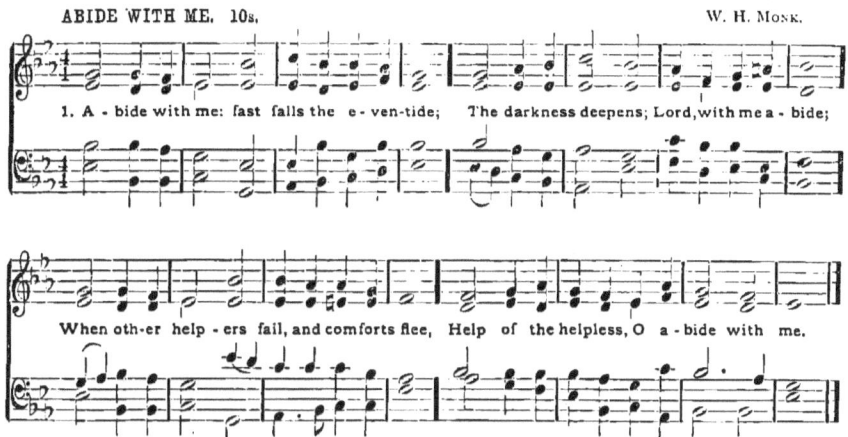

1. A-bide with me: fast falls the e-ven-tide; The darkness deepens; Lord, with me a-bide; When oth-er help-ers fail, and comforts flee, Help of the helpless, O a-bide with me.

641

2 Swift to its close, ebbs out life's little day;
Earth's joys grow dim, its glories pass away:
Change and decay in all around I see;
O thou, who changest not, abide with me.

3 I need thy presence every passing hour;
What but thy grace can foil the tempter's power?
Who like thyself my guide and stay can be?
Thro' cloud and sunshine, Lord, abide with me.

4 I fear no foe, with thee at hand to bless:
Ills have no weight, and tears no bitterness,
Where is death's sting? where, grave, thy victory?
I triumph still, if thou abide with me.

5 Hold thou thy Cross before my closing eyes;
Shine through the gloom, and point me to the skies;
Heaven's morning breaks, and earth's vain shadows flee;
In life, in death, O Lord, abide with me.
Henry F. Lyte.

ZION. 8s, 7s & 4s.   THOMAS HASTINGS, 1830.

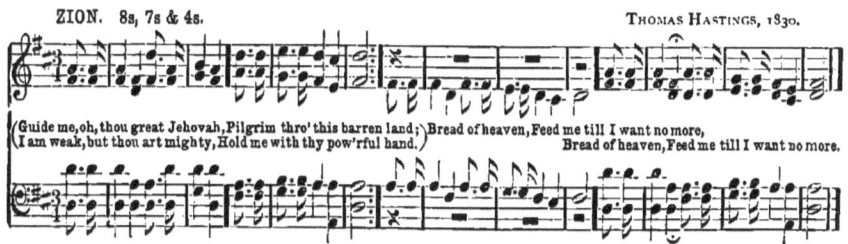

(Guide me, oh, thou great Jehovah, Pilgrim thro' this barren land;) Bread of heaven, Feed me till I want no more,
(I am weak, but thou art mighty, Hold me with thy pow'rful hand.) Bread of heaven, Feed me till I want no more.

642   *The Pilgrim's Prayer.*

2 Open now the crystal fountain,
  Whence the healing waters flow:
Let the fiery cloudy pillar
  Lead me all my journey through.
    Strong Deliverer!
Be thou still my strength and shield.

3 When I tread the verge of Jordan,
  Bid my anxious fears subside:
Cleave the flood, and stay the waters,
  Land me safe on Canaan's side.
    Songs of praises
I will ever give to thee.
William Williams, 1773.

EXPERIENCE AND LIFE.

HURSLEY. L. M — German.

1. To thine eternal arms, O God,
Take us, thine erring children, in;
From dangerous paths too boldly trod,
From wandering tho'ts and dreams of sin.

643 *I will go unto my Father.*

2 Those arms were round our childish ways,
A guard through helpless years to be;
Oh, leave not our maturer days.
We still are helpless without thee!

3 We trusted hope and pride and strength:
Our strength proved false, our pride was vain,
Our dreams have faded all at length,—
We come to thee, O Lord, again!

4 A guide to trembling steps yet be,
Give us of thine eternal powers!
So shall our paths all lead to thee,
And life smile on like childhood's hours.

T. W. Higginson, 1847.

644 *Imploring the Divine Presence.*

1 When Israel, of the Lord beloved,
Out from the land of bondage came,
Her fathers' God before her moved,
An awful guide, in smoke and flame.

2 By day, along the astonished lands;
The cloudy pillar glided slow;
By night, Arabia's crimsoned sands
Returned the fiery column's glow.

3 Thus present still, though now unseen,
When brightly shines the prosperous day,
Be thoughts of thee a cloudy screen,
To temper the deceitful ray.

4 And oh! when gathers on our path,
In shade and storm, the frequent night,
Be thou, long-suffering, slow to wrath,
A burning and a shining light.

Sir Walter Scott, 1820.

645 *Where is the Blessedness ye spake of?*

1 O, where is now that glowing love
That marked our union with the Lord?
Our hearts were fixed on things above,
Nor could the world a joy afford.

2 Where is the zeal that led us then
To make our Saviour's glory known?
That freed us from the fear of men,
And kept our eye on him alone?

3 Where are the happy seasons spent
In fellowship with him we loved?
The sacred joy, the sweet content,
The blessedness that then we proved?

4 Behold, again we turn to thee;
O, cast us not away, though vile;
No peace we have, no joy we see,
O Lord, our God, but in thy smile.

Thomas Kelly, 1806.

646 *He knoweth how to deliver the Godly.*

1 My God, my hope, my Father thou;
To thee, lo, now my soul I bow;
Be thou my strength, be thou my way;
Protect me through my life's short day.

2 In fierce temptation's darkest hour,
Save me from sin and Satan's power;
Tear every idol from thy throne,
And reign, my Father, reign alone.

3 My suffering time shall soon be o'er;
Then shall I sigh and weep no more;
My ransomed soul shall soar away,
To sing thy praise in endless day.

Anon.

AFFLICTION AND COMFORT.

COME, YE DISCONSOLATE. 11s & 10s. Samuel Webbe, 1800.

1. Come, ye dis-con-so-late, wher-e'er ye lan-guish; Come to the mer-cy-seat, fer-vent-ly kneel;
Here bring your wounded hearts, here tell your an-guish, Earth has no sor-row that heav'n can not heal.

647

2 Joy of the desolate, light of the straying,
Hope of the penitent, fadeless and pure,
Here speaks the Comforter, tenderly saying,
Earth has no sorrow that heaven can not cure.

3 Here see the bread of life; see waters flowing
Forth from the throne of God, pure from above;
Come to the feast of love; come, ever-knowing
Earth has no sorrow but heaven can remove.
Thomas Moore.

YARMOUTH 7s & 6s. Dr. L. Mason.

1. In heavenly love abiding,   And safe is such confiding,   The storm may roar without me,
No change my heart shall fear,   For nothing changes here:
My heart may low be laid, But God is round about me, But God is round about me, But God is round about me, And can I be dismay'd?

648

2 Wherever he may guide me,
No want shall turn me back;
My Shepherd is beside me,
And nothing can I lack:
His wisdom ever waketh,
His sight is never dim:
He knows the way he taketh,
And I will walk with him.

3 Green pastures are before me,
Which yet I have not seen;
Bright skies will soon be o'er me,
Where darkest clouds have been:
My hope I cannot measure;
My path to life is free;
My Saviour has my treasure,
And he will walk with me.
Anna L. Waring.

EXPERIENCE AND LIFE.

JEWETT. 6s.   Arr. fr. WEBER.

1. My Jesus, as thou wilt! Oh! may thy will be mine; In-to thy hand of love I would my all re-sign; Thro' sor-row or thro' joy, Con-duct me as thine own, And help me still to say, My Lord, thy will be done!

649

2 My Jesus, as thou wilt!
  Though seen through many a tear,
Let not my star of hope
  Grow dim or disappear;
Since thou on earth hast wept,
  And sorrowed oft alone,
If I must weep with thee,
  My Lord, thy will be done!

3 My Jesus as thou wilt!
  All shall be well for me;
Each changing future scene
  I gladly trust with thee.
Straight to my home above
  I travel calmly on,
And sing, in life or death,
  My Lord, thy will be done!
Jane Borthwick.

650

1 Thy way, not mine, O Lord,
  However dark it be!
Lead me by thy own hand,
  Choose out the path for me.

I dare not choose my lot:
  I would not if I might;
Choose thou for me, my God,
  So shall I walk aright.

2 The kingdom that I seek
  Is thine; so let the way
That leads to it be truly thine,
  Else I must surely stray.
Take thou my cup, and it
  With joy or sorrow fill,
As best to thee may seem;
  Choose thou my good and ill.

3 Choose thou for me my friends,
  My sickness or my health;
Choose thou my cares for me,
  My poverty or wealth.
Not mine, not mine the choice,
  In things or great or small;
Be thou my Guide, my Strength,
  My Wisdom and my All.
Horatius Bonar.

AFFLICTION AND COMFORT.

NAOMI. C. M.   H. G. NÄGELI, 1832. Arr. by Dr. MASON, 1836.

1. O teach me, Father, to submit, And bow to thy behest;
The rod is heavy, but the stroke Will fit me for my rest.

651 *Submission.*

2 At times he cometh in the dark,
Upon the stormy wave;
Welcome the storm that brings my Lord;
He cometh but to save.

3 At times on Tabor's height I stand;
His form is clothed in light;
The cloud of glory circles me,
And puts my fears to flight.

4 Then teach me, Father, to submit,
Whate'er my portion be;
Thy service make my chief delight,
And bind my heart to thee.
   N. Day.

652 *Affliction worketh Glory.*

1 IN trouble and in grief, O God,
Thy smile hath cheered my way;
And joy hath budded from each thorn
That round my footsteps lay.

2 The hours of pain have yielded good
Which prosperous days refused;
As herbs, though scentless when entire,
Spread fragrance when they're bruised.

3 The oak strikes deeper as its boughs
By furious blasts are driven;
So life's tempestuous storms the more
Have fixed my heart in heaven.

4 All-gracious Lord, whate'er my lot
In other times may be,
I'll welcome still the heaviest grief
That brings me near to thee.
   Anon.

653 *Himself hath suffered.*

1 CHRIST leads me through no darker rooms
Than he went through before;
No one into his kingdom comes
But through his opened door.

2 Come, Lord, when grace hath made me meet
Thy blessed face to see;
For, if thy work on earth be sweet,
What must thy glory be?

3 Then I shall end my sad complaints;
And weary, sinful days;
And join with those triumphant saints
That sing Jehovah's praise.

4 My knowledge of that life is small,
The eye of faith is dim;
But 'tis enough that Christ knows all,
And I shall be with him.
   Richard Baxter, 1681.

654 *My Times are in Thy Hand.*

1 MY times of sorrow and of joy,
Great God, are in thy hand;
My choicest comforts come from thee,
And go at thy command.

2 If thou shouldst take them all away,
Yet would I not repine;
Before they were possessed by me,
They were entirely thine.

3 Nor would I drop a murmuring word
Though all the world were gone,
But seek enduring happiness
In thee, and thee alone.
   Benjamin Beddome.

EXPERIENCE AND LIFE.

NAPLES. L. M.   L. V. WHEELER.

Be still, my heart:—these anxious cares To thee are burdens, thorns, and snares;
They cast dishonor on thy Lord, And contradict his gracious word.

655   *My Grace is sufficient for Thee.*

2 Brought safely by his hand thus far,
Why wilt thou now give place to fear?
How canst thou want if he provide,
Or lose thy way with such a Guide?

3 Did ever trouble yet befall,
And he refuse to hear thy call?
And has he not his promise passed,
That thou shalt overcome at last?

4 He who has helped me hitherto
Will help me all my journey through,
And give me daily cause to raise
New trophies to his endless praise.
                       John Newton.

656   *Light beyond the Cloud.*

1 Thy will be done: I will not fear
The fate provided by thy love;
Tho' clouds and darkness shroud me here,
I know that all is bright above.

2 Father, forgive the heart that clings,
Thus trembling, to the things of time;
And bid my soul, on angel wings,
Ascend into a purer clime.

3 E'en now, above, there's radiant day,
While clouds and darkness brood below;
Then, Father, joyful on my way
To drink the bitter cup I go.
                       Jane Roscoe.

657   *Resignation.*

1 My God, I thank thee; may no thought
E'er deem thy chastisement severe;
But may this heart, by sorrow taught,
Calm each wild wish, each idle fear.

2 Thy mercy bids all nature bloom;
The sun shines bright, and man is gay;
Thine equal mercy spreads the gloom
That darkens o'er his little day.

3 Full many a throb of grief and pain
Thy frail and erring child must know;
But not one prayer is breathed in vain,
Nor does one tear unheeded flow.

4 Thy various messengers employ;
Thy purposes of love fulfil;
And 'mid the wreck of human joy,
Let kneeling faith adore thy will.
                      Andrews Norton.

658

1 I cannot always trace the way
Where thou, Almighty One, dost move:
But I can always, always say,
That God is love, that God is love.

2 When fear her chilling mantle throws
O'er earth, my soul to heaven above,
As to her native home, upsprings,
For God is love, for God is love.

3 When mystery clouds my darkened path,
I'll check my dread, my doubts reprove,
In this my soul sweet comfort hath,
That God is love, that God is love.

4 Yes, God is love;—a thought like this
Can every gloomy thought remove,
And turn all tears, all woes, to bliss,
For God is love, for God is love.
                             Anon.

AFFLICTION AND COMFORT.

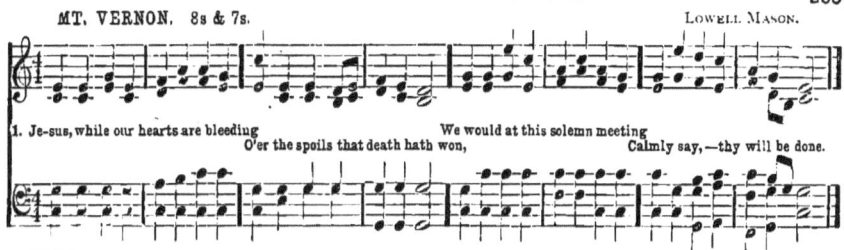

MT. VERNON. 8s & 7s.   LOWELL MASON.

1. Je-sus, while our hearts are bleeding O'er the spoils that death hath won, We would at this solemn meeting Calmly say,—thy will be done.

659 *Thy Will be Done.*

2 Though cast down, we're not forsaken;
Though afflicted, not alone;
Thou didst give, and thou hast taken;
Blessed Lord,—thy will be done.

3 Tho' to-day we're filled with mourning,
Mercy still is on the throne;
With thy smiles of love returning,
We can sing—thy will be done.

4 By thy hands the boon was given,
Thou hast taken but thine own:
Lord of earth, and God of heaven,
Evermore,—thy will be done.

T. Hastings

HOLLEY. 7s.   GEO. HEWS.

1. Oh, how safe, how hap-py he, Lord of hosts, who dwells with thee! Shel-tered 'neath al-might-y wings, Guard-ed by the King of kings!

660 *Rest in God.*

2 How to him should evil come
Who has found in thee a home?
In the refuge of thy breast,
Give me, Lord, eternal rest!

3 Hark! the voice of love divine:
"Fear not, trembler,—thou art mine!
Fear not! I am at thy side,
Strong to suffer, sure to guide.

4 "Call on me in want and woe:
I will keep thee here below;
And, thy day of conflict past,
Bear thee to myself at last."

Henry F. Lyte, 1834.

661 *It is God that worketh with You.*

1 HUMAN soul, to whom is given
Holy hungerings after heaven,
Faithful to the end endure,
Make thy heavenly calling sure.

2 God, to keep thee safe from harms,
Spreads his everlasting arms,
Feeds with secret strength divine,
Waits to whisper "Thou art mine."

3 Gently will he tend the weak;
Bruiséd reeds he ne'er will break;
He will bless thee with his peace,
Fill with all his righteousness.

Wesley's Hymns.

EXPERIENCE AND LIFE.

TULLY. 7s & 6s. — Dr. L. Mason.

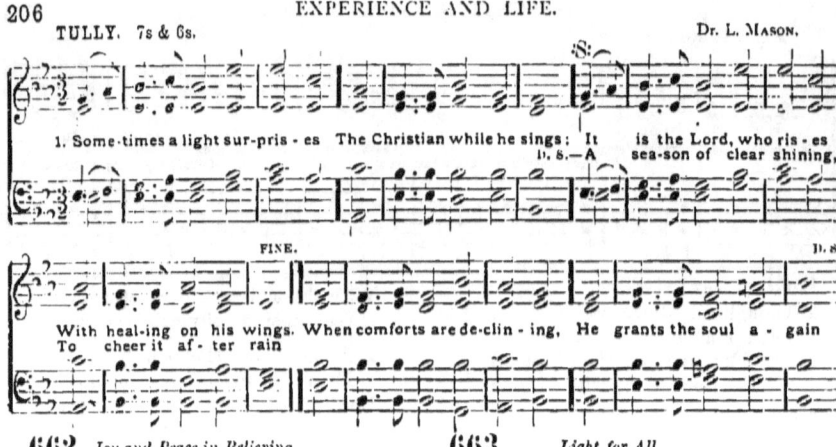

1. Some-times a light sur-pris-es The Christian while he sings; It is the Lord, who ris-es
D. S.—A sea-son of clear shining,
With heal-ing on his wings. When comforts are de-clin-ing, He grants the soul a - gain
To cheer it af-ter rain

662 *Joy and Peace in Believing.*

2 In holy contemplation,
We sweetly then pursue
The theme of God's salvation,
And find it ever new:
Set free from present sorrow,
We cheerfully can say,
"Let the unknown to-morrow
Bring with it what it may!

3 "It can bring with it nothing
But he will bear us through;
Who gives the lilies clothing
Will clothe his people too;
And God the same abiding,
His praise shall tune my voice:
For while in him confiding,
I cannot but rejoice."
    William Cowper, 1776.

663 *Light for All.*

1 The light pours down from heaven,
And enters where it may;
The eyes of all earth's children
Are cheered with one bright day.
So let the mind's true sunshine
Be spread o'er earth as free,
And fill men's waiting spirits,
As waters fill the sea.

2 Then let each human spirit
Enjoy the vision bright;
The truth which comes from heaven
Shall spread like heaven's own light;
Till earth becomes God's temple,
And every human heart
Shall join in one great service,
Each happy in his part.
    Anon.

FERGUSON. S. M. — Geo. Kingsley.

1. Be-hold, what wondrous grace The Father has bestowed On sinners of a mor-tal race, To call them sons of God.

661 *Behold, what Manner of Love.*

2 Nor doth it yet appear
How great we must be made;
But when we see our Saviour here,
We shall be like our Head.

3 If in my Father's love
I share a filial part,

Send down thy Spirit, like a dove,
To rest upon my heart.

4 We would no longer lie,
Like slaves, beneath the throne;
My faith shall Abba, Father, cry,
And thou the kindred own.
    Isaac Watts.

AFFLICTION AND COMFORT.

LINWOOD. L. M.   Arr. fr. Rossini.

1. Fa-ther, be-neath thy sheltering wing, In sweet se-cu-ri-ty we rest, And fear no e-vil earth can bring; In life, in death, su-preme-ly blest.

665 *Under his Wings shalt thou trust.*

2 For life is good, whose tidal flow
The motions of thy will obeys;
And death is good, that makes us know
The life divine which all things sways.

3 And good it is to bear the cross,
And so thy perfect peace to win;
And naught is ill, nor brings us loss,
Nor works us harm, save only sin.

4 Redeemed from that we ask no more,
But trust the love that saves to guide:
The grace that yields so rich a store
Will grant us all we need beside.
William H. Burleigh.

666   *Pardoned Sin.*

1 SWEET peace of conscience, heavenly guest,
Come, fix thy mansion in my breast;
Dispel my doubts, my fears control,
And heal the anguish of my soul.

2 Come, smiling hope, and joy sincere,
Come, make your constant dwelling here;
Still let your presence cheer my heart,
Nor sin compel you to depart.

3 O God of hope and peace divine!
Make thou these secret pleasures mine;
Forgive my sins, my fears remove,
And fill my heart with joy and love.
Ottiwell Heginbotham.

667 *Lift up your Heads, ye Gates.*

1 OH, blest the souls, for ever blest,
Where God as Ruler is confessed!
O happy hearts and happy homes,
To whom the King of Glory comes!

2 Fling wide thy portals, O my heart!
Be thou a temple set apart,
So shall thy Sovereign enter in,
And new and nobler life begin.

3 Deliverer, come! we open wide
Our hearts to thee; here, Lord, abide!
Let all thy glorious presence feel;
O King of souls, thyself reveal!
From the German.

668 *An Independent and Happy Life.*

1 How HAPPY is he born or taught,
Who serveth not another's will;
Whose armor is his honest thought,
And simple truth his highest skill.

2 Whose passions not his masters are;
Whose soul is still prepared for death
Not tied unto the world with care
Of prince's ear or vulgar breath;

3 Who God doth late and early pray
More of his grace than goods to lend
And walks with man, from day to day,
As with a brother and a friend.

4 This man is freed from servile bands
Of hope to rise, or fear to fall;
Lord of himself, though not of lands,
And having nothing, yet hath all.
Anon.

EXPERIENCE AND LIFE.

ELIZABETHTOWN. C. M.   Geo. Kingsley, 1838.

1. My God, the spring of all my joys,
The life of my de-lights,
The glo-ry of my bright-est days,
And com-fort of my nights,—

669   *All my Springs are in Thee.*

2 In darkest shades, if thou appear,
My dawning is begun;
Thou art my soul's bright morning star,
And thou my rising sun.

3 The opening heavens around me shine
With beams of sacred bliss,
While Jesus shows his love is mine,
And whispers I am his.

4 My soul would leave this heavy clay
At that transporting word,
Run up with joy the shining way,
To embrace my dearest Lord.
Isaac Watts.

670   *Sweet Prospects.*

1 When languor and disease invade
This trembling house of clay,
'Tis sweet to look beyond my pain,
And long to fly away;—

2 Sweet to look inward, and attend
The whispers of his love;
Sweet to look upward to the place
Where Jesus pleads above;—

3 Sweet, in the confidence of faith,
To trust his firm decrees;
Sweet to lie passive in his hands,
And know no will but his.

4 Sweet to rejoice in lively hope,
That, when my change shall come,
Angels will hover round my bed,
And waft my spirit home.
Augustus M. Toplady.

671   *The Inner Calm.*

1 Calm me, my God! and keep me calm,
Soft resting on thy breast;
Soothe me with holy hymn and psalm,
And bid my spirit rest.

2 Yes, keep me calm, though loud and rude
The sounds my ear that greet,
Calm in the closet's solitude,
Calm in the bustling street,—

3 Calm in the sufferance of wrong,
Like him who bore my shame;
Calm 'mid the threatening, taunting throng
Who hate thy holy name.

4 Calm as the ray of sun or star,
Which storms assail in vain;
Moving unruffled through earth's war,
The eternal calm to gain.
Horatius Bonar.

672   *Peace as a River.*

1 Give me a heart of calm repose
Amid the world's loud roar,
A life that like a river flows,
Along a peaceful shore.

2 Come, Holy Spirit, hush my heart
With gentleness divine;
Indwelling peace thou canst impart;
O, make the blessing mine.

3 Come, Holy Spirit, breathe that peace
Which flows from pardoned sin;
Then shall my soul her conflict cease,
And find a heaven within.
Anon.

AFFLICTION AND COMFORT.

ST. AGNES. C. M.   J. B. DYKES.

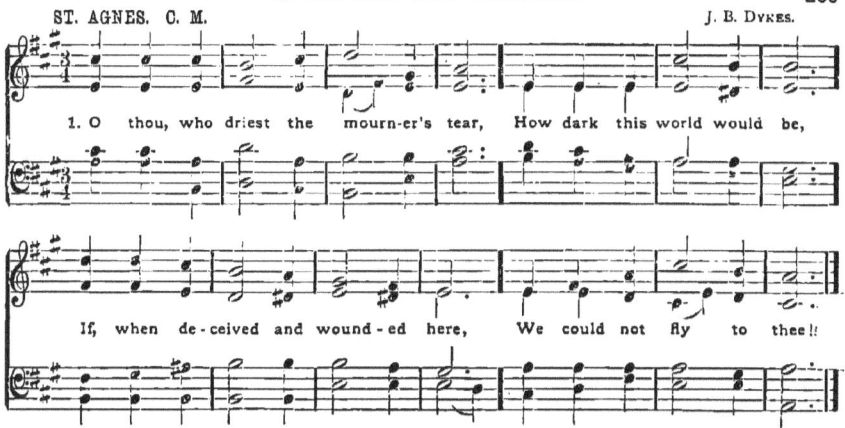

1. O thou, who driest the mourner's tear, How dark this world would be, If, when deceived and wounded here, We could not fly to thee!!

673   *Consolation.*

2 When joy no longer soothes or cheers,
And e'en the hope that threw
A moment's sparkle o'er our tears
Is dimmed and vanished too,—

3 O, who would bear life's stormy doom,
Did not thy wing of love
Come, brightly wafting through the gloom
Our peace-branch from above?

4 Then sorrow, touched by thee, grows bright,
With more than rapture's ray;
The darkness shows us worlds of light
We never saw by day.
Moore.

674   *Thou shalt hide them in Thy Presence.*

1 THY gracious presence, O my God,
All that I wish contains;
With this, beneath affliction's load,
My heart no more complains.

2 O, happy scenes above the sky,
Where thy full beams impart
Unclouded beauty to the eye,
And rapture to the heart.

3 Lord, shall the breathings of my heart
Aspire in vain to thee?
Confirm my hope that where thou art
I shall forever be.

4 Then shall my cheerful spirits sing
The darksome hours away,
And rise on faith's expanded wing
To everlasting day.
Anne Steele.

675   *A Father of the Fatherless.*

1 WHERE shall the child of sorrow find
A place for calm repose?
Thou, Father of the fatherless,
Pity the orphan's woes.

2 What friend have I in heaven or earth
What friend to trust, but thee?
My father and my mother gone,
O Lord, remember me.

3 Thy gracious promise now fulfil,
And bid my trouble cease;
In thee the fatherless shall find
Pure mercy, grace, and peace.

4 I've not a secret care or pain
But God that secret knows;
Thou, Father of the fatherless,
Pity the orphan's woes.
Anon.

676   *Whom the Lord loveth He chasteneth.*

1 O THOU whose mercy guides my way,
Though now it seem severe,
Forbid my unbelief to say,
There is no mercy here.

2 O, may I, Lord, desire the pain
That comes in kindness down,
Far more than sweetest earthly gain,
Succeeded by a frown.

3 Then, though thou bend my spirit low,
Love only shall I see;
The gracious hand that strikes the blow
Was wounded once for me.
Edmeston.

EXPERIENCE AND LIFE.

PINAO. L. M.

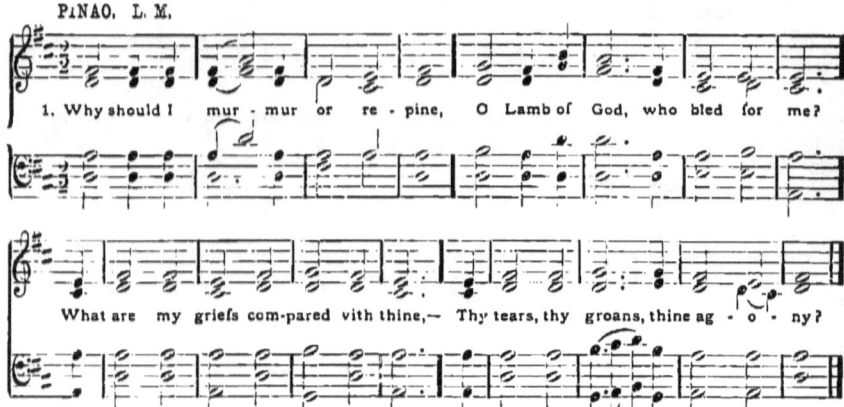

1. Why should I mur-mur or re-pine, O Lamb of God, who bled for me?
What are my griefs compared with thine,— Thy tears, thy groans, thine ag-o-ny?

677 *He shall sit as a Refiner of Silver.*

2 If thou the furnace dost employ,
  Thou sittest as refiner near,
  To purge away the base alloy,
  Till thine own image bright appear.

3 Though oft thy way is in the sea,
  Thy footsteps in the wingéd storm,
  Though crested billows threathen me,
  Love slumbers in their frowning form.

4 Submissive would I kiss the rod;
  Needful each stroke, I humbly own;
  Help me to trust thee, O my Lord,
  If now thy wisdom be unknown.
                                    Anon.

678 *Joy cometh in the Morning.*

1 O, deem not they are blest alone
  Whose lives a peaceful tenor keep;
  For God, who pities man, has shown
  A blessing for the eyes that weep.

2 The light of smiles shall fill again
  The lids that overflow with tears;
  And weary hours of woe and pain
  Are promises of happier years.

3 There is a day of sunny rest
  For every dark and troubled night;
  And grief may bide an evening guest,
  But joy shall come with early light.

4 For God has marked each sorrowing day,
  And numbered every secret tear;
  And heaven's long age of bliss shall pay
  For all his children suffer here.
                                    Bryant.

679 *Prayer for Help at all times.*

1 Is there a lone and dreary hour,
  When worldly pleasures lose their power?
  My Father, let me turn to thee,
  And set each thought of darkness free.

2 Is there an hour of peace and joy,
  When hope is all my soul's employ?
  My Father, still my hopes will roam,
  Until they rest with thee, their home.

3 The noontide blaze, the midnight scene,
  The dawn of twilight's sweet serene,
  The glow of health, the dying hour,
  Shall own my Father's grace and power.
                                    Mrs. Gilman.

680 *Hymn of Trust.*

1 O Love divine, that stooped to share
  Our sharpest pang, our bitterest tear,
  On thee we cast each earth-born care;
  We smile at pain while thou art near.

2 Though long the weary way we tread,
  And sorrow crown each lingering year,
  No path we shun, no darkness dread,
  Our hearts still whispering, Thou art near.

3 When drooping pleasure turns to grief,
  And trembling faith is changed to fear,
  The murmuring wind, the quivering leaf,
  Shall softly tell us, Thou art near.

4 On thee we fling our burdening woe,
  O love divine, forever dear,
  Content to suffer, while we know,
  Living and dying, thou art near.
                                    O. W. Holmes.

JOY, PEACE, HOPE.

REMSEN, C. M. J. P. HOLBROOK.

1. Blest is the man who shuns the place Where sinners love to meet, Who fears to tread their wicked ways, And hates the scoffer's seat.—

681 *The Godly Man blessed.*

2 But in the statutes of the Lord
Has placed his chief delight;
By day he reads or hears the word,
And meditates by night.

3 He, like a plant of generous kind,
By living waters set,
Safe from the storm and blasting wind,
Enjoys a peaceful state.

4 Sinners, in judgment, shall not stand
Among the sons of grace,
When Christ, the Judge, at his right hand,
Appoints his saints a place.
 Isaac Watts.

682 *Peace as a River.*

1 We bless thee for thy peace, O God,
Deep as the soundless sea,
Which falls like sunshine on the road
Of those who trust in thee.

2 We ask not, Father, for repose
Which comes from outward rest,
If we may have, through all life's woes,
Thy peace within our breast.

3 That peace which suffers and is strong,
Trusts where it cannot see,
Deems not the trial way too long,
But leaves the end with thee;—

4 That peace which flows serene and deep,—
A river in the soul,
Whose banks a living verdure keep,
God's sunshine o'er the whole;—

5 Such, Father, give our hearts such peace,
Whate'er the outward be,
Till all life's discipline shall cease,
And we go home to thee.
 Anon.

683 *We are Saved by Hope.*

1 The world may change from old to new,
From new to old again;
Yet hope and heaven forever true,
Within man's heart remain.

2 Hope leads the child to plant the flower,
The man to sow the seed,
Nor leaves fulfilment to her hour,
But prompts again to deed.

3 And ere upon the old man's dust
The grass is seen to wave,
We look through falling tears, to trust
Hope's sunshine on the grave.

4 O, no! it is no flattering lure,
No fancy weak or fond,
When hope would bid us rest secure,
In better life beyond.
 Mrs. Sarah Flower Adams.

684 *The secret Place of the Most High.*

1 There is a safe and secret place
Beneath the wings divine,
Reserved for all the heirs of grace;
O, be that refuge mine.

2 The least and feeblest there may bide
Uninjured and unawed;
While thousands fall on every side,
He rests secure in God.

3 He feeds in pastures large and fair
Of love and truth divine;
O child of God, O glory's heir,
How rich a lot is thine.

4 A hand almighty to defend,
An ear for every call,
An honored life, a peaceful end,
And heaven to crown it all!
 H. F. Lyte.

212 THE CHURCH.

AUSTRIA. 8s & 7s, D.   F. J. Haydn.

1. Glorious things of thee are spok-en, Zi-on, cit-y of our God:
He, whose word can-not be brok-en, Formed thee for his own a-bode. On the Rock of A-ges found-ed,
What can shake thy sure re-pose? With sal-va-tion's walls surround-ed, Thou mayst smile at all thy foes.

685 *The City of God.*

2 See! the streams of living waters,
    Springing from eternal love,
Well supply thy sons and daughters,
    And all fear of want remove.

Who can faint while such a river
    Ever flows their thirst t' assuage?—
Grace, which, like the Lord, the Giver,
    Never fails from age to age.
John Newton, 1779.

SESSIONS. L. M.   L. O. Emerson.

1. How rich the blessings, O my God, How kindly poured, and free bestowed,
Which teach this grateful heart to glow? The rivers of.... thy mercy flow!

686 *We have Peace with God through Christ.*

2 How calmly rolls the sea of life!
    Secure in thy immortal trust,
The soul has hushed her secret strife,
    Nor longer shudders at the dust.

3 Though sorrow's cloud awhile o'ercast
    The dawn of earthly hope and joy,
She knows that it must soon be past,
    And will unveil eternity.

4 Then virtue's humble toil and prayer
    Shall stand acknowledged at thy throne,
Triumphant over earthly care,
    And the blest record thou wilt own.
Jane Roscoe.

687 *Begotten us unto a lively Hope.*

1 How happy every child of grace,
    Who knows his sins forgiven!

This earth, he cries, is not my place;
    I seek my home in heaven;—

2 A country far from mortal sight,
    Yet, O, by faith I see
The land of rest, the saints' delight,
    The heaven prepared for me.

3 We feel the resurrection near,
    Our life in Christ concealed,
And with his glorious presence here
    Our earthen vessels filled.

4 On him with rapture then I'll gaze,
    Who bought the bliss for me,
And shout and wonder at his grace
    Through all eternity.
Charles Wesley.

FOUNDATION AND EXCELLENCY. 213

688 *Christ is our Corner-stone.*

2 Here, gracious God, do thou
   Forevermore draw nigh;
Accept each faithful vow,
   And mark each suppliant sigh:
In copious shower, on all who pray,
Each holy day thy blessing pour.

3 Here may we gain from heaven
   The grace which we implore,
And may that grace once given
   Be with us evermore,—
Until that day when all the blest
To endless rest are called away.
From the Latin. *Tr.* John Chandler, 1837.

689 *Our Everlasting Defense.*

2 Every human tie may perish,
   Friend to friend unfaithful prove,
Mothers cease their own to cherish,
   Heaven and earth at last remove;
     But no changes
   Can attend Jehovah's love.

3 In the furnace God may prove thee,
   Thence to bring thee forth more bright,
But can never cease to love thee;
   Thou art precious in his sight;
     God is with thee,
   God, thine everlasting Light.
Thomas Kelly 1806.

THE CHURCH.

BEALOTH. S. M. D.

1. I love thy kingdom, Lord, The house of thine a-bode, The church our blest Redeemer saved With his own precious blood. I love thy church, O God! Her walls before thee stand Dear as the apple of thine eye, And graven on thy hand.

690 *I love thy kingdom, Lord.*

2 For her my tears shall fall,
 For her my prayers ascend;
To her my cares and toils be given,
 Till toils and cares shall end.
Beyond my highest joy
 I prize her heavenly ways,
Her sweet communion, solemn vows,
 Her hymns of love and praise.

3 Jesus, thou Friend divine,
 Our Saviour and our King!
Thy hand from every snare and foe
 Shall great deliverance bring.
Sure as thy truth shall last,
 To Zion shall be given
The brightest glories earth can yield,
 And brighter bliss of heaven.
   Timothy Dwight, 1800.

691 *How beautiful upon the Mountains.*

1 How BEAUTEOUS are their feet
 Who stand on Zion's hill!
Who bring salvation on their tongues,
 And words of peace reveal!

How charming is their voice!
 How sweet the tidings are!—
"Zion, behold thy Saviour King;
 He reigns and triumphs here."

2 How happy are our ears,
 That hear this joyful sound,
Which kings and prophets waited for,
 And sought, but never found!
How blessèd are our eyes,
 That see this heavenly light!
Prophets and kings desired it long,
 But died without the sight.

3 The watchmen join their voice,
 And tuneful notes employ;
Jerusalem breaks forth in songs,
 And deserts learn the joy.
The Lord makes bare his arm,
 Through all the earth abroad;
Let every nation now behold
 Their Saviour and their God.
   Isaac Watts.

FOUNDATION AND EXCELLENCY. 215

AURELIA. 6s & 7s, D.

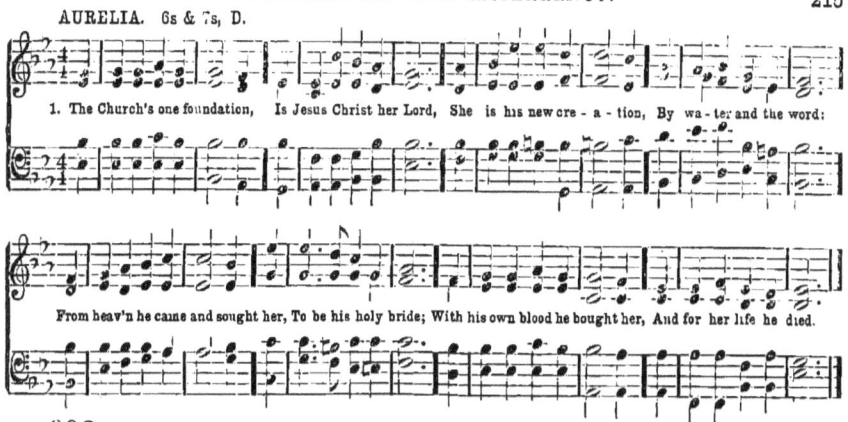

1. The Church's one foundation, Is Jesus Christ her Lord, She is his new cre-a-tion, By wa-ter and the word: From heav'n he came and sought her, To be his holy bride; With his own blood he bought her, And for her life he died.

692 *The Church is Christ's.*

2 'Mid toil and tribulation,
And tumult of her war,
She waits the consummation
Of peace for evermore;
Till with the vision glorious
Her longing eyes are blest,
And the great Church victorious
Shall be the Church at rest.

3 Yet she on earth hath union
With God the Holy One,
And mystic sweet communion
With those whose rest is won;
Oh, happy ones and holy!
Lord, give us grace that we
Like them, the meek and lowly,
On high may dwell with thee.

Samuel J. Stone, arr.

MANNHEIM. 8s & 7s, 6 l.   FRIEDRICH FILITZ.

1. Christ is made the sure foundation, Christ the head and cor-ner-stone, Chos-en of the Lord and precious, Bind-ing all the church in one, Ho-ly Zi-on's help for ev-er, And her con-fi-dence a-lone.

693 *Christ the Foundation.*

2 To this temple where we call thee,
Come, O Lord of hosts, to-day:
With thy wonted loving-kindness
Hear thy servants as they pray,
And thy fullest benediction
Shed within its walls alway.

3 Here vouchsafe to all thy servants
What they ask of thee to gain,
What they gain from thee for ever
With the blesséd to retain,
And hereafter in thy glory
Evermore with thee to reign.

John M. Neale, tr.

THE CHURCH.

ROOKINGHAM (OLD), L. M. — E. MILLER.

1. Happy the church, thou sacred place, The seat of thy Creator's grace! Thine holy courts are his abode, Thou earthly palace of.... our God.

694 *God is in the Midst of her.*

2 Thy walls are strength, and at thy gates
A guard of heavenly warriors waits;
Nor shall thy deep foundations move,
Fixed on his counsels and his love;

3 Thy foes in vain designs engage;
Against thy throne in vain they rage,
Like rising waves, with angry roar,
That dash and die upon the shore.

4 God is our shield, and God our sun;
Swift as the fleeting moments run,
On us he sheds new beams of grace,
And we reflect his brightest praise.
Isaac Watts.

695 *The Day of Espousals.*

1 Jesus, thou everlasting King!
Accept the tribute that we bring;
Accept the well-deserved renown,
And wear our praises as thy crown.

2 Let every act of worship be,
Like our espousals, Lord! to thee;
Like the dear hour, when, from above,
We first received thy pledge of love.

3 The gladness of that happy day—
Our hearts would wish it long to stay;
Nor let our faith forsake its hold,
Nor comfort sink, nor love grow cold.

4 Each following minute, as it flies,
Increase thy praise, improve our joys;
Till we are raised to sing thy name,
At the great supper of the Lamb.
Isaac Watts.

STATE STREET, S. M. — J. C. WOODMAN, 1844.

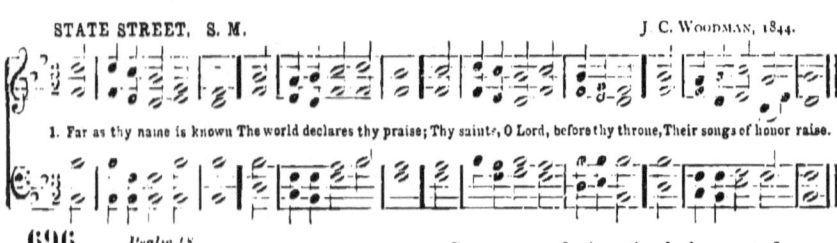

1. Far as thy name is known The world declares thy praise; Thy saints, O Lord, before thy throne, Their songs of honor raise.

696 *Psalm 48.*

2 With joy thy people stand
On Zion's chosen hill,
Proclaim the wonders of thy hand,
And counsels of thy will.

3 Let strangers walk around
The city where we dwell,
Compass and view thy holy ground,
And mark the building well;—

4 The God we worship now
Will guide us till we die—
Will be our God while here below,
And ours above the sky.
Isaac Watts.

MINISTRY. 217

MISSIONARY CHANT. L. M. — Charles Zeuner, 1832.

1. Ye Christian heralds, go, proclaim Salvation in Immanuel's name:
To distant climes the tidings bear, And plant the rose of Sharon there.

697 *I will publish the Name of the Lord.*

2 He'll shield you with a wall of fire,
With holy zeal your hearts inspire,
Bid raging winds their fury cease,
And hush the tempest into peace.

3 And when our labors all are o'er,
Then we shall meet to part no more,—
Meet, with the ransomed throng to fall,
And crown the Saviour Lord of all.
Mrs. Voke, 1816.

698 *Go into all the World and preach.*

1 Go, PREACH my gospel, saith the Lord;
Bid the whole earth my grace receive;
They shall be saved who trust my word,
And they condemned who disbelieve.

2 I'll make your great commission known,
And ye shall prove my gospel true
By all the works that I have done,
By all the wonders ye shall do.

3 Teach all the nations my commands;
I'm with you till the world shall end;
All power is trusted in my hands;
I can destroy, and I defend.

4 He spoke, and light shone round his head;
On a bright cloud to heaven he rode;
They to the farthest nations spread
The grace of their ascended Lord.
Isaac Watts.

699 *Receive him in the Lord with Gladness.*

1 WE bid thee welcome in the name
Of Jesus, our exalted Head;
Come as a servant: so he came,
And we receive thee in his stead.

2 Come as a watchman: take thy stand
Upon the tower amid the sky,
And when the sword comes on the land,
Call us to fight, or warn to fly.

3 Come as a teacher, sent from God,
Charged his whole counsel to declare;
Lift o'er our ranks the prophet's rod,
While we uphold thy hands with prayer.

4 Come as a messenger of peace,
Filled with the Spirit, fired with love;
Live to behold our large increase,
And die to meet us all above.
James Montgomery.

700 *The same commit thou to Faithful Men.*

1 O THOU who art above all light,
Our God, our Father, and our Friend
Beneath thy throne of love and light,
Let thy adoring children bend.

2 We kneel in praise, that here is set
A vine that by thy culture grew;
We kneel in prayer that thou wouldst wet
Its opening leaves with heavenly dew.

3 Since thy young servant now hath given
Himself, his powers, his hopes, his youth
To the great cause of truth and heaven,
Be thou his Guide, O God of truth.

4 And when he sinks in death, by care,
Or pain, or toil, or years oppressed,
O God, remember then our prayer,
And take his spirit to thy rest.
Anon.

THE CHURCH.

TAPPAN. C. M.   GEO. KINGSLEY.

1. Let Zi-on's watchman all a-wake, And take th' a-larm they give; Now let them from the mouth of God, Now let them from the mouth of God Their solemn charge re-ceive.

701   *They watch for your Souls.*

2 'Tis not a cause of small import
The pastor's care demands,
But what might fill an angel's heart,
And filled a Saviour's hands.

3 They watch for souls, for which the Lord
Did heavenly bliss forego;
For souls which must forever live
In rapture or in woe.

4 May they that Jesus whom they preach
Their own Redeemer see:
Lord, watch thou daily o'er their souls
That they may watch for thee.
                    Philip Doddridge.

702   *Ordination.*

1 O FATHER of the living Christ,
Fount of the living Word,
Pour on the shepherd and the flock
The Spirit of the Lord!

2 Amid this mingled mystery
Of good and ill at strife,
Help them, O God, in him to find
The Way, the Truth, the Life.

3 This way together may they tread,
That truth with joy receive,
That life of heaven, on earth begun,
Through cloud and sunshine live.

4 One may they be in faith and hope,
As one in works of love,
Till all be one in Christ and thee
In the Great Church above.
                    William Newell.

703   *Dedication.*

1 O THOU, whose own vast temple stands
Built over earth and sea,
Accept the walls that human hands
Have raised to worship thee.

2 Lord, from thine inmost glory send,
Within these courts to bide,
The peace that dwelleth, without end,
Serenely by thy side.

3 May faith grow firm, and love grow warm,
And pure devotion rise,
While round these hallowed walls the storm
Of earth-born passion dies.
                William Cullen Bryant.

704   *Removal of the Ark.*

1 ARISE, O King of grace, arise,
And enter to thy rest;
Behold, thy church, with longing eyes,
Waits to be owned and blest.

2 Enter, with all thy glorious train,
Thy Spirit and thy word;
All that the ark did once contain,
Could no such grace afford.

3 Here let the Son of David reign,
Let God's Anointed shine;
Justice and truth his court maintain,
With love and power divine.

4 Here let him hold a lasting throne,
And as his kingdom grows,
Fresh honors shall adorn his crown,
And shame confound his foes.
                       Isaac Watts.

DEDICATION. 219

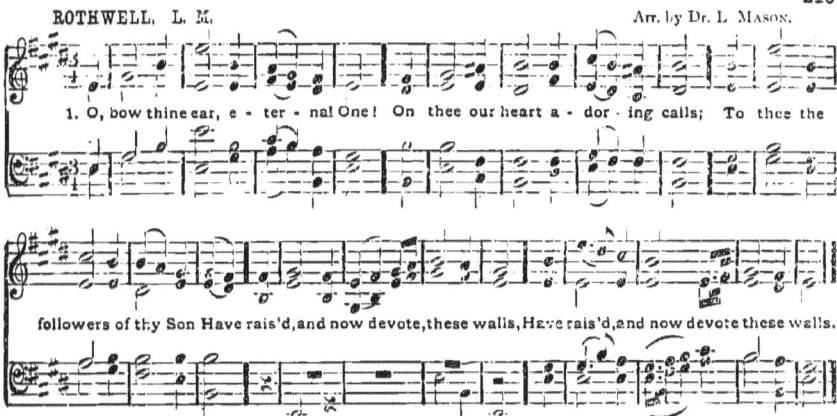

1. O, bow thine ear, e-ter-nal One! On thee our heart a-dor-ing calls; To thee the followers of thy Son Have rais'd, and now devote, these walls, Have rais'd, and now devote these walls.

705 *Dedication.*

2 Here let thy holy days be kept;
And be this place to worship given,
Like that bright spot where Jacob slept,
The house of God, the gate of heaven.

3 Here be thy praise devoutly sung;
Here let thy truth beam forth to save;
As when, of old, thy Spirit hung
On wings of light, o'er Jordan's wave.

4 And when the lips, that with thy name
Are vocal now, to dust shall turn,
On others may devotion's flame
Be kindled here, and purely burn.
John Pierpont

706 *Dedication.*

1 LORD, in thy presence we appear,
With willing hands and hearts sincere,
To consecrate beneath the skies,
An altar for thy sacrifice.

2 The universe is thine, O God,
Eternity thy vast abode;
Then what is man that he should be
The builder of a house for thee.

3 But though thy "temple is all space,
The heaven of heavens thy dwelling-place,
Yet wilt thou deign, Almighty God,
To make this building thine abode.

4 Here, where thy waiting children meet
Fix thou, O Lord, thy mercy-seat;
And in this temple we have raised,
O let thy gracious name be praised.
Rev. P. Roberts.

707 *Invocation.*

1 UNTO thy temple, Lord, we come
With thankful hearts to worship thee;
And pray that this may be our home
Until we touch eternity:—

2 The common home of rich and poor,
Of bond and free, and great and small;
Large as thy love for evermore,
And warm and bright and good to all.

3 May thy whole truth be spoken here;
Thy gospel light for ever shine;
Thy perfect love cast out all fear,
And human life become divine.
Robert Collyer, 1873.

708

1 THOU God of grace and love untold,
We to thy presence now draw nigh;
While angels, at thy throne, behold
Thee in thy majesty on high.

2 Within this house let peace abound,
And heavenly love each heart inspire;
Here may thy word in grateful sound
Beget in all a holy fire.

3 And may thy servants who proclaim
The wonders of the Christ, our Lord,
Be men of heart and soul and aim,
To lead each listener up to God.

4 May sinners here thy mercy know,
And saints thy love and peace unfold;
Upon all hearts that joy bestow
More priceless than the wealth of gold.
Rev. B. F. Clayton.

THE CHURCH.

WARSAW. H. M.   T. Clark.

1. Great King of glo-ry, come, And with thy fa-vor crown This tem-ple as thy home, This peo-ple as thine own: Beneath this roof, oh, deign to show How God can dwell with men be-low.

709   *The Great King.*

2 Here may thine ears attend
   Our interceding cries,
And grateful praise ascend,
   All fragrant, to the skies:
Here may the world melodious sound,
And spread celestial joys around.

3 Here may the listening throng
   Imbibe thy truth and love;
Here Christians join the song
   Of seraphim above;
Till all who humbly seek thy face,
Rejoice in thine abounding grace.
Benjamin Francis.

CLARK. 5th P. M. (4 lines 7s.)   T. Clark.

1. Heart and heart together bound, In your love the price be found Of your Saviour's love and woes.
Seek in God, your true repose; Of your Saviour's love and woes,

710   *One in Christ.*

2 If your bonds are yet too weak,
   If but fragile yet they prove,
Help from his good Spirit seek
   Who makes strong the chains of love.

3 O thou truest Friend, unite
   All thy consecrated band,
That their hearts be set aright
   To fulfil thy last command.

4 Let us live, O Christ, as one,
   As thou with the Father art,
That through all the world be none
   Of thy members left apart.
Zinzendorf.

711   *Thy People shall be my People.*

1 People of the living God,
   I have sought the world around,
Paths of sin and sorrow trod,
   Peace and comfort nowhere found.

2 Now to you my spirit turns—
   Turns, a fugitive unblest:
Brethren, where your altar burns,
   O, receive me into rest.

3 Lonely I no longer roam,
   Like the cloud, the wind, the wave;
Where you dwell shall be my home,
   Where you die shall be my grave.

4 Mine the God whom you adore,
   Your Redeemer shall be mine;
Earth can fill my soul no more;
   Every idol I resign.
James Montgomery.

ADMISSION OF MEMBERS.

HAPPY DAY. L. M.

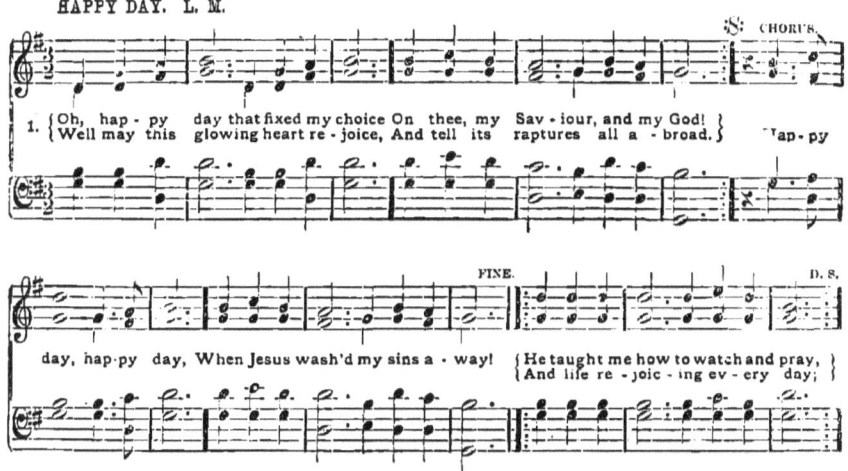

1. Oh, happy day that fixed my choice On thee, my Saviour, and my God! Well may this glowing heart rejoice, And tell its raptures all abroad. Happy day, happy day, When Jesus wash'd my sins away! He taught me how to watch and pray, And life rejoicing every day;

712 *Rejoicing in Entire Consecration.*

2 Oh, happy bond, that seals my vows
To him who merits all my love!
Let cheerful anthems fill the house,
While to his altar now I move.
    Happy day, &c.

3 'Tis done—the great transaction's done;
I am my Lord's, and he is mine;
He drew me, and I followed on,
Rejoiced to own the call divine.
    Happy day, &c.

4 Now rest—my long divided heart—
Fixed on this blissful center, rest—
Here have I found a nobler part,
Here heavenly pleasures fill my breast.
    Happy day, &c.

5 High Heaven, that heard the solemn vow,
That vow renewed shall daily hear,
Till, in life's latest hour, I bow,
And bless in death a bond so dear.
    Happy day, &c.
                  Philip Doddridge, 1740.

713 *Used when Receiving New Members.*

1 MAY those who have thy name confessed
Now find in God eternal rest;
From day to day still more increase
In faith, and love, and holiness.

2 As living members, may they share
The joys and griefs that others bear,
And active in their stations prove,
In all the offices of love.

3 From all temptations now defend,
And keep them, Lord, unto the end,
While in thy house they still improve,
Till called to join the church above.
                  Anon.

714 *Admission of Members.*

1 BELIEVING souls, of Christ beloved,
Who have yourselves to him resigned,
Your faith and practice both approved,
A hearty welcome here shall find.

2 Now saved from sin and Satan's wiles,
Though by a scorning world abhorred,
Now share with us the Saviour's smiles,
Come in, ye ransomed of the Lord.

3 In fellowship we join our hands,
And you an invitation give;
Unite with us in sacred bands;
The pledges of our love receive.

4 Do thou, who art the church's Head,
This union with thy blessing crown:
And still, O Lord, revive the dead,
Till thousands more thy name shall own.
                  Benjamin Beddome.

THE CHURCH.

MOUNT AUBURN. C. M.   Kingsley.

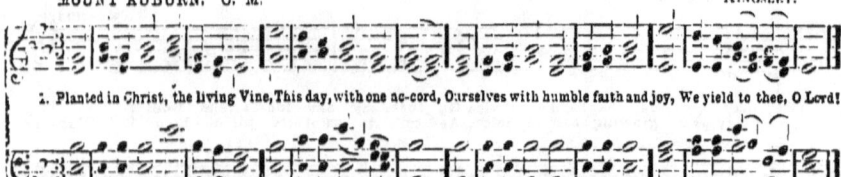

2. Planted in Christ, the living Vine, This day, with one ac-cord, Ourselves with humble faith and joy, We yield to thee, O Lord!

715 *Christian Fellowship.*

2 Joined in one body may we be,
  One inward life partake,
One be our heart, one heavenly hope
  In every bosom wake.

3 In prayer, in effort, tears, and toils,
  One wisdom be our guide;
Taught by one Spirit from above,
  In thee may we abide!
                       S. F. Smith.

716

1 Witness, ye men and angels, now;
  Before the Lord we speak;
To him we make our solemn vow,
  A vow we dare not break:—

2 That, long as life itself shall last,
  Ourselves to Christ we yield;
Nor from his cause will we depart,
  Or ever quit the field.

3 We trust not in our native strength,
  But on his grace rely,
That, with returning wants, the Lord
  Will all our need supply.

4 O, guide our doubtful feet aright,
  And keep us in thy ways,
And, while we turn our vows to prayers,
  Turn thou our prayers to praise.
                       Benjamin Beddome.

717 *Fellowship of Heaven and Earth.*

1 Happy the souls to Jesus joined,
  And saved by grace alone;
Walking in all his ways, they find
  Their heaven on earth begun.

2 The church triumphant in thy love,
  Their mighty joys we know;
They sing the Lamb in hymns above,
  And we in hymns below.

3 Thee in thy glorious realm they praise
  And bow before thy throne:
We in the kingdom of thy grace:
  The kingdoms are but one.
                       Charles Wesley.

718 *The Little Flock.*

1 Church of the Ever-living God,
  The Father's gracious choice!
Amid the voices of this earth
  How feeble is thy voice.

2 A "little flock!"—'tis well, 'tis well;
  Such be her lot and name;
Through ages past it has been so,
  And now 'tis still the same.

3 But the chief Shepherd comes at length,
  Her feeble days are o'er,
No more a handful in the earth,
  A "little flock" no more.

4 No more a lily among thorns,
  Weary and faint and few;
But countless as the stars of heaven,
  Or as the early dew.
                       Horatius Bonar.

719 *"Greater love hath no man."*

1 If human kindness meets return,
  And owns the grateful tie;
If tender thoughts within us burn,
  To feel a friend is nigh;—

2 Oh, shall not warmer accents tell
  The gratitude we owe
To him, who died our fears to quell—
  Who bore our guilt and woe!

3 While yet in anguish he surveyed
  Those pangs he would not flee,
What love his latest words displayed,—
  "Meet and remember me!"
                       Gerard T. Noel.

ORDINANCES.

TRURO. L. M. — Charles Burney.

1. 'Twas the com-mis-sion of our Lord, Go, teach the na-tions, and bap-tize! The na-tions have re-ceived the word, Since he as-cend-ed to the skies.

720 *Teach all Nations, baptizing them.*

2 Our souls he washes in his blood,
  As water makes the body clean;
And the good Spirit from our God
  Descends like purifying rain.

3 Thus we engage our souls to thee,
  And seal our covenant with the Lord;
Let angels this with rapture see,
  In heaven our solemn vows record.
                            Isaac Watts.

721 *Buried with Him by Baptism.*

1 Come, Holy Spirit, Dove divine,
On these baptismal waters shine,
And teach our hearts, in highest strain,
To praise the Lamb, for sinners slain.

2 We sink beneath the mystic flood;
O, bathe us in thy cleansing blood;
We die to sin, and seek a grave,
With thee, beneath the yielding wave.

3 And as we rise with thee to live,
O, let the Holy Spirit give
The sealing unction from above,
The breath of life, the fire of love.
                            Judson.

GOLDEN HILL. S. M. — Western Melody.

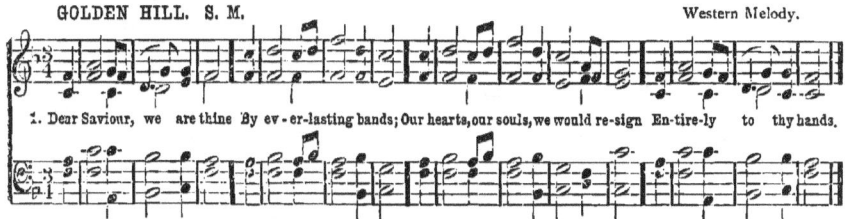

1. Dear Saviour, we are thine By ev-er-lasting bands; Our hearts, our souls, we would re-sign En-tire-ly to thy hands.

722 *Give themselves to the Lord and to us.*

2 To thee we still would cleave
  With ever-growing zeal;
If millions tempt us Christ to leave,
  O, let them ne'er prevail.

3 Death may our souls divide
  From these abodes of clay;
But love shall keep us near thy side
  Through all the gloomy way.

4 Since Christ and we are one,
  Why should we doubt or fear?
If he in heaven has fixed his throne,
  He'll fix his members there.
                            Philip Doddridge.

THE CHURCH.

COMMUNION. C. M.   S. Hill.

1. According to thy gracious word, In meek humility,
This will I do, my dying Lord— I will remember thee.

723

2 Thy body, broken for my sake,
My bread from heaven shall be;
Thy testamental cup I take,
And thus remember thee.

3 Remember thee, and all thy pains,
And all thy love to me—
Yea, while a breath, a pulse remains,
Will I remember thee.

4 And when these failing lips grow dumb
And mind and memory flee,
When thou shalt in thy kingdom come,
Jesus, remember me.
James Montgomery, 1725.

724   *Fulfil all Righteousness.*

1 Buried beneath the yielding wave
The great Redeemer lies;
Faith views him in the watery grave,
And thence beholds him rise.

2 Thus do his willing saints, to-day,
Their ardent zeal express,
And, in the Lord's appointed way,
Fulfil all righteousness.

3 With joy we in his footsteps tread,
And would his cause maintain,—
Like him be numbered with the dead,
And with him rise and reign.
Benjamin Beddome, 1818.

725   *Close of Communion.*

1 O God, accept the sacred hour
Which we to thee have given;
And let this hallowed scene have power
To raise our souls to heaven;

2 Still let us hold, till life departs,
The precepts of thy Son;
Nor let our thoughtless, thankless hearts
Forget what he has done.

3 His true disciples may we live,
From all corruption free;
And humbly learn, like him, to give
Our powers, our wills to thee.
Samuel Gilman.

726   *Baptism of Jesus.*

1 "I come," the great Redeemer cries,
"To do thy will, O Lord!"
At Jordan's flood, behold! he seals
The sure prophetic word.

2 "Thus it becomes us to fulfil
All righteousness," he said;
He spake obedient, and beneath
The yielding wave was laid.

3 Hark! a glad voice; the Father speaks,
From heaven's exalted height;
"This is my Son, my well-beloved!
My joy, my chief delight."

4 Jesus, the Saviour, well-beloved!
His name we will profess,
Like him, desirous to fulfil
Each law of righteousness.

5 No more we'll count ourselves our own,
But his in bonds of love;
O may such bonds forever draw
Our souls to things above.
Salisbury Collection.

ORDINANCES.

HAVEN. C. M. Thomas Hastings.

1. A ho-ly air is breath-ing round, A fra-grance from a-bove; Be ev-ery soul from sense un-bound Be ev-ery spir it love.

727 *The Presence of Jesus.*

2 O God, unite us heart to heart
In sympathy divine,
That we be never drawn apart,
But e'er love thee and thine.

3 But, by the cross of Jesus taught,
And all thy gracious word,
Be nearer to each other brought,
And nearer to our Lord.
A. A. Livermore.

728 *Baptism of Christ.*

1 How CALMLY wakes the hallowed morn!
How tranquil earth's repose!—
Meet emblem of the Sabbath morn,
When, early, Jesus rose.

2 How fair, along the rippling wave,
The radiant light is cast!—
A symbol of the mystic grave
Through which the Saviour passed.

3 Around this scene of sacred love
The peace of heaven is shed:
So came the Spirit, like a dove,
To rest on Jesus' head.

4 Lord, meet us in this path of thine;
We come thy rite to seal;
Move o'er the waters, Dove divine,
And all thy grace reveal.
S. F. Smith.

729 *The Lord's Table.*

1 LORD, at thy table I behold
The wonders of thy grace,
But most of all admire that I
Should find a welcome place.

2 What strange, surprising grace is this,
That such a soul has room!
My Saviour takes me by the hand,
And bids me freely come.

2 Ye saints below, and hosts of heaven,
In praise join all your powers:
No theme is like redeeming love,
No Saviour is like ours.
Stennett.

730 *The Family in Heaven and Earth.*

1 THE saints on earth and those above
But one communion make;
Joined to their Lord in bonds of love,
All of his grace partake.

2 One family, we dwell in him;
One church above, beneath;
Though now divided by the stream,
The narrow stream of death.

3 One army of the living God,
To his command we bow;
Part of the host have crossed the flood,
And part are crossing now.

4 O God, be thou our constant Guide;
Then, when the word is given,
Bid death's cold flood its waves divide,
And land us safe in heaven.
Charles Wesley.

15

THE CHURCH.

BEATITUDO. C. M.   J. B. DYKES.

1. My God, accept my heart this day,
And make it always thine,
That I from thee no more may stray,
No more from thee decline.

731 *Renewed in the Spirit of your Mind.*

2 Before the cross of Him who died,
Behold, I prostrate fall:
Let every sin be crucified,—
Let Christ be all in all.

3 Let every thought, and work, and word,
To thee be ever given;
Then life shall be thy service, Lord,
And death the gate of heaven.
                               Brydges.

732   *Baptism.*

1 PROCLAIM, saith Christ, my wondrous
   To all the sons of men;   [grace,
He that believes, and is baptized,
   Salvation shall obtain.

2 Let plenteous grace descend on those,
   Who, hoping in thy word,
This day have publicly declared,
   That Jesus is their Lord.

3 With cheerful feet may they advance,
   And run the Christian race;
And through the troubles of the way,
   Find all-sufficient grace.
                            John Newton.

WILMOT. 8s & 7s.   C. M. von WEBER, 1820.

1. Humble souls, who seek salvation Thro' the Lamb's redeeming blood, Hear the voice of revelation; Tread the path that Jesus trod.

733   *Following Christ.*

2 Jesus says, let each believer
   Be baptized into my name;
He himself in Jordan's river
   Was baptized beneath the stream.

3 Hear the blest Redeemer call you:
   Listen to his heavenly voice;
Dread no ills that can befall you,
   While you make his ways your choice.

4 Plainly here his footsteps tracing,
   Follow him without delay,
Gladly his command embracing;
   Lo! your Captain leads the way.
                              Anon.

734

1 FROM the table now retiring,
   Which for us the Lord hath spread,
May our souls, refreshment finding,
   Grow in all things like our Head!

2 His example by beholding,
   May our lives his image bear;
Him our Lord and Master calling,
   His commands may we revere.

3 Love to God and man displaying,
   Walking steadfast in his way,
Joy attend us in believing,
   Peace from God through endless **day.**
                             John Rowe.

ORDINANCES.

HAYDN. S. M.   Arr. fr. HAYDN.

1. Be-neath the symbol wave The Saviour's form was bowed; Again from out the symbol grave Rose our anointed Lord.

735   *Baptism of Jesus.*
2 Descends God's Spirit now,
  In likeness of a Dove,
To warm his breast and wreathe his brow,
  With Heaven's baptismal love.

3 With wings of holy flame,
  On him, from heaven above,
It lit, and thus God's Spirit came,—
  That heavenly-hearted Dove.
Anon.

736   *A Communion Hymn.*
1 O FOR a prophet's fire,
  O for an angel's tongue,
To speak the mighty love of Him
  Who on the cross was hung!

2 These symbols of his death,
  Oh, with what power they speak!
Prophetic lips and angels' lyres,
  Compared with these, are weak.

3 And shall they plead in vain
  With our forgetful souls?

I cannot thus ungrateful prove,
  While love my heart controls.
W. H. Furness.

737   *Delight in the Communion.*
1 O, WHAT delight is this,
  Which now in Christ we know,—
An earnest of our glorious bliss,
  Our heaven begun below.

2 When he the table spreads,
  How royal is the cheer!
With rapture we lift up our heads,
  And own that God is here.

3 The Lamb for sinners slain,
  Who died to die no more,
Let all the ransomed sons of men,
  With all his hosts, adore.

4 Let earth and heaven be joined,
  His glories to display,
And hymn the Saviour of mankind
  In one eternal day.
Charles Wesley.

WEBER. 7s.   Arr. fr. WEBER.

1. Bread of heav'n, on thee we feed, For thy flesh is meat in-deed:

Ev-er let our souls.... be fed With this true...... and liv-ing bread.

738   *I am the Living Bread.*
2 Vine of heaven, thy blood supplies
This blest cup of sacrifice;
Lord, thy wounds our healing give;
To thy cross we look and live.

3 Day by day with strength supplied
Through the life of him who died,
Lord of life, O, let us be
Rooted, grafted, built on thee!
Josiah Conder.

THE CHURCH.

1. How sweet, how heav'n-ly is the sight, When those who love the Lord, In one an-oth-er's peace de-light, And so ful-fil his word!

739 *Love as Brethren.*

2 When each can feel his brother's sigh,
And with him bear a part!
When sorrow flows from eye to eye,
And joy from heart to heart.

3 When, free from envy, scorn, and pride,
Our wishes all above;
Each can his brother's failings hide,
And show a brother's love!

4 Let love in one delightful stream,
Through every bosom flow,
And union sweet and dear esteem
In every action glow.

5 Love is the golden chain that binds
The happy souls above;
And he's an heir of heaven who finds
His bosom glow with love.
Charles Swain.

740 *Of one Heart and of one Soul.*

1 BLEST be the dear, uniting love
That will not let us part;
Our bodies may far-off remove,
We still are one in heart.

2 Joined in one Spirit to our Head,
Where he appoints we go;
We still in Jesus' footsteps tread,
And show his praise below.

3 Partakers of the Saviour's grace,
The same in mind and heart,
Not joy, nor grief, nor time, nor place,
Nor life, nor death, can part.
Charles Wesley.

741 *The Universal Bond of Love.*

1 THE glorious universe around,
The heavens with all their train,
Sun, moon, and stars, are firmly bound,
In one mysterious chain.

2 In one fraternal bond of love,
One fellowship of mind,
The saints below and saints above
Their bliss and glory find.

3 Here, in their house of pilgrimage,
Thy statutes are their song;
There, through one bright, eternal age,
Thy praises they prolong.
Horatius Bonar.

742 *Being knit together in Love.*

1 OUR souls, by love together knit,
Cemented, joined in one,
One hope, one heart, one mind, one voice,
'Tis heaven on earth begun.

2 The little cloud increases still;
The heavens are big with rain;
We haste to catch the teeming shower,
And all its moisture drain.

3 A rill, a stream, a torrent flows,
But pour a mighty flood;
O, sweep the nations, shake the earth,
Till all proclaim thee Lord.

4 And when thou mak'st thy jewels up,
And sett'st thy starry crown,
When all thy sparkling gems shall shine,
Proclaim us, Lord, thine own.
Milles.

FELLOWSHIP AND UNITY.

BOYLSTON. S. M.   LOWELL MASON, 1832.

1. Blest be the tie that binds Our hearts in Christian love; The fellowship of kindred minds Is like to that above.

743 *Ye are all one in Christ Jesus.*

2 Before our Father's throne
We pour our ardent prayers;
Our fears, our hopes, our aims are one,
Our comforts and our cares.

3 We share our mutual woes,
Our mutual burdens bear;
And often for each other flows
The sympathizing tear.

4 When we asunder part,
It gives us inward pain;
But we shall still be joined in heart,
And hope to meet again.

5 From sorrow, toil, and pain,
And sin we shall be free,
And perfect love and friendship reign
Through all eternity.
Joseph Fawcett.

744 *"For ye are all one in Christ Jesus."*

1 LET party names no more
The Christian world o'erspread;
Gentile and Jew, and bond and free
Are one in Christ, their Head.

2 Among the saints on earth
Let mutual love be found—
Heirs of the same inheritance,
With mutual blessings crowned.

3 Thus will the church below
Resemble that above,
Where springs of purest pleasure rise,
And every heart is love.
Benjamin Beddome, 1818.

STEPHENS. C. M.   W. JONES.

1. Help us to help each oth-er, Lord, Each oth-er's cross to bear;
Let each his friend-ly aid af-ford, And feel his broth-er's care.

745 *Desiring Holiness.*

2 Help us to build each other up,
Our heart and life improve;
Increase our faith, confirm our hope,
And perfect us in love.

3 Up into thee, our living Head,
Let us in all things grow,
Till thou hast made us free indeed,
And spotless here below.
Charles Wesley.

746 *Love as Brethren.*

2 Father, still our faith increase;
Cleanse from all unrighteousness;
Thee the unholy cannot see;
Make, oh, make us meet for thee!

3 Mutual love the token be,
Lord, that we belong to thee:
Only love to us be given;
Lord, we ask no other heaven.
Charles Wesley, 1740.

747 *One Fold and One Shepherd.*

2 Let all that now divides us
  Remove and pass away.
Like shadows of the morning
  Before the blaze of day.
Let all that now unites us
  More sweet and lasting prove,
A closer bond of union,
  In a blest land of love.
Jane Borthwick, 1863.

748 *Universal Hallelujah.*

1 When shall the voice of singing
  Flow joyfully along?
When hill and valley, ringing
  With one triumphant song,
Proclaim the contest ended,
  And him who once was slain,
Again to earth descended,
  In righteousness to reign?

2 Then from the craggy mountains
  The sacred shout shall fly;
And shady vales and fountains
  Shall echo the reply:
High tower and lowly dwelling
  Shall send the chorus round,
All hallelujah swelling
  In one eternal sound.
J. Edmeston, 1824.

GROWTH AND FUTURE GLORY.

ST. GABRIEL. L. M.   HAYDEN, 1792-1809.

1. Triumph-ant Zi-on, lift thy head From dust, and darkness, and, the dead; Tho' humbled long, a-wake at length, And gird thee with thy Saviour's strength, And gird thee with thy Saviour's strength.

749 *Awake! put on thy Strength, O Zion.*
2 Put all thy beauteous garments on,
And let thy various charms be known:
Then, decked in robes of righteousness,
The world thy glories shall confess.

3 God, from on high, thy groans will hear;
His hand thy ruins shall repair;
Nor will thy watchful Monarch cease
To guard thee in eternal peace.
Philip Doddridge.

750 *Unto Thee shall all Flesh come.*
1 THE praise of Zion waits for thee,
Great God, and praise becomes thy house;

There shall thy saints thy glory see,
And there perform their public vows.

2 O thou whose mercy bends the skies
To save when humble sinners pray,
All lands to thee shall lift their eyes,
And grateful isles of every sea.

3 Soon shall the flocking nations run
To Zion's hill and own their Lord;
The rising and the setting sun
Shall see the Saviour's name adored.
Isaac Watts.

ZION. 8s, 7s & 4s.   Dr. HASTINGS.

On the mountain's top appearing, Lo! the sacred herald stands, Mourning captive, God himself shall loose thy bands,
Welcome news to Zi-on bearing, Zi-on long in hostile lands. Mourning captive, God himself shall loose thy bands.

751
2 God, thy God, will now restore thee;
He himself appears thy Friend;
All thy foes shall flee before thee;
Here their boasts and triumphs end;
Great deliverance
Zion's King will surely send.

3 Peace and joy shall now attend thee;
All thy warfare now is past:
God thy saviour will defend thee;
Victory is thine at last;
All thy conflicts
End in everlasting rest.
Thomas Kelly.

752 *The Dayspring from on High.*
1 CHRISTIAN, see! the orient morning
Breaks along the heathen sky;
Lo, the expected day is dawning—
Glorious Dayspring from on high;
Hallelujah!
Hail the Dayspring from on high!

2 Lord of every tribe and nation,
Spread thy truth from pole to pole;
Spread the light of thy salvation
Till it shine on every soul;
Hallelujah!
Hail the Dayspring from on high!
Anon.

THE CHURCH.

SOLITUDE. C. M.   L. B. Starkweather.

1. Fa-ther of me and all man-kind, And all the hosts a-bove, Let ev-ery un-derstanding mind U-nite to praise thy love.

Used by per. Oliver Ditson Co., owners of Copyright.

753   *Thy Kingdom Come.*

2 Thy kingdom come, with power and grace,
   To every heart of man;
Thy peace and joy and righteousness,
   In all our bosoms reign,—

3 The righteousness that never ends,
   But makes an end of sin;
The joy that human thought transcends,
   Into our souls bring in;

4 The kingdom of established peace,
   Which can no more remove;
The perfect powers of godliness,
   The omnipotence of love.
                     Charles Wesley.

754   *The Kingdom Come.*

1 O God, the darkness roll away,
   Which clouds the human soul,
And let the bright, the perfect day
   Speed onward to its goal.

2 Let every hateful passion die,
   Which makes of brethren foes;
And war no longer raise its cry,
   To mar the world's repose,

3 Let faith and hope and charity
   Go forth through all the earth;
And man, in heavenly bearing, be
   True to his heavenly birth.

4 Yea, let thy glorious kingdom come,
   Of holiness and love;
And make this world a portal meet
   For thy bright courts above.
                     William Gaskell.

NASSAU. 7s, 6l.   J. Rosenmüller.

1. God of mer-cy, God of grace, Show the brightness of thy face; Shine up-on us, Fa-ther, shine,
Fill us with thy light di-vine; And thy saving health ex-tend Un-to earth's re-motest end.

755   *Thy Kingdom Come.*

2 Let the people praise thee, Lord!
Let thy love on all be poured;
Let awakened nations sing
Glory to their heavenly King,
At thy feet their tribute pay,
And thy holy will obey.

3 Let the people praise thee, Lord!
Earth shall then her fruits afford,
God to man his blessing give,
Man to God devoted live;
All below, and all above,
One in joy and light and love.
                     Henry F. Lyte, 1834.

GROWTH AND FUTURE GLORY.

REVIVE THY WORK. S. M. — JAMES McGRANAHAN, by per.

1. Revive thy work, O Lord, Thy mighty arm make bare; Speak with the voice that wakes the dead, And make thy people hear.

Cho.—Re-vive thy work, revive thy work, And give refreshing show'rs; The glory shall be all thine own, The blessing shall be ours.

756

2 Revive thy work, O Lord,
Disturb this sleep of death;
Quicken the smold'ring embers now
By thine Almighty breath.—CHO.

3 Revive thy work, O Lord,
Create soul-thirst for thee;
And hung'ring for the bread of life,
Oh, may our spirits be.—CHO.

4 Revive thy work, O Lord,
Exalt thy precious name;
And by the Holy Ghost, our love
For thee and thine inflame.—CHO.

Rev. J. C. Ryle.

CALL TO VICTORY. 7s & 5s. — L. O. EMERSON.

1. Saints, for whom the Saviour bled, In your Captain's footsteps tread: Fol-low Je-sus, and be led On to vic-to-ry!
See your foemen take the ground; While the sig-nal trumpets sound, Hear his accents pour a-round, Cheering mel-o-dy.

Used by per. Oliver Ditson Co., owners of Copyright.

757

2 Christian soldier, on with me!
Soon your enemies must flee;
Your reward before you see
  Sparkling from on high!
Boldly take the glorious field;
You may fall—but must not yield;
You shall write upon your shield,
  Victory, though you die!

3 By the ransom which he gave,
By his triumph o'er the grave,
Trust his mighty power to save;
  Firm and faithful be;
And when death's dark hour is nigh,
When the tear-drop dims the eye,
You shall in the parting sigh,
  Grasp the victory.

Anon.

THE CHURCH.

LEIGHTON. S. M. GREATOREX COLLECTION.

1. Come, kingdom of our God, Sweet reign of light and love; Shed peace, and hope, and joy abroad, And wisdom from a - bove.

758 *Thy Kingdom Come.*

2 Over our spirits first
Extend thy healing reign;
There raise and quench the sacred thirst
That never pains again.

3 Come, kingdom of our God,
And make the broad earth thine;
Stretch o'er her lands and isles the rod
That flowers with grace divine.

4 Soon may all tribes be blest
With fruits from life's glad tree;
And in its shade like brothers rest,
Sons of one family.
John Johns, 1837.

759 *Lord, revive thy Work.*

1 O LORD, thy work revive
In Zion's gloomy hour,
And make her dying graces live
By thy restoring power.

2 Awake thy chosen few
To fervent, earnest prayer;
Again their sacred vows renew,
Thy blessed presence share.

3 Thy Spirit then will speak
Through lips of feeble clay,
And hearts of adamant will break,
And rebels will obey.

4 Lord, lend thy gracious ear;
O, listen to our cry;
O, come and bring salvation here:
Our hopes on thee rely.
Phœbe H. Brown.

HAMDEN. 8s, 7s & 4s. LOWELL MASON.

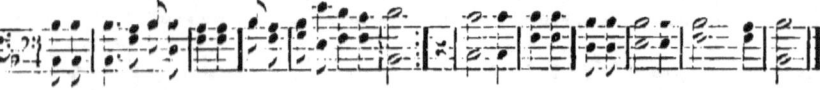

1. { Yes, my native land, I love thee; All thy scenes, I love them well; }
   { Home, and friends, and happy country, Can I bid you all fare-well? } Can I leave you, Far in heathen lands to dwell?

760 *The Missionary's Farewell.*

2 Scenes of sacred peace and pleasure,
Holy days and Sabbath bell,
Richest, brightest, sweetest treasure,
Can I—can I say, Farewell?
Can I leave you,
Far in heathen lands to dwell?

3 Yes, I hasten from you gladly,
To the strangers let me tell
How he died—the blessed Saviour—
To redeem a world from hell:
Let me hasten
Far in heathen lands to dwell.

4 Bear me on, thou restless ocean,
From the scenes I love so well;
Heaves my heart with warm emotion,
While I go far hence to dwell:
Glad I bid thee,
Native land, farewell, farewell!
S. F. Smith.

MISSIONS.

MUNICH. 7s & 6s, D.   Arr. fr. MENDELSSOHN.

1. Our country's voice is pleading, Ye men of God, a-rise!
   His prov-i-dence is lead-ing, The land be-fore you lies; Day-gleams are o'er it bright'ning,
   And promise clothes the soil; Wide fields, for har-vest whitening, In-vite the reaper's toil.

761 "*Home Missions.*"

2 The love of Christ unfolding,
  Speed on from east to west,
Till all, his cross beholding,
  In him are fully blest.
Great Author of Salvation,
  Haste, haste the glorious day,
When we, a ransomed nation,
  Thy sceptre shall obey.
Mrs. Maria F. Anderson

762 '*Departing Missionaries.*"

1 ROLL on, thou mighty ocean;
  And, as thy billows flow,
Bear messengers of mercy
  To every land below.

Arise, ye gales, and waft them
  Safe to the destined shore;
That man may sit in darkness,
  And death's black shade no more.

2 O thou eternal Ruler,
  Who holdest in thine arm
The tempests of the ocean,
  Protect them from all harm!
Thy presence, Lord, be with them,
  Wherever they may be;
Though far from us, who love them,
  Still let them be with thee.
James Edmeston.

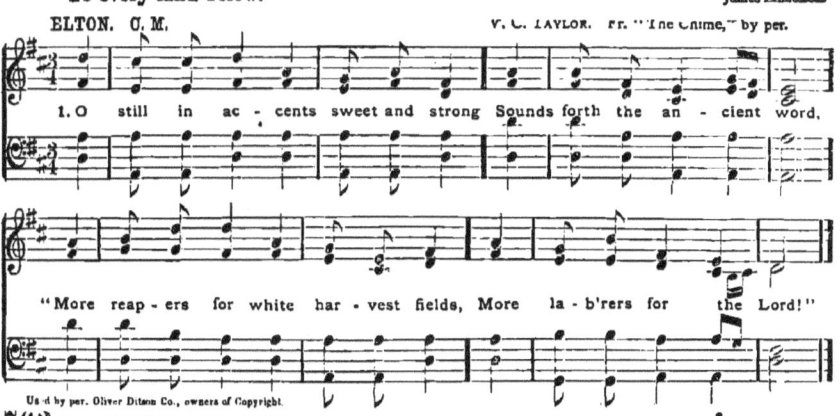

ELTON. C. M.   V. C. TAYLOR. Fr. "The Chime," by per.

1. O still in ac-cents sweet and strong Sounds forth the an-cient word,
"More reap-ers for white har-vest fields, More la-b'rers for the Lord!"

_{Used by per. Oliver Ditson Co., owners of Copyright.}

763   *More Laborers.*

2 We hear the call; in dreams no more
  In selfish ease we lie,
But, girded for our Father's work,
  Go forth beneath His sky.

3 Where prophets' word, and martyrs' blood,
  And prayers of saints were sown,
We, to their labors entering in,
  Would reap where they have strown.

4 O thou whose call our hearts has stirred!
  To do thy will we come,
Thrust in our sickles at thy word,
  And bear our harvest home.
Samuel Longfellow.

CHRISTIAN PHILANTHROPY.

WARD. L. M.   From a Scotch Tune, by Dr. L. Mason.

1. Thy Father's house! thine own bright home! And thou hast there a place for me!
Though yet an exile here I roam, That distant home by faith I see.

764   *"Many Mansions."*

2 I see its domes resplendent glow,
Where beams of God's own glory fall;
And trees of life immortal grow,
Whose fruits o'erhang the sapphire wall.

3 I know that thou, who on the tree
Didst deign our mortal guilt to bear,
Wilt bring thine own to dwell with thee,
And waitest to receive me there!

4 Thy love will there array my soul
In thine own robe of spotless hue;
And I shall gaze, while ages roll,
On thee, with raptures ever new!

5 Oh, welcome day! when thou my feet
Shalt bring the shining threshold o'er;
A Father's warm embrace to meet,
And dwell at home forever more!
Ray Palmer.

765   *Zion's Glory.*

1 Zion! awake, thy strength renew;
Put on thy robes of beauteous hue;
And let the admiring world behold
The King's fair daughter clothed in gold.

2 Church of our God! arise and shine,
Bright with the beams of truth divine;

Then shall thy radiance stream afar,
Wide as the heathen nations are.

3 Gentiles and kings thy light shall view,
And shall admire and love thee too;—
They come, like clouds across the sky,
As doves that to their windows fly.
William Shrubsole, jr.

766   *Psalm 72.*

1 Great God! whose universal sway
The known and unknown worlds obey;
Now give the kingdom to thy Son;
Extend his power, exalt his throne.

2 As rain on meadows newly mown,
So shall he send his influence down;
His grace, on fainting souls, distills
Like heavenly dew on thirsty hills.

3 The heathen lands, that lie beneath
The shades of overspreading death,
Revive at his first dawning light,
And deserts blossom at the sight.

4 The saints shall flourish in his days,
Dressed in the robes of joy and praise;
Peace, like a river, from his throne,
Shall flow to nations yet unknown.
Isaac Watts.

MISSIONS.

FOUNT. 8s & 7s. D.

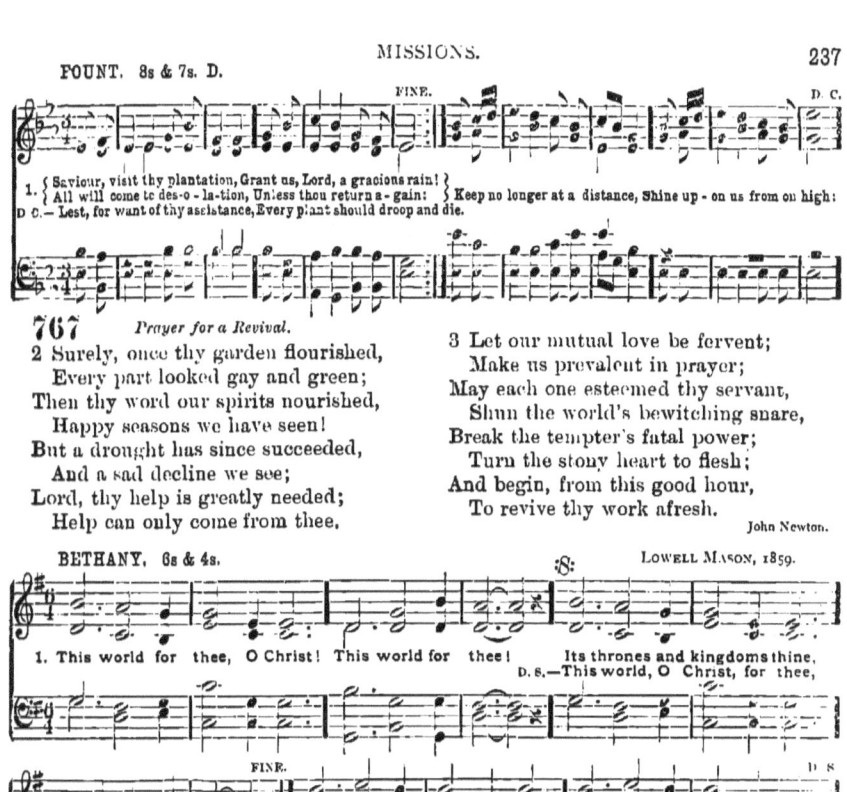

1. Saviour, visit thy plantation, Grant us, Lord, a gracious rain!
All will come to des-o-la-tion, Unless thou return a-gain:
Keep no longer at a distance, Shine up-on us from on high;
D. C.— Lest, for want of thy assistance, Every plant should droop and die.

767 *Prayer for a Revival.*

2 Surely, once thy garden flourished,
Every part looked gay and green;
Then thy word our spirits nourished,
Happy seasons we have seen!
But a drought has since succeeded,
And a sad decline we see;
Lord, thy help is greatly needed;
Help can only come from thee.

3 Let our mutual love be fervent;
Make us prevalent in prayer;
May each one esteemed thy servant,
Shun the world's bewitching snare,
Break the tempter's fatal power;
Turn the stony heart to flesh;
And begin, from this good hour,
To revive thy work afresh.
John Newton.

BETHANY. 6s & 4s. LOWELL MASON, 1859.

1. This world for thee, O Christ! This world for thee! Its thrones and kingdoms thine,
D. S.—This world, O Christ, for thee,

Thine ev-er be; As ful-ness of the sea,— This world, O Christ, for thee.
This world for thee.

Used by per. Oliver Ditson Co., owners of Copyright

768 *This world for Christ.*

2 For this thy bannered hosts,
Lift up thy name,
Wherever sin hath gone,
With sting and shame;
That men may bow to thee,—
This world, O Christ, for thee,
This world for thee!

3 Thy church can never stay
Content at rest,
Till all the nations wide,
In thee are blest,
From river to the sea,—
This world, O Christ, for thee,
This world for thee!

4 Come forth, thou King of kings,
And lead us on,
The army of thy saints
Till earth is won
In blessed victory,—
This world, O Christ, for thee,
This world for thee!

5 Hark! to the battle cry,
The strife begun;
O hearts, be brave and strong,
Till conflict done;
Till then, our cry shall be,—
This world, O Christ, for thee,
This world for thee.
Francis B. Wheeler, D.D.

CHRISTIAN PHILANTHROPY.

ITALY. 6s & 4s. — Felice Giardini, 1760.

1. Lord of all power and might, Father of love and light, Speed on thy word: Oh, let the gospel sound / All the wide world around, Wherever man is found! God speed his word.

769 *Speed on Thy Word.*

2 Onward shall be our course,
Despite of fraud or force;
God is before:
His word ere long shall run,
Free as the noon-day sun;
His purpose must be done:
God bless his word.
Hugh Stowell, 1854.

770 *Go ye into all the World.*

1 Sound, sound the truth abroad:
Bear ye the word of God
Through the wide world:
Tell what our Lord hath done;
Tell how the day was won,
And from his lofty throne
Satan is hurled.

2 Far over sea and land—
'Tis our Lord's own command—
Bear ye his name;
Bear it to every shore;
Regions unknown explore;
Enter at every door:
Silence is shame.

3 Ye who, forsaking all
At your loved Master's call,
Comforts resign,
Soon will the work be done;
Soon will the prize be won;
Brighter than yonder sun
Then shall ye shine.
Anon.

771 *Thy Kingdom come.*

1 Our Father, unto Thee
Our earnest prayer shall be,
Thy kingdom come.
O'er all earth's broad domains,
Where sin has left its stains,
Till naught that's pure remains,
Thy kingdom come.

2 Let Christians ne'er forget,
The word of God holds yet
Its power of old.
Send forth the gospel light,
However dark the night,
There God's own truth and might
Shall hope unfold.

3 Dispel the mists that blind
The heathen's darkened mind
In sin and woe.
Haste the Millennial morn,
When error's power is shorn,
And nations yet unborn
The Christ shall know.

4 Then hoary age and youth,
In spirit and in truth,
Shall worship thee.
O speed the blessèd day,
When from sin's blighting sway,
Forever and for aye,
Earth shall be free.
Rev. H. E. Haley.

MISSIONS.

MISSIONARY HYMN. 7s & 8s. [IAMBIC.] — LOWELL MASON, 1824.

1. From Greenland's icy mountains, From In-dia's cor-al strand, Where Afric's sunny fountains Roll down the gol'den sand,— From many an ancient riv-er, From many a palmy plain,— They call us to de-liv-er Their land from error's chain.

772 *Missionary Hymn.*

2 What though the spicy breezes
Blow soft o'er Ceylon's isle,
Though every prospect pleases,
And only man is vile;
In vain, with lavish kindness,
The gifts of God are strown:
The heathen in his blindness,
Bows down to wood and stone.

3 Shall we, whose souls are lighted
With wisdom from on high,—
Shall we to men benighted
The lamp of life deny?
Salvation! O, salvation!
The joyful sound proclaim,
Till earth's remotest nation
Has learned Messiah's name.

4 Waft, waft, ye winds, his story,
And you, ye waters, roll,
Till, like a sea of glory,
It spreads from pole to pole;
Till o'er our ransomed nature
The Lamb, for sinners slain,
The mighty King and Saviour,
In bliss returns to reign.
Bishop Reginald Heber, 1819.

773

1 LORD of the living harvest,
That whitens o'er the plain,
Where angels soon shall gather
Their sheaves of golden grain,

Accept these hands to labor,
These hearts to trust and love,
And deign with them to hasten
Thy kingdom from above.

2 As laborers in thy vineyard
Send us out, Christ, to be
Content to bear the burden
Of weary days for thee.
We ask no other wages
When thou shalt call us home,
But to have shared the travail
Which makes thy kingdom come.
J. S. B. Monsell.

774

1 OH, that the Lord's salvation
Were out of Zion come,
To heal his ancient nation,
To lead his outcasts home!
How long the holy city
Shall heathen feet profane?
Return, O Lord, in pity,
Rebuild her walls again.

2 Let fall thy rod of terror,
Thy saving grace impart;
Roll back the vail of error,
Release the fettered heart;
Let Israel, home returning,
Their lost Messiah see;
Give oil of joy for mourning,
And bind thy Church to thee.
Henry F. Lyte, 1834.

240 CHRISTIAN PHILANTHROPY.

ALL SAINTS. L. M. W. KNAPP, 1768.

1. O Spirit of the living God, In all thy plenitude of grace,
Wher-e'er the foot of man hath trod, Descend on our benighted race.

775 *Wilt Thou not revive us again?*
2 Give tongues of fire and hearts of love
 To preach the reconciling word;
Give power and unction from above,
 Where'er the joyful sound is heard.

3 Be darkness, at thy coming, light;
 Confusion, order, in thy path;
Souls without strength inspire with might;
 Bid mercy triumph over wrath.

4 Baptize the nations; far and nigh
 The triumphs of the cross record:
The name of Jesus glorify,
 Till every kindred call him Lord.
    James Montgome

776 *Home Missions.*
1 Look from thy sphere of endless day,
 O God of mercy and of might!
In pity look on those who stray,
 Benighted in this land of light.

2 Send forth thy heralds, Lord, to call
 The thoughtless young, the hardened old,
A scattered, homeless flock, till all
 Be gathered to thy peaceful fold.

3 Send them thy mighty word to speak,
 Till faith shall dawn, and doubt depart,
To awe the bold, to stay the weak,
 And bind and heal the broken heart.

4 Then all these wastes, a dreary scene,
 That makes us sadden as we gaze,
Shall grow with living waters green,
 And lift to heaven the voice of praise.
    William C. Bryant.

777 *City Mission.*
1 Go, MESSENGER of peace and love,
 To people plunged in shades of night;
Like angels sent from fields above,
 Be thine to shed celestial light.

2 Go to the hungry—food impart;
 To paths of peace the wanderer guide;
And lead the thirsty, panting heart
 Where streams of living waters glide.

3 Thy love a rich reward shall find
 From him who sits enthroned on high;
For they who turn the erring mind
 Shall shine like stars above the sky.
    Balfour.

778 *Christ's Coming.*
1 JESUS! thy church, with longing eyes,
 For thine expected coming waits;
When will the promised light arise,
 And glory beam from Zion's gates?

2 Ev'n now, when tempests round us fall,
 And wintry clouds o'ercast the sky,
Thy words with pleasure we recall,
 And deem that our redemption's nigh.

3 Oh, come and reign o'er every land;
 Let Satan from his throne be hurled;
All nations bow to thy command,
 And grace revive a dying world.

4 Teach us, in watchfulness and prayer,
 To wait for the appointed hour;
And fit us, by thy grace, to share
 The triumphs of thy conquering power.
    Wm H. Bathurst.

CHARITIES AND REFORMS. 241

MARINER'S SONG. 8s & 7s, D.   L. O. E.

1. Tossed up-on life's rag-ing bil-low, Sweet it is, O Lord, to know,
Thou didst press a sai-lor's pil-low, And canst feel a sai-lor's woe.
D. C.—Thou the faith-ful watch art keep-ing,— 'All, all's well,' thy con-stant cheer.

Nev-er slumb'ring, nev-er sleep-ing, Though the night be dark and drear,

Used by per. Oliver Ditson Co., owners of Copyright.

779   *He Stills the Waves.*

2 And though loud the wind is howling,
  Fierce though flash the lightnings red,
Darkly though the storm-cloud's scowling
  O'er the sailor's anxious head,
Thou canst calm the raging ocean,
  All its noise and tumult still,
Hush the tempest's wild commotion,
  At the bidding of thy will.

3 Thus my heart the hope will cherish,
  While to thee I lift mine eye,
Thou wilt save me ere I perish,
  Thou wilt hear the sailor's cry.
And though mast and sail be riven,
  Life's short voyage soon be o'er;
Safely moored in heaven's wide haven,
  Storm and tempest vex no more.
                   G. W. Bethune.

780   *All for Christ.*

1 WITH my substance I will honor
  My Redeemer and my Lord;
Were ten thousand worlds my manor,
  All were nothing to his word.
While the heralds of salvation
  His abounding grace proclaim,
Let his friends, of every station,
  Gladly join to spread his fame.
    16

2 Be his kingdom now promoted;
  Let the earth her Monarch know;
Be my all to him devoted;
  To my Lord my all I owe.
Praise the Saviour, all ye nations;
  Praise him, all ye hosts above;
Shout, with joyful acclamations,
  His divine, victorious love.
                   Francis.

781   *Quit you like Men; be strong.*

1 WE are living, we are dwelling
  In a grand and awful time,
In an age on ages telling:
  To be living is sublime.
Hark! the onset! will ye fold your
  Faith-clad arms in lazy lock?
Up! O, up! thou drowsy soldier;
  Worlds are charging to the shock.

2 Worlds are charging, heaven beholding;
  Thou hast but an hour to fight;
Now, the blazoned cross unfolding,
  On! right onward for the right.
On! let all the soul within you
  For the truth's sake go abroad:
Strike! let every nerve and sinew
  Tell on ages—tell for God.
                   Coxe.

CHRISTIAN PHILANTHROPY.

ASHWELL. L. M. Dr. L. Mason.

1. Rock'd in the cra-dle of the deep, I lay me down in peace to sleep;
Se-cure I rest up-on the wave, For thou, O Lord, hast power to save.

782 *Cradle of the Deep.*

2 I know thou wilt not slight my call,
For thou dost mark the sparrow's fall;
And calm and peaceful is my sleep,
Rocked in the cradle of the deep.

3 In ocean caves still safe with thee
The germ of immortality;
And calm and peaceful is my sleep,
Rocked in the cradle of the deep.
Mrs. Willard.

783 *Lord, save us; we perish.*

1 The billows swell, the winds are high;
Clouds overcast my wintry sky:
Out of the depths to thee I call;
My fears are great, my strength is small.

2 O Lord, the pilot's part perform,
And guide and guard me through the storm;
Defend me from each threatening ill;
Control the waves; say, Peace, be still.

3 Amid the roaring of the sea,
My soul still hangs her hope on thee;
Though tempest-tossed and half a wreck,
My Saviour through the floods I seek.
Cowper.

784 *Look not upon the Wine.*

1 Slavery and death the cup contains;
Dash to the earth the poisoned bowl;
Softer than silk are iron chains,
Compared with those that chafe the soul.

2 Hosannas, Lord, to thee we sing,
Whose power the giant fiend obeys;
What countless thousands tribute bring
For happier homes and brighter days!

3 Thou wilt not break the bruiséd reed,
Nor leave the broken heart unbound:
The wife regains a husband freed,
The orphan clasps a father found.

4 Spare, Lord, the thoughtless, guide the blind,
Till man no more shall deem it just
To live by forging chains to bind
His weaker brother in the dust.
Hymns of the Spirit.

785 *Their Sacrifices shall be accepted.*

1 When, driven by oppression's rod,
Our fathers fled beyond the sea,
Their care was first to honor God,
And next to leave their children free.

2 Above the forest's gloomy shade
The altar and the school appeared;
On that the gifts of faith were laid,
In this their precious hopes were reared.

3 The altar and the school still stand,
The sacred pillars of our trust,
And Freedom's sons shall fill our land
When we are sleeping in the dust.

4 Before thine altar, Lord, we bend,
With grateful song and fervent prayer,
For thou, who wast our fathers' Friend,
Wilt make our children still thy care.
Lunt.

CALEDONIA. P. M.

1. Friends of free-dom swell the song, Young and old the train pro-long, Make the Temp'rance ar-my strong, And on to vic-to-ry. Lift your ban-ners, let them wave, Onward march a world to save! Who would fill a drunkard's grave, And bear his in-fa-my.

786 *Friends of Freedom.*

2 Shrink not when the foe appears,
Spurn the coward's guilty fears;
Hear the shrieks, behold the tears
    Of ruined families.
Raise the cry in every spot—
I " Touch not, taste not, handle not."
Who would be a drunken sot—
    The worst of miseries.

3 Give the aching bosom rest,
Carry joy to every breast,
Make the wretched drunkard blest,
    By living soberly.
Raise the glorious watchword high,
" Touch not, taste not, till you die,"
Let the echo reach the sky,
    And the earth keep jubilee.

4 God of mercy, hear us plead,
For thy help we intercede;
See how many bosoms bleed,
    And heal them speedily.
Haste, oh, haste the happy day,
When beneath its gentle ray,
Temp'rance all the world shall sway,
    And reign triumphantly.

Anon.

CHRISTIAN PHILANTHROPY.

GREENWOOD. S. M.
Root & Sweetser's Coll.

1. Mourn for the thou-sands slain, The youth-ful and the strong; Mourn for the wine-cup's fear-ful reign, And the de-lud-ed throng.

787 *Wine is a Mocker.*

2 Mourn for the ruined soul—
Eternal life and light
Lost by the fiery, maddening bowl,
And turned to hopeless night.

3 Mourn for the lost, but call,
Call to the strong, the free;
Rouse them to shun that dreadful fall;
And to the refuge flee.

4 Mourn for the lost, but pray,
Pray to our God above
To break the fell destroyer's sway,
And show his saving love.

S. C. Brace.

WARE. 8s, 7s & 4s.
Arr. by W. B. Bradbury.

1. Star of peace, to wanderers wea-ry, Bright the beams that smile on me; Cheer the pi-lot's vis-ion dreary, Far, far at sea; Cheer the pi-lot's vision dreary, Far, far at sea.

788 *The Guiding Star.*

2 Star of hope, gleam on the billow;
Bless the soul that sighs for thee;
Bless the sailor's lonely pillow,
Far, far at sea.

3 Star of faith, when winds are mocking
All his toil, he flies to thee;
Save him, on the billows rocking,
Far, far at sea.

4 Star divine, O, safely guide him;
Bring the wanderer home to thee;
Sore temptations long have tried him,
Far, far at sea.

Jane Cross Simpson.

CHARITIES AND REFORMS.

LITCHFIELD. C. M.   Dr. L. Mason.

1. We come, O Lord, before thy throne, And, with united pleas,
We meet and pray for those who roam Far-off upon the seas.

789   *Prayer for Seamen.*

2 O, may the Holy Spirit bow
The sailor's heart to thee,
Till tears of deep repentance flow
Like raindrops in the sea.

3 Then may a Saviour's dying love
Pour peace into his breast,
And waft him to the port above
Of everlasting rest.

Phœbe H. Brown.

GOD SPEED THE RIGHT.   8s & 4s.   From the German.
DUET.

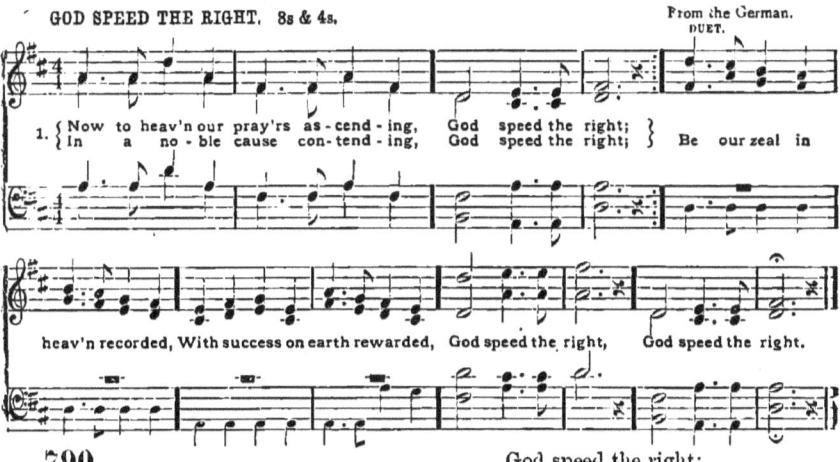

1. Now to heav'n our pray'rs ascending, God speed the right;
In a noble cause contending, God speed the right;
Be our zeal in heav'n recorded, With success on earth rewarded, God speed the right, God speed the right.

790

2 Be that prayer again repeated,
God speed the right;
Ne'er despairing, though defeated,
God speed the right;
Like the good and great in story,
If we fail, we fail with glory,
God speed the right.

3 Patient, firm, and persevering,
God speed the right;
Ne'er th' event nor danger fearing,
God speed the right;
Pains, nor toils, nor trials heeding
And in heav'n's own time succeeding,
God speed the right.

4 Still our onward course pursuing,
God speed the right;
Ev'ry foe at length subduing,
God speed the right;
Truth our cause, whate'er delay it,
There's no power on earth can stay it,
God speed the right.

W. E. Hickson.

CHRISTIAN PHILANTHROPY.

WESLEY. 8s & 7s, D.   John Zundel.

1. Lord, in mercy thou hast spoken; Ages witness as they roll; Bleeding hearts and spirit broken, Touched by thee, O God, are whole. By thy pitying spirit guided, Jesus sought the sufferer's door; And the mourner's sorrows bore.
D. S.—Comfort for the poor provided,

791 *The opening of the Prison.*

2 So thy mercy's angel, bending,
  Heard a friendless prisoner's call,
And through night's cold vault descending,
  Loosed from chains thy servant Paul.

Father, as thy love is endless,
  Working by thy servants thus,
The forsaken and the friendless
  Deign to visit, e'en by us.
Pierpont.

CANONBURY. L. M.   Robert Schumann.

1. O Lord of Hosts, almighty King, Behold the sacrifice we bring; To every arm thy strength impart, Thy spirit shed through every heart.

792 *The Sword of the Lord.*

2 Wake in our breasts the living fires,
The holy faith that warmed our sires;
Thy hand hath made our nation free;
To die for her is serving thee.

3 Be thou a pillared flame to show
The midnight snare, the silent foe;
And when the battle thunders loud,
Still guide us in the moving cloud.

4 God of all nations, sovereign Lord,
In thy dread name we draw the sword,
We lift the starry flag on high
That fills with light our stormy sky.

5 From treason's rent, from murder's stain,
Guard thou its folds till peace shall reign—
Till fort and field, till shore and sea,
Join our loud anthem, Praise to thee.
O. W. Holmes.

THE NATIONS. 247

AMERICA. 6s & 4s.   English Hymn.

1. My country! 'tis of thee, Sweet land of liberty, Of thee I sing; Land where my fathers died! Land of the pilgrim's pride! From ev-'ry mountain side Let free-dom ring.

793   *National Hymn.*

2 My native country, thee,
   Land of the noble free,
      Thy name I love:
I love thy rocks and rills,
Thy woods and templed hills;
   My heart with rapture thrills
      Like that above.

3 Let music swell the breeze,
   And ring from all the trees
      Sweet freedom's song;
Let mortal tongues awake,
Let all that breathe partake,
   Let rocks their silence break,
      The sound prolong.

4 Our father's God, to thee,
   Author of liberty,
      To thee we sing;
Long may our land be bright
With freedom's holy light,
   Protect us by thy might,
      Great God, our King!
             S. F. Smith, 1833.

794   *Our Native Land.*

1 GOD bless our native land!
   Firm may she ever stand,
      Through storm and night:
When the wild tempests rave,
Ruler of wind and wave,
   Do thou our country save
      By thy great might!

2 For her our prayer shall rise
   To God, above the skies;
      On him we wait:
Thou who art ever nigh,
Guarding with watchful eye,
   To thee aloud we cry,
      God save the State!
            John S. Dwight, 1844.

795   *Thou leadest Joseph like a Flock.*

1 O GOD, beneath thy guiding hand,
   Our exiled fathers crossed the sea;
And when they trod the wintry strand,
   With prayer and psalm they worshipped thee.

2 Laws, freedom, truth, and faith in God
   Came with those exiles o'er the waves;

And where their pilgrim feet have trod,
   The God they trusted guards their graves.

3 And here thy name, O God of love,
   Their children's children shall adore,
Till these eternal hills remove,
   And spring adorns the earth no more.
             L. Bacon.

VARIOUS OCCASIONS.

STEPHENS. C. M.   W. JONES.

1. Lord, while for all mankind we pray, Of every clime and coast,
Oh! hear us for our native land,— The land we love the most.

796   *Prayer for our Country.*

2 Oh! guard our shore from every foe,
With peace our borders bless,
With prosperous times our cities crown,
Our fields with plenteousness.

3 Unite us in the sacred love
Of knowledge, truth and thee;
And let our hills and valleys shout
The songs of liberty.

4 Lord of the nations! thus to thee
Our country we commend;
Be thou her Refuge and her Trust,
Her everlasting Friend.
              John Reynell Wreford, 1837.

797   *Our Fathers have told us.*

1 O LORD, our father's oft have told,
In our attentive ears,
Thy wonders in their days performed,
And elder times than theirs.

2 For not their courage, nor their sword,
To them salvation gave,
Nor strength that from an equal force
Their fainting troops could save,—

3 But thy right hand and powerful arm,
Whose succor they implored;
Thy presence with the chosen race
Who thy great name adored.

4 As thee, their God, our fathers owned,
Thou art our sovereign King:
O, therefore, as thou didst to them,
To us deliverance bring.

5 To thee the triumph we ascribe,
From whom the conquest came;
In God we will rejoice all day
And ever bless thy name.
              Anon.

ST. MICHAEL. S. M.   DAY'S PSALTER.

1. For all thy saints, O God, Who strove in Christ to live, Who followed him, obeyed, adored, Our grateful hymn receive.

798   *Thanksgiving for all Saints.*

2 For all thy saints, O God,
Accept our thankful cry,
Who counted Christ their great reward,
And yearned for him to die.

3 They all, in life and death,
With him, their Lord, in view,

Learned, from thy Holy Spirit's breath,
To suffer and to do.

4 For this thy name we bless,
And humbly pray that we
May follow them in holiness,
And live and die in thee.
              Richard Mant.

THE NATION.

799

2 Not as the conqueror comes,
  They, the true-hearted, came,
Not with the roll of stirring drums,
  And the trump that sings of fame:
Not as the flying come,
  In silence and in fear;
They shook the depths of the desert's gloom,
  With their hymns of lofty cheer.

3 Amidst the storm they sang;
  And the stars heard, and the sea!
And the sounding aisles of the dim woods
      rang
  To the anthem of the free,

The ocean eagle soared
  From his nest by the white wave's foam,
And the rocking pines of the forest roared,
  This was their welcome home!

4 What sought they thus afar?
  Bright jewels of the mine?
The wealth of seas, the spoils of war?
  They sought a faith's pure shrine!
Ay, call it holy ground,
  The soil where first they trod!
They have left unstained, what here they
      found;
  Freedom to worship God.

          Felicia D. Hemans.

MISSIONARY CHANT. L. M.
Charles Zeuner, 1832.

1. Thanks be to Him who built the hills;
Thanks be to Him the streams who fills;
Thanks be to Him who lights each star
That sparkles in the blue afar.

800 *Thanksgiving.*

2 Thanks be to Him who makes the morn,
And bids it glow with beams new-born;
Who draws the shadows of the night,
Like curtains, o'er our wearied sight.

3 Thanks be to Him who sheds abroad,
Within our hearts, the love of God—
The Spirit of all truth and peace,
Fountain of joy and holiness.
Horatius Bonar.

801 *Thanksgiving for the Faithful.*

1 For all thy gifts we praise thee, Lord,
  With lifted song and bended knee;
But now our thanks are chiefly poured
  For those who taught us to be free.

2 For when the soul lay bound below
  A heavy yoke of forms and creeds,
And none thy word of truth could know,
  O'ergrown with tares and choked with weeds,—

3 The monarch's sword, the prelate's pride,
  The church's curse, the empire's ban,
By one poor monk were all defied,
  Who never feared the face of man.

4 With lifted song and bended knee,
  For all thy gifts we praise thee, Lord;
But chief for those who made us free—
  The champions of thy holy word.
James Freeman Clarke.

DORT. 6s & 4s.
Lowell Mason.

1. The God of har-vest praise; In loud thanksgiving raise Hand, heart, and voice: The valleys laugh and sing; Forests and mountains ring; The plains their tribute bring; The streams rejoice.

802 *Thanksgiving.*

2 Yea, bless his holy name,
And joyous thanks proclaim
    Through all the earth:
To glory in your lot
Is comely; but be not
God's benefits forgot
    Amid your mirth.

3 The God of harvest praise;
Hands, hearts, and voices raise
    With sweet accord;
From field to garner throng,
Bearing your sheaves along,
And in your harvest song
    Bless ye the Lord.
James Montgomery.

803

2 He bids the sun to rise and set;
In heaven his power is known;
And earth, subdued to him, shall yet
Bow low before his throne.
For he is good, &c.

Anon

VARIOUS OCCASIONS.

BENEVENTO. 7s, D. Samuel Webbe.

1. While, with ceaseless course, the sun Hasted thro' the former year, Many souls their race have run,
D.S.—We a little longer wait;
Nevermore to meet us here; But how little none can know.
Fixed in an eternal state, They have done with all below;

804 *New Year.*

2 As the wingéd arrow flies
  Speedily the mark to find:
As the lightning from the skies
  Darts, and leaves no trace behind,—
Swiftly thus our fleeting days
  Bear us down life's rapid stream;
Upward, Lord, our spirits raise,
  All below is but a dream.

3 Thanks for mercies past receive;
  Pardon of our sins renew;
Teach us henceforth how to live,
  With eternity in view:
Bless thy word to old and young;
  Fill us with a Saviour's love;
When our life's short race is run,
  May we dwell with thee above.
                              John Newton.

GERMANY. L. M. Beethoven.

1. Great God, we sing that mighty hand By which supported still we stand;
The opening year thy mercy shows; Let mercy crown it till it close.

805 *"I continue unto this day."*

2 By day, by night, at home, abroad,
  Still we are guarded by our God;
By his incessant bounty fed,
  By his unerring counsel led.

3 With grateful hearts the past wo own:
  The future, all to us unknown,
We to thy guardian care commit,
  And, peaceful, leave before thy feet.

4 In scenes exalted or depressed,
  Be thou our joy, and thou our rest;
Thy goodness all our hopes shall raise,
  Adored through all our changing days.
                              Philip Doddridge.

THE YEAR. 253

LUCAS. 5s & 12s.   James Lucas. Arr. by S J. Vail.

806 *Come, let us anew.*

2 Our life is a dream;
Our time, as a stream,
Glides swiftly away,
And the fugitive moment refuses to stay:
The arrow is flown;
The moment is gone;
The millenial year
Rushes on to our view, and eternity's near.

3 Oh that each, in the day
Of his coming, may say,
"I have fought my way through;
I have finished the work thou didst give me
to do;"
Oh that each from his Lord
May receive the glad word,
"Well and faithfully done;
Enter into my joy and sit down on my
throne."
.Charles Wesley, 1750.

VARIOUS OCCASIONS.

MERTON. C. M.   H. K. Oliver.

1. Thee we a-dore, e-ter-nal Name, And hum-bly own to thee How fee-ble is our mor-tal frame, What dy-ing worms are we.

807   *He fleeth also as a Shadow.*

2 The year rolls round, and steals away
   The breath that first it gave;
Whate'er we do, where'er we be,
   We're traveling to the grave.

3 Our wasting lives grow shorter still,
   As months and days increase;
And every beating pulse we tell
   Leaves but the number less.

4 Waken, O Lord, our drowsy sense
   To walk this dangerous road;
And if our souls are hurried hence,
   May they be found with God.
                  Isaac Watts.

808   *Seed-time and Harvest.*

1 Fountain of mercy, God of love,
   How rich thy bounties are,
The rolling seasons, as they move,
   Proclaim thy constant care.

2 When in the bosom of the earth
   The sower hides the grain,
Thy goodness marks its secret birth,
   And sends the early rain.

3 The spring's sweet influence, Lord, is thine;
   The plants in beauty grow;
Thou giv'st the summer's suns to shine,
   The mild, refreshing dew.

4 We own and bless thy gracious sway;
   Ere man and all nature hails;
Seed-time nor harvest, night nor day,
   Summer nor winter fails.
                  Anna Flowerdew, 1812.

809   *The Close of the Year.*

1 O God, to thee our hearts would pay
   Their gratitude sincere,
Whose love hath kept us, night and day
   Throughout another year.

2 Of every breath and every power
   Thou wast the gracious Source;
From thee came every happy hour
   Which smiled along its course.

3 For joy and grief alike we pay
   Our thanks to thee above,
And only pray to grow each day
   More worthy of thy love.
                  William Gaskell.

810   *Beginning of the Year.*

1 Break, new-born year, on glad eyes break!
   Melodious voices move!
On, rolling Time! thou canst not make
   The Father cease to love.

2 Our hearts in tears may oft run o'er;
   But Lord, thy smile still beams;
Our sins are swelling evermore;
   But pardoning grace still streams.

3 Lord, from this year more service win,
   More glory, more delight!
O make its hours less sad with sin,
   Its days with thee more bright!

4 O golden then the hours must be!
   The year must needs be sweet;
Yes, Lord, with happy melody
   Thine opening grace we greet.
                  T. H. Gill.

THE SEASONS. 255

BERNARD. 7s & 6s, D.   J. P. HOLBROOK.

1. Full-handed, glowing autumn God's loving-kindness crowns;
O'er all the earth his goodness
In fruitfulness abounds. In golden fields of harvest His bounty largely flows; O'er painted woods his glory In gorgeous radiance glows.

811 *As a Shock of Corn in its Season.*

2 In th' good man's face so shineth
The glory of the Lord;
So in his heart aboundeth
The fruitage of the word.

Like full-ripe corn in harvest,
When comes life's reaping time,
He shall be safely garnered
In heaven's purer clime.

T. C. Moulton.

WESTMINSTER. 8s & 7s.   J. P. HOLBROOK.

1. See the leaves around us falling, Dry and withered, to the ground, Thus to thoughtless mortals calling, In a sad and solemn sound.—

812 *We all do fade as a Leaf.*

2 Youth, on length of days presuming,
Who the paths of pleasure tread,
View us, late in beauty blooming,
Numbered now among the dead.

3 Though as yet no losses grieve you,
Gay with health and many a grace,
Let no cloudless skies deceive you;
Summer gives to autumn place.

4 Yearly in our course appearing,
Messengers of shortest stay,
Thus we preach in mortal hearing:
Ye, like us, shall pass away.

5 On the tree of life eternal,
O, let all our hopes be laid;
This alone, forever vernal,
Bears a leaf that shall not fade.

Rome.

VARIOUS OCCASIONS.

ZEBULON. H. M.   Dr. L. Mason.

1. How pleasing is thy voice, O Lord, our heavenly King, That bids the frosts retire, And wakes the lovely spring! The rains return, the ice distills, And plains and hills forget to mourn.

813 *Thou visitest the Earth and waterest it.*

2 Thy showers make soft the fields:
  On every side, behold,
The ripening harvests wave
  Their loads of richest gold.
The laborers sing with cheerful voice,
And, blest, rejoice in God, their King.

3 With life he clothes the spring,
  The earth with summer warms;
He spreads th' autumnal feast,
  And rides in wintry storms.
His gifts divine through all appear,
And round the year his glories shine.
                   Dwight.

814 *Thou hast made Summer.*

1 Lord of the worlds below,
  On earth thy glories shine;
The changing seasons show
  Thy skill and power divine.
The rolling years are full of thee;
In all we see a God appears.

2 They came, in robes of light,
  The Summer's flaming days;
The sun, thine image bright,
  Thy majesty displays;
And oft thy voice in thunder rolls;
But still our souls in thee rejoice.
                   Anon.

HENRY. C. M.   S. B. Pond.

1. When brighter suns and milder skies Proclaim the opening year, What various sounds of joy arise! What prospects bright appear!

815 *Lo, the Winter is past.*

2 Earth and her thousand voices give
  Their thousand notes of praise;
And all that by his mercy live
  To God their offering raise.

3 The streams, all beautiful and bright,
  Reflect the morning sky;
And there, with music in his flight,
  The wild bird soars on high.

4 Thus, like the morning, calm and clear
  That saw the Saviour rise,
The spring of heaven's eternal year
  Shall dawn on earth and skies.

5 No winter there; no shades of night
  Obscure those mansions blest,
Where, in the happy fields of light,
  The weary are at rest.
                   Peabody.

THE FAMILY.

816 *Sweet Home.*

2 Sweet bonds that unite all the children of peace,
And their precious Jesus whose love cannot cease;
Though oft from thy presence in sadness I roam,
I long to behold thee in glory, my home.—REF.

3 I sigh from this body of sin to be free,
Which hinders my joy and communion with thee;
Though now my temptations like billows may foam,
All, all will be peace, when I'm with thee at home.—REF.

4 I long, dearest Lord, in thy beauties to shine;
No more as an exile in sorrow to pine;
But in thy dear image arise from the tomb;
With glorified millions to praise thee at home.—REF.

D. Denham.

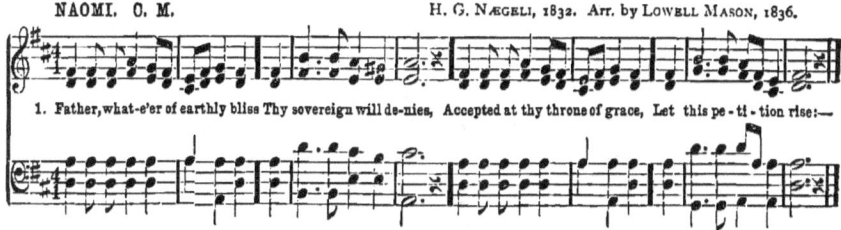

817 *The one Petition.*

2 "Give me a calm, a thankful heart,
From every murmur free;
The blessings of thy grace impart,
And make me live to thee;

3 "Let the sweet hope that thou art mine,
My life and death attend;
Thy presence through my journey shine,
And crown my journey's end."

Anne Steele.

VARIOUS OCCASIONS.

ERNAN. L. M. — Dr. Lowell Mason.

1. Wher-e'er the Lord shall build my house, An al-tar to his name I'll raise; There, morn and eve-ning, shall as-cend The sac-ri-fice of prayer and praise.

818 *The Altar at Home.*

2 With duteous mind, the social band
Shall search the records of thy law;
There learn thy will, and humbly bow
With filial reverence and awe.

3 Here may God fix his sacred seat,
And spread the banner of his love;
Till, ripened for a happier state,
We meet the family above.
T. Scott.

819 *Suffer little Children to come unto me.*
1 Jesus, thou Shepherd of the sheep,
Thy little flock in safety keep;
These lambs within thine arms now take,
Nor let them e'er thy fold forsake.

2 Secure them from the scorching beam,
And lead them to the living stream;
In verdant pastures let them lie,
And watch them with a shepherd's eye.

3 Lord, bring thy sheep that wander yet;
And let their number be complete;
Then let the flock from earth remove,
And reach the heavenly fold above.
Anon.

BOYLSTON. S. M. — Lowell Mason, 1832.

1. It is the hour of prayer: Draw near and bend the knee, And fill the calm and ho-ly air With voice of mel-o-dy.

820 *The Hour of Prayer.*
2 O'erwearied with the heat
And burden of the day,
Now let us rest our wandering feet,
And gather here to pray.

3 O, blessed is the hour
That lifts our hearts on high;
Like sunlight when the tempests lower,
Prayer to the soul is nigh.
Anon.

THE FAMILY.

FULTON, 7s. W. B. Bradbury.

1. God of mer-cy, hear our prayer For the chil-dren thou hast given;
Let them all thy bless-ings share— Grace on earth and bliss in heaven.

821 *He shall save the Children.*

2 In the morning of their days
May their hearts be drawn to thee;
Let them learn to lisp thy praise
In their earliest infancy.

3 When we see their passions rise,
Sinful habits unsubdued,
Then to thee we lift our eyes,
That their hearts may be renewed.

4 For this mercy, Lord, we cry;
Bend thine ever-gracious ear;
While on thee our souls rely,
Hear our prayer, in mercy hear.
Anon.

822 *"They are thine."*

1 DEAR Saviour, if these lambs should stray
From thy secure inclosure's bound,
And, lured by worldly joys away,
Among the thoughtless crowd be found,—

2 Remember still that they are thine,
That thy dear, sacred name they bear;
That the seal of love divine,
The sign of covenant grace, they wear.

3 In all their erring, sinful years,
O, let them ne'er forgotten be;
Remember all the prayers and tears
Which made them consecrate to thee.

4 And when these lips no more can pray,
These eyes can weep for them no more,
Turn thou their feet from folly's way,
The wanderers to thy fold restore.
Mrs. A. B. Hyde.

823 *"Them also I must bring."*

1 SEE the kind Shepherd, Jesus, stands,
And calls his sheep by name,
Gathers the feeble in his arms,
And feeds each tender lamb.

2 He leads them to the gentle stream
Where living water flows,
And guides them to the verdant fields
Where sweetest herbage grows.

3 The weakest lamb amid the flock
Shall be its Shepherd's care;
While folded in our Saviour's arms,
We're safe from every snare.
Anon.

VARIOUS OCCASIONS.

SILOAM. C. M.
I. B. Woodbury.

1. By cool Siloam's shady rill How sweet the lily grows!
How sweet the breath beneath the hill Of Sharon's dewy rose!

824 *Early Religion.*

2 Lo! such the child whose early feet
The paths of peace have trod;
Whose secret heart, with influence sweet,
Is upward drawn to God.

3 By cool Siloam's shady rill
The lily must decay;
The rose that blooms beneath the hill,
Must shortly fade away.

4 O thou who givest life and breath,
We seek thy grace alone,
In childhood, manhood, age, and death,
To keep us still thine own.
Reginald Heber.

825 *Happy is the man that findeth Wisdom.*

1 O, happy is the man who hears
Instruction's warning voice,
And who celestial wisdom makes
His early, only choice.

2 Wisdom hath treasures greater far
Than east and west unfold,
And her rewards more precious are
Than all the gain of gold.

3 She guides the young with innocence
In pleasure's paths to tread;
A crown of glory she bestows
Upon the hoary head.

4 According as her labors rise,
So her rewards increase;
Her ways are ways of pleasantness,
And all her paths are peace.
Scotch Paraphrases.

826 *The Entrance of Thy Words giveth Light.*

1 How shall the young secure their hearts,
And guard their lives from sin?
Thy word the choicest rules imparts
To keep the conscience clean.

2 'Tis like the sun, a heavenly light,
That guides us all the day,
And through the dangers of the night
A lamp to lead our way.

3 Thy word is everlasting truth;
How pure is every page!
That holy book shall guide our youth,
And well support our age.
Isaac Watts.

827 *Early Piety.*

1 When we devote our youth to God,
'Tis pleasing in his eyes;
A flower, when offered in the bud,
Is no vain sacrifice.

2 'Tis easier work if we begin
To fear the Lord betimes;
For sinners who grow old in sin
Are hardened in their crimes.

3 It saves us from a thousand snares
To mind religion young;
Grace will preserve succeeding years
And make our virtues strong.

4 To thee, almighty God, to thee
May we our hearts resign;
'Twill please us to look back and see
That our whole lives were thine.
Isaac Watts.

YOUTH AND OLD AGE. 261

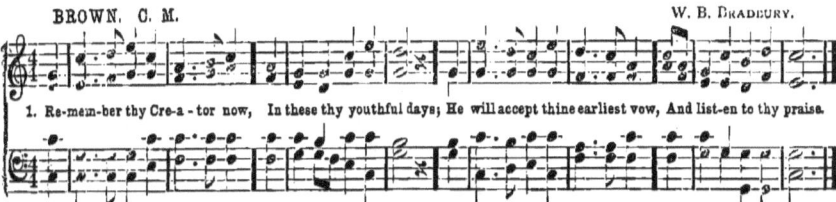

BROWN. C. M.   W. B. Bradbury.

1. Re-mem-ber thy Cre-a-tor now, In these thy youthful days; He will accept thine earliest vow, And list-en to thy praise.

828 *Remember now thy Creator.*

2 Remember thy Creator now,
And seek him while he's near;
For evil days will come, when thou
Shalt find no comfort here.

3 Remember thy Creator now,
His willing servant be:
Then, when thy head in death shall bow,
He will remember thee.

4 Almighty God, our hearts incline
Thy heavenly voice to hear;
Let all our future days be thine,
Devoted to thy fear.
Anon.

829 *Cast me not off in the Time of Old Age.*

1 My God, my everlasting hope,
I live upon thy truth;
Thy hands have held my childhood up,
And strengthened all my youth.

2 Still has my life new wonders seen
Repeated every year;
Behold, my days that yet remain—
I trust them to thy care.

3 Cast me not off when strength declines,
When hoary hairs arise:
And round me let thy glory shine
Whene'er thy servant dies.
Isaac Watts.

NEW HAVEN. 6s & 4s.   Thomas Hastings.

1. Shepherd of ten-der youth, Guid-ing in love and truth Thro' devious ways— Christ, our tri-umphant King, We come thy name to sing, And here our children bring, To shout thy praise.

830 *Thou art the Guide of my Youth.*

2 Ever be near our side,
Our Shepherd and our Guide,
Our staff and song:
Jesus, thou Christ of God,
By thine endearing word
Lead us where thou hast trod;
Make our faith strong.

3 So now, and till we die,
Sound we thy praises high,
And joyful sing:
Let all the holy throng,
Who to thy church belong,
Unite and swell the song
To Christ our King.
C. Alexandrinus.

CROYLAND. L. M.   VARIOUS OCCASIONS.   Arr. fr. NEUKOMM.

1. Hark! 'tis your heavenly Father's call, How soft the charming ac-cents fall; "Ask and re-ceive, my son," he cries, With lov-ing heart and melt-ing eyes.

Used by per. Oliver Ditson Co., owners of Copyright.

831   *Early Piety.*

2 Lord, I accept thine offered grace,
   I come to seek my Father's face,
   Nor will he turn his ear away
   Who taught my heart and lips to pray.

3 One thing I ask, and wilt thou hear,
   And grant my soul a gift so dear?
   Wisdom, descending from above,
   The sweetest token of thy love;

4 Wisdom betimes to know the Lord,
   To fear his name and keep his word;
   To lead my feet in paths of truth,
   And guide and guard my wandering youth.

5 Then shouldst thou grant a length of days,
   My life shall still proclaim thy praise;
   Or early death my soul convey
   To realms of everlasting day.
                      Ottiwell Heginbotham, 1799.

832   *The Measure of my Days.*

1 ALMIGHTY Maker of my frame,
   Teach me the measure of my days;
   Teach me to know how frail I am,
   And spend the remnant to thy praise.

2 My days are shorter than a span;
   A little point my life appears;
   How frail at best is dying man!
   How vain are all his hopes and fears!

3 O, spare me, and my strength restore,
   Ere my few hasty minutes flee;
   And when my days on earth are o'er,
   Let me forever dwell with thee.
                      Anne Steele.

833   *The Time is short.*

1 GOD of eternity, from thee
   Did infant Time his being draw;
   Moments, and days, and months, and years,
   Revolve by thine unvaried law.

2 Silent and slow they glide away;
   Steady and strong the current flows,
   Lost in eternity's wide sea,
   The boundless gulf from whence it rose.

3 With it the thoughtless sons of men
   Upon the rapid stream are borne,
   Swift to that everlasting home,
   Whence not one soul can e'er return.

4 Great Source of wisdom, teach my heart
   To know the price of every hour,
   That time may bear me on to joys
   Beyond its measure and its power.
                      Philip Doddridge, 1755.

834   *He fleeth also as a shadow.*

1 LIKE shadows gliding o'er the plain;
   Or clouds that roll successive on,
   Man's busy generations pass,
   And while we gaze, their forms are gone.

2 He lived, he died, beheld the sun,
   The abstract of the historian's page;
   Alike in God's all-seeing eye,
   The infant's day, the patriarch's age.

3 O Father, in whose mighty hand
   The boundless years and ages lie,
   Teach us thy boon of life to prize,
   And use the moments as they fly.
                      John Taylor.

BREVITY OF LIFE. 263

FLUMLEY. L. M.   L. O. EMERSON.

Used by per. Oliver Ditson Co., owners of Copyright.

835 *Heaven Alone Unfading.*

2 The evening cloud, the morning dew,
The withering grass, the fading flower
Of earthly hopes are emblems true,
The glory of a passing hour.

3 But though earth's fairest blossoms die
And all beneath the skies is vain,

There is a land whose confines lie
Beyond the reach of care and pain.

4 Then let the hope of joys to come
Dispel our cares, and chase our fears
If God be ours, we're traveling home,
Though passing through a vale of tears.
David E. Ford.

SOLITUDE. C. M.   I. B. STARKWEATHER.

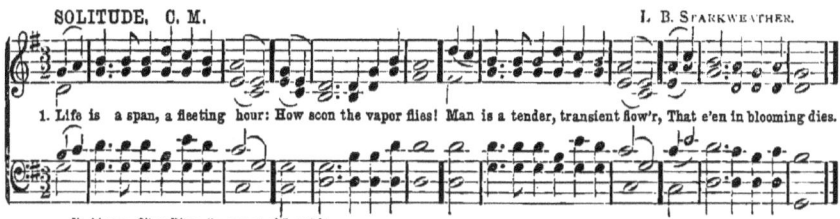

Used by per. Oliver Ditson Co., owners of Copyright.

836 *Thou hast made my Days as a Hand-breadth.*

2 The once loved form, now cold and dead
Each mournful thought employs;
And nature weeps her comforts fled,
And withered all her joys.

3 Hope looks beyond the bounds of time,
When what we now deplore
Shall rise in full, immortal prime,
And bloom to fade no more.

4 Cease then, fond nature, cease thy tears;
Religion points on high;
There everlasting spring appears,
And joys that never die.
Anne Steele.

837 *What is your Life?*

1 How SHORT and hasty is our life!
How vast our soul's affairs!
Yet senseless mortals vainly strive
To lavish out their years.

2 Our days run thoughtlessly along,
Without a moment's stay;
Just like a story, or a song,
We pass our lives away.

3 God from on high invites us home,
But we march heedless on,
And, ever hastening to the tomb,
Stoop downward as we run.

4 Draw us, O God, with sovereign grace.
And lift our thoughts on high,
That we may end this mortal race,
And see salvation nigh.
Isaac Watts.

264

BRADFORD. C. M.   MORTALITY.   HANDEL.

1. Let oth-ers boast how strong they be, Nor death nor dan-ger fear;
But we con-fess, O Lord, to thee, What fee-ble things we are.

838 *As a Flower of the Field so he flourisheth.*
2 Fresh as the grass our bodies stand,
And flourish bright and gay;
A blasting wind sweeps o'er the land,
And fades the grass away.

3 Our life contains a thousand springs,
And dies if one be gone;
Strange that a harp of thousand strings
Should keep in tune so long!

4 But 'tis our God supports our frame—
The God who made us first;
Salvation to th' almighty Name
That reared us from the dust.
                          Isaac Watts.

839 *"Number our days."*
1 BENEATH our feet and o'er our head
Is equal warning given;
Beneath us lie the countless dead,
Above us is the heaven.

2 Death rides on every passing breeze,
And lurks in every flower;
Each season has its own disease,
Its peril every hour.

3 Turn, mortal turn! thy soul apply
To truths divinely given;
The dead, who underneath thee lie,
Shall live for hell or heaven!
                          Reginald Heber.

AMSTERDAM. 7s & 6s, D.   Dr NARES.

1. Time is winging us a-way To our e-ter-nal home:
Life is but a winter's day, A journey to the tomb;
Youth and vig-or soon will flee,
Blooming beau-ty lose its charms; All that's mortal soon will be En-closed in death's cold arms.

840 *"We all do fade as a leaf."*
2 Time is winging us away
To our eternal home:
Life is but a winter's day,
A journey to the tomb;

But the Christian shall enjoy
Health and beauty soon above;
Far beyond the world's alloy,
Secure in Jesus' love.
                          J. Burton.

DEATH.

ST. SYLVESTER. 8s & 7s.   J. B. DYKES.

1. Days and mo-ments quick-ly fly - ing, Blend the liv - ing with the dead;
Soon shall we who sing be ly - ing, Each with-in our nar - row bed.

841 *Last Day of the Year.*

2 Soon our souls to God who gave them
   Will have sped their rapid flight;
  Able now by grace to save them,
   Oh, that while we can we might!

3 Jesus, infinite Redeemer,
   Maker of this mighty frame;
  Teach, oh, teach us to remember
   What we are, and whence we came:—

4 Whence we came, and whither wending;
   Soon we must through darkness go,
  To inherit bliss unending,
   Or eternity of woe.
                              Caswall.

CHINA. C. M.

1. Why do we mourn de - part - ing friends, Or shake at death's a - larms?
'Tis but the voice that Je - sus sends To call them to his arms.

842

2 Are we not tending upward too,
   As fast as time can move?
  Nor would we wish the hours more slow,
   To keep us from our Love.

3 Why should we tremble to convey
   Their bodies to the tomb?

  There the dear flesh of Jesus lay,
   And left a long perfume.

4 The graves of all his saints he blessed,
   And softened every bed;
  Where should the dying members rest
   But with the dying Head?
                              Isaac Watts.

MORTALITY.

ZEPHYR. L. M.   W. B. Bradbury, 1844.

1. How blest the righ-teous when he dies! When sinks a trust-ing soul to rest, How mild-ly beam the clos-ing eyes! How gen-tly heaves th'ex-pir-ing breast!

843 *Death of the Righteous.*

2 So fades a summer cloud away,
   So sinks the gale when storms are o'er.
So gently shuts the eye of day,
   So dies a wave along the shore.

3 A holy quiet reigns around,
   A calm which life nor death destroys;
And naught disturbs that peace profound
   Which his unfettered soul enjoys,

4 Triumphant smiles the victor's brow,
   Fanned by some guardian angel's wing;
O grave, where is thy victory now?
   And where, O death, where is thy sting?
                       Anna L. Barbauld.

844 *To die is Gain.*

1 Why should we start, and fear to die?
   What timorous worms we mortals are!
Death is the gate of endless joy,
   And yet we dread to enter there.

2 The pains, the groans, and dying strife
   Fright our approaching souls away;
We still shrink back again to life,
   Fond of our prison and our clay.

3 O, if my Lord would come and meet,
   My soul should stretch her wings in haste,
Fly fearless through death's iron gate,
   Nor feel the terrors as she passed.

4 Jesus can make a dying bed
   Feel soft as downy pillows are,
While on his breast I lean my head,
   And breathe my life out sweetly there.
                       Isaac Watts.

845 *Let my last End be like his.*

1 How sweet the hour of closing day,
   When all is peaceful and serene,
And when the sun, with cloudless ray,
   Sheds mellow lustre o'er the scene!

2 Such is the Christian's parting hour;
   So peacefully he sinks to rest;
When faith, endued from heaven with pow'r
   Sustains and cheers his languid breast.

3 A beam from heaven is sent to cheer
   The pilgrim on his gloomy road;
And angels are attending near,
   To bear him to their bright abode.
                       Wm. H. Bathurst.

846

1 The hour of my departure 's come,
   I hear the voice that calls me home;
At last, O Lord! let trouble cease,
   And let thy servant die in peace.

2 Not in mine innocence I trust;
   I bow before thee in the dust;
And thro' my Saviour's blood alone,
   I look for mercy at thy throne.

3 I leave the world without a tear,
   Save for the friends I held so dear;
To heal their sorrows, Lord, descend,
   And to the friendless prove a friend.

4 I come, I come at thy command,
   I give my spirit to thy hand;
Stretch forth thine everlasting arms,
   And shield me in the last alarms.
                       Logan.

DEATH. 267

VOX ANGELICA. 11s, 10 & 9s.

1. Hark, hark, my soul, angelic songs are swelling
O'er earth's green fields and ocean's wave-beat shore;
How sweet the truth those blessed strains are telling
Of that new life when sin shall be no more.
CHORUS. Angels of gladness, angels of light, Singing to welcome the pilgrims of the night.

847   *The Pilgrims of the Night.*

2 Darker than night life's shadows fall around us,
  And, like benighted men we miss our mark;
  God hides himself, and grace hath scarcely found us,
  Ere death finds out his victims in the dark.—CHO.

3 Rest comes at length, though life be long and dreary,
  The day must dawn, and darksome night be past:
  All journeys end in welcomes to the weary,
  And heaven, the heart's true home, will come at last.—CHO.

4 Angels! sing on, your faithful watches keeping;
  Sing us sweet fragments of the songs above;
  While we toil on, and soothe ourselves with weeping,
  Till life's long night shall break in endless love.—CHO.

  Frederick W. Faber, 1854.

BARTIMEUS. 8s & 7s.   STEPHEN JENKS.

1. Let me go where saints are going, To the mansions of the blest; Let me go where my Redeemer, Has prepared his people's rest.

848

2 Let me go where none are weary,
  Where is raised no wail or woe,
  Let me go and bathe my spirit
  In the raptures angels know.

3 Let me go, for bliss eternal
  Lures my soul away, away,
  And the victor's song triumphant
  Thrills my heart, I cannot stay.

4 Let me go where tears and sighing
  Are forever more unknown,
  Where the joyous songs of glory
  Call me to a happier home.

5 Let me go, oh, speed my journey,
  Saints and seraphs lure away,
  Let me go, oh, speed my going!
  Let me go where all is love.

  L. Hartsough.

MORTALITY.

AVEREEN. L. M.

1. Asleep in Jesus! blessed sleep! From which none ever wake to weep; A calm and undisturbed repose, Unbroken by the last of foes.

Used by per. Oliver Ditson ... owners of Copyright

849 *Them which sleep in Jesus.*

2 Asleep in Jesus! O, how sweet
 To be for such a slumber meet!
With holy confidence to sing
 That death hath lost its venomed sting!

3 Asleep in Jesus! peaceful rest,
 Whose waking is supremely blest;
No fear, no woe, shall dim that hour
 Which manifests the Saviour's power.

4 Asleep in Jesus! far from thee
 Thy kindred and their graves may be;
But thine is still a blessed sleep,
 From which none ever wake to weep.
                                             Mrs. Mackay.

850 *The Flower fadeth.*

1 As the sweet flower that scents the morn,
 But withers in the rising day,
Thus lovely was this infant's dawn,
 Thus swiftly fled its life away.

2 It died ere its expanding soul
 Had ever burned with wrong desires,
Had ever spurned at Heaven's control,
 Or ever quenched its sacred fires.

3 It died to sin, and died to care;
 But for a moment felt the rod;
Then, rising on the viewless air,
 Spread its light wings and soared to God.
                                             John W. Cunningham.

REST. L. M.   W. B. BRADBURY.

1. Dear is the spot where Christians sleep, And sweet the strains their spirits pour; O, why should we in anguish weep? They are not lost, but gone before.

851 *They are not lost, but gone before.*

2 Secure from every mortal care,
 By sin and sorrow vexed no more,
Eternal happiness they share
 Who are not lost, but gone before.

3 To Zion's peaceful courts above
 In faith triumphant may we soar,
Embracing, in the arms of love,
 The friends not lost, but gone before.
                                             B. Clark.

DEATH.

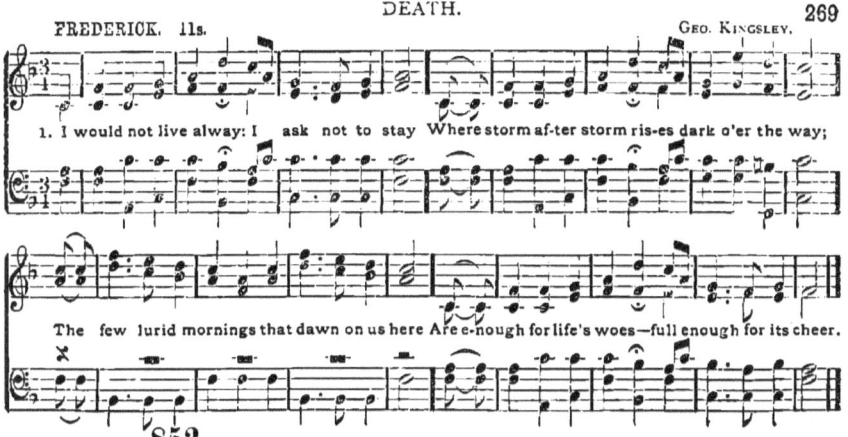

852
2 I would not live alway: no, welcome the tomb;
Since Jesus hath lain there, I dread not its gloom:
There sweet be my rest till he bid me arise
To hail him in triumph descending the skies.

3 Who, who would live alway, away from his God,
Away from yon heaven, that blissful abode,
Where the rivers of pleasure flow o'er the bright plains,
And the glory of noontide eternally reigns;

4 Where the saints of all ages in harmony meet,
Their Saviour and brethren transported to greet;
While the anthems of rapture unceasingly roll,
And the smile of the Lord is the feast of the soul?
W. A. Muhlenberg, 1823.

853 *He that believeth in Me shall never die.*
2 This is not death's dark portal—
   Life's golden gate to me:
Link after link is broken,
   And I at last am free.

Jesus, thou wilt receive me,
   And welcome me above;
This sunshine, which now fills me,
   Is thine own smile of love.
Horatius Bonar.

MORTALITY.

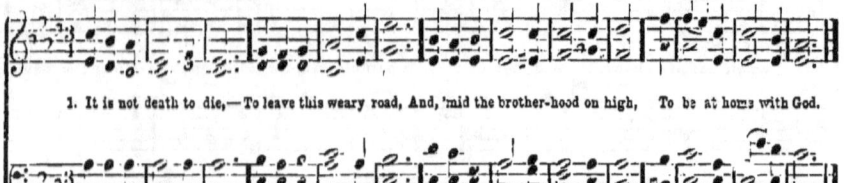

854 *"Whoso believeth in me shall never die."*

2 It is not death to close
  The eye long dimmed by tears,
And wake, in glorious repose
  To spend eternal years.

3 It is not death to fling
  Aside this sinful dust,
And rise, on strong, exulting wing,
  To live among the just.

4 Jesus, thou Prince of Life,
  Thy chosen can not die;
Like thee, they conquer in the strife,
  To reign with thee on high.
G. W. Bethune, tr.

855 *Well done.*

1 SERVANT of God, well done!
  Rest from thy loved employ:
The battle fought, the victory won,
  Enter thy Master's joy.

2 Tranquil amidst alarms,
  Death found him on the field,
A veteran slumbering on his arms,
  Beneath his red-cross shield.

3 The pains of death are past;
  Labor and sorrow cease;
And life's long warfare closed at last,
  His soul is found in peace.

4 Soldier of Christ, well done!
  Praise be thy new employ;
And while eternal ages run,
  Rest in thy Saviour's joy.
James Montgomery, 1825.

856 *Is it well with the Child?*

1 Go to thy rest, fair child,
  Go to thy dreamless bed,
While yet so gentle, undefiled,
  With blessings on thy head.

2 Ere sin had seared the breast,
  Or sorrow woke the tear,
Rise to thy throne of changeless rest,
  In yon celestial sphere.

3 Shall love, with weak embrace,
  Thy upward wing detain?
No, gentle angel; seek thy place
  Amid the cherub train.
Anon.

857 *Our Salvation nearer than when we believed.*

1 ONE sweetly solemn thought
  Comes to me o'er and o'er:
Nearer my parting hour am I
  Than e'er I was before;—

2 Nearer my Father's house,
  Where many mansions be;
Nearer the throne where Jesus reigns;
  Nearer the crystal sea;—

3 Nearer that hidden stream,
  Winding through shades of night,
Rolling its cold, dark waves between
  Me and the world of light.

4 Jesus, to thee I cling:
  Strengthen my arm of faith;
Stay near me while my way-worn feet
  Press through the stream of death.
Phœbe Carey.

DEATH. 271

EMILIA. 8s & 7.   John W. Tufts.

1. Darling child, in slumber seeming Far away in happy dreaming, Still and breathless is thy sleeping, Heedless of our watch and weeping, Lord, have mercy upon us!

Used by per. W. L. Greene & Co., owners of Copyright

858

2 While our hearts with grief are breaking,
Thou to heavenly joy art waking;
Clouds of sorrow o'er us glooming
Shadow not thy life's sweet blooming.
Lord, in mercy comfort us.

3 Israel's shepherd safely fold thee,
In his bosom gently hold thee,
And our feet in mercy guiding,
Bring us where thou art abiding.
Heavenly Father, hear our prayer.
E. P. Parker.

BURTON. 8s & 7.   E. P. Parker.

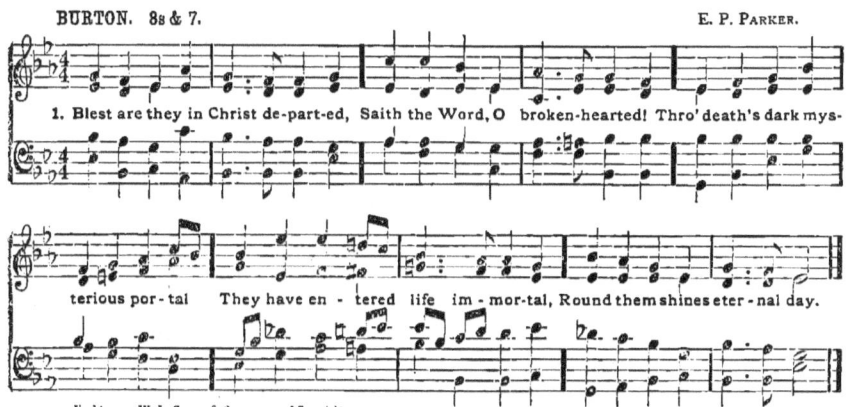

1. Blest are they in Christ departed, Saith the Word, O broken-hearted! Thro' death's dark mysterious portal They have entered life immortal, Round them shines eternal day.

Used by per. W. L. Greene & Co., owners of Copyright.

859

2 Hard their warfare, great their burden,
But the splendid goal and guerdon
They have reached; and now, victorious,
Wear the crowns and garlands glorious
Which shall never fade away.

3 No more fears, nor doubts, nor crying,
No more sin, nor pain, nor dying,

No more tears on any faces,
In those holy, heavenly places
Where love reigns for evermore.

4 Lord, on us thy mercy lighten,
With thy love our sorrows brighten;
Make our hope of heaven grow clearer,
Heaven itself becomes the dearer,
For the loved ones gone before.
E. P. Parker.

272 MORTALITY.

PHILLIPS. C. M.   I. B. WOODBURY.

1. Behold the western evening light! It melts in deep'ning gloom; So calmly Christians sink away, Descending to the tomb.

Used by per. Oliver Ditson Co., owners of Copyright.

860
2 The winds breathe low; the yellow leaf
Scarce whispers from the tree;
So gently flows the parting breath
When good men cease to be.

3 How mildly on the wandering cloud
The sunset beam is cast!
So sweet the memory left behind
When loved ones breathe their last.

4 Night falls, but soon the morning light
Its glories shall restore;
And thus the eyes that sleep in death
Shall wake to close no more.
                          Wm. P. O. Peabody.

861   *Not lost, but gone before.*
1 ANOTHER hand is beckoning us,
Another call is given;
And glows once more with angel steps
The path that leads to heaven.

2 Oh, half we deemed she needed not
The changing of her sphere,
To give to heaven a shining one,
Who walked an angel here!

3 Unto our Father's will alone
One thought hath reconciled,—
That he whose love exceedeth ours
Hath taken home his child.

4 Fold her, O Father! in thine arms,
And let her henceforth be
A messenger of love between
Our human heart and thee.
                        John G. Whittier.

862   *They shall shine as the Stars.*
1 THE dead are like the stars by day,
Withdrawn from mortal eyes;
But not extinct, they hold their way
In glory through the skies.

2 Spirits from bondage thus set free
I may, I must believe,
Are somewhere in immensity,
And know, and love, and live.

3 Ah, 'tis in heaven, where Christ is gone,
Our friends with angels dwell;
There we may hope to meet again
Those here we loved so well.
                        James Montgomery.

863   *Sorrow not, even as Others.*
1 DEAR as thou wast, and justly dear,
We will not weep for thee:
One thought shall check the starting tear:
It is, that thou art free.

2 And thus shall faith's consoling power
The tears of love restrain:
O, who that saw thy parting hour,
Could wish thee back again?

3 Triumphant in thy closing eye
The hope of glory shone;
Joy breathed in thine expiring sigh,
To think the fight was won.

4 Gently the passing spirit fled,
Sustained by grace divine;
O, may such grace on me be shed,
And make my end like thine!
                        Dale.

DEATH. 273

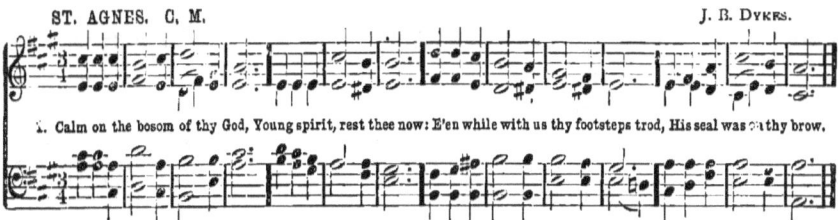

1. Calm on the bosom of thy God, Young spirit, rest thee now: E'en while with us thy footsteps trod, His seal was on thy brow.

864 *Death of the Young.*
2 Dust to its narrow house beneath;
 Soul to its place on high:
 They that have seen thy look in death
 No more may fear to die.

3 Lone are the paths, and sad the bowers,
 Whence thy meek smile is gone;
 But O, a brighter home than ours,
 In heaven, is now thine own.
 Hemans.

865 *Death of the Young.*
1 WHEN blooming youth is snatched away
 By death's resistless hand,
 Our hearts the mournful tribute pay
 Which pity must demand.

2 Let this vain world engage no more:
 Behold the opening tomb:
 It bids us seize the present hour:
 To-morrow death may come.

3 O, let us fly—to Jesus fly!
 Whose powerful arm can save;
 Then shall our hopes ascend on high,
 And triumph o'er the grave.

4 Great God, thy sovereign grace impart,
 With cleansing, healing power;
 This only can prepare the heart
 For death's surprising hour.
 Anne Steele.

1. When thou, my righteous Judge, shalt come To take thy ransom'd people home, Shall I a-mong them stand? { Shall such a worthless worm as I, Who sometimes am a-fraid to die, } Be found at thy right hand?

866 *The Day shall try them.*
2 I love to meet among them now,
 Before thy gracious feet to bow
 Though weakest of them all;
 But—can I bear the piercing thought?—
 What if my name should be left out,
 When thou for them shalt call!

3 Among them, Lord, let me be found,
 Whene'er the archangel's trump shall sound,
 To see thy smiling face;
 Then loudest of the throng I'll sing,
 While heaven's resounding mansions ring
 With shouts of sovereign grace.
 Selina, Countess of Huntingdon, 1772.

274 SCOTLAND. 12s & 11s. MORTALITY.

1 Thou art gone to the grave; but we will not deplore thee,
Tho' sorrows and darkness encompass the tomb;
The Saviour has pass'd thro' its portals before thee, And the lamp of his love is thy guide thro' the gloom, And the lamp of his love is thy guide thro' the gloom.

867

2 Thou art gone to the grave; we no longer behold thee,
Nor tread the rough paths of the world by thy side;
But the wide arms of mercy are spread to enfold thee,
And sinners may hope, for the Sinless hath died.

3 Thou art gone to the grave; and, its mansion forsaking,
Perchance thy tried spirit in doubt lingered long;
But the sunshine of glory beamed bright on thy waking,
And full on thine ear burst the seraphim's song.

4 Thou art gone to the grave; but we will not deplore thee,
Since God was thy Refuge, thy Guardian, thy Guide;
He gave thee, he took thee, and he will restore thee;
And death has no sting, for the Saviour hath died.
                                                   Bishop Reginald Heber.

IOWA. 8s.   A. D. FILMORE.

1. We speak of the realms of the blest, That country so bright and so fair, And oft are its glories confessed, But what must it be to be there? But what must it be to be there?

868
2 We speak of its freedom from sin,
  From sorrow, temptation, and care,
  From trials without and within,
  But what must it be to be there?
3 We speak of its service of love,
  The robes which the glorified wear,

The church of the first-born above;
But what must it be to be there!
4 Do thou, Lord, 'mid sorrow and woe,
  Still for heaven my spirit prepare,
  And shortly I also shall know,
  And feel, what it is to be there.
                                       Anon.

DEATH.

DORRNANCE. 8s & 7s.   I. B. WOODBURY.

1. Sister, thou wast mild and lovely, Gentle as the summer's breeze, Pleasant as the air of evening, When it floats among the trees.

869   *On the Death of a Sister.*

2 Peaceful be thy silent slumber,
Peaceful in the grave so low:
Thou no more wilt join our number,
Thou no more our songs shalt know.

3 Dearest sister, thou hast left us,
Here thy loss we deeply feel;
But 'tis God that hath bereft us,
He can all our sorrows heal.

4 Yet again we hope to meet thee,
When the day of life has fled;
Then in heaven with joy to greet thee,
Where no farewell tear is shed.
S. F. Smith.

870   *Homewards.*

1 DROPPING down the troubled river,
To the tranquil, tranquil shore,
Where the sweet light shineth ever,
And the sun goes down no more.

2 Dropping down the winding river,
To the wide and welcome sea,
Where no tempest wrecketh ever,
Where the sky is fair and free.

3 Dropping down the eddying river,
With a helmsman true and tried—
Even Him who, to deliver
Precious souls from death, hath died,

4 Dropping down the rapid river,
To the dear and deathless land,
Where the living live forever
At the Father's own right hand.
Horatius Bonar.

DOVER. S. M.   Arr. by T. HASTINGS.

1. And will the Judge descend? And must the dead a-rise? And not a sin-gle soul es-cape His all discern-ing eyes?

871   *Knowing the Terror of the Lord, we persuade Men.*

2 How will my heart endure
The terrors of that day,
When earth and heaven, before his face,
Astonished, shrink away?

3 But, ere the trumpet shakes
The mansions of the dead,
Hark! from the gospel's cheering sound
What joyful tidings spread!

4 Come, sinners, seek his grace
Whose wrath ye can not bear:
Fly to the shelter of his cross,
And find salvation there.
Philip Doddridge.

872   *"Come, Lord Jesus."*

1 COME, Lord, and tarry not!
Bring the long-looked-for day;
Oh, why these years of waiting here,
These ages of delay?

2 Come, for thy saints still wait;
Daily ascends their sigh;
The Spirit and the Bride say, Come!
Dost thou not hear the cry?

3 Come, and make all things new,
Build up this ruined earth,
Restore our faded paradise,—
Creation's second birth.

4 Come, and begin thy reign
Of everlasting peace;
Come, take the kingdom to thyself,
Great King of Righteousness!
Horatius Bonar.

FUTURITY.

ANVERN. L. M. — Arr. by Dr. L. Mason.

1. There is a land mine eye hath seen, In vis-ions of en-raptured thought, So bright that all which spreads between Is with its radiant glo-ry fraught,— Is with its radiant glo-ry fraught;—

873 *Vision of Heaven.*

2 A land upon whose blissful shore
There rests no shadow, falls no stain;
There those who meet shall part no more,
And those long parted meet again.

3 Its skies are not like earthly skies,
With varying hues of shades and light;
It hath no need of suns to rise
To dissipate the gloom of night.

4 There sweeps no desolating wind
Across that calm, serene abode;
The wanderer there a home may find,
Within the paradise of God.
G. Robins, Jr.

874 *The Future World.*

1 There is a glorious world on high,
Resplendent with eternal day;
Faith views the blissful prospect nigh,
While God's own word reveals the way.

2 There shall the servants of the Lord,
With never-fading lustre, shine;
Surprising honor, vast reward,
Conferred on man by love divine!

3 On wings of faith and strong desire,
Oh, may our spirits daily rise,
And reach at last the shining choir
In the bright mansions of the skies.
Anne Steele.

WOODLAND. C. M. — N. D. Gould.

1. There is an hour of peaceful rest, To mourning wand'rers giv'n; There is a tear for souls distressed, A balm for ev-e-ry wounded breast; 'Tis found a-bove—in heaven.

875 *Prospect of Heaven.*

2 There is a home for weary souls,
By sin and sorrow driven;
When tossed on life's tempestuous shoals,
Where storms arise and ocean rolls,
And all is drear—but heaven.

3 There fragrant flowers immortal bloom,
And joys supreme are given;
There rays divine disperse the gloom;
Beyond the dark and narrow tomb
Appears the dawn—of heaven.
W. B. Tappan.

HEAVEN. 277

APPLETON. L. M. WILLIAM BOYCE.

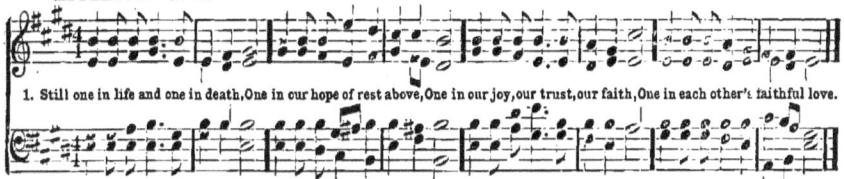

1. Still one in life and one in death, One in our hope of rest above, One in our joy, our trust, our faith, One in each other's faithful love.

876 *Heaven a Social State.*

2 Yet must we part, and, parting, weep;
  What else has earth for us in store?
Our farewell pangs how sharp and deep!
Our farewell words how sad and sore!

3 Yet shall we meet again in peace,
  To sing the song of festal joy,
Where none shall bid our gladness cease,
And none our fellowship destroy.

4 There hand in hand firm-linked at last,
  And heart to heart enfolded all,
We'll smile upon the troubled past,
And wonder why we wept at all.
  Horatius Bonar.

877 *Holiness a Condition of Heaven.*

1 HEAVEN is a place of rest from sin;
  But all who hope to enter there
Must here that holy course begin
Which shall their souls for rest prepare.

2 Clean hearts, O God, in us create;
  Right spirits, Lord, in us renew;
Commence we now that higher state,
Now do thy will as angels do.

3 In Jesus' footsteps may we tread,
  Learn every lesson of his love,
And be from grace to glory led,
From heaven below to heaven above.
  James Montgomery.

GETHSEMANE. 7s, 6l. RICHARD REDHEAD.

1. Heavenward doth our journey tend; We are strangers here on earth; Thro' the wilderness we wend

Towards the Canaan of our birth: Here we roam a pilgrim band; Yonder is our native land.

878 *The Homeward Journey.*

2 Heavenward! doth God's spirit cry,
  When I hear him in his word,
Showing thus the rest on high,
  Where I shall be with my Lord;
When his word fills all my thought,
Oft to heaven my soul is caught.

3 Heavenward death shall lead, at last,
  To the home where I would be;
All my sorrows overpast,
  I shall triumph there with thee;
Jesus, thou hast gone before,
That we, too, might heavenward soar.

4 Heavenward! heavenward! Only this
  Is my watchword on the earth;
For the love of heavenly bliss
  Counting all things little worth;
Heavenward all my being tends,
Till in heaven my journey ends.
  Schmolck.

FUTURITY.

SWEET REST. 7s & 6s. W. B. BRADBURY.

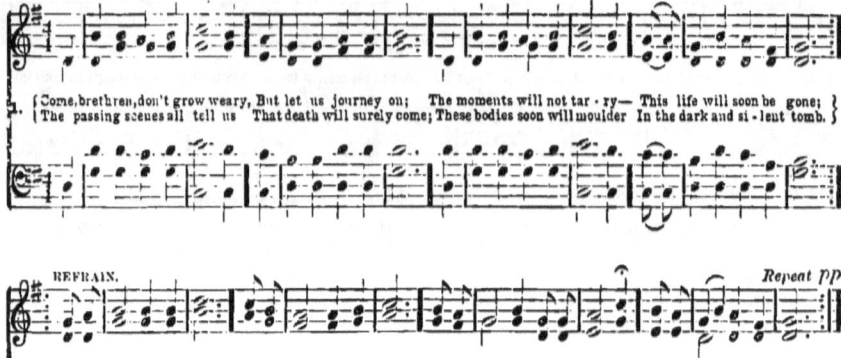

1. { Come, brethren, don't grow weary, But let us journey on; The moments will not tar-ry— This life will soon be gone;
   { The passing scenes all tell us That death will surely come; These bodies soon will moulder In the dark and si-lent tomb.

REFRAIN. *Repeat pp*
There is sweet rest in heav'n, There is sweet rest in heav'n, There is sweet rest, there is sweet rest, There is sweet rest in heav'n.

879   *Sweet Rest.*

2 Loved ones have gone before us,
   They beckon us away;
O'er aerial plains they're soaring,
   Blest in eternal day:
But we are in the army,
   And dare not leave our post;
We'll fight until we conquer
   The foe's most mighty host.—REF.

3 Our Captain's gone before us,
   He kindly calls us home
To yonder world of glory,
   And sweetly bids us come.
The world, the flesh, and Satan
   Will strive to hedge our way,
But we'll o'ercome these powers,
   And hourly watch and pray.—REF.

4 And Jesus will be with us,
   E'en to our journey's end,
In every sore affliction
   His present help to lend.
He never will grow weary,
   Though often we request;
He'll give us grace to conquer,
   And take us home to rest.—REF.
            Anon.

880   *"A City."*

1 JERUSALEM, the glorious!
   The glory of the elect,—
O dear and future vision
   That eager hearts expect!
Ev'n now by faith I see thee,
   Ev'n here thy walls discern;
To thee my thoughts are kindled,
   And strive, and pant, and yearn!

2 The Cross is all thy splendor,
   The Crucified, thy praise;
His laud and benediction
   Thy ransomed people raise;—
Jerusalem! exulting
   On that securest shore,
I hope thee, wish thee, sing thee,
   And love thee evermore!

3 O sweet and blessed Country!
   Shall I e'er see thy face?
O sweet and blessed Country!
   Shall I e'er win thy grace?
Exult, O dust and ashes!
   The Lord shall be thy part;
His only, his for ever,
   Thou shalt be, and thou art!
            John M. Neale. *ar.*

HEAVEN.

EWING. 7s & 6s, D. [IAMBIC.] Bp. ALEXANDER EWING, 1861.

1. Je-ru-sa-lem the gold-en! With milk and hon-ey blest, Be-neath thy con-tem-pla-tion Sink heart and voice op-prest. I know not, oh, I know not What joys a-wait us there, What ra-dian-cy of glo-ry, What bliss be-yond com-pare.

881 *Jerusalem the Golden.*

2 They stand, those halls of Zion,
  All jubilant with song,
And bright with many an angel,
  And all the martyr throng.
The Prince is ever in them,
  The daylight is serene;
The pastures of the blessed
  Are decked in glorious sheen.

3 There is the throne of David;
  And there, from care released,
The shout of them that triumph,
  The song of them that feast.
And they who, with their Leader,
  Have conquered in the fight,
Forever and forever
  Are clad in robes of white.
      Bernard of Clugny, 1150. *Tr.* J. M. Neale, 1851.

882 *"Short Toil."*

1 BRIEF life is here our portion;
  Brief sorrow, short-lived care;
The life, that knows no ending,
  The tearless life, is there:

Oh, happy retribution!
  Short toil, eternal rest;
For mortals, and for sinners,
  A mansion with the blest!

2 And there is David's fountain,
  And life in fullest glow;
And there the light is golden,
  And milk and honey flow;
The light, that hath no evening,
  The health, that hath no sore,
The life, that hath no ending,
  But lasteth evermore.

3 There Jesus shall embrace us,
  There Jesus be embraced,—
That spirit's food and sunshine;
  Whence earthly love is chased:
Yes! God my King and Portion,
  In fullness of his grace,
We then shall see for ever,
  And worship face to face.
      John M. Neale, *tr.*

FUTURITY.

HOME. C. M. D. — L. V. WHEELER.

1. Je-ru-sa-lem, my hap-py home, Name ev-er dear to me; When shall my labors have an end, In joy, and peace, in thee? Oh, when, thou cit-y of my God, Shall I thy courts ascend, Where ev-er-more the an-gels sing, Where Sabbaths have no end?

883 *Home.*

2 There happier bowers than Eden's bloom,
  Nor sin nor sorrow know:
Blest seats! thro' rude and stormy scenes,
  I onward press to you.
Why should I shrink at pain or woe?
  Or feel at death dismay?
I've Canaan's goodly land in view,
  And realms of endless day.

3 Apostles, martyrs, prophets there,
  Around my Saviour stand;
And soon my friends in Christ below,
  Will join the glorious band.
Jerusalem! my happy home!
  My soul still pants for thee;
Then shall my labors have an end,
  When I thy joys shall see.
          "F. B. P." *r.* 1616.

JERUSALEM. C. M. — From Episcopal Hymnal.

Je-ru-sa-lem! my happy home! Name ever dear to me! When shall my la-bors have an end, In joy, and peace, in thee!

HEAVEN. 281

"FOREVER WITH THE LORD." S. M. D.   I. B. Woodbury.

1. "For-ev-er with the Lord!" A-men. So let it be; Life for the dead is in that word, 'Tis im-mor-tal-i-ty. Here in the bod-y pent, Ab-sent from Him I roam; Yet night-ly pitch my mov-ing tent A day's march near-er home, near-er home, near-er home, A day's march near-er home.

Used by per. Oliver Ditson Co., owners of Copyright

884 *So shall we ever be with the Lord.*

2 "Forever with the Lord!"
Father, if 'tis thy will,
The promise of that faithful word,
Ev'n here to me fulfil.
Be thou at my right hand;
So shall I never fail:
Uphold thou me, and I shall stand;
Help, and I shall prevail.

3 So, when my latest breath
Shall rend the vail in twain,
By death I shall escape from death,
And life eternal gain.
Knowing "as I am known,"
How shall I love that word,
And oft repeat before the throne,
"Forever with the Lord!"
James Montgomery.

885 *In my Father's House are many Mansions.*

1 My Father's house on high—
Home of my soul! how near,
At times, to faith's foreseeing eye
Thy golden gates appear!
Yet clouds still intervene,
And all my comfort flies;
Like Noah's dove I flit between
Rough seas and stormy skies.

2 Anon the clouds depart,
The winds and waters cease;
While sweetly o'er my gladdened heart
Expands the bow of peace.
And then I feel that he,—
Remembered or forgot,—
The Lord is never far from me,
Though I perceive him not.
James Montgomery.

FUTURITY.

ADRIAN. S. M. J. E. GOULD.

1. Come to the land of peace; From shadows come away;
Where all the sounds of weeping cease, And storms no more have sway.

886 *Come, ye Blessed.*

2 Fear hath no dwelling here;
But pure repose and love
Breathe through the bright, celestial air,
The spirit of the dove.

3 Come to the bright and blest,
Gathered from every land;
For here thy soul shall find its rest
Amid the shining band.

4 In this divine abode
Change leaves no saddening trace;
Come, trusting spirit, to thy God,
Thy holy resting-place.
Anon.

887 *The Bliss of Heaven.*

1 There is no night in heaven;
In that blest world above
Work never can bring weariness,
For work itself is love.

2 There is no grief in heaven;
For life is one glad day,
And tears are of those former things
Which all have passed away.

3 There is no sin in heaven;
Behold that blessed throng!
All holy is their spotless robe,
All holy is their song.

4 There is no death in heaven;
But, when the Christian dies,
The angels wait his parted soul,
And waft it to the skies!
Francis M. Knollis.

888 *Heaven Everywhere.*

1 Our heaven is everywhere,
If we but love the Lord,
Unswerving tread the narrow way,
And ever shun the broad.

2 'Tis where the trusting heart
Bows meekly to its grief,
Still looking up with earnest faith
For comfort and relief.

3 Wherever truth abides,
Sweet peace is ever there:
If we but love and serve the Lord,
Our heaven is everywhere.
Miss Fletcher.

889 *Awake and Sing.*

1 Rest for the toiling hand,
Rest for the anxious brow,
Rest for the weary, way-worn feet,
Rest from all labor now;

2 Soon shall the trump of God
Give out the welcome sound
That shakes thy silent chamber-walls,
And breaks the turf-sealed ground.

3 Ye dwellers in the dust,
Awake! come forth and sing;
Sharp has your frost of winter been,
But bright shall be your spring.

4 'Twas sown in weakness here;
'Twill then be raised in power;
That which was sown an earthly seed
Shall rise a heavenly flower.
Horatius Bonar.

HEAVEN. 283

ZERAH. C. M. Dr. L. MASON.

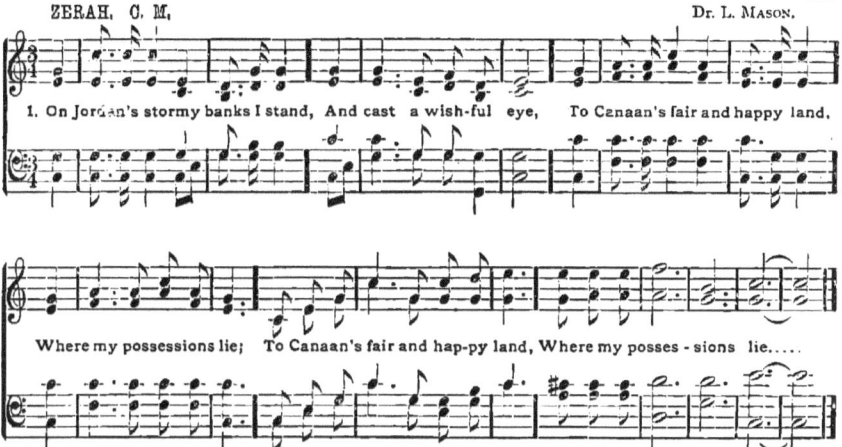

1. On Jordan's stormy banks I stand, And cast a wish-ful eye, To Canaan's fair and happy land, Where my possessions lie; To Canaan's fair and hap-py land, Where my posses-sions lie.....

890 *Prospect of Heaven.*

2 Oh! the transporting, rapturous scene,
That rises to my sight;
Sweet fields arrayed in living green,
And rivers of delight.

3 No chilling winds nor poisonous breath;
Can reach that healthful shore;
Sickness and sorrow, pain and death,
Are felt and feared no more.

4 When shall I reach that happy place,
And be forever blest?
When shall I see my Father's face,
And in his bosom rest?

Samuel Stennett.

891 *The Land that is very far off.*

1 FAR from these narrow scenes of night
Unbounded glories rise,
And realms of infinite delight,
Unknown to mortal eyes.

2 Fair, distant land! could mortal eyes
But half its charms explore,
How would our spirits long to rise
And dwell on earth no more.

3 No clouds those blissful regions know:
Realms ever bright and fair;
For sin, the source of mortal woe,
Can never enter there.

4 Prepare us, Lord, by grace divine,
For thy bright courts on high;
Then bid our spirits rise and join
The chorus of the sky.

Anne Steele.

892 *The Promised Land.*

1 THERE is a land of pure delight,
Where saints immortal reign;
Infinite day excludes the night,
And pleasures banish pain.

2 There everlasting spring abides,
And never-withering flowers:
Death, like a narrow sea, divides
This heavenly land from ours.

3 But timorous mortals start and shrink
To cross this narrow sea;
And linger shivering on the brink,
And fear to launch away.

4 Oh, could we make our doubts remove,
Those gloomy doubts that rise,
And see the Canaan that we love,
With unbeclouded eyes;

5 Could we but climb where Moses stood,
And view the landscape o'er,
Not Jordan's stream nor death's cold flood
Should fright us from the shore.

Isaac Watts, 1709.

FUTURITY.

WANDERER. S. M. — P. HOLBROOK.

1. How long, O Lord, our God, Holy, and true, and good, Wilt thou not judge thy suffering church, Her sighs, and tears, and blood?

893 *How long, O Lord.*

2 Saint after saint on earth
Has lived, and loved, and died;
And as they left us one by one,
We laid them side by side.

3 We laid them down to sleep,
But not in hope forlorn;
We laid them but to ripen there,
Till the last glorious morn.

4 We long to hear thy voice,
To see thee face to face,
To share thy crown and glory then,
As now we share thy grace.
Horatius Bonar.

894 *Thought of Heaven.*

1 I LOVE to think of heaven,
Where white-robed angels are,
Where many a friend is gathered safe
From fear, and toil, and care.

2 I love to think of heaven,
Where my Redeemer reigns,
Where rapturous songs of triumph rise,
In endless, joyous strains.

3 I love to think of heaven,
The greetings there we'll meet,
The harps—the songs forever ours—
The walks—the golden streets.

4 I love to think of heaven,
That promised land so fair,
Oh, how my raptured spirit longs
To be forever there.
Rev. L. Hartsough.

VESPER. 8s & 7s. — Arr. fr. FLOTOW.

1. This is not my place of rest-ing: Mine's a cit-y yet to come; On-ward to it I am hast-ing— On to my e-ter-nal home.

895 *We seek a City to come.*

2 In it all is light and glory;
O'er it shines a nightless day:
Every trace of sin's sad story,
All the curse, hath passed away.

3 There the Lamb, our Shepherd, leads us
By the streams of life along,
On the freshest pastures feed us,
Turns our sighing into song.

4 Soon we pass this desert dreary,
Soon we bid farewell to pain;
Never more are sad and weary,
Never, never sin again.
Horatius Bonar.

HEAVEN. 285

1. High in yonder realms of light, Dwell the raptur'd saints above, Far beyond our fee-ble sight, Hap-py in Im-manuel's love; Pil-grims in this vale of tears, Once they knew, like us be-low, Gloom-y doubts, dis-tress-ing fears, Torturing pain, and heav-y woe.

896 *The Songs and Bliss of Heaven.*

2 'Mid the chorus of the skies,
    'Mid th' angelic lyres above,
Hark! their songs melodious rise,
    Songs of praise to Jesus' love:
Happy spirits! ye are fled,
    Where no grief can entrance find;
Lulled to rest the aching head,
    Soothed the anguish of the mind.

3 All is tranquil and serene,
    Calm and undisturbed repose,
There no cloud can intervene,
    There no angry tempest blows:
Every tear is wiped away,
    Sighs no more shall heave the breast,
Night is lost in endless day,
    Sorrow in eternal rest.
                        Thomas Raffles.

897 *The Victory of the Saints.*

1 PALMS of glory, raiment bright,
    Crowns that never fade away,
Gird and deck the saints in light,
    Priests and kings, and conquerors they:
Yet the conquerors bring their palms
    To the Lamb amidst the throne,
And proclaim, in joyful psalms.
    Vict'ry through his cross alone.

2 Kings for harps their crowns resign,
    Crying, as they strike the chords,—
" Take the kingdom—it is thine,—
    King of kings, and Lord of lords!"
Round the altar priests confess,—
    If their robes are white as snow,
'Twas the Saviour's righteousness,
    And his blood, that made them so.

3 Who were these?—On earth they dwelt,
    Sinners once of Adam's race,
Guilt, and fear, and suffering felt,
    But were saved by sovereign grace:
They were mortal, too, like us;
    Ah! when we like them must die,
May our souls, translated thus,
    Triumph, reign, and shine on high.
                        James Montgomery.

898   Eye hath not Seen.

2 But the good Spirit of the Lord
    Reveals a heaven to come;
The beams of glory in his word
    Allure and guide us home.

3 Pure are the joys above the sky,
    And all the region peace;
No wanton lips, nor envious eye,
    Can see or taste the bliss.

4 Those holy gates forever bar
    Pollution, sin, and shame;
None shall obtain admittance there
    But followers of the Lamb.
                                  Isaac Watts.

899   The Unseen World.

1 THERE is a state unknown, unseen,
    Where parted souls must be;
And but a step doth lie between
    That world of souls and me.

2 I see no light, I hear no sound,
    When midnight shades are spread;
Yet angels pitch their tents around
    And guard my quiet bed.

3 Impart the faith that soars on high,
    Beyond this earthly strife,
That holds sweet converse with the sky,
    And lives eternal life.
                                  John Taylor.

900

2 Glorious city, home eternal,
    Where the saints shall dwell for aye,
Singing joyful hallelujahs
    To the Lamb through endless day;
Crowns of life, and palms of glory,
    Spotless robes will there be given.
Hallelujah! hallelujah!
    'Tis the saints' eternal heav'n!
                                   Anon.

HEAVEN. 287

HOME OF THE SOUL. 12s & 8s. PHILIP PHILLIPS, by per.

1. I will sing you a song of that beau-ti-ful land, The far a-way home of the soul, Where no storms ev-er beat on the glit-ter-ing strand, While the years of e-ter-ni-ty roll, While the years of e-ter-ni-ty roll.

901 *Home of the Soul.*

2 Oh, that home of the soul, in my visions and dreams,
Its bright jasper walls I can see,
Till I fancy but thinly the vale intervenes
Between the fair city and me.

3 There the great trees of life in their beauty do grow,
And the river of life floweth by,
For no death ever enters the city, you know,
And nothing that maketh a lie.

4 That unchangeable home is for you and for me,
Where Jesus of Nazareth stands;
The King of all kingdoms forever is he,
And he holdeth our crowns in his hands.

5 Oh, how sweet it will be in that beauti-ful land,
So free from all sorrow and pain!
With songs on our lips and with harps in our hands,
To meet one another again.
Mrs. Ellen H. Gates.

---

902 *Sweet By-and-By.*
[Tune—SWEET BY-AND-BY. Key of G.]

1 THERE'S a land that is fairer than day,
And by faith we may see it afar,
For the Father waits over the way,
To prepare us a dwelling-place there
REF.—In the sweet by-and-by
We shall meet on that beautiful shore.

2 We shall sing on that beautiful shore
The melodious songs of the blest,
And our spirits shall sorrow no more;
Not a sigh for the blessing of rest.

3 To our bountiful Father above,
We will offer our tribute of praise
For the glorious gift of his love,
And the blessings that hallow our days.

4 We shall meet, we shall sing, we shall reign
In the land where the saved never die!
We shall rest free from sorrow and pain,
Safe at home in the sweet by-and-by.
S. Fillmore Bennett.

MISCELLANEOUS.

IS MY NAME WRITTEN THERE? 7s & 6s.

Frank M. Davis, by per.

1. Lord, I care not for rich-es, Neither silver nor gold, I would make sure of heav-en, I would en-ter the fold; In the book of thy king-dom, With its pa-ges so fair, Tell me, Je-sus, my Sav-iour, Is my name writ-ten there? Is my name writ-ten there? Is my name writ-ten there? In the book of thy king-dom, Is my name writ-ten there?

903

2 Lord, my sins they are many
  Like the sands of the sea,
But thy blood, O my Saviour,
  Is sufficient for me;
For thy promise is written
  In bright letters that glow,
Tho' your sins be as scarlet,
  I will make them like snow.

3 Oh, that beautiful city,
  With its mansions of light,
With its glorified beings
  In pure garments of white;
Where no evil thing cometh
  To despoil what is fair,
Where the angels are watching,
  Is my name written there?

Mrs. M. A. Kidder.

MISCELLANEOUS. 289

WORLD OF LIGHT. P. M.   O. Snow, by per.

1. There is a beau-ti-ful world, Where saints and an-gels sing, A world where peace and pleasure reign, And heav'nly prais-es ring. We'll be there, we'll be there, Palms of vic-t'ry, Crowns of glo-ry, we shall wear In that beau-ti-ful world on high.

904

2 There is a beautiful world
Where sorrow never comes;
A world where tears shall never fall,
In sighing for our home.—Cho.

3 There is a beautiful world,
Unseen to mortal sight,
And darkness never enters there,
That home is fair and bright. —Cho.

4 There is a beautiful world
Of harmony and love;
Oh! may we safely enter there,
And dwell with God above.—Cho.
O. Snow.

905 Tune—Sweet Hour of Prayer. Key of D.

1 Sweet hour of prayer! Sweet hour of
That calls me from a world of care, [prayer!
And bids me at my Father's throne
Make all my wants and wishes known:
In seasons of distress and grief
My soul has often found relief,
And oft escaped the tempter's snare,
By thy return, sweet hour of prayer.

2 Sweet hour of prayer! Sweet hour of
Thy wings shall my petition bear [prayer!
To Him whose truth and faithfulness
Engage the waiting soul to bless;
And since he bids me seek his face,
Believe his word and trust his grace,
I'll cast on him my every care,
And wait for thee, sweet hour of prayer.

3 Sweet hour of prayer! Sweet hour of
May I thy consolation share, [prayer!
Till from Mount Pisgah's lofty height
I view my home and take my flight:
This robe of flesh I'll drop, and rise
To seize the everlasting prize,
And shout while passing through the air,
Farewell, farewell, sweet hour of prayer!
W. W. Walford, 1845.

MISCELLANEOUS.

JESUS ONLY. 8s & 7s. H. P. Pierce, by per.

1. "Je-sus on-ly," is the mot-to Now en-grav-en on my shield; Where he leads me I will fol-low, Fighting bravely on the field; Weak and tempted, weak and tempted, Thro' his strength I'll nev-er yield.

906 *Jesus only.*

2 "Jesus only," when I'm doubtful,
  Can my feeble faith make strong;
Only He can wisely counsel,
  Make me right where I've been wrong.
    He's my Saviour,
  Praises loud to Him belong.

3 "Jesus only," with thanksgiving
  All my care on Him I roll,
With His peace, past understanding,
  He now "garrisons" my soul.
    Blest Redeemer!
  Glad I yield to His control.

4 "Jesus only," let His praises
  Sound to earth's remotest shore,
Souls from sin and shame He raises,
  Saves them by His mighty power
    Hallelujah!
  Love and trust Him evermore.
              —Anon.

REVIVE US AGAIN. 11s. English Melody.

1. We praise thee, O God! for the Son of thy love, For Je-sus, who died, and is now gone a-bove.

CHORUS.

Hal-le-lu-jah! thine the glo-ry! Hal-le-lu-jah! A-men.
Hal-le-lu-jah! thine the glo-ry! Omit............ Re-vive us a-gain.

907

2 We praise thee, O God! for thy spirit of light,
Who has shown us the Saviour, and scattered our night.—Cho.

3 All glory and praise to the Lamb that was slain,
Who hath borne all our sins, and has cleansed every stain.—Cho.

4 Revive us again: fill each heart with thy love!
May our souls be rekindled with fire from above.—Cho.
                                W. P. Mackay, 1863.

MISCELLANEOUS.

WHILE THE DAYS ARE GOING BY. 8s & 7s.   JNO. R. SWENEY.

1. There are lone-ly hearts to cher-ish, While the days are go-ing by;
There are wea-ry souls who per-ish, While the days are go-ing by. If a
smile we can re-new, As our jour-ney we pur-sue, Oh, the good that we may do,
While the days are go-ing by. While go-ing by, while go-ing by, While go-ing
by, while go-ing by, Oh, the good we may be do-ing, While the days are go-ing by.

908

2 There's no time for idle scorning,
   While the days are going by;
Let our face be like the morning,
   While the days are going by.
Oh, the world is full of sighs,
   Full of sad and weeping eyes;
Help your fallen brothers rise,
   While the days are going by.—Cho.

3 All the loving links that bind us,
   While the days are going by;
One by one we leave behind us,
   While the days are going by.
But the seeds of good we sow;
   Both in shade and shine will grow,
And will keep our hearts aglow,
   While the days are going by.—Cho.

Anon.

CLOSER, STILL CLOSER. 11s.   W. A. Ogden, by per.

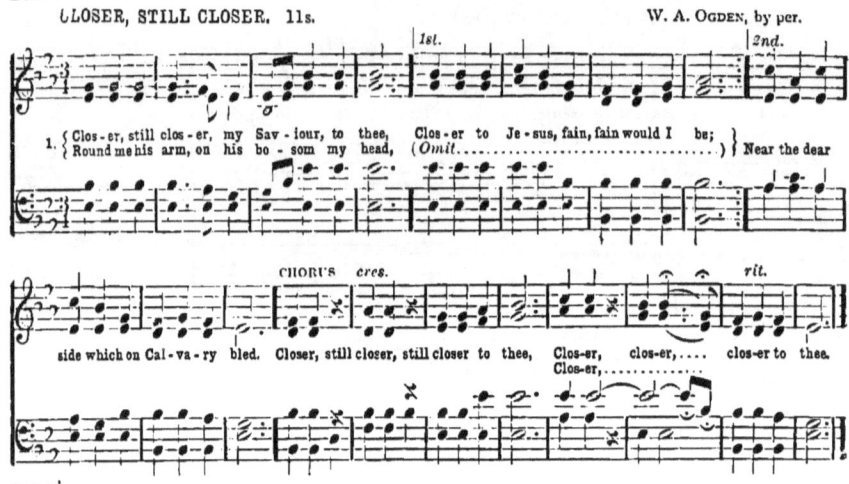

909

2 Closer by day, tho' my sky be all bright,
Closer, still closer. when falleth the night;
Earth has no spot where without him I'm safe,
Time has no moment I need not his grace.
—Cho.

3 When to the Jordan of death I descend,
Danger I'll fear not, if Christ be my friend;
Breasting the billows, my death-song shall be,
Closer, still closer, my Saviour, to thee.
—Cho. L. R. C.

OUR HIDING-PLACE. 7s.   W. A. Ogden, by per.

910

2 When the thunders, mutt'ring deep,
O'er my soul their terrors creep,
And I sink in deep despair,
Is there refuge anywhere?—Cho.

3 Oh, the refuge where I rest,
Oh, the calmness of my breast,
When in trembling, tearful prayer
I have found a refuge there.—Cho.

Rev. H. O. Hoffman.

911

2 Its fountains are deep and its waters are pure;
And sweet to the weary soul;
It flows from the throne of Jehovah alone!
Oh, come where its bright waves roll.
—Ref.

3 This beautiful stream is the River of Life!
It flows for all nations free!
A balm for each wound in its water found;
Oh, sinner, it flows for thee!—Ref.

4 Oh, will you not drink of this beautiful stream,
And dwell on its peaceful shore?
The Spirit says, Come all ye weary ones, home,
And wander in sin no more.—Ref.

Anon.

MISCELLANEOUS.

HOW CAN I KEEP FROM SINGING? 8s & 7s.   Rev. R. Lowry, by per.

1. My life flows on in endless song; Above earth's lam-en-ta-tion, I catch the sweet, tho' far-off, hymn, (Omit............) That hails a new cre-a-tion; Thro' all the tu-mult and the strife, I hear the mu-sic ring-ing; It finds an ech-o in my soul—How can I keep from sing-ing?

912

2 What tho' my joys and comforts die?
   The Lord my Saviour liveth;
What tho' the darkness gather round?
   Songs in the night he giveth;
No storm can shake my inmost calm,
   While to that refuge clinging;
Since Christ is Lord of heaven and earth
   How can I keep from singing?

3 I lift my eyes; the cloud grows thin,
   I see the blue above it;
And day by day this pathway smooths
   Since first I learned to love it,
The peace of Christ makes fresh my heart,
   A fountain ever springing;
All things are mine since I am his—
   How can I keep from singing?
                              Anon.

913 [Tune—What a Friend we have in Jesus. Key of F.]

1 What a friend we have in Jesus,
   All our sins and griefs to bear;
What a privilege to carry
   Everything to God in prayer!
Oh, what peace we often forfeit,
   Oh, what needless pain we bear—
All because we do not carry
   Everything to God in prayer.

2 Have we trials and temptations?
   Is there trouble anywhere?
We should never be discouraged—
   Take it to the Lord in prayer.
Can we find a friend so faithful,
   Who will all our sorrows share?
Jesus knows our every weakness—
   Take it to the Lord in prayer.

3 Are we weak and heavy laden,
   Cumbered with a load of care?
Precious Saviour, still our refuge—
   Take it to the Lord in prayer.
Do thy friends despise, forsake thee?
   Take it to the Lord in prayer;
In His arms He'll take and shield thee,
   Thou wilt find a solace there.
                         Horatius Bonar.

CHANTS.

914 GLORIA IN EXCELSIS.   PART I.   Ancient English.

1 GLORY be to | God on | high, || and on earth | peace, good- | will towards | men.
2 We praise thee, we bless thee, we | worship | thee, || we glorify thee, we give thanks to | thee for | thy great | glory.

PART II.

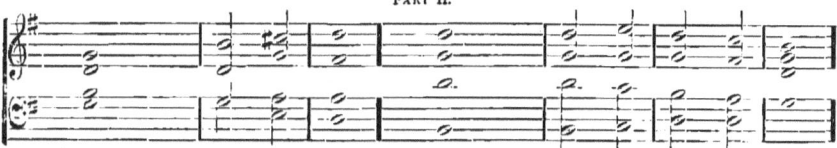

3 O Lord God, | heavenly | King, || God the | Father | Al- — | mighty!
4 O Lord, the only begotten Son, | Jesus | Christ; || O Lord God, Lamb of | God, Son | of the | Father,

PART III.

5 That takest away the | sins ·· of the | world, || have mercy | upon | us.
6 Thou that takest away the | sins ·· of the | world, || have mercy | upon | us.
7 Thou that takest away the | sins ·· of the | world, || re- | cieve our | prayer.
8 Thou that sittest at the right hand of | God the | Father, || have mercy | upon | us. |

RETURN TO PART I.

9 For thou | only ·· art | holy: || thou | only | art the | Lord:
10 Thou only, O Christ, with the | Holy | Ghost, || art most high in the | glory ·· of | God the | Father. || A- | men.

915 GLORIA PATRI. Irr.   H. W. GREATOREX.

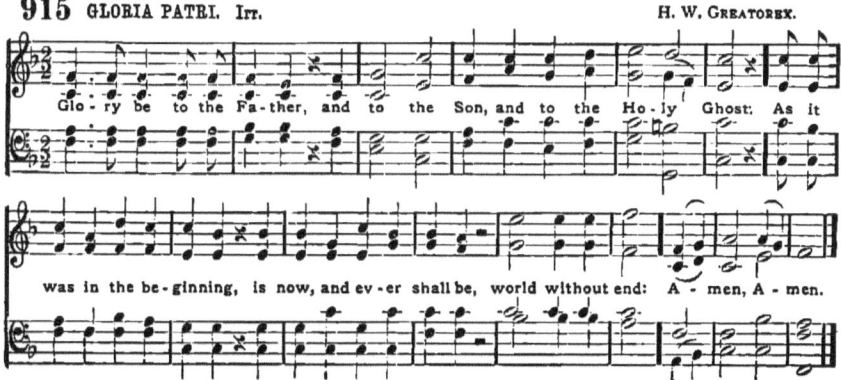

Glo-ry be to the Fa-ther, and to the Son, and to the Ho-ly Ghost: As it was in the be-ginning, is now, and ev-er shall be, world without end: A-men, A-men.

916 THE LORD'S PRAYER.

Adapted by H. R. PALMER.

Used by per. H R Palmer.

1 Our Father, who art in heaven, hallowed | be Thy | name; || Thy kingdom come, Thy will be done on | earth, as it | is in | heaven;

2 Give us this day our | daily | bread; || And forgive us our trespasses, as we forgive | them that | trespass a- | gainst us.

3 And lead us not into temptation, but deliver | us from | evil; || For Thine is the kingdom, and the power, and the glory, for | ever and | ever. A- | men.

917 "THY WILL BE DONE!"

L. MASON.

1 "Thy will be | done!" || In devious way the hurrying stream of | life may | run; || Yet still our grateful hearts shall say, | "Thy will be | done!"

2 "Thy will be | done!" || If o'er us shine a gladdening and a | prosperous | sun, || This prayer will make it more divine— | "Thy will be | done!"

3 "Thy will be | done!" || Though shrouded o'er our | path with | gloom, || One comfort—one is ours,—to breathe, while we adore, | "Thy will be | done!"

Sir John Bowring.

918 TRISAGION CHORUS. [RESPONSE.]

R. TAYLOR.

919 DOMINUS REGIT ME.

Lowell Mason.

Psalm 23.

1 The Lord is my Shepherd; I | shall not | want; || he maketh me to lie down in green pastures; he leadeth me beside the | still— | waters.
2 He restoreth my soul; he leadeth me in the paths of righteousness for his | name's— | sake. || Yea, though I walk through the valley of the shadow of death, I will fear no evil: for thou art with me; thy rod and thy | staff they | comfort me.
3 Thou preparest a table before me, in the presence of mine enemies; thou anointest my head with oil; my | cup · · runneth | over. || Surely goodness and mercy shall follow me all the days of my life; and I will dwell in the house of the | Lord for | ever. || A- | men.

920 VENITE, EXULTEMUS DOMINO.

W. Boyce.

Psalm 95.

1 O come, let us sing un- | to the | Lord: || Let us make a joyful noise to the | rock of | our sal- | vation.
2 Let us come before his presence | with thanks- | giving, || Let us make a joyful noise | unto | him with | psalms.
3 For the Lord is a | great— | God, || And a great | King a- | bove all | gods.
4 In his hand are the deep places | of the | earth; || The heights of the | mountains are | his— | also.
5 The sea is his, | and he | made it; || And his hands | formed · · the | dry— | land.
6 O come, let us worship | and bow | down; || Let us kneel be- | fore the | Lord, our | Maker.
*7 For he | is our | God, || And we are the people of his pasture, and the | sheep of | his— | hand.

CHANTS.

921 TE DEUM LAUDAMUS. *Ancient English.*

The Ancient "Te Deum."

1 WE praise thee, | O— | God; ‖ we acknowledge | thee to | be the | Lord. ‖
All the earth doth | worship | thee, ‖ the Father | ever- | last- — | ing. ‖

2 To thee all angels | cry a- | loud, ‖ the heavens, and | all the | powers there- | in. ‖
To thee cherubim and seraphim, con- | tinually · · do | cry, ‖ Holy, holy, holy, Lord | God of | Saba- | oth; ‖

3 Heaven and earth are full of the majesty | of thy | glory. ‖ The glorious company of the apostles praise thee. The goodly fellowship of the | prophets | praise— | thee. ‖
The noble army of martyrs | praise— | thee. ‖ The holy church throughout all the | world · · doth ac- | knowledge | thee. ‖

4 The Father, of an | infi- · · nite | majesty; ‖ thine adorable, | true and | only | son; ‖
Also the Holy | Ghost, the | Comforter. ‖ Thou art the King of glory, O Christ, thou art the ever-blessed | Son · · of the | Fa- — | ther. ‖

5 When thou tookest upon thee to de- | liver | man, ‖ thou didst humble thyself to be | born — | of a | virgin. ‖
When thou hadst overcome the | sharpness · · of | death, ‖ thou didst open the kingdom of | heaven · · to | all be- | lievers. ‖

6 Thou sittest at the right hand of God, in the | glory · · of the | Father. ‖ We believe that thou shalt | come to | be our | judge. ‖
We therefore pray thee, | help thy | servants, ‖ whom thou hast redeemed | with thy | precious | blood. ‖

7 Make them to be numbered | with thy | saints, ‖ in | glory | ever- | lasting. ‖
O Lord, save thy people, and | bless thine | heritage; ‖ govern them and | lift them | up for- | ever. ‖

8 Day by day we | magni- · · fy | thee; ‖ and we worship thy name ever, | world with- | out— | end. ‖
Vouchsafe, O Lord, to keep us this | day with-out | sin; ‖ O Lord, have mercy upon us, have | mer-cy up- | on— | us. ‖

9 O Lord, let thy mercy | be up- | on us, ‖ as our | trust— | is in | thee. ‖
O Lord, in | thee · · have I | trusted; ‖ let me | never | be con- | founded. ‖ A- | men. ‖

CHANTS.

922 LAETATUS SUM. John Randall

Psalm 122.

1 I was glad when they said | unto | me, || Let us go unto the | house — | of the | Lord.
2 Our feet are standing with- | in thy | gates, || O — | — Je- | rusa- | lem;
3 Jerusalem that art builded | as a | city || That | is com- | pact to- | gether:
4 Whither the tribes go up, even the | tribes · · of the | Lord, || For a testimony unto Israel, to give thanks unto the | name — | of the | Lord.
5 For there are set | thrones for | judgment, || The thrones of the | house of | Da- — | vid.
6 Pray for the peace of Je- | rusa- lem: || They shall | prosper · · that | love — | thee.
7 Peace be with- | in thy | walls, || And prosperity with- | in thy | pala- | ces.
8 For my brethren and com- | panions' | sakes, || I will now say, | Peace — | be with- | in thee.
*9 For the sake of the house of the | Lord our | God || I will | seek — | thy — | good.

923 *Psalm 103.*

1 Bless the Lord, | O my | soul; || And, all that is within me, | bless his | holy | name.
2 Bless the Lord, | O my | soul, || And for- | get not | all his | benefits:
3 Who forgiveth all | thine in- | iquities; || Who | healeth · · all | thy dis- | eases;
4 Who redeemeth thy life | from de- | struction; || Who crowneth thee with loving | kindness · · and | tender | mercies;
5 Who satisfieth thy mouth with | good — | things; || So that thy youth is re- | newéd | like the | eagle.
6 The Lord executeth righteous | acts and | judgments || For | all that | are op- | pressed.
7 He made known his ways | unto | Moses, || His doings unto the | children · · of | Isra- | el.
8 The Lord is full of com- | passion and | gracious || Slow to anger, and | plenteous | in — | mercy.
. . . .
19 The Lord hath established his | throne · · in the | heavens; || And his kingdom | ruleth | over | all.
20 Bless the Lord, ye angels of his, ye might- | y in | strength, || That fulfill his word, hearkening unto the | voice of | his — | word.
21 Bless ye the Lord, all | ye his | hosts; || Ye ministers of | his, that | do his | pleasure.
22 Bless the Lord, all ye his works, in all places of | his do- | minion: || Bless the | Lord, — | O my | soul.

CHANTS.

924 JUBILATE DEO.
JOHN ROBINSON.

Psalm 100.

1 MAKE a joyful noise unto the Lord, | all ye | lands. || Serve the Lord with Gladness; come before his | presence | with — | singing.

2 Know ye that the Lord | he is | God: || It is he that hath made us, and we are his; we are his people, | and the | sheep · · of his | pasture.

3 Enter into his gates with thanksgiving, and into his | courts with | praise: || Give thanks unto him, and | bless — | his — | name.

4 For the Lord is good; his mercy en- | dureth for- | ever, || And his truth unto | all — | gener- | ations.

925
Psalm 98.

1 O SING unto the | Lord a new | song; || for he hath | done — | marvel-ous | things: || His right hand and his | holy | arm, || hath | wrought sal- | vation | for him.

2 He hath remembered his mercy and his faithfulness toward the | house of | Israel: || All the ends of the earth have seen the sal- | vation | of our | God.

3 Make a joyful noise unto the Lord, | all the | earth: || Break forth and sing for | joy, yea | sing — | praises.

4 Sing praises unto the Lord | with the | harp; || With the harp, and the | voice — | of mel- | ody.

5 With trumpets, and | sound of | cornet || Make a joyful noise be- | fore the | King, the | Lord.

6 Let the sea roar, and the | fullness · · there- | of; || The world, and | they that | dwell there- | in.

7 Let the floods | clap their | hands, || Let the hills sing for joy to- | gether · · be- | fore the | Lord;

8 For he cometh to | judge the | earth: || He shall judge the world with righteousness, and the | peoples | with — | equity.

INDEX OF SUBJECTS.

Abba, Father............293, 664
Abide with us.......139, 234, 641
Absence, from Christ...564, 638
Absence, from God......519, 543
Accepted Time......359, 372, 590
Activity...547, 590, 594, 600-604,
 609, 620-622, 625, 627, 725
Adoption....................664
Adoration 4, 67, 82
Advent of Christ......See *Christ*.
Affliction 647-680
Benefits of..444, 652, 657, 673,
 676, 677
Christ's help in 254, 292,
 296, 367, 439, 680, 779, 783
Comfort in..647, 652, 656,
 673, 680, 836
God's help in 70, 411, 422,
 443, 453, 526, 656, 657, 673,
 674, 679, 680, 817
Ordered by God.....459, 651,
 654, 657
Submission under...651, 654,
 656, 674, 817
Thankfulness for..........657
Age................See *Old Age*.
All is well...................463
All Saints' Day..............798
All things work for God..444, 457
Angels:
 At Ascension of Christ.....245
 At Birth of Christ...215, 217,
 219, 222, 223, 226
 At Coronation of Christ....255
 At Death 845
 At Gethsemane..............238
 At Resurrection of Christ,
 251, 256
 Ministering 899
Anti-slavery..384, 488, 644, 781,
 790
Ark.........................586
Armor, Christian..578, 598, 605,
 607, 612, 613, 615, 618, 620, 630
Ashamed of Christ......569, 624
Aspiration...341, 506, 516, 519,
 520, 523, 525, 531, 543, 547, 549,
 550, 552, 556, 559, 573, 610, 906
Atonement..........281, 286, 293
Autumn.............808, 811-813
Awakening...359, 361, 362, 372,
 378, 380

Backsliding...550, 632, 637, 638,
 645
Banner.................614, 629
Baptism...720, 721, 724, 728, 732,
 733, 735
 Of Christ 726, 728, 735
 Of Holy Spirit.............322
Bearing the Yoke............357
Benediction ...64, 125-130, 133,
 134, 143, 146
Benevolence..488, 492, 500, 780,
 791
Bereavement..836, 842, 851, 860,
 862, 863, 867, 876
Bible: 335-346.
 Authority of...............336

Bible:
 Comfort from ...337, 339, 340,
 342, 344, 346
 Foundation of Hope...336, 346
 Inspiration of 340
 Light......................343, 344
 Love for 338, 339, 345
 Treasure...................346
 Word of Life...........332, 344
Blindness removed...........519
Brotherly Love..475, 739, 742, 743
Blessing sought 117, 187

Calmness....................671
 In death..........843, 845, 860
Charity:
 Christ's example of..485, 498,
 500
 Concerning opinions...477, 744
 To the erring......478, 486, 491
 To the poor........488, 492, 498
Cheerfulness 440, 634, 662
 From God's presence...669, 674
 In view of death...853, 854, 857
Childlikeness 415, 460, 490,
 531, 537
Children..........819, 822, 823
 Christ's Child........223, 224
 Death of children...856, 858, 864
 Prayer for..............821. 822
 Shepherd's care for 819, 823
Christ 214, 311
 Advent of—first....214, 216, 228
 " " —second ..220, 778,
 871, 872
 Altogether lovely...264, 279,
 524, 565
 Ascension..............245, 246
 Baptism of............728, 735
 Birth of..........223, 224, 227
 Blood of...............268, 286
 Compassion of..278, 351, 360, 367
 Condescension of...........237
 Coronation of.........255, 258
 Crucifixion of.239, 241, 254, 406
 Entering Jerusalem 242
 Example of....232, 263, 274,
 284, 485, 498, 734, 740
 Faithfulness of............632
 Forgiving spirit of 241, 478
 Glory of..........255, 258, 261
 Life and ministry.....225, 263
 Love of....232, 245, 267, 298,
 483, 488, 499, 587
 Meekness of...........231, 263
 Mission of....220, 225, 263, 309
 Moses and.................306
 Name of, dear...265, 266, 281,
 295, 300, 305
 One with His people...722, 740
 Poverty of.................240
 Presence of...........641, 680
 Prophesied of..............222
 Reign of........277, 384, 758
 Resurrection of......245, 246,
 249, 250, 251, 253, 257, 294
 Sufferings of.....237, 240, 592,
 593, 710, 723
 Sympathy of...270, 281, 419, 791

Christ—Names and Emblems:
 Advocate...................236
 All in all..259, 280, 291, 292, 449
 Bread of Life..........734, 738
 Brother....................307
 Captain of Salvation....595-630
 Conqueror............261, 295
 Conqueror of Death....251, 294
 Corner-stone 688
 Dayspring 752
 Daystar 288
 Door.......................653
 Forerunner.................571
 Friend......237, 298, 301, 302,
 307, 589, 710, 913
 Guest 234, 641
 Head of the Church..549, 722,
 740, 744
 Immanuel.........275, 281, 565
 Intercessor 293
 King ...218, 242, 244, 246, 255,
 258, 277, 290, 295, 667, 695
 Lamb 306, 417
 Life 260, 271, 325, 534
 Light of Life....280, 291, 325,
 330, 536
 Light of the World..271, 290,
 296, 675
 Man of sorrows 238, 255
 Physician 230
 Priest.............243, 266, 270, 295
 Prince of Peace 290
 Prophet 290, 295
 Redeemer...262, 266, 287, 567,
 303
 Refiner....................677
 Refuge 292, 910
 Rest 233, 280, 296, 367
 Resurrection 294
 Rock.......................286
 Sacrifice 247, 293, 295
 Shepherd ...285, 287, 632, 819,
 823, 830, 895
 Son of David 15, 884, 704
 Son of God 229, 276, 281,
 284, 410, 570
 Son of Man 281, 567
 Stranger...................278
 Son of Righteousness 283
 The Crucified 579
 Treasure 271
 Truth 260, 325, 516
 Vine 715, 738
 Way 260, 325, 520
Christlikeness...282, 498, 540, 722
Christmas 216, 229
Church 685
 Abode of Christians.....75, 711
 Conflicts of...........748, 751
 Enlarged......389, 718, 750, 758
 Founded on Christ 688, 692
 Glory of.......685, 696, 752, 758
 Joining the 21, 712, 713,
 714, 722
 Organization of 688, 696
 Prayer for 774
 Security of........685, 689, 694
 Triumphant 751
 Waiting for Christ 872, 893
Cisterns 348

INDEX OF SUBJECTS.

City—heavenly....527, 880, 883, 895, 900
Close of Worship....116, 135, 141
Comfort............See *Affliction*.
Comforter.....................329
Communion....See *Lord's Table*.
Of Saints.....................816
With Christ..299, 564, 569-571, 578
With God.......518, 570, 578, 582, 586
With one another...415, 715, 727, 740
Coming to Christ......402, 408, 424, 428
Completeness........308, 451, 637
Confession............404, 422
Confidence in God...635, 648, 670
Conflict of Ages..........751, 781
Conquerors...595, 605, 613, 618, 627, 757, 855, 897
Conscience........318, 341, 494, 666, 826
Voice of....................504
Consecration..195, 398, 401, 413, 425, 712, 725, 731
Contentment 415, 487
Conversion....See *Regeneration*.
Country—defense of..........792
Flag of.......................792
Love of..................793, 794
Prayer for 796
Courage..532, 591, 594, 603, 612, 617, 621, 622, 757, 770, 781
Creed—perfect................516
Cross....366, 375, 540, 579, 584, 585, 587, 588, 589, 592, 593, 620, 723, 775
And Crown 585, 607
Bearing the.....407, 425, 585
Glorying in....587, 588, 599, 624
Joy before..............579, 589
Crown....468, 585, 595, 596, 605, 611, 612, 625
Crucified with Christ....540, 731

Daily bread—prayer for......455
Death......842, 844-846, 850-856, 860-863, 865, 867, 869, 870
Better than to live alway...852
Gain 852, 853
Going home............853, 870
Not extinction.......853, 854, 870
Of children..........850, 858
Of Christian friends..859, 861, 862, 867, 869
Of Minister..................855
Of righteous.........843, 860
Of sister..............861, 869
Of youth..........864, 865, 869
Peacefulness of Christians, 843, 860, 863
Rest in 849
Sleep....................849, 851
Support in..................857
Time of—uncertain 839
Triumph over..844, 816, 853, 855
Decision....522, 638, 712, 716, 722
Dedication..7, 38, 688, 696, 703, 704, 706, 708
Dependence..315, 318, 476, 556, 623, 638, 643
Despondency.................610
Devotion........25, 29, 38, 70, 74
Dignity of man 183, 203
Discipline....458, 459, 647, 652, 657, 682
Door, open...................373
Doxologies 64, 128, 129, 136
Duty—cheerfulness in........489

End of the wicked 374
End of the world............871
Endurance 614
Erring 478, 491
Eternity..............806, 833
Evening....61, 98, 104, 116, 119, 120, 121, 123
Sabbath............13, 39, 140
Example............474, 627
Excuses 354
Expostulation ...348, 358, 359, 363, 364, 368, 369, 377, 378, 379, 834

Faith 665
And hope and love.........544
In times of trial....435, 437, 439, 457, 657, 665
Longing for 435, 436, 447
Power of..........158, 437, 471
Triumphs of................669
Walking by 440, 458
Without sight..........576, 682
Without works—dead 44
Faithfulness 508, 528, 600, 855
Family....112, 502, 511, 816-818, 820, 821
Fasting 201, 397
Feast—Gospel 347, 354, 356
Fellowship ...475, 492, 710, 711, 715, 717, 739, 740, 741, 742, 743, 744
Fickleness 638, 639
Following Christ ...469, 482, 574
Forgiveness.........See *Pardon*.
Forgiving Spirit............478
Frailty 638, 838
Friendship 475, 502, 743

Gain and Loss........375, 407, 540
Gethsemane 238, 592, 593
Gentleness.........478, 486, 491
Glory of God...........914, 915
Glorifying God............421
God 147, 213
All in all....67, 70, 152, 164, 495
Arm of........127, 442, 545, 643
Care of....173, 206, 466, 575, 829
Condescension of........183
Creator................151, 163
Dwelling with His people..531
Eternity of..............150
Everywhere 169
Faithfulness of 670, 678, 806
Father.....209, 457, 525, 664, 675, 679
Fulness of.195, 447, 654, 669, 674
Gentleness of 184, 206
Goodness of 154, 173, 176, 187, 190, 805, 808
Greatness of ..54, 93, 148, 156, 191, 766
Guardian....75, 124, 138, 160, 635, 648
Guide ..181, 205, 530, 633, 642, 644, 655
Helper 443, 452, 548, 679
Holiness of....1, 84, 86, 166, 918
In Nature..151, 162, 163, 165, 166, 193
King......55, 174, 199, 709
Long-suffering of 405
Love........188, 203, 531, 658
Love of..95, 167, 177, 272, 276, 451, 480, 501, 791
Majesty of..............54, 174
Mercy of....81, 168, 171, 182, 211
Omnipresence of 159, 201
Omniscience of...157, 159, 161
Pity of 404, 493

God:
Power of............54, 69, 149
Presence of 456, 664, 817
Protection of...454, 643, 648, 661, 797, 805
Providence of...173, 196, 206, 208, 662, 829, 838
Providence of—mysterious, 189, 194, 458
Refuge......155, 170, 202, 461, 464, 684
Rock....210, 212, 348, 448, 464, 511, 685
Searcher of hearts.........159
Shepherd......178, 207, 648, 919
Source of blessing....70, 175, 181, 200, 208, 395, 467
Speaking to the soul...570, 586
Wisdom of..............54, 147
With the true worker 609
Godlikeness 540
Godly sorrow........406, 419, 552
Go Forward 628
Good part...............361, 375
Good works............44, 476
Gospel 347-390
Efficacy 391
Feast......347, 349, 354-356, 372
Light of....324, 383, 387, 388
Message 380
Nigh thee 386
Spread of..389, 392, 395, 742, 761
Grace ...31, 58, 66, 194, 201, 211, 289, 467
Gratitude 65, 187
Grieving the spirit 361
Growth....................549

Harvest..............802, 808, 811
Gospel 391
Last..................431, 872
Spiritual ..370, 761, 773, 777, 811
Healing of sorrow..........647
Heart:
Broken and contrite..328, 397, 426, 552, 555
Hardness of 561
Heaven 873-902
Anticipated......687, 730, 764, 868, 882, 883
Blessedness of..887, 890, 892, 902
Conditions 312, 877, 898
Connection with earth...717, 861, 862, 883
Earnest of..................313
Eternity of 855
Everywhere 888
Foretaste of 52, 894
Free from sin...868, 877, 891, 895, 898
Free from sorrow....868, 878, 882, 886, 895
Glory of 868, 873, 874, 881, 891, 895, 904
Heirship of................684
Home in...764, 816, 818, 882, 883, 885, 901
Hope of......210, 393, 561, 648, 656, 678, 683, 835, 878, 885, 890
Longing for......506, 527, 848, 852, 890
Near.............153, 857, 899
Not sensuous 898
Rest in 561, 875, 877, 896
Reunion in....851, 852, 862, 869, 873, 876, 886
Rewards in............678, 882
Saints in..............688, 730
Sociableness of........876, 882
Heirs..................465, 684
Highway of holiness........520

INDEX OF SUBJECTS.

Holiness............465, 474, 476
Desires for..........543, 549, 745
Holy Spirit....317, 321, 327, 328
Baptism of...................322
Comforter 329
Dove........................320
Earnest of inheritance.....313
God's willingness to give....48
Guide.............312, 315, 331
Invitations..............371, 380
Invocation of...314, 315, 320,
322, 327, 333, 672
Power of.....................318
Prayer for 43, 313, 316
Quickener................814, 322
Regeneration of.............430
Sanctifier 327, 333
Home 816
Home Hymn...................118
Honor, to Christ 306
To the good........627, 798, 801
Hope........597, 664, 683, 687, 836
In God 610
Steadfast................624, 683
Triumphant..............661, 687
Humility ...415, 452, 460, 487, 552

Image of Christ....540, 722, 816
Of God...................430, 540
Imitation of Christ 540, 653
Immortal life........508, 836, 862
Inconstancy..................639
Invitation to sinners..350, 351,
371, 372, 376, 379, 382
To the sorrowful 377
To the wanderer 353, 368
To the weary 357, 367
Invocation 91, 707

Jews return 718
Joy...................662, 669, 681
In Christ....252, 266, 302, 307,
481, 497
In God.......86, 71, 72, 447, 669
In Heaven 170, 194, 836, 898
Of the convert..............431
Of the redeemed...144, 390, 608
Jubilee 390
Judge not....................477
Judgment................866, 871

Kindness............ 476, 478, 491
Kingdom of Christ 384, 748
Of God...............753-755, 758
Of God within.....536, 567, 569
Knowledge of God...........518
How to live.................556
Of self..................432, 518

Labor, dignity of............485
Law, in the heart........341, 513
Liberty......................512
Life, brevity of...804, 806, 807,
812, 832-840, 882
Eternal 210, 884
Hidden with Christ..560, 569,
579, 687
Pilgrimage of..See *Pilgrimage.*
Real and earnest 594
River of...170, 389, 395, 428, 870
Uncertainty of 839
Well spent..................600
Light for all.................663
Light, in darkness.......515, 612
Walking in..................580
Little things of value..415, 491, 608
Flock...................718, 819
Longing after God 156, 509,
518, 531, 535, 538, 513, 673, 610
Christ 259, 565, 568, 630
Looking unto Jesus 259
20

Lord's Supper:
Communion at 727, 736, 737
In memory of Christ........723
Institution of..............719
Retiring from.........725, 734
Strengthened by 738
Lord's Table 80, 729, 730, 734
Loss..........See *Gain and Loss.*
Love, awakens love 579
Casting out fear.........501, 561
Constraining power of Christ,
579
Debt of.....................311
Divine......................478
Evidences of................489
Excellency of...............470
For Country 793, 794
Forgiving 478
For the Church.....75, 690, 711
Law of......................492
Longed for 415, 488, 565
Of enemies 476, 489
To Christ ..499, 500, 569, 572,
576, 909
To God 498, 505, 551
To Man......................488
Lukewarmness......805, 394, 645

Man, dignity of..........167, 183
Martyrs......................798
Mary at the Tomb...........254
Meditation 18, 109, 339, 565,
569, 586
Mercy call of........350, 378, 416
Implored 638
Mercy-seat...........46, 517, 647
Millennial Glory..384, 748, 749,
751, 752, 758
Ministering Spirits...See *Angels.*
Ministers......691, 697-699, 700,
701, 770, 775
Death of....................855
Ordination of 700, 702
Ministry of good.....777, 780, 791
Of the departed.........861, 862
Missionaries................431
Missions.....761, 762, 770-773, 775
City 761, 780
Foreign 768
Home 761, 776
Morning....97, 99, 101-104, 106,
108, 111
Sabbath 12, 26, 41
Moses and Christ.............306
Mourners, comforted........678
Mourning...........See *Affliction.*

Name, in Book of Life 903
Of Christian.....265, 266, 275,
281, 295, 300, 305, 418, 499
Bearing the.................496
Nation...............See *Country.*
Nature's worship............197
Nearness to God...543, 547, 550,
568, 573
Neighbor...........476, 488, 492
New Birth.....See *Regeneration.*
New Year........601, 606, 804-807

Obedience...............12, 485
Offering, acceptable..12, 21, 34,
115
Old age....10, 399, 491, 606, 808,
811, 829
One thing needful...........362
Opening hymns...........1-138
Oppression.......See *Anti-slavery.*
Ordinances...............720-738
Ordination ....See *Ministers.*
Orphans................675, 784
Overcoming............613, 655

Paradoxes 482
Pardon............430, 434, 672
Parting 876
Pastor 701
Patience 552, 568
Peace...................179, 384
As a river............672, 682
In believing 422, 686
Pearl of price..............346
Penitence.....396, 397, 400, 404,
409, 422
Perfection 393, 451, 468, 540,
549, 637
Pilgrimage....527, 601, 642, 835,
873, 884
Pilgrim Fathers......785, 797, 799
Pilgrims of the Night 847
Pillar, guiding..........642, 644
Pleasures of religion ...52, 875,
437, 557
Worldly.............398, 556, 563
Poor 498, 791
Praise 17, 54-95, 128, 750
Call to............78, 77, 87
Exhortation ...26, 79, 80, 93, 94
To Christ....48, 214, 235, 267,
300, 302-307, 310, 737, 780, 830
To God....40, 55, 60-62, 76, 78,
83, 85, 186, 204, 800, 802,
920, 921
Universal............82, 88, 92
(See *Adoration.*)
Prayer 507-575
Delight in.............110, 562
For Guidance 105, 554
Gate of Heaven 524
Hour of 11, 529, 905
House of....................85
Humble 525
Importunity in............612
Invitation to..........511, 541
Life of the Christian...532, 546
Lord's Prayer....507, 521, 916
Nature of 14, 545
Seasons for 511
Secret............11, 109, 544, 569
Teach us to pray....19, 546, 552
Unutterable...............544
Preachers...........See *Ministers.*
Pride............452, 487, 525, 643
Prisoner 791
Prize...........506, 614, 625, 770
Probation 312, 358, 364, 378
Procrastination 350, 358, 359,
363, 372, 381
Prodigal Son............368, 423
Progress..594, 596, 601, 618, 620,
625, 637
Promise, bow of........422, 888
Promises................410, 437
Sure....................514, 683
Prosperity, dangerous........644
Punishment..................374
Purity........476, 526, 547, 577
Long for 314, 510

Race, Christian...601, 603, 607,
625, 846
Reconciliation 298, 298
Redeemer, liveth.......247, 262
Redemption ....See *Salvation.*
Refining....................689
Reformers...............798, 801
Refreshing..........384, 638, 742
Regeneration 426-434
New Birth......427, 433, 506, 567
Rejoicing..............See *Joy.*
Religion, Comfort of 880
Call to......................828
Early......819, 822, 823-828, 830
Pleasures of.....52, 70, 375, 437

INDEX OF SUBJECTS.

Resignation....70, 209, 403, 459, 490, 532, 583, 636, 654, 657, 817
Resolve........................408
Rest............586, 604, 665
  In Christ..........238, 385, 568
  In death....................849
  In God..........660, 670, 671
  In Heaven....561, 879, 886, 887
  Longing for......374, 561, 670
  On the Sabbath..........8, 67
Resurrection............812, 889
  Hope........................836
  Morning of..........102, 116
  Of Christ....44, 245, 251, 276
  " " —pledge of ours...251
Returning...352, 353, 394, 632, 638, 711
Revelation..............See *Bible.*
Revival......................742
  Prayer for....756, 759, 767, 907
Rewards.....................614
Riches renounced...398, 407, 412
Religion better than....375, 393, 490, 540, 556
Right........................790
Righteousness;
  Thirsting for..............393
River of Life................911

Sabbath......................23
  Blessedness of....11, 27, 44, 107
  Welcomed................41, 47
Sacrifice—true...............12
  Evening....................115
  Of the heart............12, 397
Salvation...209, 289, 347, 378, 461
  By Christ..217, 264, 267, 268, 276
  Day of.....................372
  Nearer than when we believed, 857
Sanctification...451, 468, 519, 637
Sanctuary...................1-53
  Blessing sought in......7, 43
  Delight in............5, 6, 42
  God present in..........9, 24
  Meeting Christ in.........46
Schools......................785
Scriptures.............See *Bible.*
Seamen....778, 779, 782, 783, 789
Seasons..........808, 813, 814
Seed.................134, 143, 145
Seedtime and Harvest........808
Self-communion..........518, 569
Self-denial..............584, 593
Self examination............394
Sickness....................670
Simplicity..............415, 460
Sin cause of trouble.........665
  Confession of..............667
Sincerity.........341, 465, 552
Singing...........51, 68, 912
Slavery.........See *Antislavery.*
Soldiers......613, 615, 618, 626, 630, 781
Song of songs...............248
Sorrow......See *Sufferings*, also *Afflictions.*
Soul, immortal..............504
  Worth of...................432

Sowing and reaping...299, 431, 608, 631
Spring.............808, 813, 815
Stand up for Jesus..........629
Star of Bethlehem...........221
Stars revealed by darkness..673
Stewards..........503, 508, 780
Still small voice....361, 570, 586
Strength, in weakness........452
  Prayer for................525
Submission...209, 445, 452, 457, 487, 512, 552, 559, 583, 649, 817
Suffering and Glory:
  Asked when needful......676
  Benefits of..........652, 657
  Better than joy............652
  Christ's example in.....592, 593, 653
  Comfort from Christ's...588, 589, 653
  Compensation for—in Heaven, 678
  Leads to God..............573
  Leads to Heaven..........573
  Leads to peace......458, 665
  Makes perfect.............677
  Of Christ.............See *Christ.*
  Christ's........587, 592, 593
  Welcomed......651, 652, 680
  With Christ................585
Summer......................814
Sweet Home..................816
Symbols.................728, 735
Sympathy....475, 710, 727, 742, 743, 744, 791, 908

Talents......................559
Temperance........781, 784, 786
Temptation......552, 562, 635
  Reliance on God in..461, 507, 510, 558, 596, 612
  Strength in................635
  Succor in..............643, 646
  Triumph over...............595
Thanksgiving....115, 151, 166, 171, 176, 190, 211, 796, 800-803, 808, 811-813, 815
Thirsting................351, 373
Time, flight of....804-807, 812, 833, 837, 840
  Improvement of............806
  Treasures, in Heaven......648
  Of the world...............556
Trust in God......172, 209, 414, 422, 446, 442, 654, 686
  At all times........450, 679
  Childlike......459, 460, 490
  For direction........648, 655
  For salvation........429, 451
  For strength........448, 452
  For success.........441, 623
  In discouragement...538, 610
  In trouble..447, 450, 452, 453, 457, 458, 538, 610
Truth, blessing sought of.134, 143
  Boldness in defence of.....781
  Desiring to know..........516
  Triumph of......441, 769, 790

Unbelief..........436, 561, 676
Unfaithfulness......320, 639, 645
Union with Christ...568, 722, 740
  Through suffering..........584
Unity, Christian..539, 710, 715, 727, 730, 741, 742, 744, 747

Victory............See *Conquerors.*
Vows......................21, 712
Voyage of life..........779, 788

Walking with God....550, 566, 581, 746
Wanderers....322, 352, 353, 368, 373, 394, 632, 638, 711, 819, 823
Wants, spiritual.............510
War....................792, 797
Warfare..590, 594-596, 598, 601, 605, 607, 608, 611, 613, 614, 615, 616, 618, 626, 630, 781
Warning....361, 363, 364, 812, 839
Watchfulness......510, 511, 525, 611
Watchman............229, 701
Way of death................365
  Of life......260, 290, 365, 520
Weakness of Men.............638
Well done...................374
Will of God be done...192, 209, 319, 452, 459, 472, 507, 542, 552, 559, 650, 656, 659
Winners................444, 609
Winters................813, 815
Witnesses.........438, 625, 798
Work.....415, 590, 604, 608, 609, 619, 631
Workers with God....444, 545, 608, 609, 763
World, end of...............871
  Honors of..................556
  Pleasures of......393, 556, 562
  Renounced..................98
  Treasures of...............556
  Vanity of.............518, 835
Worship, public............1-146
  Acceptable.......10, 21, 22, 34
  Blessings sought in...16, 25, 33
  Close of................126-146
  Delight in.......15, 45, 46, 565
  Family......112, 511, 816-818, 820, 821
  God only....................59
  Joy in.............18, 19, 53
  Quiet......................213
  Willing.........15, 25, 26, 50

Year, close of....804, 807, 809, 841
  Opening of......601, 606, 805, 806, 810
Youth....606, 822, 824, 826-828, 830, 840
  Bible, guide of............826
  Call to....................828
  Death of......850, 856, 864, 865
  Savior's care for..........823
  Seeking God in........824, 831

Zion, beloved..........689, 690
  Call to awake........749, 765
  City of God................627

INDEX OF SCRIPTURE TEXTS.

GENESIS.
1 : 3............324
1 : 31...........158
5 : 24......550, 581
6 : 3............361
8 : 22...........806
19 : 17..........363
28 : 10-12.......573
28 : 16............9
28 : 17.....524, 705
28 : 22...........11
32 : 28..........545
47 · 9...........841

EXODUS.
12 : 26..........719
13 : 21..........644
14 : 15.....618, 628
20 : 11...........44
22 : 29..........802
25 : 22..........517

LEVITICUS.
25 : 9...........390

NUMBERS.
23 : 10......843, 845

DEUTERONOMY.
12 : 9...........374
28 : 8...........794
31 : 6...........622
32 : 3...........697
33 : 27..........643
34 : 1...........890

JUDGES.
7 : 18...........792

RUTH.
1 : 16...........711

1ST SAMUEL.
7 : 12...........467
15 : 22...........12

2D SAMUEL.
22 : 31..........392
23 : 4............97

1ST KINGS.
3 : 9............556
8 : 27...........156
19 : 12..........533

2D KINGS.
4 : 26...........856

1ST CHRONICLES.
16 : 27..........183

2D CHRONICLES.
6 : -............706

NEHEMIAH.
9 5.............78

ESTHER.
4 : 16...........408
6 : 1............149

JOB.
5 : 26...........811
7 : 21............99
14 : 2......807, 834
19 : 25..........247
20 : 8...........806

PSALMS.
1 : -............681
4 : -............100
4 : 4............394
5 : 3............106
8 : 3............196
14 : 7...........774
15 : -......465, 476
17 : -............393
17 : 8...........122
18 : 46..........212
19 : -......163, 335
19 : 2...........108
22 : 19..........443
23 : -...178, 207, 919
24 : -......246, 261
24 : 7, 9........667
25 : 5...........516
27 : 1...........461
27 : 4............75
27 : 11..........515
29 : 9...........703
30 : 5............69
31 : 2...........464
31 : 15..........654
31 : 20..........674
32 : 8...........642
32 : 11...........52
33 : 5...........190
34 : 7...........635
36 : -............66
36 : 6...........189
36 : 9...........447
39 : 4...........832
39 : 5...........836
40 : 8...........398
41 : 17...........22
42 : -......538, 611
42 : 2...........519
44 : 1...........797
46 : -...........170
46 : 1, 7, 11....202
46 : 4...........910
46 : 5...........694
48 : 12..........696
50 : 7...........751
51 : 1...........404
51 : 10..........426
51 : 17.....397, 555
55 : 17..........511
57 : -.........60, 62
61 : 2...........210
63 : 1.......20, 824
63 : 8..450, 456, 479
65 : -.............76
65 : 2...........750

65 : 9...........813
66 : -...........307
68 : 5...........675
68 : 34..........174
69 : 30..........803
71 : -...........302
71 : 9...........829
72 : -...........766
72 : 4...........821
72 : 8...........277
72 : 17..........384
73 : 25..........495
74 : 17..........814
78 : 18..........257
80 : 1...........795
84 : -.......42, 77
84 : 1..............6
84 : 3.............46
84 : 11.............5
85 : 6..756, 767, 775
85 : 8...........586
87 : 3...........685
87 : 7...........669
88 : 13..........110
89 : -.......144, 187
89 : 6...........191
89 : 21..........637
90 : 1...........155
90 : 2...........150
90 : 5...........804
91 : -...........466
91 : 1...........684
91 : 4...........665
92 : -............57
93 : 35...........69
95 : -...4, 77, 920
95 : 6...........208
97 : -............55
97 : 1...........165
98 : -......218, 925
100 : -..63, 77, 924
100 : 4...........25
103 : 56,79,80,168,923
103 : 8-12........81
103 : 13.........182
103 : 14.........184
103 : 15.........838
104 : 19.........151
104 : 34....53, 670
106 : 4..........565
107 : 7..........633
111 : 9..........160
116 : 1..........493
116 : 12..........21
117 : -...........64
118 : -...........14
118 : 24..........17
119 : -..........342
119 : 33.........341
119 : 96.........344
119 : 97..338, 339
119 : 130........826
119 : 133........145
119 : 151........680
121 : -..........462
121 : 5..........198
122 : -......15, 922
122 : 2...........18

122 : 7......38, 707
125 : -...........442
125 : 2...........689
126 : -...........431
127 : 1...........623
130 : 1...........422
131 : 1...........487
132 : 8...........704
133 : -...........502
136 : -...........171
136 : 1...........211
139 : 7...........157
139 : 12..........114
139 : 23..........526
141 : -...........103
145 : -............93
145 : 9...........176
147 : 15..........769
148 : -...82, 92, 94
150 : -............90
1ι : 6..............85

PROVERBS.
3 : 13............825
8 : 17............827
17 : 17...........475
18 : 21...........298
23 : 31...........784

ECCLESIASTES.
9 : 10......358, 364
11 : 6............631
12 : 1............828

SONG OF SOLOMON.
1 : 3.............300
1 : 7.............273
2 : 11............815
5 : 16............264

ISAIAH.
2 : 5.............580
5 : 24............566
6 : 3.........86, 918
9 : 2.............296
9 : 6......224, 229
21 : 11...........229
26 : 9............518
33 : 17...........891
35 : 1............389
35 : 8............520
35 : 8-10.........617
40 : 8............850
40 : 31..418, 603, 620
45 : 7............124
48 : 13...........672
48 : 18...........692
49 : 16...........690
51 : 3............926
52 : 1............749
52 : 7............601
53 : 4............235
53 : 8............246
55 : -............391
55 : 1.347,349,355,379
55 : 12...........748
57 : 20...........350
58 : 13........3, 41

59 : 20...........266
61 : 1............791
63 : 7............272
64 : 6......812, 840
65 : 1............204

JEREMIAH.
2 : 2.............695
2 : 13............348
3 : 4.............830
3 : 22............490
23 : 24...........169
29 : 13............37
31 : 18-20........352

LAMENTATIONS.
3 : 23............124

EZEKIEL.
11 : 19...........396
33 : 11...........369
36 : 33...........761
44 : 24..............8

DANIEL.
12 : 3............862

MICAH.
6 : 6..............34

HABAKKUK.
3 : 2...756, 759, 767

ZECHARIAH.
4 : 10............608
13 : 1............268

MALACHI.
3 : 3.............677
3 : 10............780

New Testament.

MATTHEW.
2 : 9.............214
3 : -.............728
3 : 3.............220
3 : 15............724
3 : 15-16-17.....726
3 : 16............735
4 : 16............383
5 : 8.............577
5 : 16............401
6 : 6.............544
6 : 9.............209
6 : 9-13.507,521, 916
6 : 10. 319, 403, 459,
         542, 753, 754,
         758, 917
6 : 11............455
6 : 13.............88
6 : 28............662
7 : -.............365
7 : 7........43, 514
8 : 19............469
8 : 25............783
9 : 24............869

INDEX OF SCRIPTURE TEXTS.

9:38............763
10:37.........425
11:28, 233, 357, 360, 383.
11:28-30.......367
11:29............428
14:23............109
18:3.....415, 460
18:20......7, 30, 40
20:6.............606
21:28............604
21:42............48
22:4.............354
22:37............505
24:41............839
25:21............855
25:34............886
25:40............500
26:11............498
26:41.....525, 611
28:6..........6, 245
28:9.............258
28:20..........299, 571

Mark.
7:35............458
8:37............432
8:38............599
9:24............436
10:14...........819
11:22...........435
13:37...........503
14:36...........649
16:3............250
16:15.....698, 770

Luke.
1:78............752
2:-...217, 223, 226
2:10............215
2:14, 216, 219, 228, 914.
4:18......225, 263
6:37............478
9:23............585
9:57............413
10:29...........488
10:42......362, 375
11:1.......546, 552
11:2......559, 771
12:32.....648, 718
14:-............356
14:33...........407
14:40...........252
15:-......367, 423
17:5.............23
17:21...........567
18:1............541
18:13...........400
18:34...........658
19:10...........309
19:41...........419
22:19...........723
22:32...........262
22:39...........258

22:42............636
23:28............867
23:42......301, 411
24:23............256
24:29..139, 234, 641
24:32.......32, 570
24:34............251
24:51............253

John.
1:1.............332
1:4.............271
1:16............481
3:7.............433
3:17......186, 276
4:21........10, 201
6:37............402
6:51............738
6:63......314, 322
6:68............424
8:12......290, 536
9:4.......500, 619
10:3............126
10:9............297
10:10...........534
10:15...........285
10:16.....747, 823
11:26.....853, 854
11:36...........232
12:-............212
12:32...........366
13:34...........496
14:2......764, 885
14:6......260, 702
14:17...........313
14:26.....315, 329
14:31...........734
15:12...........710
15:13...........499
16:13.....312, 331
16:14...........334
17:21...........715
17:24...........568
19:27...........816
19:30...........239
20:11...........254
21:15...........409
21:16...........483

Acts.
1:9.............250
2:47............712
3:1.......820, 905
4:12............275
7:32............740
7:60............860
16:9............772
17:24-28........67
17:28...........558
21:14...........650
21:25...........359
26:22...........805

Romans.
5:1.............686
6:4.............721

8:24............683
8:26............333
8:28......444, 457
8:31............609
8:37............605
10:8............386
13:11...........857
14:4............477
15:16...........327

1st Corinthians.
1:23............579
2:9.............898
2:10............899
6:10............787
7:29............833
9:26............612
10:4......286, 591
10:21...........729
12:26...........492
13:-............470
13:5............486
13:12...........194
15:3............406
16:13...........781
16:23...........575

2d Corinthians.
2:14............267
4:4.......343, 358
4:17............652
4:18............557
5:7.............440
5:11............871
5:14............480
5:15............472
5:17............484
6:2...372, 376, 377
7:10............400
8:5.......717, 722
8:9.............240
12:9............655
12:10...........452
13:2............125

Galatians.
2:20............439
3:28......743, 744
4:15............645
6:2.......547, 745
6:14.....587, 588

Ephesians.
2:5.............289
2:8.............485
2:13............589
2:20.....688, 693
3:8.............303
3:9.............130
3:15............730
3:19............195
4:6.............161
4:8.......257, 294
4:23............731

5:32............692
6:11............613
6:13............629
6:16............598

Philippians.
1:21............844
1:22............399
1:23............842
2:5......292, 510
2:9.............295
2:13............661
2:29............699
3:10............584
3:14............625
4:13............284

Colossians.
1:5.............875
1:22............451
2:2.............742
2:10............308
3:3......560, 569
3:11...259, 280, 291

1st Thessalonians.
4:13............863
4:14............849
4:17............884
5:17............615

1st Timothy.
1:18............596
2:1.............796
6:12............716
6:15............768

2d Timothy.
1:12............624
2:2.............700
2:3......614, 630
2:5.............626
3:16............340
4:1.............866
4:5.............494
4:7.............846

Titus.
2:10............474

Hebrews.
2:10............595
2:18............653
4:9......2, 561, 819
4:15............270
7:25......236, 293
8:10............513
11:4............627
11:10...........880
11:16...........892
12:1............438
12:6............676
12:14...........877

12:28............868
13:1............746
13:12...........601
13:14, 19,327,704,895

James.
1:16............166
1:17......175, 558
2:26............441
4:7.............651
4:14...825, 837, 841

1st Peter.
1:3.............687
1:8.............576
2:7...265, 281, 305
2:21......274, 621
2:25............632
3:4.............671
3:8.............739
4:13............593
4:19............657
5:5.............297
5:7.............206

2d Peter.
1:19............288
2:9.............646

1st John.
1:3.......578, 552
2:6.............550
3:1.......177, 661
3:20............172
4:8......208, 658
4:10............167
4:12............468
4:16............188
4:18............501

Jude.
1:20:-....320, 549

Revelation.
3:8.............373
3:20............278
4:8.......1, 84, 921
4:11.............83
5:9.............310
5:9-14..........248
5:11............304
15:3............306
21:-............883
21:1......779, 901
21:2............900
21:4...656, 878, 902
21:10............881
21:22.............27
21:27............903
22:1......395, 911
22:17............371
22:20............872

INDEX OF TUNES.

	PAGE.
ABIDE With Me. 10s	199
Addison. S. M.	159
Adrian. S. M.	123, 282
Advocate. L. M. 6l	144
Aletta. 7s	92
All Saints. L. M	8, 240
America. 6s, 4s	247
Ames. L. M	186
Amsterdam. 7s, 6s, D.	66, 158, 264
Anatolius. 7s, 6s, 8s	40
Antioch. C. M	68
Anvern. L. M.	276
Appleton. L. M	277
Ariel. C. P. M.	100
Arley. L. M	41
Arlington. C. M.	153
Asaph. H. M	67
Ascension. P. M.	80
Ashford. L. M.	103
Ashwell. L. M.	242
Athens. C. M. D.	135
Aurelia. 7s, 6s, D	145, 215
Austria. 8s, 7s, D	212
Autumn. 8s, 7s, D	185, 197
Ava. 6s, 4s	119
Avereen. L. M	208
Avison. 11s, 10s	79
Avon. C. M.	129
Avondale. C. M.	12
Azmon. C. M	141
BADEA. S. M.	19
Balerma. C. M.	172
Bartholomew. 10s.	48
Bartimeus. 8s, 7s	267
Bealoth. S. M.	214
Beatitudo. C. M.	220
Beautiful Stream. P. M	238
Belmont. C. M.	194
Benevento. 7s, D.	252
Bera. L. M.	9
Bernard. 8s, D.	255
Bethany. 6s, 4s	179, 237
Bishop. L. M.	165
Blumenthal. 7s, D.	285
Bonar. S. M. D	196
Boner. C. M.	98
Boylston. S. M.	229, 258
Bradford. C. M.	264
Brattle Street. C. M. D.	24
Bremen. C. P. M.	57
Bridgewater. L. M.	114
Brown. C. M.	228, 266
Browne. S. M. D	249
Brownell. L. M. 6l	34, 152
Buckfield. L. M	90
Burton. 6s, 7s.	271
Byefield. L. M. D	52
CALEDONIA. P. M	243
Call to Victory. 7s, 5s	233
Calvary. 6s, 4s.	146
Cambridge. C. M.	87
Canonbury. L. M.	240
Carol. C. M. D.	69
Cherith. C. M.	189
Chester. 8s, 7s.	63

	PAGE.
Chesterfield. C. M	111
China. C. M.	265
Christmas. C. M	69
Clark. 7s.	220
Cleansing Fountain. C. M.	86
Closer, Still Closer. 11s	292
Come,Ye Disconsolate.11s,10s.	201
Communion. C. M.	224
Constancy. L. M.	187
Contrast. 8s, D	176
Conway. C. M.	173
Corfu. C. M.	130
Coronation. C. M	83
Coventry. C. M.	174
Cowper. C. M.	86
Creation. L. M. 6l.	51
Croyland. L. M	202
Curtis. L. M	22, 90
DARWELL. H. M.	82
Day of Rest. C. M.	10
Dedham. C. M	49
Dennis. S. M.	64, 196
Detroit. C. M.	118
Devizes. C. M.	99
Dix. 7s, 6l	185
Dorrnance. 8s, 7s.	275
Dort. 6s, 4s.	250
Dover. S. M.	181, 273
Downs. C. M.	11
Downs. 7s	167
Drostane. L. M.	77
Duke Street. L. M.	41, 77
Dundee. C. M.	46
Dykeman. S. M.	193
EASTER Hymn. 7s	80
Edinburgh. 11s.	19
Egmont. L. M.	23
Elizabethtown. C. M	208
Eltham. 7s, D.	44
Elton. C. M.	171, 259
Emilia. 8s, 7s	271
Ernan. L. M.	149, 258
Estella. L. M.	20
Ethel. L. M.	188
Evening Hymn. L. M.	40
Ewing. 7s, 6s, D	279
FADING, Still Fading. P. M...	34
Farland. 8s, 7s, 4s	82
Federal Street. L. M.	53
Ferguson. S. M.	266
Forever with the Lord.S.M.D.	281
Fount. 8s, 7s, D	237
Frederick. 11s.	269
Frost. 7s, 6s.	230
Fullness. 8s, 7s.	57
Fulton. 7s.	259
GEER. C. M.	175, 198
Geneva. C. M.	59
Gerhardt. 8s.	74
Germany. L. M.	6, 252
Gethsemane. 7s, 6l	277
Gloria in Excelsis (chant)	295
Gloria Patri	295

	PAGE.
Glorious City. 8s, 7s, D	286
God Be with You. P. M.	180
God Speed the Right. 8s, 4s	245
Golden Hill. S. M.	223
Good Shepherd. L. M. 6l	56
Gorton. S. M.	93
Goshen. 11s.	121
Gottschalk. 7s	168, 191
Gratitude. L. M.	42
Greenville. 8s, 7s, 4s	18, 46
Greenwood. S. M.	244, 270
HADDAM. H. M.	31
Halle. 7s, 6l	116
Hamburg. L. M.	125
Hamden. 8s, 7s, 4s	234
Happy Day. L. M.	221
Harwell. 8s, 7s	70
Haven. C. M	225
Hayden. S. M	227
Heber. C. M.	138
Hebron. L. M	33, 150
He Leadeth Me. L. M	63
Hendon. 7s.	62, 230
Henley. 11s, 10s	123
Henry. C. M	140, 256
Herald Angels. 7s, D.	71
Higgins. 7s.	95
Holly. 7s.	205
Home. C. M. D.	280
Home of the Soul. 12s, 8s	287
Horton. 7s	108, 117
How Can I Keep from Singing. 8s, 7s	294
Hummel. C. M.	110
Hummel. C. M. (Zeuner's)	137, 154
Hursley. L. M.	200
Hymn. C. M.	84
I AM Trusting. 7s	136
Imlah. L. M.	127
Integer Vitæ. 8s, 6s	131
Iowa. 8s	274
Irenæus. H. M	213
Is My Name Written There. 7s, 6s	288
Italy. 6s, 4s	29, 238
I Will Follow Thee. S. M	148
JERUSALEM. C. M.	280
Jesus Only. 8s, 7s	290
Jewett. 6s	202
Joy Land. H. M.	65
KEENE. L. M	47
Kellogg. H. M.	106
LABAN. S. M.	190
Langran. 10s	121
Leighton. S. M.	157, 234
Lenox. H. M.	90, 124
Let Every Heart Rejoice.	251
Linwood. L. M.	207
Lisbon. S. M	18
Lischer. M.	16
Litchfield, C. M.	245
Louvan. L. M	139

INDEX OF TUNES.

	PAGE.
Loving-kindness. L. M.	88
Lucas. 5s, 12s	253
Luton. L. M.	78
Lux Benigna. P. M.	161
Lydian. L. M.	48
MAITLAND. C. M	183
Mendebras. 7s, 6s, D.	195
Mannheim. 8s, 7s, 6f.	245
Manoah. C. M	156, 160, 286
Mariner's Song. 8s, 7s, D.	241
Marlon. L. M	55
Marlow. C. M	182
Martyn. 7s, D.	81, 94
Meditation. 11s, 8s	88
Mear. C. M	9
Mendon. L. M.	102
Meribah. C. P. M.	273
Merton. C. M	30, 254
Middleton. 8s, 7s, D.	97
Migdol. L. M	7
Missionary Chant. L. M.	75, 217, 250
Missionary Hymn. 7s, 6s.	239
Montague. 7s, 6s, D.	269
Mornington. S. M.	119
Mount Auburn. C. M.	222
Mt. Vernon. 8s, 7s	205
Munich. 7s, 6s, D.	235
Myers. H. M	101
NAOMI. C. M.	203, 257
Naples. L. M	201
Nassau. 7s, 6f.	232
Nettleton. 8s, 7s, D.	57
New Haven. 6s, 4s	105, 261
Nicæa. Pec	5
Northfield. C. M	104
Nuremberg. 7s	13
OLD HUNDRED. L. M	42
Olive's Brow. L. M.	76
Olivet. 6s, 4s.	139
Olmutz. S. M.	12
Olney. S. M.	107
Omniscience, No. 1. C. M.	170
Omniscience, No. 2. C. M.	170
Orient. 11s, 10s.	66
Orland. L. M	161
Ortonville. C. M	85
Our Hiding-Place. 7s.	292
PARK Street. L. M.	32
Passion Chorale. 7s, 6s, D	75
Pax Dei. 10s	106
Peterborough. C. M	35
Phillips. C. M.	272
Pilgrim. 8s, 7s.	134

	PAGE.
Pisao. L. M.	210
Pleading. 8s, 7s, 4s	120
Plumley. L. M.	263
RATHBUN. 8s, 7s	184
Redeemer. 8s, 7s	158
Redemption. L. M.	183
Refuge. 7s.	94
Regent Square. 8s, 7s, 4s. 176, 235	
Rensen. C. M	211
Rest. L. M	268
Retreat. L. M	162
Return. C. M.	113
Revive Thy Work. S. M	233
Revive Us Again. 11s.	290
Rockingham. L. M	73, 89
Rockingham (old). L. M	216
Rosefield. 7s, 6f.	144, 168
Rothwell. L. M	219
SABBATH. 7s, 6f.	11
Salisbury. L. M. D	39
Savannah. 10s.	28
Scotland. 12s, 11s	274
Seasons. L. M.	143
Sessions. L. M.	212
Seymour. 7s.	28
Shawmut. S. M	45
Shirland. S. M	160
Sicily. 8s, 7s, 4s	43
Siloam. C. M	260
Silver Street. S. M.	26
Solitude. C. M	282, 263
Southgate. 8s, 4s.	41
Spanish Hymn. 7s, 6f.	62, 132
Spohr. C. M. 6f.	166
Sprague. S. M.	17
St. Agnes. C. M.	200, 273
St. Catharine's. H. M. 3d. P M	30, 145
St. Crispin. L. M	196
St. Gabriel. L. M.	231
St. Gertrude. 6s, 5s, D	193
St. John's. C. M.	61
St. Leon. C. M.	85
St. Martin's. C. M.	58, 60
St. Michael. S. M	218
St. Sylvester. 8s, 7s.	265
St. Thomas. S. M	99, 136
State Street. S. M.	36, 216
Stella. L. M. 6f.	165
Stephens. C. M.	229, 248
Stockwell. 8s, 7s	37
Stonefield. L. M.	151
Subjection. S. M.	65
Swanwick. C. M.	155
Sweet Home. 11s, 5s.	175, 257
Sweet Rest. 7s, 6s	278

	PAGE.
TAMPICO. C. M	87
Tamworth. 8s, 7s, 4s	213
Tappan. C. M	218
Telman's Chant. 7s	81
Thatcher. S. M.	134
Theodora. 7s	147
Toplady. 7s, 6f.	92
Truro. L. M	223
Tully. 7s, 6s	206
UXBRIDGE. L. M.	109
VARINA. C. M. D.	50, 131
Vesper. 8s, 7s	284
Vesper Hymn. 8s, 7s.	58
Victoria. P. M	83
Vox Angelica. 11s, 10s, 9s.	267
WALES. 8s, 4s.	116
Wanderer. S. M.	284
Ward. L. M.	54, 236
Wardwell. 7s	51
Ware. 8s, 7s, 4s	244
Ware. L. M.	126
Warrington. L. M	178
Warsaw. H. M	229
Warwick. C. M	25
Watchman Tell Us. 7s, D.	72
Wayne. H. M	17, 125
Webb. 7s, 6s.	72, 122
Weber. 7s.	227
Wells. L. M	177
Welton. C. M	163
Wesley. 8s, 7s, D.	246
Westfield. L. M	21
Westminster. 8s, 7s.	255
While the Days Are Going By. 6s, 7s.	291
Willis. 7s	152
Wilmot. 8s, 7s.	27, 226
Wimborne. 8s, 7s.	192
Windham. L. M.	116
Woodland. C. M.	35, 276
Woodside. C. M.	135
Woolworth. L. M.	115, 128
Work Song. 7s, 6s	192
World of Light. P. M.	289
YARMOUTH. 7s, 6s	201
Ydolem. C. M.	112
Yoakley. L. M	91
ZEBULON. H. M	256
Zephyr. L. M.	266
Zerah. C. M.	70, 283
Zion. 8s, 7s, 4s	124, 199, 231

CHANTS AND RESPONSES.

	PAGE.		PAGE.		PAGE.
Dominus Regit Me	297	Responses	302	Thy Will Be Done	296
Gloria In Excelsis	295	Te Deum Laudamus	298	Trisagion Chorus	296
Gloria Patri	295	The Lord Will Comfort Zion [sentence]	301	Venite, Exultemus Domino	297
Jubilate Deo	300	The Lord's Prayer	296		
Lætatus Sum	299				

METRICAL INDEX.

L. M.

	PAGE
All Saints	8, 240
Ames	186
Auvern	276
Appleton	277
Arley	41
Ashford	103
Ashwell	242
Avereen	208
Bera	9
Bishop	165
Bridgewater	111
Buckfield	90
Canonbury	246
Constancy	187
Croyland	262
Curtis	22, 90
Drostane	77
Duke Street	11, 77
Egmont	23
Ernan	149, 258
Estella	20
Ethel	188
Evening Hymn	40
Federal Street	53
Germany	6, 252
Gratitude	42
Hamburg	125
Happy Day	221
Hebron	33, 150
He Leadeth Me	63
Hursley	200
Imlah	127
Keene	47
Linwood	207
Louvan	139
Loving-kindness	88
Luton	78
Lydian	48
Marion	55
Mendon	102
Migdol	7
Missionary Ch.	75, 217, 230
Naples	204
Old Hundred	42
Olive's Brow	76
Orland	164
Park Street	32
Pinao	210
Plumley	263
Redemption	183
Rest	208
Retreat	182
Rockingham	73, 89
Rockingham (old)	216
Rothwell	219
Seasons	143
Sessions	212
St. Crispin	166
St. Gabriel	231
Stonefield	151
Truro	223
Uxbridge	109
Ward	54, 236
Ware	126
Warrington	178
Wells	177
Welton	163
Westfield	21
Windham	116
Woodworth	115, 128
Yoakley	91
Zephyr	236

L. M., 6 lines.

	PAGE
Advocate	144
Brownell	34, 152
Creation	51
Good Shepherd	56
Stella	165

L. M. D.

	PAGE
Byfield	52
Salisbury	39

C. M.

	PAGE
Antioch	68
Arlington	158
Avon	129
Avondale	12
Azmon	141
Balerma	172
Beatitudo	226
Belmont	194
Boner	98
Bradford	264
Brown	228, 261
Cambridge	87
Cherith	189
Chesterfield	111
China	265
Christmas	69
Cleansing Fountain	86
Communion	224
Conway	173
Corfu	130
Coronation	83
Coventry	174
Cowper	86
Day of Rest	10
Dedham	49
Detroit	118
Devizes	99
Downs	11
Dundee	46
Elizabethtown	208
Elton	171, 235
Geer	175, 198
Geneva	225
Haven	225
Heber	138
Henry	140, 256
Hummel	110
Hummel (Zeu.)	137, 154
Hymn	84
Jerusalem	280
Litchfield	245
Maitland	183
Manoah	156, 169, 286
Marlow	182
Mear	9
Morton	30, 254
Mount Auburn	222
Naomi	203, 247
Northfield	164
Omniscience, No. 1	170
Omniscience, No. 2	170
Ortonville	85
Peterborough	35
Phillips	272
Remsen	211
Return	117
Siloam	260
Solitude	282, 262
St. Agnes	209, 273
St. John's	61
St. Leon	85
St. Martin's	58, 60
Stephens	229, 248
Swanwick	155
Tampico	87
Tappan	218
Warwick	25
Woodland	95, 276
Woodside	155
Ydolem	112
Zerah	70, 283

C. M. D.

	PAGE
Athens	135
Brattle Street	24
Carol	69
Home	280
Varina	50, 131

C. P. M.

	PAGE
Ariel	100
Bremen	57
Meribah	273

S. M.

	PAGE
Addison	159
Adrian	128, 282
Badea	19
Boylston	229, 258
Dennis	61, 196
Dover	181, 275
Dykeman	133
Ferguson	206
Golden Hill	223
Gorton	93
Greenwood	214, 270
Hayden	227
I Will Follow Thee	138
Laban	140
Leighton	157, 234
Lisbon	18
Mornington	119
Olmutz	142
Olney	107
Revive Thy Work	233
Shawmut	45
Shirland	160
Silver Street	26
Sprague	17
St. Michael	248
St. Thomas	99, 136
State Street	36, 216
Subjection	65

S. M. D.

	PAGE
Bealoth	214
Bonar	196
Browne	219
Forever with the Lord	281

H. M.

	PAGE
Asaph	67
Darwell	82
Haddam	31
Irenæus	213
Joy Land	65
Kellogg	106
Lenox	96, 124
Lischer	16
Myers	101
St. Catharine's	90, 145
Warsaw	220
Wayne	17, 125
Zebulon	256

P. M.

	PAGE
Ascension	80
Beautiful Stream	286
Caledonia	243
Fading, Still Fading	34
God Be With You	109
Lux Benigna	161
Victoria	83
World of Light	289

6s & 4s.

	PAGE
America	247
Ava	119
Bethany	179, 237
Calvary	146
Dort	270
Italy	29, 238
New Haven	105, 261
Olivet	139

7s D.

	PAGE
Benevento	252
Blumenthal	285
Litham	44
Herald Angels	71
Martyn	81, 94
Watchman Tell Us	72

7s.

	PAGE
Aletta	92
Clark	220
Downs	167
Easter Hymn	80
Fulton	259
Gottschalk	168, 191
Hendon	62, 230
Higgins	95
Holley	205
Horton	108, 117
I Am Trusting	136
Nuremburg	13

METRICAL INDEX.

	PAGE		PAGE		PAGE		PAGE
Our Hiding Place	282	Work Song	192	Jesus Only	280	Hamden	234
Refuge	91	Yarmouth	201	Mount Vernon	265	Pleading	120
Seymour	28			Pilgrim	131	Regent Square	176, 235
T'eman's Chant	81	**7s & 6s, D.**		Rathbun	181	Sicily	43
Theodoro	147	Amsterdam	66, 158, 264	Redeemer	158	Tamworth	213
Wardwell	51	Aurelia	145, 215	St. Sylvester	265	Ware	244
Weber	27	Bernard	235	Stockwell	37	Zion	124, 199, 231
Willis	152	Ewing	279	Vesper	284		
		Mendlebras	195	Vesper Hymn	38	**10s.**	
7s. 6l.		Montague	299	Westminster	255	Abide With Me	199
Dix	185	Munich	235	While the Days Are		Bartholomew	48
Gethsemane	277	Passion Chorale	75	Going By	201	Langran	121
Halle	116			Wilmot	27, 226	Pax Dei	106
Nessus	232	**8s & 4s.**		Wimborne	192	Savannah	28
Rosefield	144, 168	God Speed the Right	245				
Sabbath	14	Southgate	41	**8s & 7s, D.**		**11s & 10s.**	
Spanish Hymn	62, 152	Wales	145	Austria	212	Avison	79
Toplady	92			Autumn	185, 197	ComeYeDisconsolate	201
		8s & 7s.		Fount	237	Henley	123
7s & 6s.		Bartimeus	267	Glorious City	286	Orient	66
Frost	230	Burton	271	Mariner's Song	241		
Gerhardt	74	Chester	183	Middleton	97	**11s.**	
Is My Name Written		Dorrnance	275	Nettleton	117	Closer, Still Closer	292
There	288	Emilia	271	Wesley	246	Edinburgh	19
Missionary Hymn	239	Fullness	57			Frederick	269
Sweet Rest	278	Harwell	70	**8s, 7s & 4s.**		Goshen	121
Tully	206	How can I keep		Farland	82	Revive Us Again	290
Webb	72, 122	from singing	204	Greenville	18, 46		

INDEX OF FIRST LINES.

	HYMN		HYMN
Abide not in the realms of......Burleigh	602	Amazing grace! how sweet the...Newton	485
Abide with me: fast falls the......Lyte	641	Am I a soldier of the cross......Watts	626
Abide with us; the evening......Raffles	234	Amidst a world of hope and fear...Moore	528
A broken heart, my God......Watts	397	And canst thou, sinner! slight......Hyde	376
According to thy gracious......Montgomery	723	And must I part with all......Beddome	407
A charge to keep I have......C. Wesley	508	And will the judge descend....Doddridge	871
Again as evening's shadow..S. Longfellow	98	Angels! roll the rock away......Scott	250
Again our earthly cares......Newton	25	Another hand is beckoning us...Whittier	861
Again the Lord of life......Barbauld	26	Another six day's work is done...Stennett	8
A glory gilds the sacred page......Cowper	343	Approach not the altar with......Osgood	53
Ah! whither should I go......C. Wesley	424	Arise, and bless the Lord......Montgomery	79
A holy air is breathing round..Livermore	727	Arise, my soul, arise......C. Wesley	293
Alas, and did my Savior bleed......Watts	406	Arise, O king of grace, arise......Watts	704
All around us fair......Book of Hymns	590	Arise, ye saints, arise......Kelly	614
All as God wills! who wisely......Whittier	192	Arm of the Lord, awake......Shrubsole	127
All hail the power of Jesus......Perronet	258	As body when the soul......Drummond	441
All nature feels attractive......Drennan	492	As every day thy mercy......Ch. Psalmist	104
All-seeing God, 'tis thine to know...Scott	477	Ask, and ye shall receive......	514
All ye nations praise the......Montgomery	85	Asleep in Jesus! blessed sleep...Mackay	849
Almighty God, in humble....Montgomery	556	As pants the heart for cooling......Lyte	610
Almighty God, thy word is......Carwood	145	As shadows cast by cloud......Bryant	221
Almighty Maker of my frame......Steele	832	Assist us, Lord, to act, to be......Moore	523
Always with us, always with us.....Nevin	209	As the hart, with eager......Montgomery	538

INDEX OF FIRST LINES.

HYMN	
As the sweet flower that......*Cunningham*	850
Author of good, we rest on.........*Merrick*	636
Awake, and sing the song......*Hammond*	306
Awake, my soul, and with the.........*Ken*	96
Awake, my soul, lift up thine...*Barbauld*	598
Awake, my soul, stretch every..*Doddridge*	625
Awake, my soul, to joyful lays.....*Medley*	272
Awake, my tongue, thy tribute..*Needham*	147
Awake our souls, away our fears....*Watts*	603
Awake, ye saints, awake............*Cotterill*	44
BEFORE Jehovah's awful throne...*J. Wesley*	63
Begin the day with God...............*Bonar*	111
Behold a Stranger at the door...... *Grigg*	278
Behold, the Prince of Peace......*Needham*	290
Behold the sun, how bright.........*Moore*	387
Behold the western evening......*Peabody*	860
Behold, what wondrous grace........ *Watts*	664
Behold, where in a mortal form....*Enfield*	263
Being of beings, God of love..... *C. Wesley*	195
Believing souls of Christ ....*Beddome*	714
Beneath our feet and o'er our.......*Heber*	839
Beneath the shadow of.......*S. Longfellow*	584
Beneath the symbol wave.................	735
Beset with snares on every......*Doddridge*	522
Be still, my heart, these anxious.*Newton*	655
Be thou, O God, by night, by day.........	547
Be thou, O God, exalted high..............	62
Beyond, beyond that boundless...*Conder*	533
Bless, O my soul, the living God.... *Watts*	56
Blest are the pure in heart............*Keble*	577
Blest are the sons of peace........... *Watts*	502
Blest are the souls that hear......... *Watts*	144
Blest are they in Christ departed..*Parker*	859
Blest be the dear uniting love...*C. Wesley*	740
Blest be the tie that binds..........*Fawcett*	743
Blest Comforter divine............*Sigourney*	329
Blest day of God, most calm................	27
Blest hour! when mortal man......*Raffles*	11
Blest is the man who shuns the..... *Watts*	681
Blest Jesus, when my.........*Heginbotham*	497
Blow ye the trumpets, blow.....*C. Wesley*	390
Bread of heaven, on thee we.......*Conder*	738
Break, new-born year, on glad.........*Gill*	810
Brethren, while we sojourn here...*Swain*	616
Brief life is here our portion.....*Neale, tr.*	882
Brightest and best of the sons.......*Heber*	214
Broad is the road that leads........... *Watts*	365

HYMN	
Brother, thou hast wandered...*J. F. Clarke*	368
Buried beneath the yielding......*Beddome*	724
By cool Siloam's shady rill............*Heber*	824
CALM me, my God! and keep me..*Bonar*	671
Calm on the bosom of my God...*Hemans*	864
Calm on the listening ear..............*Sears*	219
Child of sin and sorrow......... *T. Hasting*	377
Children of the heavenly King...*Cennick*	617
Christian, see! the orient morning........	752
Christ is made the sure............*Neale, tr.*	693
Christ is our corner-stone.... *Chandler, tr.*	688
Christ leads me through.............*Baxter*	653
Christ, the Lord, is risen to-day..*C. Wesley*	251
Church of the ever-living God......*Bonar*	718
Closer, still closer, my Saviour...*L. R. C.*	909
Come, and let us sweetly join...*C. Wesley*	40
Come at the morning hour............ *Watts*	511
Come, blessed Spirit.................*Beddome*	315
Come, brethren, don't grow weary........	879
Come, Christians, brethren......... *White*	135
Come, dearest Lord, descend and... *Watts*	130
Come, every pious heart............*Stennett*	311
Come, gracious Spirit................*Browne*	312
Come, happy souls, approach........ *Watts*	186
Come hither, all ye weary souls..... *Watts*	357
Come, Holy Ghost, in love..........*Palmer*	323
Come, Holy Spirit, calm my.......*Burdett*	314
Come, Holy Spirit, come................*Reed*	326
Come, Holy Spirit, come................*Hart*	327
Come, Holy Spirit, come...........*Beddome*	328
Come, Holy Spirit, Dove divine... *Judson*	721
Come, Holy Spirit, heavenly Dove..*Watts*	320
Come, humble sinner, in whose.....*Jones*	408
Come, join ye saints, with heart...*Medley*	308
Come, kingdom of our God............*Johns*	758
Come, let us anew...................... *C. Wesley*	806
Come, let us join our cheerful........ *Watts*	304
Come, let us lift our joyful........ *Watts*	73
Come, let us pray: 't is sweet to...*Conder*	541
Come, let us sing the song....*Montgomery*	248
Come, Lord, and tarry not...........*Bonar*	872
Come, mighty Spirit, penetrate....*Bonar*	322
Come, O my soul! in sacred.....*Blacklock*	54
Come, sacred Spirit, from........*Doddridge*	321
Come, said Jesus' sacred voice..*Barbauld*	367
Come, sinners, to the gospel....*C. Wesley*	356
Come, sound his praise abroad...... *Watts*	77

314

INDEX OF FIRST LINES.

| HYMN. | HYMN. |

Come, thou almighty King........C. *Wesley* 80
Come, thou Fount of every.......*Robinson* 467
Come, thou soul transforming......*Evans* 134
Come to the house of prayer.......*Taylor* 49
Come to the land of peace................... 886
Come unto me when shadows..*Waterman* 385
Come we that love the Lord.........*Watts* 52
Come, ye disconsolate, where 'er...*Moore* 647
Come, ye sinners, poor and needy...*Hart* 379
Come, ye that know and fear......*Burder* 188

DARLING child in slumber..........*Parker* 858
Days and moments quickly........*Caswall* 841
Dear as thou wast, and justly.........*Dale* 863
Dear is the spot where Christians..*Clark* 851
Dear Saviour, if these lambs should..*Hyde* 822
Dear Saviour, we are thine......*Doddridge* 722
Delay not, delay not, O sinner...*Hastings* 381
Depths of mercy! can there be..*C. Wesley* 416
Did Christ o'er sinners weep.....*Beddome* 419
Dismiss us with thy blessing........*Heber* 132
Do not I love thee, O my Lord..*Doddridge* 489
Dropping down the troubled........*Bonar* 870

EARLY, my God, without delay......*Watts* 20
Ere earth's foundations yet were laid.... 167
Ere mountains reared their forms......... 150
Ere to the world again we go............. 131
Eternal God, almighty Cause......*Browne* 59
Eternal Source of life ...*Coppe's Selections* 554
Eternal Spirit, we confess............*Watts* 318

FADING, still fading............................. 105
Faith adds new charms to...........*Turner* 437
Far as thy name is known ....*Watts* 696
Far from mortal cares retreating..*Taylor* 50
Far from my thoughts, vain world..*Watts* 565
Far from these narrow scenes........*Steele* 891
Father, adored in.........*Birmingham Coll.* 521
Father and Friend, thy light....*Bowring* 109
Father, at thy footstool see......*C. Wesley* 539
Father, beneath thy sheltering..*Burleigh* 665
Father, bless thy word to all................ 137
Father! glory be to thee...... ......*Mason* 136
Father, hear the........*Hymns of the Spirit* 591
Father, I know that all my life...*Waring* 415
Father in heaven, to thee my.....*Furness* 551
Father of all our mercies .....*Montgomery* 558

Father of eternal grace..........*Montgomery* 540
Father of light, conduct my feet............ 553
Father of lights, we sing thy ...*Doddridge* 166
Father of me and all mankind..*C. Wesley* 753
Father of mercies, in thy word......*Steele* 345
Father, thy paternal care...........*Malan* 200
Father, thy wonders do not singly..*Very* 153
Father, we look up to thee......*C. Wesley* 537
Father, whate'er of earthly bliss.....*Steele* 817
Feeble, helpless, how shall I......*Furness* 284
For all thy gifts we praise thee.....*Clarke* 801
For all thy saints, O God...............*Mant* 798
Forever with the Lord.........*Montgomery* 884
Fountain of mercy, God of.....*Flowerdew* 808
Frequent the day of grace returns..*Brown* 23
Friends of freedom swell the song......... 786
From all that dwell below the skies..*Watts* 64
From all that's mortal, all that's vain.... 582
From every stormy wind that......*Stowell* 517
From Greenland's icy mountain...*Heber* 772
From the cross uplifted high.......*Hawcis* 366
From the table now retiring..........*Rowe* 734
Full-handed, glowing autumn....*Moulton* 811

GENTLY, Lord! oh, gently lead...*Hastings* 633
Give forth thine........*Hymns of the Spirit* 504
Give me a heart of calm repose............ 672
Give me the wings of faith to rise..*Watts* 438
Give thanks to God most high......*Watts* 211
Give to our God immortal praise...*Watts* 171
Give to the Lord......*Sabbath Hymn Book* 375
Give to the winds thy fears......*Gerhardt* 453
Glorious city, home unclouded.............. 900
Glorious things of thee are.........*Newton* 685
Glory be to God on high (chant).......... 914
Glory be to the Father...... .....*Greatorex* 915
Glory to thee, my God, this night...*Ken* 122
God be with you till we meet......*Rankin* 575
God bless our native land............*Dwight* 794
God calling yet; shall I not..*Borthwick, tr.* 405
God in the gospel of his Son.....*Beddome* 337
God is love; his mercy...............*Bowring* 203
God is my strong salvation...*Montgomery* 461
God is the refuge of his saints......*Watts* 170
God moves in a mysterious way..*Cowper* 189
God of eternity, from thee......*Doddridge* 833
God of mercy, God of grace.... ....*Lyte* 755
God of mercy, hear our prayer.............. 821

INDEX OF FIRST LINES.

HYMN.			HYMN.	
God of my life, through all......	*Doddridge*	65	Heart and heart together........ *Zinzendorf*	710
God of our salvation, hear us.........	*Kelly*	146	Heaven is a place of rest....... *Montgomery*	877
God of the earth, the sky....	*S. Longfellow*	164	Heavenward doth our journey.. *Schmolck*	878
God of the morning, at whose......	*Watts*	97	He dies, the friend of sinners dies. *Watts*	245
God reigns on earth; he.........	*Hathaway*	165	He has come! the Christ of God.... *Bonar*	228
God that madest earth and...........	*Heber*	138	He leadeth me, oh blessed......... *Gilmore*	205
Go forward, Christian soldier......	*Tuttiett*	628	He lives! the great Redeemer lives.. *Steele*	236
Go labor on; spend and be spent...	*Bonar*	604	He liveth long who liveth well............	600
Go, messenger of peace and love.	*Balfour*	777	Help us to help each other...... *C. Wesley*	745
Go, preach my gospel, saith the.....	*Watts*	698	He sendeth sun, he sendeth......... *Adams*	459
Go to dark Gethsemane........	*Montgomery*	592	High in the heavens, eternal God.. *Watts*	66
Go to thy rest, fair child..................		856	High in yonder realms of light...... *Raffles*	896
Grace! 'tis a charming sound..	*Doddridge*	289	Holy and reverend is the name. *Needham*	160
Gracious Saviour, thus before...	*Bateman*	117	Holy Father, heavenly King...............	202
Gracious Spirit, Love divine........	*Stocker*	331	Holy Father, thou hast taught me. *Neale*	635
Great God, attend while Zion........	*Watts*	5	Holy, holy, holy Lord............... *Williams*	86
Great God, in vain man's narrow.	*Kippis*	148	Holy, holy, holy, Lord God........... *Heber*	1
Great God, let all my.........	*Heginbotham*	175	Holy Spirit! gently come........ *Hammond*	334
Great God, let not thy grace............		555	Holy Spirit, Light divine............... *Reed*	333
Great God, my Father and...	*Exeter Coll.*	525	How beauteous are their feet........ *Watts*	691
Great God, the followers of......	*Ware, Jr.*	7	How beauteous were the marks...... *Coxe*	231
Great God, thy penetrating eye......	*Scott*	159	How blest the righteous......... *Barbauld*	843
Great God, we sing that.........	*Doddridge*	805	How blest the sacred tie that... *Barbauld*	475
Great God whose universal sway...	*Watts*	706	How calmly wakes the hallowed.... *Smith*	728
Great King of glory, come.........	*Francis*	709	How can I sink with such a prop... *Watts*	412
Great Ruler of all nature's......	*Doddridge*	184	How charming is the place......... *Stennett*	46
Great Source of being and of love.		395	How did my heart rejoice to hear.. *Watts*	15
Great Source of unexhausted...	*Exeter Coll.*	181	How gentle God's commands . *Doddridge*	206
Guide me, oh thou great..........	*Williams*	642	How glorious is the hour........... *Bulfinch*	430
			How happy every child of....... *C. Wesley*	687
Had I the tongues of Greeks and...	*Watts*	470	How happy is he born or taught...........	668
Hail the day that sees him rise.	*C. Wesley*	253	How long, O Lord, our God......... *Bonar*	893
Hail to the Lord's anointed..	*Montgomery*	384	How long shall dreams of....... *Doddridge*	348
Happy the church, thou sacred.....	*Watts*	694	How lost was my condition...................	230
Happy the souls to Jesus.........	*C. Wesley*	717	How pleasant, how divinely fair.... *Watts*	6
Hark, hark, my soul, angelic.........	*Faber*	847	How pleasing is thy voice........... *Dwight*	813
Hark, hark, the notes of joy..........	*Reed*	217	How precious is the Book divine. *Fawcett*	340
Hark, my soul; it is the Lord......	*Cowper*	483	How rich the blessing, O my God. *Roscoe*	686
Hark, the glad sound! the.......	*Doddridge*	225	How shall the young secure their.. *Watts*	826
Hark, the herald angels sing....	*C. Wesley*	227	How shall we praise the Lord... *Bowring*	120
Hark! the vesper hymn is.....	*Montgomery*	119	How short and hasty is our life..... *Watts*	837
Hark! through the courts of heaven......		423	How sweet, how calm the sacred morn..	107
Hark, 'tis your heavenly.....	*Heginbotham*	831	How sweet, how heavenly is the... *Swain*	739
Hark! what celestial sounds.....	*Williams*	215	How sweetly flowed the............ *Bowring*	233
Hark! what mean those holy......	*Cawood*	226	How sweet the hour of closing... *Bathurst*	845
Haste, traveler, haste; the night..	*Collyer*	363	How sweet the melting lay...................	110
Hath not thy heart within........	*Bulfinch*	570	How sweet the name of Jesus..... *Newton*	265
Hear, O sinner! mercy hails you.....	*Reed*	378	How sweet to be allowed to pray.. *Follen*	542

HYMN	HYMN
How sweet to leave the world.........*Kelly* 524	I would not live alway.........*Muhlenberg* 852
How sweet upon this sacred...*Mrs Follen* 28	
How tedious and tasteless the.....*Newton* 564	JERUSALEM, my happy home."*F.B.P.*"*tr.* 883
How vain is all beneath the skies...*Ford* 835	Jerusalem, the glorious..........*Neale, tr.* 880
Ho, ye that pant for living streams.*Watts* 355	Jerusalem, the golden..............*Neale, tr.* 881
Human soul, to whom....*Wesley's Hymns* 661	Jesus, and shall it ever be...........*Grigg* 599
Humble souls, who seek salvation........ 733	Jesus! I love thy charming....*Doddridge* 305
	Jesus, I my cross have taken..........*Lyte* 425
I AM coming to the cross.........*McDonald* 429	Jesus, Lamb of God for me.........*Palmer* 417
I ask a perfect creed.......................*Bonar* 516	Jesus, lover of my soul............*C. Wesley* 292
I ask not now for gold to gild.....*Whittier* 490	Jesus, my all to heaven is gone..*Cenwick* 520
I ask not wealth, but power to take.*Cary* 471	Jesus, my heart within me.........*Palmer* 572
I bless the Crucified................... ......*Bonar* 579	Jesus, my Lord, how rich thy.*Doddridge* 500
I cannot always trace the way............. .. 658	Jesus! name of wondrous love........*How* 418
I cannot walk in darkness long......*Mason* 185	Jesus only, is the motto. 906
I come, the great Redeemer *Salsbury Coll.* 726	Jesus shall reign where'er the sun.*Watts* 277
If human kindness meets return.....*Noel* 719	Jesus! thou art the sinner's.....*Burnham* 301
I heard the voice of Jesus say......*Bonar* 428	Jesus, thou everlasting King.........*Watts* 695
I know that my Redeemer lives..*Medley* 247	Jesus, thou joy of loving hearts..*Palmer* 481
I know that my Redeemer lives...*C. Wesley* 262	Jesus, thou shepherd of the......*Hastings* 819
I love the Lord; he heard my cries.*Watts* 493	Jesus, thy boundless love to me.*J. Wesley* 484
I love the sacred Book of God.........*Kelly* 338	Jesus! thy church with longing.*Bathurst* 778
I love thy kingdom, Lord...........*Dwight* 690	Jesus, we thy promise claim.....*Wesleyan* 30
I love to steal awhile away...........*Brown* 109	Jesus, while our hearts are bleeding...... 659
I love to think of heaven........*Hartsough* 894	Join all the glorious names...........*Watts* 295
I'm not ashamed to own my Lord....*Watts* 624	Joyful be the hours to-day............*Kelly* 252
In all my Lord's appointed ways.*Ryland* 413	Joy to the world! the Lord is come.*Watts* 218
In all my vast concerns with thee..*Watts* 157	Just as I am, without one plea......*Elliott* 402
In heavenly love abiding...........*Waring* 648	
In sleep's serene oblivion...*Hawkesworth* 102	KINGDOMS and thrones to God......*Watts* 174
In the cross of Christ I glory.....*Bowring* 588	Know, my soul, thy full salvation....*Lyte* 634
In this peaceful.........*Hymns of the Spirit* 35	
In thy courts let peace be.........*Bowring* 38	LAMP of our feet, whereby we.....*Barton* 344
In trouble and in grief, O God.............. 652	Leader of Israel's host, and......*Wesleyan* 530
I praise and bless thee.*Hymns of the Spirit* 427	Lead, kindly light, amid the.....*Newman* 515
I sing the mighty power of God.....*Watts* 158	Let everlasting glories crown.........*Watts* 336
Is there a lone and dreary hour..*Gilman* 679	Let every heart rejoice and sing............. 803
Is there ambition in my heart......*Watts* 487	Let every mortal ear attend..........*Watts* 347
It came upon the midnight clear.....*Sears* 222	Let me be with thee where thou art..... 568
It is not death to die............*Bethune, tr.* 854	Let me go where saints are....*Hartsough* 848
It is the hour of prayer........................ 820	Let not despair nor fell revenge.....*Watts* 583
I want a principle within.........*C. Wesley* 494	Let others boast how strong they..*Watts* 838
I was a wandering sheep...........*Bonar* 632	Let party names no more ....*Beddome* 744
I will follow thee, my Saviour............... 469	Let Zion's watchmen all.........*Doddridge* 701
I will resolve with all my heart......*Steele* 401	Life is a span, a fleeting hour.........*Steele* 836
I will sing you a song of the. ....*Gates* 901	Life is the time to serve the Lord..*Watts* 358
I worship thee, sweet will of God..*Faber* 414	Life of all that lives...*Hymns of the Spirit* 534
I would love thee, God and Father........ 505	Lift up your heads, eternal.*Tate & Brady* 261

INDEX OF FIRST LINES. 317

HYMN.		HYMN.	
Lift your glad voices in triumph on high	249	Mid scenes of confusion and......*Denham*	816
Light of life, seraphic fire........*C. Wesley*	536	Mighty God, the first, the last.....*Gaskell*	161
Light of those whose dreary......*Toplady*	296	Mourn for the thousands slain......*Brace*	787
Like shadows gliding o'er the......*Taylor*	834	Must Jesus bear the cross alone.....*Allen*	585
Like the eagle, upward, onward...*Bonar*	620	My blessed Saviour, is thy love............	499
Lo! from the upper skies.........*Wheeler*	216	My country! 't is of thee.............*Smith*	793
Lo, God is here! let us adore......*Wesley*	9	My dear Redeemer and my Lord... *Watts*	274
Long as I live I'll bless thy name... *Watts*	93	My faith looks up to thee............*Palmer*	439
Long have I sat beneath the.........*Watts*	639	My Father bids me come......................	509
Look from thy sphere of............*Bryant*	776	My Father, cheering name............*Steele*	209
Look ye saints, the sight is.............*Kelly*	255	My Father's house on high...*Montgomery*	885
Lord, at this closing hour..............*Fitch*	142	My God, accept my early vows........ *Watts*	103
Lord, at thy table I behold.........*Stennett*	729	My God, accept my heart..........*Brydges*	731
Lord, before thy presence come... *Taylor*	29	My God, how endless is thy love.... *Watts*	124
Lord, bid thy light arise............*Bathurst*	330	My God, in whom are all the......... *Watts*	60
Lord, dismiss us with thy............*Shirley*	133	My God, is any hour so sweet......*Elliott*	520
Lord, I approach thy mercy-seat..*Newton*	410	My God, I thank thee; may........*Norton*	657
Lord, I believe a rest remains... *C. Wesley*	561	My God, my everlasting hope........ *Watts*	829
Lord, I believe; thy power.........*Wreford*	436	My God, my Father, while I stray..*Elliott*	403
Lord, I care not for riches..........*Kidder*	903	My God, my hope, my Father, thou.......	646
Lord, I have made thy word my... *Watts*	342	My God, my strength............... *C. Wesley*	510
Lord, in heaven, thy dwelling....*Bowring*	87	My God, permit me not to be...... *Watts*	618
Lord, in mercy thou hast..........*Pierpont*	791	My God, the spring of all my joys..*Watts*	669
Lord, in the morning thou shalt.... *Watts*	106	My gracious Lord, I own........*Doddridge*	399
Lord, in thy presence we appear..*Roberts*	706	My Jesus, as thou wilt............*Borthwick*	649
Lord, lead the way the Saviour.*Crosswell*	498	My life flows on in endless song............	912
Lord, my weak tho't in vain........*Palmer*	149	My Maker and my King..... ....*Steele*	208
Lord of all being, throned afar ...*Holmes*	67	My opening eyes with rapture.....*Hutton*	3
Lord of all power and might ....*Stowell*	769	My Saviour, my almighty Friend... *Watts*	302
Lord of our supreme desire......*C. Wesley*	482	My soul, be on thy guard............*Heath*	611
Lord of the living harvest...........*Monsell*	773	My soul, how lovely is the place ... *Watts*	24
Lord of the worlds above............. *Watts*	42	My soul, repeat his praise............. *Watts*	81
Lord of the worlds below.....................	814	My soul, weigh not thy life..........*Swain*	612
Lord, teach us how to pray...*Montgomery*	552	My times of sorrow and of joy...*Beddome*	654
Lord, thou art good; all nature....*Brown*	154		
Lord, thy glory fills the heaven......*Mant*	84	NEARER, my God, to thee............*Adams*	573
Lord, we come before thee now............	37	Nor eye hath seen, nor ear hath.... *Watts*	898
Lord, what offering shall we........*Taylor*	34	Not only for some task sublime......*Gill*	449
Lord, when my raptured thought...*Steele*	196	Not to condemn the sons of men.... *Watts*	276
Lord, while for all mankind...... *Wreford*	796	Not with our mortal eyes............. *Watts*	576
Lord, with glowing heart, I 'd........*Keys*	204	Now is the accepted time............*Dobell*	372
Love divine, all love excelling...*C. Wesley*	468	Now is the time approaching...*Borthwick*	747
		Now may the Lord, our........*Montgomery*	126
MAJESTIC sweetness sits..............*Stennett*	264	Now to heaven our prayer.........*Hickson*	790
Make us by thy transforming........*Steele*	282	Now to our loving.......*Hymns and Tunes*	72
Mark the soft falling snow......*Doddridge*	391	Now to the Lord a noble song....... *Watt.*	58
Mary to the Saviour's tomb.........*Newton*	254	Now to the Lord who makes......... *Watts*	243
May those who have thy name..............	713	Now with creation's early song............	99

INDEX TO FIRST LINES.

HYMN	HYMN
O now thine ear, Eternal One....*Pierpont* 705	Oh, when shall I see Jesus.................. 630
O Christ, our King, Creator.........*Palmer* 244	Oh, where shall rest be........*Montgomery* 374
O Christ, with each returning...*Chandler* 101	O Jesus, Lord of all below............... 259
O come, Creator, Spirit blest.....*Breviary* 317	O let my trembling soul be........*Bowring* 458
O could I find from day to day..*Cleveland* 543	O let your mingling voices rise.....*Roscoe* 309
O could I speak the matchless......*Medley* 307	O Lord, I would delight in thee...*Ryland* 447
O deem not they are blest alone..*Bryant* 678	O Lord, my best desires fulfill.....*Cowper* 445
O do not let the word depart....*Mrs. Reed* 259	O Lord of hosts, almighty King...*Holmes* 792
O'er the gloomy hills of ....*Williams* 388	O Lord, our fathers oft have told........... 797
O everlasting Light.................*Steele* 291	O Lord, thy heavenly grace......*Oberlin* 398
O Father, humbly we repose ......*Gaskell* 457	O Lord, thy work revive..........*Brown* 759
O Father, lift our souls above............ 179	O Love divine, that stooped to....*Holmes* 680
O Father of the living Christ........*Newell* 702	O Love divine, whose constant...*Whittier* 473
O for a closer walk with God......*Cowper* 550	O love, how cheering is the..... *C. Wesley* 531
O for a faith that will not ....*Bathurst* 435	O love of God, how strong............*Bonar* 177
O for a heart to praise my........*C. Wesley* 426	O love that casts out fear............*Bonar* 501
O for a prophet's fire............ ....*Furness* 736	Once more before we part.............*Hart* 141
O for a shout of joy.....................*Young* 95	Once more my soul the rising. .....*Watts* 108
O for a thousand tongues to....*C. Wesley* 300	One prayer I have, all............*Montgomery* 559
Oft in sorrow, oft in woe............... 618	One sweetly solemn thought........*Carey* 857
O God, accept the sacred hour....*Gilman* 725	One there is above all others ....*Newton* 298
O God, beneath thy guiding hand.*Bacon* 795	On Jordan's stormy banks ....*Stennett* 890
O God, by whom the seed is........*Heber* 143	On the dark wave of Galilee........*Russell* 240
O God, the darkness roll away....*Gaskell* 754	On the dewy breath of even........ 115
O God, thou art my God......*Montgomery* 456	On the mountain's top appearing...*Kelly* 751
O God, to thee our hearts...........*Gaskell* 809	Onward, Christian............*Baring-Gould* 622
O gracious God, in whom I live......*Steele* 548	Onward, Christian, though.........*Johnson* 621
O happy is the man..*Scotch Pharaphrases* 825	Open, Lord, my inward ear....*C. Wesley* 213
O have you not heard of that 911	Oppressed with guilt and full of fears.... 346
Oh bless the Lord, my soul...........*Watts* 30	O sacred Head, now ......*Alexander* 237
Oh, blest the souls.......*From the German* 667	O Source divine, and Life of all...*Sterling* 480
Oh cease, my wandering......*Mecklenburg* 873	O Source of uncreated Light.......*Dryden* 316
Oh, come, and dwell with me...*C. Wesley* 512	O speak of Jesus: other names..t.......... 281
Oh come! loud anthems....*Tate & Brady* 4	O speed thee, Christian, on the way...... 607
Oh, could our thoughts and.. ....*Steele* 557	O spirit of the living God.......*Montgomery* 775
O help us, Lord, each hour of....*Milman* 443	O still in accents sweet........*S. Longfellow* 763
Oh, for a glance of heavenly day....*Hart* 396	O strong to save and bless...........*Bonar* 464
Oh! for that tenderness of..... .*C. Wesley* 409	O teach me, Father, to submit..........*Day* 651
Oh, give thanks to him who........*Conder* 199	O that I could forever dwell.............. 569
Oh, happy day that fixed my..*Doddridge* 712	O that I could repent..............*C. Wesley* 420
O Holy Father! Friend unseen....*Elliott* 414	O that it were as it hath.......*Montgomery* 479
O Holy Father! mid the calm...*Burleigh* 121	O thou, from whom all..............*Haweis* 411
O how I love thy holy law ....*Watts* 339	O thou great Friend to all the......*Parker* 325
O how safe, how happy he............*Lyte* 660	O thou, in all thy might so far ...*Hosmer* 446
Oh, sometimes gleams upon our..*Whittier* 597	O thou in whose presence my......*Swain* 273
Oh that my heart was right ......*Toplady* 519	O thou, that hearest prayer........*Burton* 43
Oh, that the Lord's salvation............*Lyte* 774	O thou, to whom all creatures..*Doddridge* 183
Oh that the Lord would guide ......*Watts* 341	O thou, to whom in ancient.. ...*Pierpont* 10

HYMN.		HYMN.	
O thou to whose all-searching ...*J. Wesley*	526	Rise, my soul, and stretch thy...*Seagrave*	506
O thou who art above all height	700	Rise, O my soul, pursue the......*Needham*	627
O thou, who dried the mourner's..*Moore*	673	Rocked in the cradle of the........*Willard*	782
O thou who hast at thy..............*Cotterill*	472	Rock of ages, cleft for me...........*Toplady*	286
O thou whose mercy guides.....*Edmeston*	676	Roll on, thou mighty ocean......*Edmeston*	762
O thou, whose own vast temple...*Bryant*	703		
O thou whose tender mercy..........*Steele*	638	SAFELY through another week....*Newton*	33
Our country's voice is...............*Anderson*	761	Saints, for whom the Saviour bled.........	757
Our Father, unto thee..................*Haley*	771	Salvation! O the joyful sound....... *Watts*	269
Our God is good, in earth and.....*Gurney*	176	Saviour, breathe an evening.....*Edmeston*	114
Our God, our help, in ages past..... *Watts*	155	Saviour, I follow on...............*Robinson*	574
Our heaven is everywhere.........*Fletcher*	888	Saviour, visit thy plantation........*Newton*	767
Our heavenly Father calls......*Doddridge*	578	Say not the law divine ....*Barton*	386
Our heavenly Father, hear...*Montgomery*	507	Say, sinner! hath a voice within....*Hyde*	361
Our Lord is risen from the...... *C. Wesley*	246	Scorn not the slightest word or deed......	608
Our souls, by love together knit ...*Miller*	742	See, from Zion's sacred mountain...*Kelly*	389
Out of the depths of woe......*Montgomery*	422	"See how he loved!" exclaimed...*Bache*	232
O what a treasure all divine......*Beddome*	271	See the kind Shepherd, Jesus stands.....	823
O what delight is this..............*C. Wesley*	737	See the leaves around us falling....*Horne*	812
O where is now that glowing love...*Kelly*	645	Servant of God, well done.....*Montgomery*	855
		Shall hymns of grateful love......*Cummins*	310
PALMS of glory, raiment........*Montgomery*	897	Shepherd of tender youth....*Alexandrinus*	830
People of the living God......*Montgomery*	711	Shepherd of the ransomed flock............	285
Planted in Christ, the living.........*Smith*	715	Show pity, Lord! O Lord, forgive...*Watts*	404
Pleasant are thy courts above.........*Lyte*	36	Silent, like men in solemn haste...*Bonar*	601
Plunged in a gulf of dark despair...*Watts*	267	Sing to the Lord a joyful song.....*Monsell*	61
Praise God, from whom all..... ....*Ken*	128	Sing to the Lord, ye distant lands.. *Watts*	220
Praise the Lord; ye..............*Dublin Coll.*	82	Sinners, the voice of God............*Fawcett*	350
Praise to thee, thou great...........*Fawcett*	83	Sinners, turn: why will ye die.*C. Wesley*	369
Praise waits in Zion, Lord! for...... *Watts*	76	Sinners, will you slight the .. ..*Allen*	380
Praise ye Jehovah's name... ....*Goode*	90	Sister, thou wast mild'and lovely..*Smith*	869
Prayer is appointed to convey........*Hart*	532	Slavery and death.....*Hymns of the Spirit*	784
Prayer is the soul's sincere...*Montgomery*	546	Sleep not, soldier of the cross......*Gaskell*	615
Press on, press on! ye sons.........*Gaskell*	596	Soft as fades the sunset......*S. Longfellow*	118
Proclaim, saith Christ, my..........*Newton*	732	Softly fades the twilight ray ....*Smith*	39
		Soldiers of Christ, arise .. ..*C. Wesley*	613
QUIET, Lord, my froward heart....*Newton*	460	So let our lips and lives express..... *Watts*	474
		Sometimes a light surprises.........*Cowper*	662
RAISE your triumphant songs.. ..... *Watts*	51	Sound, sound the truth abroad......*Kelly*	770
Rejoice, believer, in the Lord......*Newton*	71	Sovereign and transforming grace..*Hedge*	31
Remember thy Creator now..............	828	Sow in the morn thy seed.....*Montgomery*	631
Rest for the toiling hand...............*Bonar*	889	Speak gently—it is better far.........*Bates*	491
Returning, not departing...........*Bonar*	853	Speak with us, Lord, thyself ...*C. Wesley*	586
Return, my roving heart.........*Doddridge*	394	Spirit of peace, and health........*J. Wesley*	319
Return, O wanderer now...*W. B. Collyer*	353	Stand up, and bless the Lord*Montgomery*	78
Return, O wanderer, to........*W. Hastings*	352	Stand up, my soul, shake off thy...*Watts*	595
Revive thy work, O Lord..............*Ryle*	756	Stand up, stand up for Jesus......*Duffield*	629
Ride on. ride on in majesty.........*Milman*	242	Star of peace to wanderers.........*Simpson*	788

HYMN.		HYMN.
Still one in life and one in death...*Bonar*	876	The morning light is breaking......*Smith* 383
Supreme in wisdom, as in power..........	448	The offerings to thy throne......*Bowring* 22
Sure, the blest Comforter is nigh...*Steele*	313	The praise of Zion waits for thee...*Watts* 750
Sweet hour of prayer! sweet......*Walford*	905	There are lonely hearts to cherish......... 908
Sweet is the day of sacred rest......*Watts*	57	There is a beautiful world...............*Snow* 904
Sweet is the light of Sabbath ...*Edmeston*	13	There is a book, who runs may.....*Keble* 193
Sweet is the prayer whose holy stream..	544	There is a fountain filled with blood...... 268
Sweet is the work.....*Spirit of the Psalms*	45	There is a glorious world on high...*Steele* 874
Sweet peace of conscience...*Heginbotham*	660	There is a God, all nature speaks...*Steele* 151
Sweet the moments, rich in..........*Allen*	589	There is a land mine eye........*Robins, Jr.* 873
Sweet was the time when I first..*Newton*	434	There is a land of pure delight......*Watts* 892
		There is an eye that never..........*Wallace* 545
TARRY with me, O my Saviour......*Smith*	116	There is an hour of peaceful......*Tappan* 875
Teach me, my God and King.....*Herbert*	421	There is a safe and secret place.......*Lyte* 684
Tell me not in mournful........*Longfellow*	594	There is a state unknown............ *Taylor* 899
Thanks be to him who built thee.*Bonar*	800	There is none other name than thine..... 275
That blessed law of thine........*C. Wesley*	513	There is no night in heaven....... *Knolles* 887
The billows swell, the winds ......*Cowper*	783	There's a fullness in God's mercy..*Faber* 182
The breaking waves dashed......*Hemans*	799	There's a land that is fairer than.*Bennett* 902
The Christian warrior—see..*Montgomery*	605	There's not a hope with comfort..*Taylor* 571
The church's one foundation......*Stone*	692	There's nothing bright, above........*Moore* 152
The Crucified is gone..*Tr. John Chandler*	560	The saints on earth and those..*C. Wesley* 730
The day is past and gone............*Leland*	112	The Saviour calls; let every car......*Steele* 351
The day is past and gone............... *Blew*	113	The Saviour speaks to every...*Hathaway* 433
The day is past and over............*Neale*	123	The spacious firmament on........*Addison* 163
The day of praise is done...........*Ellerton*	140	The Spirit in our hearts.. ......*Onderdonk* 371
The day, O Lord, is spent............*Neale*	130	The strife is o'er, the battle... ...*Pott, tr.* 257
The dead are like the stars...*Montgomery*	802	The world may change from old...*Adams* 683
Thee we adore, eternal name... ......*Watts*	807	They, who on the......*Spirit of the Psalms* 466
Thee will I love, my strength.....*J. Wesley*	180	They who seek the throne......*Meth. Coll.* 201
The floods, O Lord, lift up their..*Burgess*	69	Thine earthly Sabbaths, Lord..*Doddridge* 2
The glorious universe around........*Bonar*	741	Think gently of the erring one...*Fletcher* 486
The God of glory walks his round.*Heber*	606	Thirsting for a living spring......*Appleton* 535
The God of harvest praise.....*Montgomery*	802	This is not my place of resting......*Bonar* 895
The happy morn has come..........*Hawris*	294	This is the day the Lord hath........*Watts* 17
The harp at Nature's advent......*Whittier*	197	This is the glorious day.......................... 48
The heaven of heavens cannot..*Drennan*	156	This world for thee, O Christ.... *Wheeler* 768
The heavens declare thy glory......*Watts*	335	Thou art gone to the grave...........*Heber* 867
The hour of my departure's come.*Logan*	846	Thou art, O God! the life and.......*Moore* 162
The King of heaven his table..*Doddridge*	354	Thou art the Way; to thee alone..*Doane* 260
The light pours down from heaven.......	663	Thou dear Redeemer, dying........*Cennick* 266
The Lord! how wondrous are his...*Watts*	168	Thou God of grace and love........*Clayton* 708
The Lord is King; lift up thy.....*Conder*	55	Thou hidden source of calm...*C. Wesley* 280
The Lord Jehovah lives............*Hastings*	212	Thou strong and loving Son of....*Noralis* 567
The Lord my pasture shall........*Addison*	178	Thou, whose almighty word......*Marriott* 324
The Lord my shepherd is............*Watts*	207	Through all the various shifting....*Collett* 173
The Lord of glory is my light........*Watts*	75	Through all this life's eventful..*Gaskell* 566
The morning dawns upon....*Montgomery*	241	Thro' the love of God, our... ....*Peters* 463

INDEX TO FIRST LINES.   321

HYMN.	HYMN.
Thus far the Lord has led me on....*Watts* 100	We lift our hearts to thee.........*J. Wesley* 288
Thy bounteous hand with food.....*Heber* 455	We praise and bless thee, gracious Lord 637
Thy Father's house! thine own...*Palmer* 764	We praise thee, Lord, with.........*Franck* 88
Thy goodness, Lord, our souls....*Gibbons* 190	We praise thee, O God! for the....*Mackey* 907
Thy gracious presence, O my God..*Steele* 674	We speak of the realms of the blest........ 868
Thy presence ever living..........*Doddridge* 125	We the weak ones, we the sinners...*Gill* 563
Thy way, not mine, O Lord.........*Bonar* 650	We 've no abiding city here ....*Kelley* 527
Thy way, O God, is in the sea....*Fawcett* 194	What a friend we have in Jesus....*Bonar* 913
Thy will be done: I will not fear..*Roscoe* 656	What equal honors shall we bring..*Watts* 235
Time is winging us away............*Burton* 840	What is the thing of............*Montgomery* 432
'Tis by the faith of joys to come...*Watts* 440	What precept, Jesus, is like....*Livermore* 478
'Tis finished! so the Saviour ......*Stennett* 239	What shall I render to my God.....*Watts* 21
'Tis midnight; and on Olive's....*Tappan* 238	What sinners value, I resign.........*Watts* 393
To God, the great, eternal.....*Summerbell* 129	When all thy mercies, O my......*Addison* 187
To God, the only wise..................*Watts* 451	When, as returns this.......*Mrs. Barbauld* 12
To our Redeemer's glorious ....*Steele* 303	When blooming youth is snatched.*Steele* 865
Tossed upon life's raging............*Bethune* 779	When brighter suns and..........*Peabody* 815
To thee and to thy love...................... 452	When driven by oppression's rod...*Lunt* 785
To thee, O God, we homage.....*Doddridge* 283	When God revealed his gracious...*Watts* 431
To thine eternal arms, O God..*Higginson* 643	When Israel, of the Lord beloved...*Scott* 644
To thy temple I repair.........*Montgomery* 82	When I survey the wondrous......... *Watts* 587
To us a child of hope is born........*Logan* 224	When languor and disease........*Toplady* 670
Triumphant Zion, lift thy......*Doddridge* 749	When my love to Christ grows weak..... 593
Try us, O God, and search the..*C. Wesley* 549	When, overwhelmed with grief.....*Watts* 210
'Twas the commission of our.........*Watts* 720	When shall the voice of...........*Edmeston* 748
	When strangers stand and hear.....*Watts* 279
UNSHAKEN as the sacred hill.........*Watts* 442	When thou, my righteous Judge..*Selina* 866
Unto thy temple, Lord, we come.*Collyer* 707	When torn is the bosom by.........*Lutton* 562
Upon the gospel's sacred page....*Bowring* 392	When we devote our youth to..... *Watts* 827
Up to the hills I lift mine eyes............. 198	Where for refuge shall 1 fly......*Hoffman* 910
Upward I lift mine eyes..............*Watts* 462	Where're the Lord shall build my..*Scott* 818
	Where shall the child of sorrow............ 675
VAINLY through night's weary......*Auber* 623	While life prolongs its precious...*Dwight* 364
	While my Redeemer's near ....*Steele* 287
WALK in the light! so shalt thou..*Barton* 580	While shepherds watched their......*Tate* 223
Walk with your God along the road.*Gill* 581	While thee I seek............*Mrs. Williams* 70
Watchman, tell us of the night..*Bowring* 229	While we walk with God in....*C. Wesley* 746
Weak and irresolute is man........*Cowper* 638	While, with ceaseless course, the.*Newton* 804
We all, O Father! all are thine......*Dyer* 454	Whither, O whither should I...*C. Wesley* 172
We are living, we are dwelling.......*Coxe* 781	Who is thy neighbor? He.........*Peabody* 488
Weary of earth, and laden with.....*Stone* 382	Whom have we, Lord, in heaven.....*Lyte* 495
We bid thee welcome in........*Montgomery* 699	Who, O Lord, when life is o'er........*Lyte* 465
We bless thee for this.........*Mrs. Gilman* 14	Who shall ascend the heavenly.....*Watts* 476
We bless thee for thy peace, O God....... 682	Why do we mourn departing.........*Watts* 842
We bow before thy mercy-seat.*Batchelor* 74	Why should I murmur or repine... 677
We come, O Lord, before thy......*Brown* 789	Why should we start, and fear to...*Watts* 844
Welcome, delightful morn.......*Hayward* 41	Why will ye waste on trifling.*Doddridge* 362
Welcome, sweet day of rest...........*Watts* 47	With broken heart and contrite....*Elvi* 1 400

HYMN.		HYMN.
Within thy house, O Lord, our God......	16	YE boundless realms of joy............*Tate* 92
With joy we hail the sacred day.....*Lyte*	18	Ye Christian heralds, go, proclaim..*Voke* 697
With joy we meditate the grace.... *Watts*	270	Ye nations round the earth...........*Watts* 68
With love the Saviour's heart o'erflowed	496	Ye servants of the Lord ....*Doddridge* 503
With my substance I will...........*Francis*	780	Yes, for me, for me he careth........*Bonar* 297
With reverence let the saints........ *Watts*	191	Yes, my native land, I love thee...*Smith* 760
With sacred joy we lift our eyes...*Jarvis*	19	Yes, the Redeemer rose..........*Doddridge* 256
With tearful eyes I look.. .*Mrs. C. Elliott*	360	Ye tribes of Adam, join..... *Tate & Brady* 94
Witness, ye men and angels......*Beddome*	716	Ye wretched, hungry, starving......*Steele* 349
Word by God the Father sent........*Coxe*	332	Your harps, ye trembling saints.*Toplady* 450
Word of life, most........*From the German*	370	
Word, whose creative thrill.........*Brooks*	91	ZION! awake, thy strength........*Shrubsole* 765
Work, for the night is coming..... *Walker*	619	Zion stands with hills surrounded..*Kelly* 689
Workman of God, O lose not.........*Faber*	609	

CHANTS AND RESPONSES.

	HYMN.		HYMN.
BLESS the Lord, oh my soul. Psalm 103	923	O come, let us sing unto the Lord.	
Father, hear us.............................	928	Psalm 95............................	920
Glory be to God on high....................	914	O sing, unto the Lord a new song.	
Glory be to the Father	915	Psalm 98............................	925
Grant, we beseech thee............... 927,	930	Our Father, who art in heaven............	916
Hear our prayer, heavenly Father........	929	The Lord is my Shepherd. Psalm 23....	919
Holy, holy, holy, Lord God.................	918	The Lord will comfort Zion...............	926
I was glad when they said unto me.		Thy will be done........................	917
Psalm 122.................................	922	We praise thee, O God	921
Make a joyful noise unto the Lord.			
Psalm 100.................................	924		

RESPONSIVE READINGS.

SELECTION 1.

Psalm VIII.

O Lord, our Lord, how excellent is thy name in all the earth!

Who hast set thy glory upon the heavens.

Out of the mouth of babes and sucklings hast thou established strength, because of thine adversaries.

That thou mightest still the enemy and the avenger.

When I consider thy heavens, the work of thy fingers, the moon and the stars, which thou hast ordained;

What is man that thou art mindful of him? and the son of man, that thou visitest him?

For thou hast made him but little lower than God, and crownest him with glory and honor.

Thou madest him to have dominion over the works of thy hands;

Thou hast put all things under his feet: all sheep and oxen, yea, and the beasts of the field;

The fowl of the air, and the fish of the sea, whatsoever passeth through the paths of the seas.

O Lord, our Lord, how excellent is thy name in all the earth!

Psalm XXIV.

The earth is the Lord's, and the fulness thereof; the world, and they that dwell therein.

For he hath founded it upon the seas, and established it upon the floods.

Who shall ascend into the hill of the Lord? and who shall stand in his holy place?

He that hath clean hands and a pure heart;

Who hath not lifted up his soul unto vanity, and hath not sworn deceitfully.

He shall receive a blessing from the Lord, and righteousness from the God of his salvation.

This is the generation of them that seek after him, that seek thy face, O God of Jacob.

Lift up your heads, O ye gates; and be ye lift up, ye everlasting doors: and the King of glory shall come in.

Who is the King of glory? the Lord strong and mighty, the Lord mighty in battle.

Lift up your heads, O ye gates; yea, lift them up, ye everlasting doors: and the King of glory shall come in.

Who is this King of glory? the Lord of hosts, he is the King of glory.

Psalm cl.

Praise ye the Lord. Praise God in his sanctuary: praise him in the firmament of his power.

Praise him for his mighty acts:

Praise him according to his excellent greatness. Praise him with the sound of the trumpet:

Praise him with the psaltery and harp.

Praise him with the timbrel and dance: praise him with stringed instruments and the pipe.

Praise him upon the loud cymbals:

Praise him upon the high sounding cymbals. Let everything that hath breath praise the Lord. Praise ye the Lord.

SELECTION 2.
Psalm xix.

The heavens declare the glory of God; and the firmament sheweth his handywork.

Day unto day uttereth speech, and night unto night sheweth knowledge.

There is no speech nor language; their voice cannot be heard.

Their line is gone out through all the earth, and their words to the end of the world.

In them hath he set a tabernacle for the sun.

Which is as a bridegroom coming out of his chamber, and rejoiceth as a strong man to run his course.

His going forth is from the end of the heaven, and his circuit unto the ends of it:

And there is nothing hid from the heat thereof.

The law of the Lord is perfect, restoring the soul:

The testimony of the Lord is sure, making wise the simple.

The precepts of the Lord are right, rejoicing the heart:

The commandment of the Lord is pure, enlightening the eyes.

The fear of the Lord is clean, enduring forever:

The judgments of the Lord are true, and righteous altogether.

More to be desired are they than gold, yea, than much fine gold:

Sweeter also than honey and the honeycomb.

Moreover by them is thy servant warned:

In keeping of them there is great reward.

Who can discern his errors? clear thou me from hidden faults.

Keep back thy servant also from presumptuous sins; let them not have dominion over me:

Then shall I be perfect, and I shall be clear from great transgression.

Let the words of my mouth and the meditation of my heart be acceptable in thy sight,

O Lord, my rock, and my redeemer.

Psalm lxvii.

God be merciful unto us, and bless us, and cause his face to shine upon us;

That thy way may be known upon earth, thy saving health among all nations.

Let the peoples praise thee, O God; let all the peoples praise thee.

O let the nations be glad and sing for joy:

For thou shalt judge the peoples with equity, and govern the nations upon earth.

Let the peoples praise thee, O God; let all the peoples praise thee.

The earth hath yielded her increase: God, even our own God, shall bless us.

God shall bless us: and all the ends of the earth shall fear him.

Psalm c.

Make a joyful noise unto the Lord, all ye lands.

Serve the Lord with gladness: come before his presence with singing.

Know ye that the Lord he is God: it is he that hath made us, and we are his;

We are his people, and the sheep of his pasture.

Enter into his gates with thanksgiving, and into his courts with praise:

Give thanks unto him, and bless his name.

For the Lord is good; his mercy endureth forever; and his faithfulness unto all generations.

SELECTION 3.

Psalm XLVII.

O clap your hands, all ye peoples; shout unto God with the voice of triumph.

For the Lord Most High is terrible; he is a great King over all the earth.

He shall subdue the peoples under us, and the nations under our feet.

He shall choose our inheritance for us, the excellency of Jacob whom he loved.

God is gone up with a shout, the Lord with the sound of a trumpet.

Sing praises to God, sing praises: sing praises unto our King, sing praises.

For God is the King of all the earth: sing ye praises with understanding.

God reigneth over the nations: God sitteth upon his holy throne.

The princes of the peoples are gathered together to be the people of the God of Abraham:

For the shields of the earth belong unto God; he is greatly exalted.

Psalm xxxiii.

Rejoice in the Lord, O ye righteous: praise is comely for the upright.

Give thanks unto the Lord with harp: sing praises unto him with the psaltery of ten strings.

Sing unto him a new song, play skillfully with a loud noise.

For the word of the Lord is right; and all his work is done in faithfulness.

He loveth righteousness and judgment: the earth is full of the lovingkindness of the Lord.

By the word of the Lord were the heavens made;

And all the host of them by the breath of his mouth.

He gathereth the waters of the sea together as an heap:

He layeth up the deeps in store-houses.

Let all the earth fear the Lord: let all the inhabitants of the world stand in awe of him.

For he spake, and it was done; he commanded, and it stood fast.

The Lord bringeth the counsel of the nations to nought:

He maketh the thoughts of the peoples to be of none effect.

The counsel of the Lord standeth fast forever, the thoughts of his heart to all generations.

Blessed is the nation whose God is the Lord;

The people whom he hath chosen for his own inheritance.

The Lord looketh from heaven: he beholdeth all the sons of men:

From the place of his habitation he looketh forth upon all the inhabitants of the earth;

He that fashioneth the hearts of them all, that considereth all their works.

There is no king saved by the multitude of an host:

A mighty man is not delivered by great strength.

An horse is a vain thing for safety: neither shall he deliver any by his great power.

Behold, the eye of the Lord is upon them that fear him, upon them that hope in his mercy;

To deliver their soul from death, and to keep them alive in famine.

Our soul hath waited for the Lord: he is our help and our shield.

For our heart shall rejoice in him, because we have trusted in his holy name.

Let thy mercy, O Lord, be upon us, according as we have hoped in thee.

SELECTION 4.
Psalm LXV.

Praise waiteth for thee, O God, in Zion: and unto thee shall the vow be performed.

O thou that hearest prayer, unto thee shall all flesh come.

Iniquities prevail against me: as for our transgressions, thou shalt purge them away.

Blessed is the man whom thou choosest and causest to approach unto thee, that he may dwell in thy courts:

We shall be satisfied with the goodness of thy house, the holy place of thy temple.

By terrible things thou wilt answer us in righteousness, O God of our salvation:

Thou that art the confidence of all the ends of the earth, and of them that are afar off upon the sea:

Which by his strength setteth fast the mountains; being girded about with might:

Which stilleth the roaring of the seas, the roaring of the waves, and the tumult of the peoples.

They also that dwell in the uttermost parts are afraid at thy tokens:

Thou makest the outgoings of the morning and evening to rejoice. Thou visitest the earth, and waterest it,

Thou greatly enrichest it; the river of God is full of water:

Thou providest them corn, when thou hast so prepared the earth.

Thou waterest her furrows abundantly;

Thou settlest the ridges thereof: thou makest it soft with showers; thou blessest the springing thereof.

Thou crownest the year with thy goodness; and thy paths drop fatness.

They drop upon the pastures of the wilderness: and the hills are girded with joy.

The pastures are clothed with flocks; the valleys also are covered over with corn;

They shout for joy, they also sing.

Psalm xxxii.

Blessed is he whose transgression is forgiven, whose sin is covered.

Blessed is the man unto whom the Lord imputeth not iniquity, and in whose spirit there is no guile.

When I kept silence, my bones waxed old through my roaring all the day long.

For day and night thy hand was heavy upon me: my moisture was changed as with the drought of summer.

I acknowledged my sin unto thee, and mine iniquity have I not hid:

I said, I will confess my transgressions unto the Lord; and thou forgavest the iniquity of my sin.

For this let every one that is godly pray unto thee in a time when thou mayest be found:

Surely when the great waters overflow they shall not reach unto him.

Thou art my hiding place; thou wilt preserve me from trouble;

Thou wilt compass me about with songs of deliverance.

I will instruct thee and teach thee in the way which thou shalt go; I will counsel thee with mine eye upon thee.

Be ye not as the horse, or as the mule, which have no understanding:

Whose trappings must be bit and bridle to hold them in, else they will not come near unto thee.

Many sorrows shall be to the wicked: but he that trusteth in the Lord, mercy shall compass him about.

Be glad in the Lord, and rejoice, ye righteous:

And shout for joy, all ye that are upright in heart.

SELECTION 5.
Psalm LI.

Have mercy upon me, O God, according to thy loving kindness:

According to the multitude of thy tender mercies blot out my transgressions.

Wash me thoroughly from mine iniquity, and cleanse me from my sin.

For I acknowledge my transgressions: and my sin is ever before me.

Against thee, thee only, have I sinned, and done that which is evil in thy sight:

That thou mayest be justified when thou speakest, and be clear when thou judgest.

Behold, I was shapen in iniquity; and in sin did my mother conceive me.

Behold, thou desirest truth in the inward parts: and in the hidden part thou shalt make me to know wisdom.

Purge me with hyssop, and I shall be clean: wash me, and I shall be whiter than snow.

Make me to hear joy and gladness; that the bones which thou hast broken may rejoice.

Hide thy face from my sins, and blot out all mine iniquities.

Create in me a clean heart, O God; and renew a right spirit within me.

Cast me not away from thy presence; and take not thy holy spirit from me.

Restore unto me the joy of thy salvation: and uphold me with a free spirit.

Then will I teach transgressors thy ways; and sinners shall be converted unto thee.

Deliver me from bloodguiltiness, O God, thou God of my salvation; and my tongue shall sing aloud of thy righteousness.

O Lord, open thou my lips; and my mouth shall shew forth thy praise.

For thou delightest not in sacrifice; else would I give it: thou hast no pleasure in burnt offering.

The sacrifices of God are a broken spirit:

A broken and a contrite heart, O God, thou wilt not despise.

Do good in thy good pleasure unto Zion: build thou the walls of Jerusalem.

Then shalt thou delight in the sacrifices of righteousness, in burnt offering and whole burnt offering:

Then shall they offer bullocks upon thine altar.

Psalm CXXII.

I was glad when they said unto me, Let us go unto the house of the Lord.

Our feet are standing within thy gates, O Jerusalem;

Jerusalem, that art builded as a city that is compact together:

Whither the tribes go up, even the tribes of the Lord, for a testimony unto Israel, to give thanks unto the name of the Lord.

For there are set thrones for judgment, the thrones of the house of David.

Pray for the peace of Jerusalem: they shall prosper that love thee.

Peace be within thy walls, and prosperity within thy palaces.

For my brethren and companions' sakes, I will now say, Peace be within thee.

For the sake of the house of the Lord our God I will seek thy good.

Psalm CXXXIII.

Behold, how good and how pleasant it is for brethren to dwell together in unity!

It is like the precious oil upon the head, that ran down upon the beard, even Aaron's beard;

That came down upon the skirt of his garments; like the dew of Hermon, that cometh down upon the mountains of Zion:

For there the Lord commanded the blessing, even life for evermore.

SELECTION 6.
Psalm LXXXIV.

How amiable are thy tabernacles, O Lord of hosts!

My soul longeth, yea, even fainteth for the courts of the Lord;

My heart and my flesh cry out unto the living God.

Yea, the sparrow hath found her an house, and the swallow a nest for herself, where she may lay her young.

Even thine altars, O Lord of hosts, my King, and my God.

Blessed are they that dwell in thy house: they will be still praising thee.

Blessed is the man whose strength is in thee; in whose heart are the highways to Zion.

Passing through the valley of weeping they make it a place of springs; yea, the early rain covereth it with blessings.

They go from strength to strength, every one of them appeareth before God in Zion.

O Lord God of hosts, hear my prayer: Give ear, O God of Jacob.

Behold, O God, our shield, and look upon the face of thine anointed.

For a day in thy courts is better than a thousand.

I had rather be a doorkeeper in the house of my God, than to dwell in the tents of wickedness.

For the Lord God is a sun and a shield: the Lord will give grace and glory: no good thing will he withhold from them that walk uprightly.

O Lord of hosts, blessed is the man that trusteth in thee.

Psalm XLVI.

God is our refuge and strength, a very present help in trouble.

Therefore will we not fear, though the earth do change, and though the mountains be moved in the heart of the seas:

Though the waters thereof roar and be troubled, though the mountains shake with the swelling thereof.

There is a river, the streams whereof make glad the city of God, the holy place of the tabernacles of the Most High.

God is in the midst of her; she shall not be moved: God shall help her and that right early.

The nations raged, the kingdoms were moved: he uttered his voice, the earth melted.

The Lord of hosts is with us; the God of Jacob is our refuge.

Come, behold the works of the Lord, what desolations he hath made in the earth.

He maketh wars to cease unto the end of the earth:

He breaketh the bow, and cutteth the spear in sunder; he burneth the chariots in the fire.

Be still, and know that I am God: I will be exalted among the nations, I will be exalted in the earth.

The Lord of hosts is with us; the God of Jacob is our refuge.

Psalm XIV.

The fool hath said in his heart, There is no God.

They are corrupt, they have done abominable works; there is none that doeth good.

The Lord looked down from heaven upon the children of men, to see if there were any that did understand, that did seek after God.

They are all gone aside; they are together become filthy; there is none that doeth good, no, not one.

Have all the workers of iniquity no knowledge? who eat up my people as they eat bread, and call not upon the Lord

There were they in great fear: for God is in the generation of the righteous.

Ye put to shame the counsel of the poor, because the Lord is his refuge.

Oh that the salvation of Israel were come out of Zion!

When the Lord bringeth back the captivity of his people, then shall Jacob rejoice, and Israel shall be glad.

SELECTION 7.

Psalm XLIII.

Judge me, O God, and plead my cause against an ungodly nation:

O deliver me from the deceitful and unjust man.

For thou art the God of my strength; why hast thou cast me off?

Why go I mourning because of the oppression of the enemy?

O send out thy light and thy truth; let them lead me:

Let them bring me unto thy holy hill, and to thy tabernacles.

Then will I go unto the altar of God, unto God my exceeding joy:

And upon the harp will I praise thee, O God, my God.

Why art thou cast down, O my soul? and why art thou disquieted within me? hope thou in God:

For I shall yet praise him, who is the health of my countenance, and my God.

Psalm XXVII.

The Lord is my light and my salvation; whom shall I fear?

The Lord is the strength of my life; of whom shall I be afraid?

When evil-doers came upon me to eat up my flesh, even mine adversaries and my foes, they stumbled and fell.

Though an host should encamp against me, my heart shall not fear:

Though war should rise against me, even then will I be confident.

One thing have I asked of the Lord, that will I seek after;

That I may dwell in the house of the Lord all the days of my life,

To behold the beauty of the Lord, and to inquire in his temple.

For in the day of trouble he shall keep me secretly in his pavilion:

In the covert of his tabernacle shall he hide me; he shall lift me up upon a rock.

And now shall mine head be lifted up above mine enemies round about me;

And I will offer in his tabernacle sacrifices of joy;

I will sing, yea, I will sing praises unto the Lord.

Hear, O Lord, when I cry with my voice:

Have mercy also upon me, and answer me.

When thou saidst, Seek ye my face; my heart said unto thee, Thy face, Lord, will I seek.

Hide not thy face from me; put not thy servant away in anger:

Thou hast been my help; cast me not off, neither forsake me, O God of my salvation.

For my father and my mother have forsaken me, but the Lord will take me up.

Teach me thy way, O Lord; and lead me in a plain path, because of mine enemies.

Deliver me not over unto the will of mine adversaries;

For false witnesses are risen up against me, and such as breathe out cruelty.

I had fainted, unless I had believed to see the goodness of the Lord in the land of the living.

Wait on the Lord: be strong, and let thine heart take courage; yea, wait thou on the Lord.

SELECTION 8.
Psalm xxiii.

The Lord is my shepherd; I shall not want.

He maketh me to lie down in green pastures; he leadeth me beside the still waters.

He restoreth my soul: he guideth me in the paths of righteousness for his name's sake.

Yea, though I walk through the valley of the shadow of death, I will fear no evil;

For thou art with me: thy rod and thy staff they comfort me.

Thou preparest a table before me in the presence of mine enemies;

Thou hast anointed my head with oil; my cup runneth over.

Surely goodness and mercy shall follow me all the days of my life:

And I will dwell in the house of the Lord forever.

Psalm i.

Blessed is the man that walketh not in the counsel of the wicked.

Nor standeth in the way of sinners, nor sitteth in the seat of the scornful.

But his delight is in the law of the Lord;

And in his law doth he meditate day and night.

And he shall be like a tree planted by the streams of water, that bringeth forth its fruit in its season.

Whose leaf also doth not wither; and whatsoever he doeth shall prosper.

The wicked are not so; but are like the chaff which the wind driveth away.

Therefore the wicked shall not stand in the judgment,

Nor sinners in the congregation of the righteous.

For the Lord knoweth the way of the righteous:

But the way of the wicked shall perish.

Psalm xv.

Lord, who shall sojourn in thy tabernacle? who shall dwell in thy holy hill?

He that walketh uprightly and worketh righteousness, and speaketh truth in his heart.

He that slandereth not with his tongue, nor doeth evil to his friend, nor taketh up a reproach against his neighbor.

In whose eyes a reprobate is despised; but he honoreth them that fear the Lord.

He that sweareth to his own hurt, and changeth not,

He that putteth not out his money to usury, nor taketh reward against the innocent.

He that doeth these things shall never be moved.

APOSTLES' CREED.

I believe in God the Father Almighty, maker of heaven and earth;

And in Jesus Christ, his only Son, our Lord.

Who was conceived by the Holy Ghost, Born of the Virgin Mary,

Suffered under Pontius Pilate,

Was crucified, dead and buried:

The third day he arose again from the dead:

He ascended into heaven, and sitteth on the right hand of God the Father Almighty;

From thence he shall come to judge the quick and the dead.

I believe in the Holy Ghost; the holy catholic church; the communion of saints; the forgiveness of sins; the resurrection of the body; and the life everlasting. AMEN.

SELECTION 9.
THE LAW OF GOD.
Exodus xx: 3-17.

Thou shalt have none other gods before me.

Thou shalt not make unto thee a graven image, nor the likeness of any form that is in heaven above, or that is in the earth beneath, or that is in the water under the earth;

Thou shalt not bow down thyself unto them, nor serve them;

For I the Lord thy God am a jealous God, visiting the iniquity of the fathers upon the children, upon the third and upon the fourth generation of them that hate me;

And shewing mercy unto thousands of them that love me and keep my commandments.

Thou shalt not take the name of the Lord thy God in vain;

For the Lord will not hold him guiltless that taketh his name in vain.

Remember the sabbath day, to keep it holy.

Six days shalt thou labor, and do all thy work;

But the seventh day is a sabbath unto the Lord thy God;

In it thou shalt not do any work, thou, nor thy son, nor thy daughter, thy manservant, nor thy maidservant, nor thy cattle, nor thy stranger that is within thy gates;

For in six days the Lord made heaven and earth, the sea, and all that in them is, and rested the seventh day.

Wherefore the Lord blessed the sabbath day, and hallowed it.

Honor thy father and thy mother: that thy days may be long upon the land which the Lord thy God giveth thee.

Thou shalt do no murder.

Thou shalt not commit adultery.

Thou shalt not steal.

Thou shalt not bear false witness against thy neighbor.

Thou shalt not covet thy neighbor's house, thou shalt not covet thy neighbor's wife, nor his manservant, nor his maidservant, nor his ox, nor his ass, nor anything that is thy neighbor's.

The Summary of the Law.
Matt. xxii. 37-40.

And he said unto him, Thou shalt love the Lord thy God with all thy heart, and with all thy soul, and with all thy mind.

This is the great and first commandment.

And a second like unto it is this, Thou shalt love thy neighbor as thyself.

On these two commandments hangeth the whole law, and the prophets.

SELECTION 10.
Decalogue of Beatitudes and Promises.
Matt. v. 3-12.

Blessed are the poor in spirit: for theirs is the kingdom of heaven.

Blessed are they that mourn: for they shall be comforted.

Blessed are the meek: for they shall inherit the earth.

Blessed are they that hunger and thirst after righteousness: for they shall be filled.

Blessed are the merciful: for they shall obtain mercy.

Blessed are the pure in heart: for they shall see God.

Blessed are the peacemakers: for they shall be called sons of God.

Blessed are they that have been persecuted for righteousness' sake: for theirs is the kingdom of heaven.

Blessed are ye when men shall reproach you, and persecute you, and say all manner of evil against you falsely, for my sake.

Rejoice and be exceeding glad: for great is your reward in heaven: for so persecuted they the prophets which were before you.

The Lord's Prayer.
Matt. vi. 9-13.

Our Father which art in heaven.

Hallowed be thy name. Thy kingdom come.

Thy will be done, as in heaven, so on earth.

Give us this day our daily bread.

And forgive us our debts, as we also have forgiven our debtors.

And bring us not into temptation, but deliver us from the evil one.

The Eternal Thing.
I. Cor. xiii.

If I speak with the tongues of men and of angels, but have not love, I am become sounding brass, or a clanging cymbal.

And if I have the gift of prophecy, and know all mysteries and all knowledge; and if I have all faith, so as to remove mountains, but have not love, I am nothing.

And if I bestow all my goods to feed the poor, and if I give my body to be burned, but have not love, it profiteth me nothing.

Love suffereth long, and is kind; love envieth not; love vaunteth not itself, is not puffed up,

Doth not behave itself unseemly, seeketh not its own, is not provoked, taketh not account of evil;

Rejoiceth not in unrighteousness, but rejoiceth with the truth;

Beareth all things, believeth all things, hopeth all things, endureth all things.

Love never faileth; but whether there be prophecies, they shall be done away; whether there be tongues, they shall cease; whether there be knowledge, it shall be done away.

For we know in part, and we prophesy in part;

But when that which is perfect is come, that which is in part shall be done away.

When I was a child, I spake as a child, I felt as a child, I thought as a child: now that I am become a man, I have put away childish things.

For now we see in a mirror, darkly; but then face to face: now I know in part; but then shall I know even as also I have been known.

But now abideth faith, hope, love, these three; and the greatest of these is love.

www.ingramcontent.com/pod-product-compliance
Lightning Source LLC
Chambersburg PA
CBHW021158230426
43667CB00006B/447